Restructuring for World Peace
On the Threshold of the Twenty-First Century

THE HAMPTON PRESS
COMMUNICATION SERIES

Communication, Peace, and Development
Majid Tehranian, supervisory editor

Restructuring for World Peace

On the Threshold of the Twenty-First Century

EDITED BY

KATHARINE AND MAJID TEHRANIAN

HAMPTON PRESS, INC.
CRESSKILL, NEW JERSEY

Library of Congress Cataloging-in-Publication Data

Restructuring for world peace : challenges for the twenty-first
   century / edited by Katharine and Majid Tehranian.
      p.   cm. -- (The Hampton Press communication series.
   Communication, peace, and development)
      Based on a conference held at the University of Hawaii, June 2-5,
   1991.
      Includes bibliographical references and index.
      ISBN 1-8813-3-84-5.   -- ISBN 1-8813-3-85-3
      1. Peace. 2. Security, International. 3. Human rights.
   4. Social justice.   I. Tehranian, Majid.   II. Tehranian, Katharine.
   III. Series.
   JX1952.R385 1992
   327.1'72–dc20   92-15818
                                                              CIP

Hampton Press, Inc.
23 Broadway
Cresskill, NJ 07626

Maluna a'e o nā lāhui apau ke ola ke kanaka
"Above all nations is humanity"

The Spark M. Matsunaga Institute for Peace of the University of Hawai'i is an academic community designed to develop and share knowledge about the root causes of violence, the conditions of peace, and the use of nonviolent means for resolving conflicts. Founded in 1985, the institute operates with openness to all views and with a commitment to academic freedom and rigor. It is committed to improving education in peace studies for graduate, undergraduate, secondary, and primary school students; undertaking research to promote understanding of issues of violence, nonviolence, social justice, ecological vitality, freedom, and human dignity; participating with community groups to communicate with all segments of our society on these issues; and publishing scholarly and creative works on peace in all media.

Contents

This volume is dedicated to the memory of
Senator Spark M. Matsunaga
statesman, soldier, scholar, poet
and tireless activist for peace and justice.

PREFACE

Plans for this book were drawn up early in the summer of 1990. To honor the late U.S. Senator Spark M. Matsunaga of Hawai'i after whom the peace institute at the University of Hawai'i had just been named, a steering committee was formed to plan for an international conference around the timely theme of "Restructuring for Peace: Challenges for the Twenty-first Century." The conference was held a year later on June 2-5, 1991. It brought together some 30 leading peace scholars from around the world.

When we began to plan the conference, there was an air of optimism around the world. The Cold War had ended, the media and the politicians were speaking of an impending peace dividend, there was a breakout of democracy in Eastern Europe, and there seemed to be a genuine historical opportunity to reconfigure international relations for peace, freedom, and, with a little bit of luck, even justice!

The events since then, including the Persian Gulf War and its tragic aftermath, as well as the upheavals in the former Soviet Union and Eastern Europe, have tempered that optimism. The conference steering committee chose its particular theme because we believed that the beginning of any new historical era presents unprecedented opportunities for fresh thinking on continuing and emerging problems. It also calls for proactive rather than reactive planning by peace scholars and activists. It is in this context that we focused on the concept of "restructuring for peace" as an organizing theme for a series of annual conferences that together might present a coherent body of ideas, visions, and plans for the future.

The first item on the conference agenda, therefore, was to define the problem, identify the critical issues, and explore alternative strategies for the struggle to achieve greater international and domestic security, freedom, justice, and community.

The next step was to produce a book to be used in peace studies and international relations courses, introducing the challenges of the new era. For us at the University of Hawai'i, this meant a textbook for the introductory course in our proposed Master's Program in Peace and Conflict Resolution. There is a parallel therefore between the conceptual designs of the Master's Program and this book, both of them inspired by the work of Johan Galtung.

The final goal was to produce a volume that would set an agenda for peace studies. We took some pains to define the conference theme in such a way as to invite both creative and disciplined thinking. In response to the conference call, papers were produced around the four universal values of an emerging democratic culture: restructuring for peace with *security, freedom, justice,* and *community.* These values became the organizing principles for the conference and for the volume that is before you. The papers were presented, discussed, and critiqued at both plenary as well as small group sessions. They were then revised and critiqued by the group leaders, outside critics, and the editors. The output thus represents the collective wisdom of a group of prominent peace scholars who represent a wide range of national, disciplinary, and ideological perspectives.

As the first in a series of conferences and books, the present work takes a broad view of the main challenges facing the world in the coming decades. The terms "structure" and "restructuring" perhaps call for a special explanation. Lacking the experimental laboratories of the natural sciences, social scientists often take resort to a triple concept, *structure-function-process,* to capture both the static and dynamic aspects of society. The structure of a society may be considered to be a static snapshot of that society at a moment in time. It is the organized context, the institutional arrangement, in which perennial processes such as socialization of children and legitimation of governments take place. Change, as we all know, is the only unchangeable law of history. Human societies are in a constant state of flux, however imperceptibly. To decipher these changes, social scientists have often focused on those perennial "functions" that differentiate the structures of society, such as the political, economic, or social institutions. That in turn has led to a division of labor among social scientists between political scientists, economists, sociologists, and others. However, to look at society through the prisms of structures and functions provides only a static and fragmented disciplinary view, hence the need for dynamic and interdisciplinary perspectives. To obtain a dynamic view of society-in-time, social scientists focus on "process," that is, on changes in structures from Time 1 to Time 2, and so on. That process may be identified as "structuration" or "structuring," the latter implying an active agency.

By focusing on structural problems, this book calls attention to the *continuing* military, political, economic, and cultural barriers to security, freedom, justice, and community. By employing a verb, it emphasizes human agency in the deliberate processes of *restructuring.* By using a continuous present tense, it suggests a process of structuration in which human interventions play a critical role.

The title also is linked with a planned series of volumes on the critical issues facing the post-Cold War era. With the decline of the universalist ideological pretensions of the two camps of the Cold War, ethnic conflict is clearly coming to the fore as one of the most pressing sources of conflict. Several volumes in this series will focus on problems of ethnic conflict and peace at the local, state, national, and global levels. The first volume, *Restructuring for Ethnic Peace: A Public Debate at the University of Hawai'i,* was the result of a series of public forums held in the spring of 1991, focusing on current ethnic conflicts on American campuses. Others will focus on problems of ethnic conflict and peace in the state of Hawai'i, North America, and other regions of the world.

To situate the contribution of this book, it might be useful to recognize that the field of peace studies is characterized by three dominant theoretical and ideological tendencies: reformist, structuralist, and transformationist. The reformist school is premised on an incremental approach to peacemaking, primarily focusing on security and disarmament issues. The structuralist school calls attention to the basic institutional barriers to peace and security, such as the conditions of structural violence, and is focused on restructuring domestic and international relations in order to achieve greater social harmony and social justice. The transformationist school is premised on the need for the spiritual and cultural transformation of individuals and society in order to incorporate new values—notably the principle of nonviolence—needed before any lasting institutional changes can be made. Although the three perspectives are not mutually exclusive and one often flows into the other, the literature of peace studies is characterized by these three distinct tendencies.

Without rejecting the reformist and transformationist premises, we have chosen to focus on restructuring for peace because this particular historical moment calls for a careful and critical re-examination of the postwar institutional arrangements. These arrangements had generated a prolonged cold war and hot wars in Korea, Vietnam, Central America, and the Middle East, not to mention the conditions of structural violence in South Africa and wherever else significant populations are held in bondage. The arrangements themselves therefore needed questioning. Lasting world peace seems to call for restructuring the institutional arrangements that exacerbate both domestic and international conflict. For example, superpower rivalries and nuclear terrorism have been major sources of instability, and the continuing disenfranchisement of large communities, such as the Kurds and the Palestinians, has been another structural barrier to stable peace.

Thus, this volume is organized around the theme of restructuring for peace with democracy, incorporating the values of security, freedom, justice, and community into the world institutional arrangements. The participants in the project were challenged to respond to the following sets of questions on the challenges facing the world in the post-Cold War era as we move towards a new century.

1. Was De Tocqueville right in his prophesy? Is democracy an inexorable force in modern history that has created its own new forms of tyranny and domination? Are the democratic norms of security, freedom, justice, and community fully compatible or in tension? If in tension, how can they be turned into creative tension? To achieve that, is there any right set of institutional checks and balances between the state, the market, the civil society, and the primordial bonds of identity and solidarity? In other words, is there one or many roads to democracy? Are there any safeguards against the totalitarian temptations characteristic of the transitional stage to modern industrial societies?

2. In an increasingly multipolar and interdependent world, how can we reconceptualize national security to include regional, global, and ecological security? Can national security still serve as a guiding star for policy? Are regional security pacts such as NATO still useful tools for regional collective security? Is the United Nations in its present form adequate to meet the challenges of global collective security? How can we channel the emerging regional economic and political blocs such as the European, the North American, and the Asia-Pacific economic communities into global cooperation for peace and security rather than into interregional rivalries and confrontations for domination?

3. Where is the place of freedom in the evolution of the concept of human rights, from the first generation of rights focusing on individual civil rights, to the second generation of rights concentrating on social and economic rights, and the third generation of rights emphasizing the rights of collectivities and communities? What about the balance between human rights and human responsibilities? In a multicultural world, how can we reconcile the universal rights of freedom with its particularistic cultural interpretations?

4. Can there be any meaningful security and freedom in the world without justice? If not, how can we correct the growing gaps within and among nations resulting from the apparent tendency of market forces towards concentration of economic and political power? Are there any institutional arrangements other than oligopolistic capitalism or monopolistic communism to deal with the perennial economic problems of optimum, ecologically, and socially responsible production and distribution? If so, how do such movements as the social democratic, Green, or communitarian movements propose to deal with the problems of economic organization, productivity, environment, and human incentives? What about the counter-intuitive behavior of social systems in which the best of intentions for social justice sometimes lead to its very opposite?

5. In a world characterized by increasing cultural homogenization through the diffusion of a global pop culture, how can the cultural integrity and sense of community of the less developed nations be preserved against the cultural domination of the more developed? Is the rise of fundamentalism a form of cultural guerilla action by the weak against the strong in order to gain solidarity in the struggles between rich and poor? How can we allow for the political expressions of cultural identity and communal solidarity without tyrannizing minorities and dissenters? How can we develop an interlocking spiral of human communities from the family and local community to national, regional, and global communities, each enriching rather than suffocating the others? Above all, how can we arrive at a set of globally understood and respected methods of conflict resolution to enhance and bind the human community? In the struggle for world peace, is it desirable to move incrementally from the construction of specific peace zones in culturally homogeneous areas of protracted conflict, such as Kurdistan and Palestine, to more generalized peace zones in regional common markets, and finally to a global commonwealth? Finally, how can we safeguard the rights of each individual and community as the condition for the fulfillment of the rights of all others?

Each chapter in this volume responds to these questions in its own unique way and in the context of the normative principles of peace with democracy, including security, freedom, justice, and community. Chapter 1 by Majid Tehranian argues that since the 18th century the world has experienced at least three cycles of democratic and counterdemocratic revolutions. The First Cycle started with the English, American, and French Revolutions, followed by the counterdemocratic restorations of European monarchies in the 19th century. The Second Cycle, starting roughly a century later during World War I, led to the fall of the Russian, German, Austrio-Hungarian, and Ottoman Empires, followed by the rise of modern totalitarian regimes under Stalin, Hitler, Mussolini, Franco, and Peron. The Third Cycle occurred during World War II and led to the fall of British, French, Dutch, Belgian, and Portuguese empires, and the rise of postcolonial states in Africa, Asia, and Latin America. We seem to be at the dawn of a Fourth Cycle. The end of the Cold War, the fall of Eastern European dictatorships, the rise of democratic movements in the former Soviet Union, Eastern Europe, China, the Philippines, and South Africa, all seem to suggest it. The counterrevolutionary trends in China (the Tiananmen Square massacre of 1989) and in the former Soviet Union (the attempted coup of 1991) also confirm some recurrent historical patterns.

In Chapter 2, Johan Galtung provides a portrait of the transformations occuring in this fourth cycle of world democratic revolutions and counterrevolutions. He identifies 14 conflict formations and seven geopolitical regions in the world as his focus of analysis. He also provides a set of concluding guideposts for pursuing peace with peaceful means. Although his model of an emerging world dis/order is not comforting, his diagnosis is sobering and his prescriptions promising.

Part I of this volume focuses on Restructuring for Peace with Security. In Chapter 3, Carolyn Stephenson provides a review of the evolution of the concept of security from negative peace concepts, the absence of war, to positive peace concepts, the presence of social harmony and justice. The emerging concepts of security include economic and ecological as well as military security. In Chapter 4, Kennedy Graham presents a thoughtful analysis of arms control and disarmament negotiations, the recent breakthroughs, and their implications for the future. Although he does not see a general disarmament plan in the offing, he is cautiously optimistic about imposing limitations on the international arms race. In Chapter 5, Angela Knippenberg studies the changing role of the United Nations in the new era. Without considering the UN as a panacea, she points out how the organization can be of extraordinary significance in the building of confidence and trust among the disputing parties. But she does not expect the UN to take the place of direct superpower negotiations. In Chapter 6, focusing on the contributions of social movements in peace building, Paul Smoker comes back to the theme of redefining the concept of security more inclusively. He also focuses on how the new electronic networks such as Bitnet, PeaceNet, and EcoNet contribute to the educational and social resources for peace studies, peacemaking, and peace building.

Part II, Restructuring for Peace with Freedom, emphasizes the role of international law, adjudication, and sanctions in the protection and extension of human rights. In Chapter 7, Patricia Hyndman provides an overview of the problems involved in achieving a more effective system for the protection of human rights, employing her experiences with LAWASIA as a point of reference. In Chapter 8, Jon Van Dyke and Gerald Berkley focus on how a newly established democratic regime should handle the gross violations of fundamental human rights by a previous authoritarian regime. They argue that a deliberate approach should be assumed so that the new atmosphere of democratic freedom is not turned into one of revenge and retribution. Their case studies of Argentina, Chile, Uruguay, and Spain provide ample evidence for this thesis. In Chapter 9, Ved Nanda provides a cogent argument for "humanitarian intervention" while safeguarding against its possible abuses. He employs the case of the Kurdish revolt in Iraq to illustrate his points. Chapters 10 to 12 focus on in-depth case studies of the Gulf War, native Hawaiians, and Japanese-American internees during World War II. Frank Newman calls for the primacy of international law in the conduct of international relations. Davianna McGregor argues for redress of the grave violations of the rights of indigenous peoples, such as native Hawaiians, native Americans, the Inuit, and the Maoris. Eric Yamamoto applies lessons from the reparations made to Japanese Americans interned during World War II to other similar cases of grave violations of the civil rights of ethnic minorities.

Part III argues for Restructuring for Peace with Justice. In Chapter 13, Björn Hettne provides an overview of the likely regional formations in the coming decades, focusing on the problems and prospects of each region for peace and development. In contrast to Galtung's view of regionalism as a dominant conflict formation in the post-Cold War era, Hettne presents a cautiously optimistic view for regional integration, peace, and development. If the new age is an Age of Regions, it may be also argued that the greatest threats to peace and security will come from world regional rivalries and conflicts. In Chapter 14, Holly Sklar provides one such argument by presenting a critique of American hegemony in the "new world order," juxtaposing it with the possibilities of a "fair world order" for which peace scholars and activists must work. In Chapter 15, Petra Kelly, a founding leader of the German Green Party, provides another critique of the dominant industrial system of Western Europe and North America, as it foments wars, pollutes the environment, and widens the global gaps between rich and poor both within and among nations. On the fate of the Third World, she quotes an African proverb, "When elephants make war, the grass gets trampled. When elephants make love, the grass gets trampled." Finally, Herb Addo presents an authentic voice of the Third World on the impediments the new world order continues to present to the fulfillment of global justice.

Part IV focuses on Restructuring for Peace with Community. The four essays in this part point to three major paradigmatic shifts in global consciousness that imply new epistemic and political communities. In Chapter 17, Michael Haas reviews the evolution of the notion of community and international integration, while arguing for a bottom-up approach to the building of regional communities. He demonstrates how the top-down approaches such as the Southeast Treaty Organization (SEATO) have failed, while the bottom-up approaches such as the Association of South East Asian Nations (ASEAN) have succeeded. In Chapter 18, John Burton provides a synopsis of his conflict resolution theories, with a focus on the emerging world problems of ethnic conflict breaking up such countries as Canada, the USSR, and Yugoslavia. He advocates a replacement of power politics with peace politics that focus on fulfilling basic human needs, including the nonnegotiable needs for cultural identity. In Chapter 19, Mark Juergensmeyer presents an analysis of the worldwide rise of religious, as opposed to secular, politics. He, too, considers primordial identity as a legitimate human need to be respected and fulfilled instead of denied and destroyed. He points to the formation of such religious states as Islamic Iran and possibly a Hindu India in which religion is recognized as a defining feature of the state. In Chapter 20, Tu Wei-Ming provides an apt conclusion to such a globally conscious collection of essays. He argues for a search for universal core values, what was known in an earlier era as the perennial philosophy, to bring humanity closer to a new consciousness of its own essential unity and common destiny in the midst of cultural diversities that must be not only tolerated and respected but also celebrated.

An ambitious, some may say overambitious, project such as this could not have been undertaken without the moral and material support of many collaborators. Aside from the authors presented in this volume, the editors are particularly grateful to the Matsunaga Peace Foundation and its able President Cherryl Matano, to the United Nations University and its Vice-Chancellor Roland Fuchs, to the Institute of Culture and Communication of the East-West Center and its past Director Tu Wei-Ming, and to President Albert J. Simone of the University of Hawaii for their financial and intellectual support of the project. We are also thankful to the able staff of the Spark M. Matsunaga Institute for Peace for their support of the project in various ways: to Associate Director Rhoda Miller for her able management of the conference, to Stanley Schab for his diligent editorial assistance in nursing this volume to the publisher, and to George Kent, Director of the Master's Program in Peace and Conflict Resolution, for acting as an exacting, in-house critic of the final manuscript.

As the medieval Sufi masters would have said, whatever light this volume sheds comes from the Divine, whatever errors therein stem from the hands of the editors!

Katharine & Majid Tehranian
Honolulu, Hawai'i

About the Editors

KATHARINE TEHRANIAN is assistant professor of American studies at the University of Hawai'i at Mānoa. Her teaching and research focus on American cultural history, with particular emphasis on the evolution of cities, architecture, art, and environment. Her many publications include *A Study of Housing in Nine Low Income Communities in Tehran* (1973), *An Annotated Bibliography of the Persian Cities of 5th-10th Centuries* (1978), and the forthcoming works *The City as Discourse* and *Images of American Landscape*.

MAJID TEHRANIAN, is currently professor of communication at the University of Hawai'i at Mānnoa and director of the Pacifica Institute of Policy Studies. His chief areas of teaching and research include the political economy of communication, peace and development, intercultural and international communication, and telecommunications policy and planning. He also specializes in Middle Eastern and Asia-Pacific affairs. His most recent publications include *Technologies of Power: Information Machines and Democratic Prospects* (1990) and the edited volumes *Letters from Jerusalem* (1989) and *Restructuring for Ethnic Peace: A Public Debate at the University of Hawai'i*.

About the Contributors

HERB ADDO is a senior research fellow in political economy at the Institute of International Relations at the University of the West Indies, Saint Augustine, Trinidad. His publications on the political economy of development include *Transforming the World Economy?* (1984), *Development as Social Transformation* (1985), which he edited, and numerous articles on the problems of Third World development.

GERALD W. BERKLEY is a professor of history at the University of Guam. Holder of both a Ph.D. in modern Chinese history from the University of Hong Kong and a J.D. from the Richardson School of Law at the University of Hawai'i, he is the author of numerous articles on comparative law and modern China.

ELIZABETH (BETTY) BUCK is a political scientist and research associate in the Institute of Culture and Communication of the East-West Center, Honolulu, Hawai'i. She is the author of *The Politics of Culture: A History of the Social and Cultural Transformation of Hawaii* and coauthor of *Music at the Margins: Popular Music and Global Cultural Diversity* (1991).

JOHN BURTON, pioneer conflict resolution theorist, was founder of the Centre for the Analysis of Conflict, University of Kent, and codirector of the Center for Development and Conflict Resolution at the University of Maryland and the George Mason Institute for Conflict Analysis and Resolution. He is the author of many seminal works on conflict resolution, including *International Relations: A General Theory* (1965), *World Society* (1972), *Deviance. Terrorism and War* (1979), *Global Conflict* (1986), and *Conflict: Resolution and Provention* (1990).

JOHAN GALTUNG, Olof Palme Professor of Peace at Stockholm University, founded the International Peace Research Institute (PRIO) in Oslo and its *Journal of Peace Research*. He was UN Environment Programme consultant to the Second Special Session on Disarmament, and has written extensively on peace issues. While visiting professor of peace at the Spark M. Matsunaga Institute in 1990, he published *Peace and Development in the Pacific Hemisphere, Nonviolence and Israel/Palestine*, and *Solving Conflicts*.

KENNEDY GRAHAM is Secretary-General of Parliamentarians for Global Action and former counselor with the New Zealand Mission to the United Nations in Geneva. He has been a diplomat, author, and teacher, serving in the Ministry of Foreign Affairs of New Zealand, teaching international relations at Victoria University in Wellington, and publishing many articles in New Zealand and the United States on international security issues. His latest book is *National Security Concepts of New Zealand* (1989).

MICHAEL HAAS, professor of political science at the University of Hawai'i at Mānoa, is the author of numerous publications in various areas of peace research, including *International Organization* (1971), *International Conflict* (1974), *International Systems* (1974), *Korean Unification* (1989), *The Pacific Way* (1989), and *The Asian Way to Peace* (1989), and the forthcoming *Cambodia, Pol Pot, and the United States* and *Genocide by Proxy*.

BJÖRN HETTNE is director of the Peace and Development Research Institute of Gothenburg University and the author of numerous works on international political economy, peace studies, and the restructuring of the European community.

PATRICIA HYNDMAN is an associate professor at the University of New South Wales faculty of law in Sydney. She has written widely on issues of international human rights law and the applicability of humanitarian law in times of armed conflict. As secretary of the

Human Rights Committee of the Law Association for Asia and the Pacific (LAWASIA) from 1982 to 1990, she helped develop the Model Human Rights Charter for the Pacific Island region.

MARK JUERGENSMEYER is dean of the School of Hawaiian, Asian, and Pacific Studies at the University of Hawai'i at Mānoa and the author of numerous works on ethics and the phenomenology of religions, including *Sikh Studies: Comparative Perspectives on a Changing Tradition* (1979), *Religion as Social Ritual* (1982), *Fighting With Gandhi* (1984), and *Fighting Fair: A Nonviolent Strategy for Resolving Everyday Conflicts* (1986)

PETRA KELLY, member of the German National Parliament from 1983-1990 and cofounder of Die Grünen (Green Party), is a long-time activist in antinuclear, peace, ecological, and feminist movements. Recipient of the Alternative Nobel Prize in 1982 and the U.S. Woman of the Year Award in 1983, she is the author of numerous works including *Fighting for Hope, Can a Third World War Be Prevented?*, *Mit dem Herzen denken*, and with Gert Bastian *Tibet Fights On.*

ANGELA KNIPPENBERG is senior political affairs officer and chief of the world disarmament campaign in the Department for Disarmament Affairs of the United Nations. She has been working for the UN since 1977, with previous assignments in the Department for Public Information, the Office of the Secretary-General, and the UN Fund for Population Activities in Indonesia.

DAVIANNA PŌMAIKA'I McGREGOR is an assistant professor of ethnic studies at the University of Hawai'i at Mānoa and a long-time activist in promoting and protecting native Hawaiian rights. She was a coordinator of the Protect Kaho'olawe 'Ohana and is currently working with the Pele Defense Fund, seeking to protect traditional customs, beliefs, and practices sacred to Pele, the volcano goddess, and other Hawaiian deities, and opposing geothermal energy development of the Kilauea, Hawai'i area.

ANDREW MACK is professor of international relations at the Australian National University. His current research interests include strategic theory; Pacific security, with a particular emphasis on arms control; nuclear and missile proliferation in the Asia-Pacific region; and Australian security issues. He is the author of numerous works on security and international relations, including *War Without Weapons* (1975), *Peace Research in the 1980s* (1985), *The Future of Arms Control* (1987), and *Security and Arms Control in the North Pacific* (1989).

VED P. NANDA is Thompson G. Marsh Professor and director of the international legal studies program at the University of Denver. He has written widely on all aspects of international law, devoting particular attention to human rights issues. Professor Nanda served as vice-president of the American Society of International Law from 1987 to 1988, and is currently the president of the World Association of Law Professors and a member of the board of governors of the World Jurist Association of the World Peace Through Law Center.

FRANK C. NEWMAN is Professor Emeritus and former dean of the Law School of the University of California at Berkeley and Justice (retired) of the California Supreme Court. His many years of teaching and writing have been instrumental in introducing the study of international human rights at U.S. law schools. He regularly attends the meetings of the Human Rights Commission in Geneva, representing various nongovernmental organizations in their efforts to protect the human rights of oppressed groups throughout the world.

SYED A. RAHIM is a senior researcher at the Institute of Culture and Communication of the East-West Center, Honolulu, Hawai'i. His current research concerns the cultural dimensions of development and modernization, examined from the perspective of communicative rationality and action. His recent publications include *Computerization and Development in Southeast Asia* (1987), and *Poststructuralist Concepts in Culture and Communication* (1989).

HOLLY SKLAR, a writer and lecturer living in Boston, is the author of *Washington's War On Nicaragua* and *Trilateralism: The Trilateral Commission and Elite Planning for World Management*, and coauthor of *Poverty in the American Dream*. She is currently coauthoring a book offering alternative approaches for community-based planning and development. Sklar is a columnist for *Z Magazine*, cohost of "Central America Update" on CCTV, and was an observer to the 1990 Nicaraguan elections and a delegate to the 1990 Soviet-American Women's Summit. She serves on the boards of the Latin America and Caribbean Program and the Nationwide Women's Program of the American Friends Service Committee.

PAUL SMOKER is Lloyd Professor of political science and world law at Antioch College and secretary-general of the International Peace Research Association. He has published more than 80 books and articles on peace studies; the most recent, *A Reader in Peace Studies* (1990), is an introductory text for college courses. He has taught extensively in the U.S., Europe, and Asia.

ROBERT STAUFFER is Professor Emeritus of political science at the University of Hawai'i at Mānoa. Many of his articles and edited books deal with the political economy of development, especially under conditions of extreme external great power interference, as in the Philippines. He has also written on alternative development strategies and on the struggle to achieve a more democratic polity when the very concept is employed as a means of maintaining the status quo.

CAROLYN STEPHENSON is assistant professor of political science at the University of Hawai'i at Mānoa. Editor of *Alternative Methods for International Security* (1982) and for many years coeditor of the journal *Peace and Change,* she has served as vice-chairperson of the Consortium on Peace Research, Education and Development; council member of the International Peace Research Association; and chair of the environmental studies section and member of the governing board of the International Studies Association.

TU WEI-MING is professor of Chinese history and philosophy at Harvard University and the author of numerous groundbreaking works on Confucian humanism, Chinese intellectual history, and comparative religion, including *Neo-Confucian Thought in Action* (1976), *Centrality and Commonality: An Essay on Chung-yung* (1976), *Humanity and Self-Cultivation* (1979), *Confucian Thought: Selfhood as Creative Transformation* (1985), and *The Way, Learning, and Politics* (1989).

JON M. VAN DYKE is professor of law at the William S. Richardson School of Law at the University of Hawai'i at Mānoa, where he teaches international and constitutional law. The author of numerous articles on human rights, he assisted with the drafting of the Model Pacific Human Rights Charter and is co-counsel in the class action case against the Marcos Estate for human rights abuses in the Philippines during the martial law period. A member of the board of directors of the Native Hawaiian Legal Corporation from 1978 to 1985, he is currently a consultant to the Office of Hawaiian Affairs on claims against the state and federal governments.

ERIC KEN YAMAMOTO is associate professor of law at the William S. Richardson School of Law at the University of Hawai'i at Mānoa. He has been active in addressing the wrongs imposed upon Japanese-Americans during World War Il and worked with a team of lawyers in California to set aside the Supreme Court's flawed decision in *Korematsu v United States* (1944). A council member of the Matsunaga Institute for Peace, he is on the board of directors of the Native Hawaiian Legal Corporation, and works with the Native Hawaiian Advisory Council on native rights issues in Hawai'i.

WORLD CONFLICT ZONES—JULY 1992

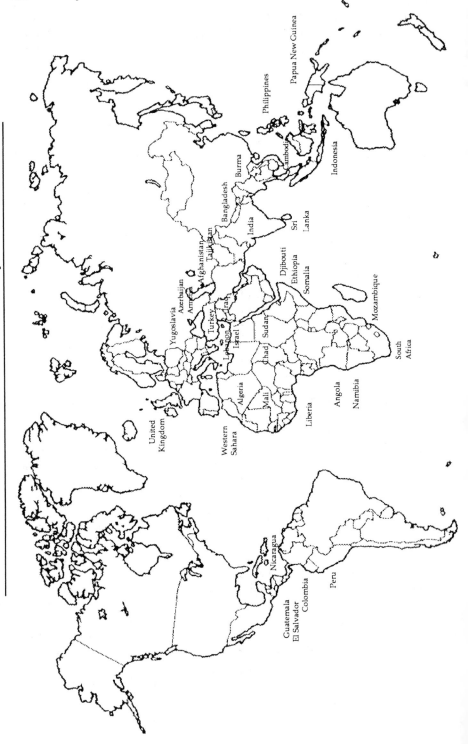

LEGEND

CW = civil war
X = war of secession or independence
10 = conflict lasting more than 10 years
F = foreign involvement
P = new peace
UN = UN peacekeeping involvement

Map   xxv

Latin America

Country	CW	X	10	I	F	P	UN
Colombia			10	I			
El Salvador						P	UN
Guatemala				I		P	UN
Nicaragua						P	UN
Peru				I			

Africa

Country	CW	X	10	I	F	P	UN
Algeria	CW						
Angola			10		F	P	UN
Chad			10	I	F		
Djibouti				I	F		
Ethiopia	X		10	I		P	
Liberia	CW				F		
Mali				I			
Mozambique	CW		10	I		P	
Namibia			10			P	UN
Somalia	CW	X		I			
South Africa	CW		10				
Sudan	CW	X	10				
Western Sahara		X	10		F	P	UN

Europe

Country	CW	X	10	I	F	P	UN
Armenia		X					
Azerbaijan		X					
Tajikistan	CW						
Turkey				I			
United Kingdom			10	I			
Yugoslavia	CW	X					

Asia

Country	CW	X	10	I	F	P	UN
Afghanistan	CW		10			P	UN
Bangladesh			10	I			
Burma			10	I			
Cambodia	CW		10		F	P	UN
India		X	10	I			
Indonesia		X	10	I			
Iraq	CW			I			
Israel				I		P	
Lebanon	CW		10		F		
Papua New Guinea	X		10				
Phillipnes			10	I			
Sri Lanka		X	10		F	P	UN

1

Restructuring for Peace: A Global Perspective

MAJID TEHRANIAN

> Ah, Love! could thou and I with Fate conspire
> To grasp this sorry Scheme of Things entire,
> Would not we shatter it to bits—and then
> Re-mould it nearer to the Heart's Desire!
>
> Omar Khayyam, *Rubaiyat*
> Translated by Edward Fitzgerald

Peace scholars often make a useful distinction between negative and positive conceptions of peace. Negative peace is simply the absence of war; positive peace is also viewed as the absence of war, but with the presence of genuine human harmony and cooperation to achieve security and justice in human affairs. The former focuses on the use of force to pursue power; the latter emphasizes the pursuit of peace and justice with peaceful means. The peace movement has been similarly divided into two conflicting camps, the advocates of peace through strength and peace through social justice (Thomas and Klare 1989; Claude 1971; Mack 1985; Stephenson 1989; Tehranian 1990a; Bardash 1991).

This chapter reviews the theoretical debate between the two camps before developing a third, *communitarian*, perspective. Theories of hegemony, balance of power, and collective security in the negative peace school are compared and contrasted with the perspectives on international law, international integration, and nonviolent resistance that characterize the positive peace school of thought. The chapter argues that without a sense of world moral and material community, durable peace cannot be achieved. This calls for communitarian, rather than coercive or hegemonic strategies of peacebuilding. A stable system of international peace requires a high level of integration based on

1

international collective security, national self-determination, economic interdependence, and shared cultural values. The chapter then focuses on the problems of restructuring for peace with the democratic values of security, freedom, justice, and community in the post-Cold War era. It concludes with an analysis of different possible scenarios on the shape of the new world order, arguing for a multipolar, communitarian, global system that can accommodate peaceful change without privileging any single national or regional power as the new hegemon.

THEORIES OF NEGATIVE AND POSITIVE PEACE

Theories of negative peace focus on the direct or indirect uses of force in international security systems. The main theoretical schools in this camp are hegemony theory, balance of power theory, and collective security theory.

Starting from the Marxist theories of capitalist development, *hegemony theory* has argued that ever since the sixteenth century, the world system has been increasingly dominated by a core of capitalist countries in Western Europe and North America, penetrating the peripheries in Africa, Asia, and Latin America through a combination of coercive and noncoercive (political, economic, and cultural) means (Wallerstein 1979). Imperialism, colonialism, and neocolonialism have served as the dominant modes of this penetration. This theoretical perspective further argues that a third group of countries, labeled semi-peripheries (e.g., Singapore, Hong Kong, South Korea, and Taiwan) have emerged in recent decades to serve as the economic entrepots of the core countries in the processes of transfer of surplus value from the less to the more developed countries. Due to resistance movements in the peripheries and competition among the core countries, the international peace and security achieved by such a system is viewed as inherently unstable. However, when a great power hegemon such as Britain in the nineteenth century or the United States in the post-World War II period achieves a high degree of military and economic superiority, it can impose its own Pax Britannica or Pax Americana on the rest of the world—at least for a while. President Bush's call for a New World Order may be considered one such effort in the post-Cold War era. The shift of emphasis from the postwar discourse of "development" to a discourse of "order" may be interpreted as a new hegemonic project in which the dualistic nature of the world system is officially acknowledged. In this new order, the less developed countries are induced (by force as well as persuasion) to accept their place as the suppliers of strategic locations, cheap labor, and raw materials while lowering their economic expectations and political claims. Despite the moral repugnance of Saddam Hussein's invasion of Kuwait, the global significance of the Gulf War may be better understood in this larger context (Cummings 1991; Abu-Lughod 1991).

Balance of power theories, premised mostly on liberal conceptions of international relations, have argued that in the absence of any moral consensus in a world of autonomous nation-states, peace and security can be achieved mainly through the use of a combination of force and persuasion in pursuit of competing national interests (Morgenthau 1978). A world power such as Britain or the United States is also faced at times with the role of the balancer-of-power among these competing powers. From time to time, a world power may have to intervene in conflicts such as World War I, World War II, or the Persian Gulf War to maintain or restore a balance. In contrast to the hegemonic theories that view imperialism as the highest stage of capitalism, balance of power theories view it as any challenge to the status quo. In the Cold War years, therefore, Soviet policies in Europe and the Middle East were considered by the balance of power theorists as imperialist, while Western policies were viewed as status quo policies. Similarly Saddam Hussein's invasion of Kuwait invoked the memory of Hitler's invasion of Poland. From a balance of power perspective, an appeasement policy was considered as reprehensible in the former case as in the latter.

In the twentieth century, however, both hegemony and balance of power theorists have recognized the need for a system of *collective security*. The proliferation of the nation-state system with its inherent instability, leading to two world wars in one century, led to the formation of the world's two leading systems of collective security, the League of Nations and the United Nations. But both organizations failed to fulfill their promises of collective security. Two particular events dramatized these failures: the invasion of Ethiopia by Mussolini in 1935, while the League of Nations stood by, and the outbreak of the Korean War in 1950, under the aegis of the United Nations, while the Soviet Union absented itself from the Security Council in protest against the UN failure to admit mainland China.

The proponents of positive peace do not deny the importance of collective security for a durable system of international peace, but they maintain that the pursuit of peace must be based on a profound commitment to justice and the use of peaceful rather than violent means (Galtung 1975; K. Boulding 1977). In this respect, therefore, the theories are unabashedly normative. Radical pacifists would opt for a total renunciation of the use of violence, while moderate pacifists concede the need for the use of force only as a last resort and under stringent conditions. Three theoretical strands are prominent: international law, international integration, and nonviolent resistance.

Theories of *international law and order* would condition the use of force in international disputes upon Article 1 of the United Nations Charter (Falk, Kratochwil, and Mendlovitz 1985). This article sets forth the maintenance of international peace and security as the primary purpose of the organization. To that end, it calls upon the member states "to take effective collective measures for the prevention and removal of threats to the peace, and for the suppression of acts of aggression or other breaches of the peace, and to bring about by peaceful means, and in conformity with the principles of justice and international law, adjustment or settlement of international disputes or situations which might lead to a breach of the peace." More explicitly, paragraph 3 in Article 2 of the Charter stipulates that "all Members shall settle their international disputes by peaceful means in such a manner that international peace, security, and justice, are not endangered." Paragraph 7 of the same article, however, declares that "nothing contained in the present Charter shall authorize the United Nations to intervene in matters which are essentially within the domestic jurisdiction of any state or shall require the Members to submit such matters to settlement under the present Charter; but this principle shall not prejudice the application of enforcement measures under Chapter VII." Article 39 in Chapter VII places this responsibility squarely upon the Security Council, under its principle of the unanimity of the five permanent members. "The Security Council," it reads, "shall determine the existence of any threat to the peace, breach of the peace, or act of aggression and shall make recommendations, or decide what measures shall be taken in accordance with Articles 41 and 42, to maintain or restore international peace and security." (The quotations from the charter are taken from Morgenthau 1978: 561-586.)

The pious wishes of the the United Nations Charter, however, have not often worked in practice. A second strand of theory in positive peace literature, therefore, focuses on what has come to be known as the *integration* or "cobweb theory" of international relations (Burton 1984). This theory maintains that while international law has delegitimized the use of force, it has not precluded it. More probably, international integration theorists argue, a cobweb of interdependence among autonomous nation-states has maximized the costs and minimized the benefits of the use of force in the settlement of international disputes. For this reason, the theory is also known as the "neo-realism" or "interdependency" theory (Keohane and Nye 1989). For empirical proof, integration theorists point with satisfaction to the world's longest, peaceful border between the United States and Canada and the remarkable achievement of peace and security among the members of the European Economic Community. Moreover, violence has broken out most often among those states with the least degree of socioeconomic interdependence and integration. Witness the Korean, Vietnamese, and Middle Eastern wars, in which a combination of external superpower rivalries and internal or regional conflicts have brought about the most bloody and protracted conflicts of the post-World War II period.

Last but not least, theories of *nonviolent resistance* have taken the notions of positive peace a step further towards a radical questioning of the use of force in the settlement of international and domestic disputes (Sharp 1985). The Gandhian theory of satyagraha has also provided both a conceptual and practical justification for the use of nonviolent means in conflict resolution (Gandhi 1984; Unnithan 1987). The case for nonviolence has been supported by such movements as the struggles for independence in India and civil rights in the United States. In these cases, however, the presence of a strong body of opinion in Britain and the United States sympathetic to the cause of the nonviolent resisters may be considered vital to their success. Due to the weakness of such a moral community in the world today, nonviolent theories and strategies have been considered by "realists" as inapplicable to international politics. The wars in Korea, Vietnam, and the Middle East have also amply demonstrated how irreconcilable moral and political positions have led to protracted conflicts. However, nonviolent methods of conflict resolution have received considerable scholarly and practical attention in specific conflict situations (Ariyaratne 1982; Sharp 1985).

COERCIVE, HEGEMONIC, AND COMMUNITARIAN ORDERS

The foregoing discussion of theories of international peace and security suggests that like a chameleon, the slogan of the New World Order also has many changing colors. Depending on who has used the slogan when, it has conjured up vastly different images. To President Bush, its most recent author, it has meant U.S. hegemony in a post-Cold War world. To the Group of 77 at the United Nations, calling for a New International Economic Order in a 1974 General Assembly resolution, it has meant a revamped international economic system to favor the less developed countries. To UNESCO, which picked it up in the 70s and 80s under the banner of a New World Communication and Information Order, it has meant *balance* as well as *freedom* in world news and information flows.

Given this confusion, it is useful to review the concept historically in order to understand its evolution. World order has historically evolved from *coercive* to *hegemonic* to what may now be called *communitarian*. All the imperial systems of the past, from the Persian to Greek, Roman, Arab, Mongol, Ottoman, French, German, British, Japanese, and American empires have been more or less coercive. They subjugated by force vast numbers of people in the peripheries to the will of a dominant center. The conquests were led sometimes by technologically and militarily superior forces, as in the case of the Persians and the Romans, but at other times by tribal encroachments on sedentary populations, as in the case of the Arab and Mongolian empires.

In the sixteenth century, however, something dramatically different happened. Europeans gained considerable scientific, technological, and economic ground vis-a-vis non-Europeans. A truly new world order was born, leading to the modern industrial world. In most successive battles, the modern Europeans won over the traditional non-Europeans. They subjugated the rest of the world to their command under new colonial and imperial systems. They also created new repressive institutions, such as the massive slavery of blacks, segregation, and apartheid. This repressive regime is not altogether dead; it still lingers on in the form of racism, sexism, and ethnic crimes such as the Holocaust and the internment of Japanese-Americans during World War II. Eventually, imperial rivalries among the Europeans led to two devastating world wars in the twentieth century. With the invention of weapons of mass destruction, war itself seemed to be an outmoded instrument of foreign policy. A new world order had to be invented. Under the League of Nations and its successor, the United Nations, the principles of collective security, de jure equality of member states, veto power of the permanent members of the Security Council, and pacific settlement of disputes became the cornerstones of this new order.

A *hegemonic* world had been born. All nation-states were declared equal in international law, but some were clearly more equal than others. Under the League and the UN, the new world order recommended both *force* and *persuasion*, collective security arrangements as well as ideological debates and legal wranglings. This new order, however, was stillborn. Without the participation of the United States, the League did not enjoy much credibility. The invasion of Ethiopia by Mussolini in 1935, and the failure of the League of Nations to act collectively against the aggressor, put the last nail on the coffin of that order. Similarly, the Cold War between the two superpowers following World War II left little opportunity for the UN Security Council to play its role as the world's policeman.

With the demise of the Cold War, is there any chance for a truly just world order? The Gulf War has demonstrated the opportunities and the pitfalls. In some respects, the new order is a continuation of the old. Immediately following the end of the war, Secretary of Defense Dick Cheney proposed $20 billion in arms sales to five "friendly" Middle Eastern countries: Israel, Turkey, Egypt, Saudi Arabia, and Kuwait.

His reasons were to bolster the U.S. allies and to keep the U.S. arms industry afloat in face of cuts in the defense budget. A newspaper cartoon told it all: Uncle Sam was portrayed taking new orders for high-tech weapons from a variety of foreign buyers. The caption read: New World Orders! The Gulf War entailed a heavy price: over 100,000 dead, another 100,000 injured, some 5 million turned into refugees, and over $55 billion mostly financed by Saudi Arabia, Kuwait, Germany, and Japan was the price paid for this New World Order.

Despite the disappointments, however, there is an emerging new world consensus on the requirements for enduring international peace and security. That consensus recognizes that enduring peace can come out of a sense of community. Hence, this potential world order may be called *communitarian*. Four elements seem essential to the construction of an effective world community: common *interests*, *norms*, *laws*, and *sanctions*. The increasing transnationalization of the world economy, interdependency, and development of regional common markets seem to be irreversible trends creating lasting common international interests and norms. Although a prolonged economic recession may argue for economic nationalism and protectionism, the old nation-state system alone appears to be no longer economically viable. Regionalism is taking its place. The European Community entered a new phase of monetary and political union in 1992. Other regions of the world are also following suit. The Association of South East Asian Nations (ASEAN) has set the pace for developing countries, a North American common market is in the offing, and an Asia-Pacific Economic Community (APEC) has been meeting to develop a Pacific community analogous to the Atlantic community (see Chapters 13 and 17). The 1991 breakup of the Soviet empire into a Commonwealth of Independent States also is a compression of these two long-term trends into a single process, including the *revolutionary* fragmentation of imperial systems into nation-states, and the *evolutionary* process of states within the same region coming together into communitarian economic and political arrangements.

There is a risk, of course, that these budding regional blocs could turn to intense economic competition and possible political confrontation rather than cooperation (as discussed in Chapters 2 and 13). However, global interdependency has become an emerging international norm to be acknowledged and respected. The new rules of interdependency emphasize peaceful settlement of disputes, the need for the global protection of the environment, use of technology, trade and development policies to overcome the gaps between the rich and the poor, and a universal application of human rights.

There is an urgent need, therefore, for an expanding body of international law, sanctions, and institutions to provide for the enforcement of these norms and for the redress of any violations (examined in Part II). The world community ultimately depends on a fragile moral community. Without solidifying these norms, it will be torn apart. However, the existing infrastructure of the international legal system is still crying out for greater use, particularly by the Great Powers who refuse to honor it when it is not in their interest.

RESTRUCTURING FOR PEACE WITH DEMOCRACY

This book is organized around the four democratic values of security, freedom, justice, and community. The domestic sources of these democratic traditions provide a useful vehicle for building the requisite institutions for a world communitarian order. Since the eighteenth century, democratic forces seem to have gained ground in the world through three long successive cycles of democratic and counterdemocratic revolutions (Rustow 1990).

The English, American, and French revolutions provided the catalysts for the first cycle, spreading the ideals of national self-determination, liberty, equality, and fraternity around the world. In Europe, however, the French Revolution was followed by the rise of Napoleon, the spread of the French revolutionary ideals, the democratic revolutions of 1848, and the counterdemocratic restorations of European monarchies.

The second cycle of democratic revolutions came about a century later during World War I, in which the struggle "to make the world safe for democracy" led to the fall of the Russian, German, Austro-Hungarian, and Ottoman empires. This cycle was similarly followed by another round of counterdemocratic movements and regimes, including the rise of Stalin in the Soviet Union, Hitler in Germany, Mussolini in Italy, and Franco in Spain.

The third global democratic revolution came with World War II, leading to the breakdown of the British, French, Dutch, Belgian, and Portuguese empires and the independence of many colonies in Africa, Asia, and Latin America. It was followed by the rise of indigenous dictatorships in the Third World, often in alliance with the First or Second Worlds.

Are we at the dawn of a fourth cycle of democratic and counterdemocratic revolutions? The end of the Cold War and the democratic movements in the Soviet Union, Eastern Europe, China, the Philippines, and South Africa suggest the return of the cycle. The ensuing instabilities in each of these countries also imply the possibilities for counterrevolution, already visible in China and the Soviet Union. These cycles may be attributed to the dialectics of development, in which the forces of economic accumulation, political mobilization, and cultural integration interact to produce the historical cycles of economic growth, political repression, and cultural integration along the lines of democratic norms and institutions (Tehranian 1990a, b). Figure 1 captures these democratic and counterdemocratic cycles in terms of periods of high accumulation, often accompanied by centralization of power, followed by periods of high mobilization characterized by rising social claims for political participation and egalitarian income distribution. The social and political dislocations of accumulation and mobilization, in turn, call for periods of high integration in which the regime in power attempts to unify the conflicting social claims by commitment to a common ideology (nationalism, communism, religion, democracy).

What Rostow (1960) called the pathology of the transition from preindustrial to industrial societies may thus be viewed as an *etatist* stage ("l'état, c'est moi!"), in which the repressive apparatus of the state ensures high levels of primitive capital accumulation under conditions of political repression. The enlightened despotisms of Western European monarchies, the communist dictatorships in the Soviet Union, China, and Cuba, the fascist regimes in Japan, Germany, Italy, and Spain, as well as the military dictatorships in some parts of the Third World are variants of the same essentially etatist stage in development. All these dictatorships have sown the seeds of their own destruction by creating an educated, professional, and mobilized intelligentsia whose political consciousness tends to be grounded in modern democratic norms. The achievement of democratic rules and institutions, however, has not moved with the same degree of certainty and uniformity in the experience of nations. More often than not, democracy is achieved through long processes of trial and error, as experienced in the historical cycles of accumulation/repression and mobilization/democratization.

Due to the worldwide diffusion of modern democratic ideas, national self-determination, freedom, equality, and community have become generally accepted values in the international community. These values closely correspond with the American and French revolutionary slogans of independence, liberty, equality, and fraternity. Collectively, therefore, they can provide the normative foundations upon which a meaningful world political community can be built. Figure 2 provides a schematic view of the dominant democratic and counterdemocratic world ideologies and political systems in the twentieth century. The axial principles of security (cum order), freedom, justice (cum equality), and community (cum fraternity) have

Accumulation

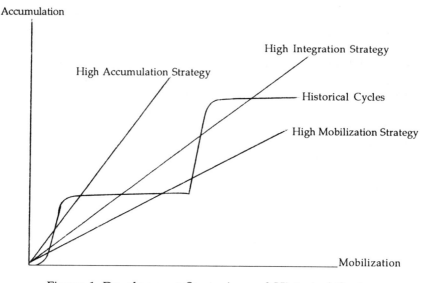

Figure 1. Development Strategies and Historical Cycles

Source: Tehranian 1990a. Reprinted by permission of Sage Publications, Inc.

come to represent the competing truth claims of modern totalitarianism, liberalism, communism, and communitarianism (Tehranian 1990c). The international system is gradually and hesitatingly institutionalizing these prevailing norms in its laws and practices. Relative to domestic political systems, the international system is clearly primitive and not as well integrated with respect to the norms of security, freedom, justice, and community. Nevertheless some foundations have already been laid on all four fronts in the United Nations system. The challenge is to recognize what has been accomplished, what needs to be done, and how to move from one point to the next.

Traditional approaches to *security* have focused on balance of power systems, the arms race, disarmament efforts, and how new military technologies, economic and political alliances, and collective security arrangements affect national, regional, and world security systems. Some more recent concepts of security, however, include economic and ecological security as an essential part of the equation (as discussed in Chapters 3 and and 6). Security from threats of economic retaliation (such as trade embargoes or stoppages of oil supplies) and humanmade ecological disasters (such as those at Three Mile Island, Chernobyl, and in the Persian Gulf) are included as important factors in the search for national and international security. Whatever definition we accept, narrow or broad, the search for national, regional,

Key:

Symbolic Color:	THE GREENS
Social System	Communitarian Democracy
Axial Principle	Community
Leadership:	Intelligentsia
Psychic Energy:	Super-Ego
Ideology:	Environmentalism
Development Strategy:	High Integration

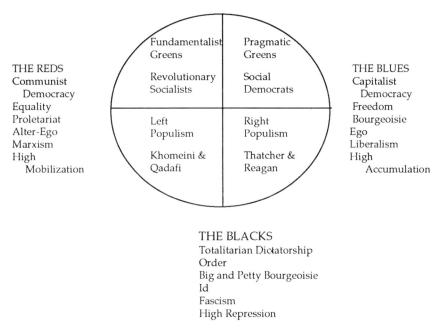

THE REDS
Communist
  Democracy
Equality
Proletariat
Alter-Ego
Marxism
High
  Mobilization

THE BLUES
Capitalist
  Democracy
Freedom
Bourgeoisie
Ego
Liberalism
High
  Accumulation

Within circle:

Fundamentalist Greens | Pragmatic Greens

Revolutionary Socialists | Social Democrats

Left Populism | Right Populism

Khomeini & Qadafi | Thatcher & Reagan

THE BLACKS
Totalitarian Dictatorship
Order
Big and Petty Bourgeoisie
Id
Fascism
High Repression

Figure 2. The Political Spectrum: A Conceptual Map

Source: Tehranian 1990 a. Reprinted by permission of Sage Publications, Inc.

and international security appears to be a primary motivating force in the behavior of state actors in the international arena.

    Freedom as a norm of international community, however, poses greater ambiguities. A distinction between negative and positive freedom—freedom *from* coercion and freedom *to* act autonomously—provides a useful basis for viewing human rights as both protective and empowering. Three successive generations of human rights legislation at the international level have focused, first, on *individual political rights* (as in the Universal Declaration of Human Rights); second, on *social and economic rights* (as in the UN Covenant on Civil and Political Rights); and third, on the *collective rights* of communities (as in the UN Covenant on Economic, Social, and Cultural Rights). Freedom as a norm of international community can therefore be measured in terms of the specific requirements of these declarations and whatever ancillary international legal documents we can locate, including regional declarations or decantations by the specialized agencies of the United Nations on such matters as the rights of ethnic groups and indigenous communities (Falk 1981).

Justice as a norm of international community poses even greater ambiguities and controversies. But an operational definition in terms of the rights of equal treatment and equal opportunity under law provides a solid legal starting point. Both these rights have been specifically defined and guaranteed in the second and third generations of human rights. They have been further defined and guaranteed in a fourth generation of human rights dealing with such structural obstacles to social and economic justice as apartheid, racism, and sexism (Shepard and Nanda 1986; Vaska and Alston 1982; Welch and Meltzer 1984). A legal approach, however, is necessary but not sufficient. Social structural impediments are generally the most serious obstacles to the fulfillment of social and economic justice. A structural approach to peace with justice, therefore, would have to take the claims of competing political ideologies and social systems into serious consideration. The failure of capitalism in the West to deal effectively with the delivery of social services to the urban poor and ethnic minorities of the inner cities has brought liberalism into disrepute even in the United States and Europe (see Chapters 14 and 15). The failure of communism in the Soviet Bloc to deal with the incentive problems in production and the fairness problems in distribution has seriously undermined communist claims to legitimacy. Both factors have opened up an unprecedented opportunity to once again take up the perennial question of the requirements for a just society. As shown in Figure 2, the axis of international debate has effectively shifted from the Cold War antagonisms between capitalism and communism to emerging social movements, which may be characterized as communitarian democratic (notably the Greens and ethnic movements) versus potentially totalitarian counterdemocratic formations (notably right-wing appeals to religious ideologies and imperial adventures) (Tehranian 1990b and Chapters 18 and 19 in this volume).

Last but not least, *community* as a norm of international conduct presents perhaps the greatest possible set of ambiguities and controversies. However, social psychologists generally agree that without a sense of community and the delicate human ties of affection, meaning, purpose, trust, and mutual obligation, atomized individuals often experience intense feelings of anomie and anxiety to the point of suicide (Durkheim 1951; Berger 1973; De Grazia 1948; Chapter 20 in this volume). The threats of a nuclear holocaust and ecological disasters as well as the visions of Planet Earth as a singular, pulsating, blue organism in a vast space of lifelessness, seem to have created a new consciousness of the common destiny of humankind. The Gaia hypothesis proposed by some biologists (Lovelock 1988) underscores this planetary unity when the earth is viewed as a single organism. The occupants of Spaceship Earth are clearly tied together in a number of interlocking communities, from local to provincial, national, regional, global, and planetary. These communities are each characterized by a different set of: (1) core values imparting a common culture and meaning system, (2) communication systems (verbal, nonverbal, and visual) and media channels (print, electronic, and integrated systems digital networks), (3) commonly agreed upon systems of human agency and intervention (command, market, planning, and legislation), and (4) generally accepted norms on methods of conflict regulation. The strengths and weaknesses of a community are clearly a function of the degree to which these four conditions are operative. As we move from the local to the global and planetary communities, however, the ties and sense of community weaken (E. Boulding 1988).

WHOSE ORDER IN THE NEW WORLD ORDER?

Communitarian democratic ideals, however, have to be measured against the realities of a world in turmoil and transition. The world community in the closing decade of the twentieth century appears to stand at a critical juncture. The Gulf War marked the end of one era and the beginning of another. With the end of the Cold War and the decline of the Soviet Bloc, the era of *bipolarity* has clearly come to an end. Are we entering a new era of *monopolarity* under the hegemonic leadership of the United States, *tripolarity* under the combined and coordinated leadership of the United States, a united Europe, and Japan, or *multipolarity* characterized by competing and cooperating regional power blocs? Does the world order continue to be fundamentally the same as it has been since the sixteenth century, as the world system theorists have argued, that is, an expanding capitalist world system led by Western Europe and the United States and lately joined by Japan and the newly industrializing countries (South Korea, Taiwan, Hong Kong, Singapore, and possibly Brazil and India)? Will the international system, as the End-of-History proponents (Fukuyama 1989) have argued, continue to move inexorably in the direction of a single global, liberal, capitalist, democratic political economy? Have ideas and visions as forces in the shaping of world history run their course, as Fukuyama has further argued, so that all that needs to be done is to work out the boring practical details of the triumph of liberal capitalism? Or alternatively, will political and cultural resistance against the hegemonic domination of liberal capitalism continue and will other moral visions and social systems emerge to take the place of what we tend today to consider the prevailing trend?

These are provocative questions to which the Gulf War may have provided some clues. As former President Nixon (1991) keenly observed, the Gulf War was not about democracy or human rights. It was a war primarily about oil and hegemony. Fundamentally, this was a war about who, if anyone, is going to be the boss in the post-Cold War era. In plain language, that is what President Bush's "new world order" means. The Gulf War was part of the dying gasp of the old world order and the birth pangs of a new one.

The postwar bipolar world system had been crumbling long before the visible breakdown of the Soviet Union. In the same way as past imperial systems (Kennedy 1987), both superpowers, the United States and the Soviet Union, lost much of their moral and political authority in an overextension of power leading to external defeats and internal weaknesses. The United States lost its credibility as a superpower by its defeat in Vietnam, mounting foreign debt, and eroding competitive edge in the world markets. The Soviet Union lost its status by its defeat in Afghanistan, the demise of communism in Eastern Europe, and the economic and political exhaustion of the USSR itself. While laissez faire capitalism lost much of its legitimacy in the Great Depression of the 1930s, communism lost its appeal with the collapse of the state-run economies of the Soviet bloc. Although laissez faire capitalism experienced an ideological revival under Reagan and Thatcher during 1980s, it has done so at the cost of considerable social dislocation and dualism (Kuttner 1991).

In the meantime, the rise of such economic superpowers as Japan and Germany leaves little doubt as to what new types of capitalism may succeed and where some of the emerging centers of gravity will be. Unified Germany, as part of an integrated 280 million strong European economy, and Japan, as the leading partner in a newly industrialized Asia-Pacific world, have competed effectively with the United States in world markets. The new capitalism is characterized by an interplay of corporate market forces and dirigist government policies. The emerging camps, however, are plagued with a triple handicap—lack of indigenous energy resources, effective military power, and a unified political will. Control of Middle East oil, historically under Anglo-American interests, will thus be critical to future world power configurations. The reluctance of Germany and Japan to join the U.S. war efforts mainly stemmed from their conflicting strategic interests with that traditional Anglo-American hegemony. While German and Japanese rearmament and European political unification may remove the other two handicaps in the long run, in the short run, the United States will continue to be a dominant global power. This is contingent, however, on U.S. economic recovery and continued political commitment to world leadership. Both factors are currently problematic.

The Gulf War clouded some of these realities. President Bush's political resolve, General Schwarzkopf's successful conduct of a high-tech military operation, and the financial and political support of the allies reasserted U.S. leadership. However, the ensuing civil war in Iraq and continued repressions in Iraq and Kuwait demonstrated that wars can be won while peace is lost. Military victories alone cannot reverse longer-term historical trends. In retrospect, the Gulf War may prove to be another ill-advised adventure in the overextension of American power. Instead of focusing on the fundamental roots of American decline—the rising wealth and income gaps and class strife, and sliding educational and industrial standards, accompanied by deindustrialization and loss of markets—the Reagan-Bush administrations have opted to pursue a policy of superpower hegemony to the neglect of U.S. domestic problems.[1]

The Gulf War served both domestic and foreign U.S. policy purposes. But the Middle East has become a litmus test for the model of the new world order as Pax Americana. Shortly after Iraq invaded Kuwait, President George Bush delivered an address to Congress on September 11, 1990, in which he called the Gulf War a "unique and extraordinary moment" in history, a rare opportunity for nations to act collectively to forestall future acts of aggression. Out of these troubled times, he predicted, "a New World Order can emerge" (Barber 1991: 6). Echoing Woodrow Wilson, Bush went on:

> A hundred generations have searched for this elusive path to peace, while a hundred wars raged across this span of human endeavor, and today that new world is struggling to be born. A world quite different from the one we have known. A world where the rule of law supplants the rule of the jungle. A world in which nations recognize their shared responsibility for freedom and justice. A world where the strong respect the rights of the weak.

These lofty ideals, however, fall flat when matched against the policies pursued in the Middle East. Following the war in Vietnam, the Nixon Doctrine committed the United States to a policy of avoiding ground warfare on the Asian land mass in favor of pursuing a policy of propping up potentates in regions such as the Middle East to act as regional policemen. In the 1970s, it was the Shah of Iran. By arming him to the teeth, the U.S. alienated not only his Arab neighbors but also the Iranian people who were suffering under his dictatorship. The Iranian revolution was a consequence of this policy, pursued from August 1953 when the Shah was reimposed on Iran by a CIA-sponsored coup d'etat. When they lost Iran in 1979, the Western powers turned to Saddam Hussein, who volunteered in the 1980s for the role of the regional gendarme. Once again, a potentate was armed with conventional and unconventional weapons, this time by a combination of Western and Soviet alliance with Iraq in its war against Iran.

In its confrontation with the revolutionary threat of Iran during the 1980s, Iraq assumed the role of a regional policeman. Saddam Hussein's war machine was built during this period by a combination of Western, Soviet, and Arab support in which the USSR, France, Britain, the United States, and Germany provided the arms, Kuwait and Saudi Arabia paid the bills to the tune of some $40 billion, and Egypt provided the manpower. In the meantime, the reality of Saddam Hussein's repression at home and aggression abroad was conveniently ignored. In fact, up to the point of invasion of Kuwait, the United States was providing mixed signals to Hussein on whether or not his claims on Kuwait would be tolerated.[2]

Between August 2, 1990, and January 16, 1991, the interlude between Hussein's invasion of Kuwait and the U.S.-led counteroffensive, the world had an opportunity to employ a combination of military, economic, and diplomatic pressures to persuade him to leave Kuwait. A massive American air and naval presence in the Persian Gulf had already deterred him from invading other Gulf states. A UN peacekeeping ground force would have paved the way for an Iraqi withdrawal from Kuwait without getting the United States directly involved in a ground war. An economic embargo would have worked sooner or later, particularly in a country such as Iraq, which is so heavily dependent on the outside world for its oil income and industrial and military imports. After all, it worked in the cases of Rhodesia and South Africa, which are far less economically dependent than Iraq. The longer it could have lasted, the weaker Hussein's war machine would have become.[3]

The stunning military victory of the U.S.-led forces in the Gulf War, the financial support received from the allies, the demise of the Soviet Union, and the successful launching of a Middle East peace conference in Washington suggest Pax Americana as the shape of the new world order. However, further reflection might suggest otherwise. First, the Gulf War was a unique situation in which an obvious villain, committing an unambiguous act of aggression against a sovereign neighbor, was chastised by an alliance joining the military superiority of the United States with the combined financial ability of Japan, Germany, Kuwait, and Saudi Arabia to defeat an economically and militarily dependent Third World dictatorship. That unique combination may never happen again. Second, the U.S. economic decline and heavy foreign debt would make it virtually impossible in the future for it to conduct a military operation of this magnitude without the full support of allies. Third, as Europe unifies and other regions, such as the Asia-Pacific under Japanese leadership and the Commonwealth of Independent States under Russian leadership, develop more coherent strategic and foreign policy, they are bound to assert their own autonomous interests in international affairs.

The emerging multipolar world must therefore be recognized for what it is. The bipolar world is gone, and no unipolar world under the aegis of Pax Americana appears possible. The United States has the military, but not the economic, prowess to act as the world's policeman. With a $3 trillion foreign debt, the Gulf War is probably the last time the U.S. will be able to launch such a costly military operation. Pressures at home for greater attendance to domestic needs and reluctance abroad to underwrite such massive and costly operations will render them unlikely.[4] Moreover, in other world trouble spots, the United States will not have such rich and willing allies.

The old hegemonic order by a single or two superpowers can no longer be sustained. The new order requires genuine collective security arrangements at both global and regional levels. This can be achieved primarily through the United Nations, itself in need of constitutional reform in order to accommodate changes in the world's changing balance of power, including the rise of Germany and Japan and the restructured Soviet Union. Regional organizations such as the Conference on Security and Cooperation in Europe (including Western as well as Eastern Europe), the Association of Southeast Asian Nations (ASEAN), the Asia-Pacific Economic Cooperation (APEC), and others will play an increasing role in the management of security and cooperation in their own respective regions.

CONCLUSION

"Civilization," as H. G. Wells has said, "is a race between education and catastrophe." In the post-Cold War era, the Gulf War and the Yugoslav civil war have once again proved his point. Despite the significant reduction of international tensions, the world still continues to be a dangerous place. For the future three distinct scenarios present themselves. The first scenario suggests an era of prolonged instability in which the rise of new ethnic consciousness and nationalism will be the major source of internal and external threats to peace and security. With the decline of the United States, the demise of the Soviet Union, and the inability of Europe and Japan to lead, no single power or combination of powers will be able to impose a world hegemony. Under this scenario, if the world recession continues, economic nationalism could combine with political nationalism leading to protectionist policies and ceaseless international friction. The second and equally compelling scenario projects a continuing peaceful evolution of the current regionalist trends towards the formation of several competing regional unions, which eventually could come into serious conflict and even open warfare. The third scenario projects a multipolar, communitarian global system that can accommodate both nation-states and new regional groups by emphasizing common interests, norms, laws, and sanctions without privileging any single national or regional power as the hegemon.

If this third scenario is considered the most desirable, restructuring of the present economic, political, and cultural institutions should proceed on both the domestic and international fronts. Since the sources of most international conflicts are domestic, the resolution of those conflicts—which are often embedded in structural violence— should take priority (as discussed in Chapter 2 and Parts II, III, and IV). There are, however, some international conflicts that stem from an unstable international system breeding mutual fear, insecurity, and violence. Part I of this book focuses on the problems of international armament, disarmament, and confidence building that need to be restructured if the world is to survive the terrible weapons we have amassed in the Cold War era.

NOTES

1. If a serious attempt is not made in the years to come to deal with the fundamental causes of American economic decline, the United States may gradually lose not only its preeminent world position but also possibly its own democratic system of government. The rise of a "warrior class" in the United States, for the first time in its history, also is a significant new factor. The military, with some 5 million active and reserve members, equipped with history's most sophisticated military technologies and organizations, may be tempted at some point to intervene in civilian politics. Under the conditions of a severe economic depression, or even of a prolonged recession, and rising levels of class and ethnic strife, and accompanying problems of violence, crime, and drugs, the military may align itself with right-wing disciplinarian or

fundamentalist religious ideologies to intervene to reestablish a disciplined society. In such an eventuality, traditional American civil liberties may be sacrificed at the altar of law and order.

2. In view of Iraq's historical claims and its previous move to invade in 1961, when Kuwait was declared independent from Britain, it is extraordinary that Hussein's intentions were misunderstood. Satellite monitoring of his troop movements in late July also must have confirmed any sense of history. A rapid deployment of U.S. air and naval forces in the Persian Gulf, accompanied by a UN Security Council resolution calling for a peaceful settlement of the Iraqi-Kuwait disputes, could have deterred Hussein—as the British deployment of forces in 1961 had deterred President Qassem from similar invasion plans.

3. By deciding to go to war on January 16, the Bush administration opted for a quick military victory, against a longer but more prudent, diplomatic course of action. Although the eventual outcome of the war was not in doubt, the rapidity with which Saddam Hussein's war machine came apart was a surprise. What lessons can we draw from this experience? First, although superior military technology and organization are critical factors in a war, the will to fight appears to be a decisive factor. Whereas in Vietnam, a technologically superior United States almost defeated the Vietcong in military terms, a dogged determination by the Vietnamese revolutionaries to carry on finally raised the level of casualties above the U.S. level of tolerance. By contrast Hussein's soldiers proved to be unwilling fighters who were ready, indeed anxious, to surrender en masse. Second, U.S. intelligence seems to have overestimated Hussein's power in the same pattern that had also led to missing the collapse of the Shah in Iran and communism in Eastern Europe. Third, the combination of a high-tech war with low U.S. casualties, careful news management by the Pentagon born out of the Vietnam war experience, and media coverage that showed it as a video game with no visible human suffering, led to a remarkable level of support for the war by the American public. Fourth, however, the war has entailed enormous material and human costs. Iraqi and Kuwaiti economies have lost much of their vital infrastructure. The oil spillage in the Gulf and the six hundred burning wells in Kuwait unleashed the world's biggest ecological disaster. The human casualties of the war and its aftermath in the Iraqi Civil ran into hundreds of thousands dead, injured, and dislocated. Fifth, the war led to a humiliating defeat for Iraq, sowing the seeds of future wars, causing the dislocation of millions of Iraqi Kurds and Shi'ites, instigating U.S. proposals for the sale of over $20 billion of arms to five allied countries (Israel, Turkey, Egypt, Saudi Arabia, and Kuwait), and opening the possibility of a new round of the arms race in the Middle East (Ajami 1990/91; al-Khalil 1991).

4. The U.S. General Accounting Office recently reported that the U.S. actually made a profit from the war (Mack 1991:3).

REFERENCES

Abu-Lughod, Janet. 1991. "Can Japan Become a Hegemon?" Paper presented at the 15th Annual Conference of the American Sociological Association, Political Economy of the World System Section. Honolulu, Hawai'i. March 28-30.

Ajami, Fuad. 1990/91. "The Summer of Arab Discontent." *Foreign Affairs* 69, no. 5 (Winter): 1-20.

Ariyaratne, A. T. 1982. *A Struggle to Awaken.* Moratuwa, Sri Lanka: Sarvodaya.

Barber, Lionel. 1991. "New World Order: The View From America." *Europe* 304 (March): 6-8.

Bardash, David P. 1991. *Introduction to Peace Studies.* Belmont, CA: Wadsworth.

Berger, Peter. 1973. *The Homeless Mind: Modernization and Consciousness.* Harmondsworth, England: Penguin.

Burton, John. 1984. *Global Conflict: The Domestic Sources of International Crisis.* College Park, MD: University of Maryland.

Boulding, Elise. 1988. *Building a Global Civic Culture: Education for an Interdependent World.* New York: Teachers College.

Boulding, Kenneth. 1977. "Twelve Friendly Quarrels with Johan Galtung." *Journal of Peace Research* 14, no. 1: 75-86.

_____. 1989. *The Three Faces of Power.* Newbury Park, CA: Sage.

Claude, Inis. 1971. *Swords into Ploughshares.* New York: Random House.

Cummings, Bruce. 1991. "The Political Economy of the Pacific Rim." Paper presented at the 15th Annual Conference of the American Sociological Association, Political Economy of the World System Section. Honolulu, Hawai'i. March 28-30.

De Grazia, Sebastian. 1948. *Political Community: A Study of Anomie.* Chicago: University of Chicago Press.

Durkheim, Emile. 1951. *Suicide: A Study in Sociology.* New York: Free Press.

Falk, Richard. 1981. *Human Rights and State Sovereignty.* New York and London: Holmes and Meier.

Falk, Richard, Frederich Kratochwil, and Saul Mendlovitz. 1985. *International Law: A Contemporary Perspective.* Boulder, CO: Westview.

Fukuyama, Francis. 1989. "The End of History." *National Interest* 16 (Summer): 3-18.

Galtung, Johan. 1975. *Essays in Peace Research* vol. 1. Copenhagen: Christian Ejlers.

Gandhi, M. K. (1927-29) 1984. *An Autobiography: The Story of My Experiments with Truth*. Harmondsworth:, England Penguin.

Kennedy, Paul. 1987. *The Rise and Fall of the Great Powers*. New York: Random House.

Keohane, Robert O., and Joseph S. Nye, Jr. 1989. *Power and Interdependence*. 2d ed. Glenview, IL: Scott, Foresman.

al-Khalil, Samir. 1991. "Iraq and Its Future." *New York Review of Books*. April 11: 10-20.

Kuttner, Robert. 1991. *The End of Laissez Faire*. New York: Random House.

Lovelock, James. 1988. *The Ages of Gaia: A Biography of Our Living Earth*. New York: Norton.

Mack, Andrew. 1985. *Peace Research in the 1980s*. Canberra: Australian National University.

_____. 1991. "After the Cold War and the Gulf War: Prospects for Security in the Asia-Pacific." Script for Radio National series on the New World Order. December 2.

Morgenthau, Hans. 1978. *Politics among Nations: The Struggle for Power and Peace*. New York: Alfred K. Knopf.

Nixon, Richard. 1991. "Why." *The New York Times*. January 6. E19.

Rostow, W. W. 1960. *The Stages of Economic Growth: A Non-Communist Manifesto*. Cambridge: Cambridge University Press.

Rustow, Dankwart A. 1990. "Democracy: A Global Revolution?" *Foreign Affairs* 69, no. 4 (Fall): 75-91.

Sharp, Gene. 1985. *Making Europe Unconquerable*. Cambridge, MA: Ballinger.

Shepard, George W. and Ved P. Nanda. 1986. *Human Rights and World Development*. Westport, CT: Greenwood.

Stephenson, Carolyn M.   1989. "The Evolution of Peace Studies." In *Peace and World Order Studies: A Curriculum Guide.* 5th ed. Eds. Daniel C. Thomas and Michael T. Klare. Boulder, CO: Westview. 9-19.

Tehranian, Majid. 1990a. "Communication, Peace, and Development: A Communitarian Perspective." In *Communicating for Peace: Diplomacy and Negotiation.* Ch. 9. Eds. Felipe Korzenny and Stella Ting-Toomey. Newbury Park, CA: Sage. 157-75.

_____. 1990b. "Communication and Revolution in the Islamic World: An Essay in Interpretation." *Asian Journal of Communication* 1: 1-33.

_____. 1990c. *Technologies of Power: Information Machines and Democratic Prospects.* Norwood, NJ: Ablex.

Thomas, Daniel C. and Michael T. Klare. 1989. *Peace and World Order Studies: A Curriculum Guide.* 5th ed. Boulder, CO: Westview.

Unnithan, T. K. N. 1987. *Change Without Violence: Gandhian Theory of Social Change.* Ahmedabad, India: Gujarat Vidyapith.

Vaska, Karel and Philip Alston, eds. 1982. *International Dimensions of Human Rights.* 2 vols. Westport, CT: Greenwood.

Wallerstein, Immanuel. 1979. *The Capitalist World Economy.* Cambridge: Cambridge University Press.

Welch, Claude E., Jr., and Robert I. Meltzer. 1984. *Human Rights and Development in Africa.* Albany, NY: State University of New York Press.

2

The Emerging Conflict Formations

JOHAN GALTUNG

CONFLICT FORMATIONS AS UNITS OF ANALYSIS

Peace is a process aimed at the reduction of human violence to human beings and to nature by peaceful means. One important source of violence is unresolved conflict. Playing into the frustration arising from unresolved conflicts, queuing up for a release, are such factors as biologically rooted aggressiveness, particularly in males; psychological deficits in empathy with victims of violence; highly hierarchical social structures; and cultures defining steep gradients between Self and Other.[1]

A conflict is by definition an incompatibility between two or more goals in a goal-seeking system. If incompatible goals are found or held within actors or parties (meaning potential actors), we have an intraconflict (intranature, intrapersonal, intrasocietal, intraregional, intraglobal), or a dilemma. If found between parties, it is an inter-conflict, or a dispute. The dispute may be between entities of the same kind (internature, interpersonal, intersocietal, interregional, inter-global), or between entities of different kinds, like human beings with nature, human beings with the state, or a state with the world (Galtung forthcoming-b, forthcoming-c).

Marx and Freud have argued rather convincingly that human awareness of conflict may be very limited. The conflict may be built into the structure of social interaction, between and within classes (Marx), or the structure of the personality (Freud), doing structural violence to the parties even if they do not perceive any incompatible goals. Sometimes only attitude and behavior are observable, not the deeper roots and forces.

Perceived or not, an incompatibility of goals does not necessarily spill over into violence. There is always the possibility of nonviolent conflict processing, or of no processing at all, letting sleeping dogs lie. But generally speaking, any conflict left unresolved leads in the long run to aggressiveness, even to direct violence. The more basic there will be conflict, in the sense of involving the basic needs for survival, well-being, freedom, and identity (Galtung 1980), the more likely the violence. The difference between frustration and conflict is significant here. In frustration a goal is left unsatisfied; a conflict is a frustration with an address. In a dilemma the Self stands in the way; in a dispute, the Other. In the real world there is always a mixture of the two, and in addition, there is general frustration floating around, leading to combinations of Self- and Other-directed aggression. What happens depends very much on the structural and cultural conditions of the conflict. The structural conditions include the extremes of hierarchy: abject repression and exploitation. The cultural conditions might include seeing the Self as chosen, anointed to destroy the Other, combined with myths of trauma and/or glory. Combined, these factors could easily make direct violence the major cause of death.[2]

At this point, however, a warning should be issued lest our view of conflict becomes too negative. Conflict or contradictions are also the great force motrice of history, a challenge to us all to resolve conflict creatively, thereby moving humans and nature alike forward toward higher levels of being. In short, using the much overworked Chinese formula: conflict=crisis=danger+opportunity.

A conflict formation is a dynamic structure of actors and parties and their incompatibilities, often called issues. A more ideal humanity might have processes for immediate conflict resolution, even with nonhuman nature. Real humanity comes with fault lines that crystallize conflicts and impede their resolution, some biologically given, some humanmade (shown in Table 1). Across these divides in the human condition, repression/exploitation is exercised, institution-alized in the structure, and internalized by the culture. Sparks fly. Examples of fault lines are class and nation, but there are more, easily identified and recognized examples.

The first fault line refers to humans against all others. The next three—gender, generation, and race—are defined by biology and are biogenetically transferable between generations. The last three are defined by structure and culture and are transmitted socioculturally. The social division into classes is vertical; territorial division into countries is in principle horizontal. For all seven fault lines, peace studies are concerned with group conflicts and the potentials for massive structural and/or direct violence.

Table 1. Fault Lines in the Human Condition

Parties	Issues
[1] Humans/Nonhumans	Environment
[2] Men/Women	Gender
[3] Middle-aged/Young/Old	Generation
[4] Light Color/Dark Color	Race
[5] High Class/Low Class	Class
[6] Culture/Culture	Nation, Ethnicity
[7] Country/Country	Territory

DIAGNOSIS OF THE CONFLICT FORMATIONS

If we were to make a Yearbook of World Conflict, Table 2 could serve as a table of contents, watching the formations as processes and focusing on the concern of peace research: violence. First are the seven "fault lines," with increasingly global and not just domestic problems, with similarities and/or causal connections. Causal chains cut across territorial, even continental borders, with communication and transportation networks relating causes in one to effects in another.

Next there are six combinations of these formations (numbers 8 to 13 in Table 2), with countries and their cores, the states, as actors. Colonial formation, now coming to an end, involves at least two countries or nations, one repressing and/or exploiting the other. State formation leads to human rights and duties problematiques for the individual. This becomes even more complex when three levels—local, state, and world—compete for allegiance. It is particularly complex when territory is combined with political class in hegemonial systems and with economic class in imperialistic systems.

Finally conflict formation 14, the dilemmas, a basic for our time, lead to direct or structural aggression and inner- and outer-directed violence, such as unhealthy/risky lifestyles, alcohol, drugs, suicide, and crime, as in the former DDR. Real life conflicts are always complex combinations of these themes, going beyond two parties disputing one goal or one party in a dilemma over two goals; both are analytically useful, like Euclidean geometry. But real conflicts are chaotic, resisting simplistic reductionism.

Human aggression against nature hits back as depletion and (toxic) pollution, the latter being part of the causal syndromes underlying the modernization diseases, and also as conflicts over scarce resources essential for basic needs. Even more basic than land is water,

Table 2. Emerging Conflict Formations for the Twenty-First Century

---

[1] Humans/Nature—The Environment Problematique
[2] Gender Conflicts—Problems of Patriarchy
[3] Generation Conflicts—Rule by the Middle-Aged
[4] Race Conflicts—Problems of Racial Dissimilarity
[5] Class Conflicts—Problems of Scarce Positional Goods
[6] Culture Conflicts—Problems of Ethnic Dissimilarity
[7] Inter-Country Conflicts—e.g., India/Pakistan over Kashmir
[8] Residual Colonial Formations—e.g., Israel, S. Africa, the Pacific
[9] States vs Individuals—The Human Rights Problematique
    - First Generation of Human Rights; civil-political
    - Second Generation of Human Rights; socioeconomic
[10] World vs States vs Local Level vs Individual
    - Third Generation of Human Rights; collective rights
[11] New World Order Hegemonial Formation
    - Superpower hegemony: U.S., EC, Japan, Moscow, Beijing, India
    - Superpower rivalry: U.S./EC? US/Japan? China/India?
      Islam/Rest?
    - Superpower alliances: U.S.+EC+Japan/Rest? U.S.+EC/Rest?
      U.S./Rest?
    - Superpower condominimum: U.S.+EC+Japan? U.S.+EC?
      U.S.+Japan? EC+Japan?
[12] Rich vs Poor—Within and Between Countries
    - Poor countries vs rich countries ("North-South")
    - Poor people vs rich people (international class conflict)
    - Poor people in poor countries vs rest (imperialism)
[13] Civilizational Formations
    - Christianity vs Islam
    - Occident vs Orient
[14] Dilemmas Leading to Apathy and Withdrawal; Spiritual Crisis

---

even more basic than water is air. Human beings may survive one month without food, only one week without water, and only some minutes without air. As to land, there will be moves from overpopulated to underpopulated areas.[3] As to water, for example, the three river systems on which most Arabs depend are controlled by non-Arabs—the Nile by Ethiopia and Southern Sudan, the Jordan by Israel, and the Euphrates-Tigris complex by Turkey. The prognosis is ominous. As to air, well-to-do people have already moved away from areas where air pollution leads to respiratory diseases.

Violence exercised by men against women is now being challenged, and peace studies has much to learn from feminist studies. But the massive killing and maiming of women as fetuses, as infants, as adults, in sex-related crimes, and inside the family continues; and so does the structural violence known as patriarchy. Men are responsible for at least 90% of the direct violence on earth, as decision makers, violent criminals, torturers, soldiers, wife beaters, and rapists. So there will be more confrontations between the genders, possibly with women having a humanizing influence on men.

Violence exercised by the middle-aged against children and the old ranges from structural forms such as marginalization (no work, for example), to the direct violence of child beating and abortion,[4] and the possible breeding of children for adoption and genetic engineering purposes. The logical conclusion is euthanasia, inviting the aged to end their own lives, purportedly to shorten their pains, but in fact discarding them as social garbage when they incur the heavy costs of modernization diseases.[5]

When uncorrelated with class and ethnicity, race—in the genetic sense of skin color, and so on—seems less important as a nucleus for crystallizing conflict formations. But there usually is a correlation, and race is, by definition, a highly visible focus. It might be wise for whites to realize that they are in a minority of perhaps 22% of the world population; that they have treated the black and the red abominably; and that their power rests to a large extent on the brown and the yellow, the racial middle classes, joining the white upper rather than the black/red under classes. South Africa is paradigmatic; that struggle is partly on behalf of the rest of the world.[6]

The rising role of culture is found in "fundamentalism:" clinging to basic values. In the two regions of heaviest economic growth, the Judeo-Christian Northwest and the Confucian-Buddhist Southeast, mainstream culture is now enshrined in the secular religion of individualist materialism/consumer fundamentalism, particularly in the West. However, in what used to be the "socialist" (meaning not socialist) and the "developing" (meaning not developing) worlds, material satisfaction of need and greed have eluded the vast majority of a frustrated population. A return to the nonmaterial values enshrined in these religions comes quickly to them both, partly as a comfort, partly as a weapon.

But there is also another factor at work. The world is shrinking as a result of the communication-transportation revolution, bringing people of different faiths closer together, leading to secularization in some, to syncretism in others, and to fundamentalism, for identity, in many. Dialectically one fundamentalism feeds the other.[7]

Class, the structurally generated unequal distribution of scarce goods, always changes character. Employment is such a case. Modern society is increasingly incapable of providing jobs for all, leading to shortening of working hours by the day, the week, the month, the year, and more important, by the lifetime. Entry into the workforce comes later and exit (retirement) earlier, with the window between the two shrinking. For still more people that window becomes zero, as they pass through life without a job. Social usefulness, social networks, and self-realization through work will be beyond that class. Leisure on the dole is no substitute. This structural violence is probably also a major factor behind apathy, alcoholism, drug use, mental disorder, and suicide.

Armed, horizontal intercountry conflicts, such as India-Pakistan and Ethiopia-Somalia, constitute only a small portion of the totality of armed conflicts; according to one study, 7 cases out of 92 for the year 1989 (Lindgren 1991: ch. 1). The other 85 were state formation (44 cases) and internal conflicts (41 cases); race, ethnicity, and class were major foci of crystallization. The role of contiguity decreases and the role of nation-state building increases.[8] Armed conflicts are increasingly acted out in complex, vertical, noncontiguous intercountry formations.

Colonial formations, depriving others of sovereignty, are waning but are not at zero, with South Africa and Israel as major examples, in addition to residual Western European colonialism, particularly in the Pacific.[9] White settler strategy has been to achieve majority through immigration and extermination, declaring majority rights against natives' historical rights.[10]

Given the choice most individuals seem to prefer the hazards of human organization to the hazards of nature. Concentration of territorially based power in the emperor/court system and in its successor, the state/cabinet system, called for a social contract as expressed in the American and French documents of 1776, 1787, and 1789, which were ultimately crystallized in the Universal Declaration of [civil and political] Human Rights of December 10, 1948. Like all contracts, the state-individual relation became a deal with rights and duties. The state gives certain rights and guarantees their implementation; the state takes loyalty, taxes, and (since 1793) human lives under universal conscription, starting with the male part of the population ("the name of the State be praised"). This quid pro quo logic may induce states that provide well for their citizens to demand very much in return. The dark colonialist and interventionist records of leading democracies confirm this. Freedom of thought, assembly, speech, and ballot are easily subordinated to security in status quo-oriented states. However, being at the top of the world pyramid, democracies usually do not initiate violence. They "respond," like feudal lords or the proverbial pub bully, provoking everyone into a fight while arguing that others started it.

The individual may temper national citizenship with local and global loyalties. Human needs register individually, ecocrises locally, development socially (but not as national aggrandizement), and peace globally. The state is ambivalent, either capable of wreaking havoc at all levels or of being an instrument for human and social development, for peace and ecobalance. The third generation of human rights is an effort to harness the state in that direction.

THE "NEW WORLD ORDER" AS CONFLICT FORMATION

The most important geopolitical conflict formation to clarify right now is the successor formation to the Cold War—the East-West conflict of 1917-1989, with peaks of intensity in the 1949-1975 period. What is our image of the New World Order? A Pax Americana using the "New World," the Americas, as a model for the whole world? An order with less developed countries (the LDCs) at the bottom, more developed countries (the MDCs) in the middle, and WDC (Washington, D.C.) at the top? Or, as will be argued here, is it a multipolar order of a unipolar hegemonial system encased in a big unipolar system with the surviving superpower on top? Or is it that and much more: militarily and politically hegemonial, with economic and cultural aspects, neither simply unipolar nor simply multipolar. Although there is no conclusive evidence, a reasonable guess is that at Malta they divided most of the world into spheres of interest, and at Yalta only most of Europe.[11] More particularly, four major regions can be described:

I. The United States will attempt hegemony over the Western Hemisphere and the Middle East, with an inner periphery in Canada-Mexico and Israel, and an outer periphery in the rest of the world.

II. The European Community will attempt hegemony over most countries in Central and Eastern Europe and the 68 countries of the ACP (African-Caribbean-Pacific) system established by the Yaounde-Lome conventions from 1964 onward, with an inner periphery in Eastern Europe and an outer periphery in the ACP. Confederate EC is moving toward an irreversible federal European Union with common finance, foreign, and defense policies. There will be expansion of membership. In principle all European democracies are eligible; in practice Turkey (Moslem) and the neutral or poor are not. The EC will retain its (North)Western European character

III. Japan will attempt hegemony over East-Southeast Asia. This might mean an inner periphery made up of the two parts of Korea (South and North), the three parts of China (PR China, Hong Kong, and Taiwan) and Singapore+Malaysia, and an outer periphery of the other four ASEAN countries, the five former socialist countries of

Mongolia, Burma, and Vietnam/Laos/Cambodia, and then Australia/ New Zealand and the other Pacific Islands, including Hawai'i. In short, the Greater East Asian Co-Prosperity Sphere or the *dai-to-a kyoeiken*.[12] The EC sphere is more global, but the Japanese sphere, based on economic power, has the largest population by far.

These first three zones, spheres, or regions will probably crystallize economically as the Dollar-zone, the ECU/DM-zone, and the Yen-zone respectively. The next four regions will not for the foreseeable future use what could be called world currencies (in plural), and may have to lean toward one or two of the first three zones. Which one(s) will be a source of conflict of major geoeconomic and geopolitical significance?

IV. The former Soviet Union will attempt hegemony over itself. This may imply Russia as the center, together with White Russia, possibly also with the Eastern Ukraine (orthodox) and Northern Kazakhstan (with heavy Russian population), and a periphery consisting of the rest of a future confederate Commonwealth of Independent States (Solzhenitsyn 1991). As for the Western Hemisphere, however, "hegemony" is incompatible with "sovereignty." Whether democratic, fascist, or under a communist renewal as a reaction to the forces of capitalism, it is very difficult to believe that this landmass will not have a center, a "Moscow," and by implication a periphery, with some breakaways.

A "hegemonial system" implies the following:

—the right, duty, and monopoly on military intervention by the hegemon in case of "instability" in their sphere of interest;

—the duty to adjudicate and punish disobedient client states and individuals, for individual and general prevention;[13]

—intervention by "gentlemen's agreement," also on behalf of other hegemons; criticism will be soft and short-lasting on an "I don't undercut you if you don't undercut me" basis;

—economic preponderance on an "I don't try to outcompete you in your region if you don't try to outcompete me in mine" basis;

—cultural regionalism for basic cultural homogeneity;

—political regionalism, that is, regional organizations for basic decision making controlled by the hegemon (and not by the United Nations), possibly with cross-representation of other hegemons; the region also defining the territory of "self-defense";[14]

—hegemons in deep trouble may be assisted by other hegemons;

—the final arbiter, the primus inter pares, the hegemon of hegemons, is the United States, not the United Nations, settling conflicts among hegemons and assisting hegemons in distress.

This "Malta system" of international feudalism has already been tested by the U.S. intervening in Panama and leading the "coalition" against Iraq, and the Soviet Union intervening in the trans-Caucasian and Baltic republics, with only muted criticism from other hegemons. When France and the Soviet Union tried to postpone/soften/avoid the Gulf War, the argument "if you don't support me I might work against you when you have trouble" no doubt carried weight. The EC entered a hegemonial mission in Yugoslavia. And Japan wields economic power: "better to buy than bomb Pearl Harbor!"

The Malta system is completed with three more regions:

V. China will attempt hegemony over itself. China has usually exercised this, except for two or three periods of disgrace, the last from the 1840s until the 1940s. China may have to accept that not only Korea and Vietnam, but also Tibet, are outside its sphere. This concept is entirely compatible with the old Confucian doctrine of Han Chinese versus the four types of barbarians: North, East, South, and West. A doctrine like this, stipulating that Chinese without leaders are superior to barbarians with leaders, dies slowly. The innermost center will remain Beijing, not Shanghai.[15]

VI. India will attempt hegemony over South Asia. This would mean an inner periphery of the other South Asian Association for Regional Cooperation (SAARC) countries on the subcontinent (Pakistan, Bangladesh, Sri Lanka, Nepal, Bhutan, and the Maldives) and an outer periphery with a heavy density of Indian nationals, such as the littoral of the Arab Sea, Bengal Bay, and Indian Ocean, and also Trinidad and Fiji.[16]

VII. A future Islamic/Arab superpower. We are talking about a possibility two to three generations hence of bringing together 1 billion Muslims and the 45 countries of the Islamic conference, possibly including a nucleus of the Arab nations (today 200 million divided into 22 states if we count Palestine), with the current process of subservience in the Gulf area possibly serving as a major impetus. It could hardly operate without a center, an inner periphery, and an outer periphery, like the others. That opens a Pandora's box of problems and rivalries in the Damascus-Baghdad-Cairo-Tehran-Istanbul pentagon of old

empires. But sooner or later a polycentric formula similar to the
European Community may emerge (also watch Turkey and the Islamic
Soviet Republics).[17] Table 3 summarizes this argument. Needless to
say, if this proves to be an adequate vision of geopolitical processes for
the 21st century, the political and military implications are
tremendous.

We are talking about a world with six or seven superpowers, four
of them with veto power in the Security Council (the EC even has two
vetoes). Five of them already have nuclear weapons (the EC double)
and the sixth, Japan, may be heading straight for DEW (directed
energy weapons) systems, such as offensive laser beams sent directly
from satellites or indirectly using geostationary mirrors.[18] Four of the
six hegemons are among the five major arms exporters, and the other
three are the major arms importers.[19] It may be argued that neither the
European Community nor the Islamic Conference have the necessary
coherence. But what they do not have they may get, even through a
mutually inspired race for coherence.

Table 3. Geopolitics 1: A Guide to the "New World Order"

Image A	Image B	Image C
(New World) Order	Development	Power
U.S.A.	Washington, D.C.; WDC	Inner Center? U.S.A.
Canada	More Developed; MDC	Center? Hegemons
Latin America	Less Developed; LDC	Periphery: the Rest
Center	**Inner Periphery**	**Outer Periphery**
The Hegemons	**More favored**	**Less favored**
I. U.S.A.	Canada-Mexico	Central, South America
	Israel, Gulf Corporation	Middle East
II. EC/EU	Eastern Europe	ACP system
	(EC-associates?)	Yaounde-Lome
III. Japan	South + North Korea	Mongolia
	Taiwan + Hong Kong + China	Indo-China, Burma
	Singapore + Malaysia	ASEAN 4
	Australia/New Zealand	Pacific Islands
IV. USSR/Moscow	Russian Republics	The Rest
V. China/Beijing	Han provinces	The Rest
VI. India/Delhi	SAARC system	littorals, islands
VII.Islamic core	Mashreq	Maghreb
World Directorate	**World Middle Class**	**World Proletariat**

Even more important than these capabilities are the motivations. The hegemons see themselves as Chosen: Israel by Yahweh; the U.S., Japan, and Islam by God, Amaterasu O-mikami (the Sun Goddess), and Allah respectively; the European Union (EU) and India as "civilization cradles;" and China (like France) simply *is* chosen. As to Russia, a part of the Bolshevik mystique was that they were chosen by History to lead humankind into the promised land of socialism. But History betrayed the Soviet Union, or the other way around. The result is a superpower in disintegration, with the mystique broken for the time being, possibly to be recreated. In addition, all seven of the hegemons have, also like Israel, have suffered deep traumas recently, and all of them have images of a glorious past worth recreating, as shown in Table 4.

Table 4. Geopolitics II: Cultural Factors in a Seven-Polar World

The Poles	Chosenness	The Traumas	The Myths
I. U.S. pole	by God, as New Canaan	Vietnam syndrome Tehran hostages	post WWII unipolarity
II. EC/EU pole	as cradle of civilization	World War II Nazism fascism, communism loss of empires U.S. junior partners	Europe as the center
III. Japan pole	by Amaterasu O-mikami	Pacific War defeat nuclear holocaust	*dai-to-a*
IV. Moscow pole	by History (betrayed)	World War II Stalinism	bipolarity Russia
V. Beijing pole	simply *is*	humiliation 1840s-1940s	perfect autonomy
VI. India pole	as cradle of civilization	colonialism underdevelopment	Hindu raj British raj
VII. Islam pole	by Allah	crusades, Zionism communism, consumerism *divide et impera* inner divisions	Islamic empires Arab nation

In short, it is an even more dangerous world. To refer to it as a "new world order" is correct only in one sense: it is more peaked, with the superhegemon, the U.S., on top. In the long run this may increase the chance that all six will turn against the U.S., making the future relation of the European Community/Union to the U.S. even more important.[20]

The "New World Order" can be seen as an effort to manage the totality of this seven-polar world from Washington, D.C. The U.S. is not only hegemon for the double Region I, but also the hegemons' hegemon, with regional deputies. The NWO is too hierarchical to be "multipolar;" it is more like six or seven parallel unipolar systems, organized in three layers. On top is Washington, D.C., followed by the hegemons that are economically or militarily more developed, such as the Moscow system, China, and India, and then the rest. The NWO is not the "North-South" conflict formation, as it gives power to the strong rather than to the rich; nor the old bipolar "East-West" conflict, as the East has disappeared or joined the South. It is too regional to be "unipolar," with the U.S. on top of the whole world. The NWO is one big pyramid with six lesser pyramids inside it, run partly by the U.S., partly by a world directorate of hegemons. The U.S. is now freer than ever to intervene in the Western hemisphere and in the Middle East, hoping that a new hegemon deputy may be created after Israel, Egypt, and Iran.[21] This highly feudal New World Order will probably collapse from inner contradictions even before it is born. This is shown by a concrete listing of the conflict formations already existing within the NWO, leaving aside new conflicts that will be created and old ones that will probably be aggravated.

GEOPOLITICS III: A NEW WORLD ORDER CONFLICT MAP

Unipolar Conflicts: inside the spheres of interest, with the hegemon using "peacekeeping forces" in the inner periphery and "rapid deployment forces" against revolts in the outer periphery.

Bipolar Conflicts: between two hegemons over jurisdiction— U.S./EU over the Caribbean-Pacific and possibly Latin America; U.S./Japan over Southeast Asia, and U.S./Japan/EU over the Pacific; U.S./Russia over some weapons; U.S./other hegemons in the Middle East (Egypt, Libya, Iran, Iraq, and successors to Iraq, Israel); EU/Russia over Baltic republics and German and Polish east borders; EU/Japan over the "Soviet Union;" EU/India over littorals and islands; EU/Islam over migrants; Japan/Russia over the Kuriles; Japan/China over oil; Russia/Islam over Central Asia; China/India over border areas; China/Islam over non-Han China; and India/Islam over Kashmir.

Multipolar Conflicts: organized conflicts with more than two hegemons—economic conflict involving U.S./EU+Japan or U.S.+EU/Japan+Russia+China+India+Islam, or civilizational conflict involving Christianity/Islam or Occident/Orient.

Coalitions of Hegemons: for example, the "North," as in the Gulf War with four hegemons cooperating (and one abstaining) to control the outer periphery of one region, thereby reinforcing hegemony. Veto power guarantees no UN action against loyal client states.

Coalitions of Peripheries: under the slogan "clients all over the world unite, you have only your hegemons to lose." But costs are higher and resources smaller than for the Center; veto power rules out UN legitimacy; the "South" exists only as outer peripheries; and the Third World is a myth. Moreover, in the New World Order power is military rather than economic, reflecting the declining economy of the U.S.

SOME COMMENTS ON PROGNOSES

Essentially four schemes have been presented: a list of fourteen conflict formations for the 21st century; Geopolitics I: a division of the world into six or seven regions with poles, hegemons, and superpowers (three global, four regional); Geopolitics II: a list of motivational cultural factors; and Geopolitics III: a conflict map for a seven-polar world. It should be noted that Geopolitics I, II, and III are elaborations of only conflict formations 11-13 as given in Table 2, and basically only of number 11. Others could be given equal attention. Particularly frightening at this rather dark hour in human history is how the other thirteen conflict formations feed into number 11. The Gulf War can serve as a very good illustration of:

[1] the way in which war insults ecosystems, and particularly vulnerable ecosystems in the regions where wars are most likely to be fought, such as deserts, oceans, and polar regions;

[2] the way in which wars reinforce patriarchy using the strong association between aggressiveness and sexuality in the human male to kill and to rape;

[3] the way in which wars make women, the very young, and the very old bystanders and victims, deprived of significant roles except as victims and bereaved family members;

[4] the way in which wars can draw on racial prejudice, making it very easy to kill en masse people of another race;

[5] the way in which wars can draw on ethnic prejudice, making it very easy to kill en masse people of another culture;

[6] the way in which wars can draw on class conflicts, fighting over scarce goods like food and water that affect livelihoods;

[7] the way in which wars can draw on intercountry rivalries;

[8] the way in which even old colonial systems help define very nasty conflict formations (e.g., Britain in the Gulf);

[9] the way in which civil-political and socioeconomic human rights yield to war priorities for all concerned;

[10] the way wars serve to reinforce the national level over and above individual, local, and world interests, to the point of making the UN subservient to the interests of some nations;

[12] the way in which wars can pit the poor against the rich, both in the sense of poor countries vs rich, poor people vs rich, and poor people in poor countries vs the other three;

[13] the way in which war may be legitimized by open reference to culture and indirect reference to deep culture; and

[14] the way in which wars may offer a temporary respite from the spiritual emptiness coming out of deep individual and collective dilemmas, producing a "sense of purpose" out of an emptiness that is reproduced when the intoxication is over.

In short, the Gulf War made use of and reinforced old conflict energies, at all points strengthening the strong at the expense of the weak, reinforcing a top-heavy world order. The New World Order can be seen as an effort to institutionalize the status quo as an unchallengeable structure. The Gulf War is paradigmatic, using the valid case of a militarily strong Iraq brutally invading a militarily weak Kuwait, to give something to the strong everywhere. No wonder it was offered on a "rent-a-war, buy now, pay later" (but not much later) basis, making some rich hegemons pay handsomely for not participating. There was some urgency in making full use of the situation; an almost ideal enemy does not come along that often.

The immediate prognosis is for some repetition of the Gulf War, led by the U.S. But against whom? For UN legitimacy an outlaw is needed, not relative to UN rules and resolutions (that would make Israel the immediate war target), but against the feudal, hegemonial NWO. This rules out wars against veto powers and clients protected by veto powers, but includes as potential war candidates anybody else. Any hegemon can ask for Security Council support in disciplining his own client, but it will be obtained only if there is sufficient general interest in using the case to solidify the general edifice. If not, do your own job; as the U.S. did in the Andes countries against the Sendero Luminoso, as it may do in Cuba, and as it helps Israel do against the Palestinians. Other victims may be Syria, Libya, and Iraq again.[22]

More interestingly, the system could also be used against nonveto hegemons, meaning fundamentally Japan, India, or any strong Arab/Islamic combination branded fundamentalist. Of the five hegemon candidates in the Western part of Islam, Egypt was beaten by a U.S. client (Israel) in 1973; Iran was almost beaten by another U.S. client (Iraq) in 1988; and Iraq was then beaten by the U.S., with Egypt helping by participating and Israel by not participating. Next in line might be Syria and Turkey, which has not been beaten since the First World War.

In Eastern Islam, Pakistan and Indonesia do not challenge the U.S, but make use of the U.S. world order in suppressing potential threats to their regimes (Indonesia ever since 1965; East Timor since 1974; Pakistan in Afghanistan lest revolutions might spread across borders). And yet the NWO will not work forever, or at all; it is too conflict-ridden.

THERAPIES

To return to the point of departure: there is no substitute for creative resolution of conflict. Table 5 indicates what this means in practice—a Herculean, even Sisyphean task, but not an impossible one.

The logic of Table 5 is not to prescribe precise solutions to conflicts, but to build the setting within which conflicts can more easily be solved. The Table addresses only structural (military, economic, and political) and cultural aspects of the general problem of violence, not the more intractable problems of the human (particularly the male) body and the human mind. There are two approaches: make the parties less aggressive, and weave them together better in equitable relations capable of creative conflict resolution.

Although Table 5 is written particularly with intercountry conflicts in mind, it also holds mutatis mutandis for conflicts with nature and for intergender, intergeneration, interracial, interethnic, and interclass conflicts. There is evidently more than enough peace work to do. But how do we make the struggle for peace a major part of the human agenda, engaging the vast majority of humankind to the point of this also becoming a solution to their spiritual crisis? The struggle is uphill. The Sisyphean metaphor is relevant, as is the Icarus metaphor. The struggle is also a lonely one, and will be discouraged by both hegemons and their clients. At times it looks hopeless, as it did to those who struggled and still struggle against slavery, colonialism, and the Cold War, making one nostalgic for the simplicity of East-West bipolarity. But they won, or are winning.

Table 5. Visioning a Peaceful World: How to Weave States Together

Power	Negative Peace	Positive Peace
	Military nonaggression	World peacekeeping forces
M	nonflow, nonintervention	nonviolent intervention
I	nonstocking of offensive arms	stationing as buffers in crisis
L	defensive, nonprovocative	stationing as hostages
I	defense	cooperation in defensive defense
T	transarmament	World Transarmament Association
A	disarmament	World Disarmament Association
R	abolition of war as an institution	World War Abolition Association
Y		
	Economic nonaggression	World economy
E	nature, human social, world	nature, human, social, world
C	production for basic needs	production for basic needs
O	distribution to most needy	distribution to most needy
N	self-reliance I	self-reliance II
O	nationally	equitably exchange
M	locally? use local factors	symbiosis, mutual benefit
I	internalizing externalities	sharing externalities equally
C		
	Cultural nonaggression	World consciousness
C	participation in dialogue	world statistics, world images
U	not backed by military or	conceptualization and foreign policy
L	economic power	world domestic politics
T	criticize, internally, externally	positive views of humanity
U	universalism and singularism	multicentric space
R	Chosen People ideas	relaxed, oscillating time
A	absolute cultural relativism	more holistic, dialectic
L		nature partnership
		equality, justice—inclusive
		minimum metaphysics
P	Internalize national interests	World institutions for world interests
O	broaden democracy	broaden democracy
L	national and local elections	chamber of governmental organization
I	party/candidate and issue votes	chamber of people's organizations
T	nuclear free municipalities	chamber of peoples
I	nuclear free professions	world elections
C	Hippocratic peace oaths	world referenda
A		world service for environment
L		and development

Today three peace communities with a very low probability of international war and a low level of structural violence across borders can be identified. Exhibit A: the twelve European Community countries among themselves; Exhibit B: the five Nordic Community countries among themselves; and Exhibit C: the six ASEAN countries among themselves, not within. These exhibits, encompassing 23 countries with about 660 million inhabitants, or 14% of the countries and 12% of the world's people, suggest a formula for peaceful relations in social formations (Galtung forthcoming-c, Galtung and Lodgaard 1970).

[1] Diversity, meaning enough difference to be complementary;
[2] Symbiosis, meaning mutually beneficial relations;
[3] Equity, meaning about equal in net benefits;
[4] Entropy, meaning a disorderly interaction configuration;
[5] Domain (number of actors) above two, but not too high;
[6] Scope (number of issues) above one, but not too high; and
[7] Transcendence, meaning joint, collective decision making.

Diversity with symbiosis is the formula for ecosystem resilience; necessary, but insufficient for humane (not the same as human in general) relations. Equity is the missing link. Yet the system has to be well-woven together so that it does not fall apart along the fault lines. At the same time an ongoing conflict processing capacity is needed. This presupposes sufficient complexity in the number of actors and issues to permit bargains of all kinds. When the numbers are too high, however, the confederate system becomes hierarchical or anarchic. Too much transcendence produces a superactor, which between states means a superstate, even a superpower such as the EU. A delicate balance is required, as in all work for peace.

POSSIBLE CONFLICT RESOLUTION PROCESSES

[1] Nonpolluting and nondepleting technologies in smaller economic cycles, making polluters/depleters understand downstream, downwind, downtime consequences of irresponsibility
[2] Parity by feminizing males, not masculinizing females, making males understand the consequences of their behavior
[3] Dignity to the young and the old through the right to work and abolition of violence to the unborn, infant, child, and aged
[4] Continue reducing correlations between race and class
[5] Work for all through labor-intensity; misery-abolition
[6] Continue reducing correlations between culture and class

[7] Search for confederal solutions to intercountry conflicts, with joint administration of contested areas and mobility

[8] Quick abolition of residual colonialism all over the world, with a Palestinian state and majority rule in South Africa

[9] Quick ratification of the International Bill of Rights all over the world; also socioeconomic rights; no military duty

[10] Strengthen the local level all over the world, broaden the scope for enlightened intermunicipal relations; UN assemblies of peoples, NGOs, TNCs, municipalities; all three generations of human rights to be ratified and guaranteed by all entities

[11] Intensive struggle against the NWO, denouncing hegemonial tendencies and veto rights; building cooperative relations among "periphery" states all over the world

[12] A world economy based more on local self-reliance and equitable exchange and ethically conscious market behavior

[13] Promoting the softer aspects of all religions; ecumenical dialogues; dialogues over traumas, myths, and future visions

[14] Promoting cultures other than fundamentalist consumerism

This is not the place to elaborate in any meaningful way the exact why, what, how, when and where, not to mention by whom, and if necessary at whose expense this could be done. Rather, the reader is invited to do all of that and much more. Any conflict formation can only be understood in terms of prognosis and its negation through suggested therapies; in other words dialectically. Try to think out a solution and at the very least the understanding of the conflict will improve.

That brings us back to the point of departure, defining peace, peace research, and peace politics. The common theme is the negation of violence. But violence has many forms: the direct violence carried by actors, the structural violence carried by structures, and the cultural violence legitimizing them both, carried by cultures. Of actors, structures, and cultures there are many. Peace is a broad agenda; peace studies a very complex area of research and education, defying but also drawing upon all disciplines; peace politics is not only a good, but also a revolutionary idea. Yet not that revolutionary. There is no demand to scrap all military as long as it is strictly defensive; no demand to scrap the market economy if behavior is sufficiently conscious of basic ethical values not to buy and sell slaves, body parts, children, weapons of mass destruction, and so on; no demand to abolish all government as long as it is more small-scale and more confederal; no demand to convert to a new religion as long as there is no insistence that any group is above all others.

Peace with peaceful means; si vis pacem, para pacem. That remains the essence of peace education, research, and action.

NOTES

Author's Note: This chapter was prepared for the Matsunaga Institute's Restructuring for Peace conference; it was also presented at the Defense College, Stockholm, December 10, 1990; at the University of Uppsala, January 31 and May 28; at IBM in Brussels and Armonk, New York, spring 1991; at the Colegio Opus, Valencia, April 6, 1991; at the Universidad de Granada, April 10, 1991; the Universität Graz, May 26, 1991; at the Friedensuniversität Bremen, June 11, 1991; at the Universität Witten-Herdecke, June 12, 1991; at the Université de Fribourg, June 21, 1991; at the APERA conference, Brisbane, June 29, 1991; and the University of Queensland, July 3, 1991. I am indebted to many discussants at all places, and particularly to George Kent and Majid Tehranian of the Matsunaga Institute for Peace for their comments; and to HSFR, Stockholm, for the Olof Palme Peace Professorship 1990-91.

1. With the distance to nature, animate and inanimate, defined in Western culture in general, and in desouling science in particular, it is little wonder that there is so much violence done to nature.

2. But not yet. Even during World War II the average number of deaths attributed to the direct violence of war was 8 million, half the number of children killed by the structural violence of avoidable disease and malnutrition during the period. I am indebted to George Kent for this point.

3. In a study using the population:land ratios for the world as a whole (disregarding the quality of land), the most overpopulated countries in the world were China, India, Japan, Bangladesh, Indonesia, Pakistan, Nigeria, (united) Germany, Vietnam, the United Kingdom, and Italy. The most underpopulated were the Soviet Union, Canada, Australia, Brazil, and the U.S. Two interesting conclusions emerge: all six hegemons to be discussed later in the chapter are population:land sensitive; and over- and underpopulated countries are quite close to each other (China, India, Japan, Germany, and the EC in general to the Soviet Union; South America to North America; Indonesia, Vietnam, Bangladesh, and Pakistan to Australia). I am indebted to Dan Campbell for his assistance.

4. Any stand against violence to sentient life also applies to abortion; like other types of violence, it is only to be resorted to as the last recourse, the decision being made by the mother in dialogue with the father (not by the woman alone nor by authorities with their ulterior motives). To be in favor of abortion and against war is as untenable as being against abortion but for war. In the "pro-life" stand there may also be the conservative idea that only God and the state may take life; the "pro-choice" stand challenges precisely that.

5. It is a telling indictment of a society not that a manual on suicide, Derek Humphry's *Final Exit*, is written, but that it becomes a best-seller.

6. This was and is understood by white conservative forces all over the world. The old order cannot be upheld. The struggle is over the post-apartheid regime.

7. An example from the 1980s would be a point-for-point comparison of the speciesism, sexism, racism, ethnic prejudice, statism, hegemonialism, and bigoted chosenism of Reagan and Khomeini. Because they understood each other, they hated each other.

8. The reason is simple: with about 170 states in the world and 1,500 nations (a low estimate), the amount of violence before cultural and territorial borders coincide is appalling. Obviously other formulas must be found.

9. In the Pacific particularly, the French and the U.S. presence is clearly geopolitically motivated; for instance, in Le Pen's election propaganda in Tahiti for the June 1989 EC elections.

10. The Pacific Hemisphere Project that I direct explores options for the "white settler majority rights, indigenous people historical rights" case, such as territorial division, bicameral legislatures, and bilingualism.

11. It was actually by the time of the prior foreign minister conference in Moscow, rather than the Yalta meeting of February 4-11, 1945, that the Red Army had already occupied most of Eastern Europe. Soviet hegemonial aspiration came to an abrupt end in 1989. U.S. aspirations were prepared by the Joint Chiefs of Staff in 1943 and 1945 (JCS 570/2 and 570/40; and NSC 68).

12. But this time created with economic means, indicating how superior the carrot is to the stick. In spite of bad memories associated with Japan and the Asia-Pacific's rational suspicions, Japan is penetrating the dai-to-a everywhere. A good example is the 93% Japanese investment rate in a major U.S. military base, Guam.

13. The Noriega case has some similarities with the Eichmann case and the death sentence for Salman Rushdie. Of course, the Israeli way of capturing those they want to arraign in court is more micromanaged, and Iran seems to execute on the spot, abroad. But the brutal U.S. invasion of Panama probably had motives far beyond the person of Noriega. Extranational adjudication is a consequence of an increasingly borderless world that still has national centers of adjudication with their particular vested interests. If nations internationalize the domain of their national law, the world will become even more violent, given the struggles over adjudication rights.

14. Article 51 of the UN Charter legitimizes the concept of "collective self-defense" without defining the collectivity, "until the Security Council has taken measures." In principle a hegemon can declare itself a part of the collectivity and veto any serious handling of the matter in the Security Council; in Lyndon Johnson's memorable words, under Article 51 the United States "could do anything it damn well pleased" (Booker 1991,: 27).

15. The cultural revolution of 1966-69 was not only a "party squabble" and a youth revolt, and not only the poor *nung* [farmers] against the powerful *shi'h* [intellectuals-bureaucrats], but also a challenge to the almighty Beijing, taken up eagerly by its rival, Shanghai, one of the centers of the revolution.

16. Thus Fiji becomes an outer perimeter of the potential Indian reach, an example of the lasting implications of British imperial tendency to move people about. Other examples: Ulster/Ireland; Gibraltar/Spain; Malvinas-Falklands/Argentina; Israel/Palestine; South Africa (but here the Dutch were the bigger movers); Hong Kong/China; Trinidad (similar to Fiji); not to mention the U.S. But that background tends to be forgotten. Whether the Fiji coup of 1987 is seen as a reaction of native Fijians to forestall an Indian takeover, a reaction of the Fijian *ratu* to preserve their privileges, a CIA intrusion to forestall radicalization of an important Pacific island, or an advance Indian operation, there will always be a New Delhi concern for so many Indians.

17. There has been a reduction from perhaps 500 Arab polities (sheikhdoms) around the turn of the century, under the relatively mild Ottoman rule, to 22 countries today (including Palestine). Comparisons with the European Community are valid not only because of the numbers and the equal size of leading countries (unlike in the Western Hemisphere with the U.S. preponderant), but also because the European powers had a very long tradition of warfare and yet built a viable union. In addition there is a general tendency to imitate Europe.

18. I would be less surprised by the revelation of an overpowering Japanese space capability outdoing potential challengers, specifically the U.S., than by the opposite, against the background of proven Japanese ability to overtake and do the unexpected (although this may say more about those who do the expecting than about Japan).

19. The SIPRI yearbook for 1990 lists the top five arms exporters in the period 1985-89 in terms of dollar values of the sales at fixed 1985 prices: Soviet Union 38.3%, U.S. 30.6%, France 9.1% England 4.5 % and China 4.0%, followed by West Germany, Czechoslovakia, Italy, Sweden, and the Netherlands). The top arms importers for the same period were India 10.0%, Iraq 6.9%, Japan 6.1%, Saudi Arabia 5.1%, Syria 3.3%, and Egypt 3.3% (and after that Czechoslovakia, North Korea, Spain, and Turkey). Thus, the top arms exporters all have veto power in the UN, making any real regulation through the UN improbable; and among the top arms importers are four of the five Islamic powers mentioned. The Big Four in the EC (France, England, Germany, Italy) are among the top eight arms exporters. All hegemons are on the two lists. The data are a little outdated: "U.S. now top arms broker as sales to Third World surge" (Associated Press 1991). Of course the Gulf War and the tendency for defense contractors to shift to export when the local buyer has a shrinking budget has much to do with the U.S. surging from 23.6% of the sales to Third World countries in 1989 to 44.8% in 1990. All figures should be taken critically.

20. The role of NATO is, and perhaps always was, to provide cover for forward U.S. bases close to the Middle East and Africa and to contain independent EC/EU, particularly German, capabilities, and not to fend off unprovoked Soviet attacks.

21. Thus Syria was built up to resist Iraq, which was built up to resist Iran, which was built up to resist communism. Leading candidates for an anti-Syrian coalition would include Turkey and Israel, not to mention Iraq again. The Gulf War will soon recede into oblivion, joining other "local wars" in the statistics. But the war logic will continue until the U.S. gives up hegemony in the region, like the Crusaders, Turks, French, and British.

22. An editorial in the *Nation* of April 29, 1991 presents an "Enemies List" using the Reagan/Peggy Noonan list of "outlaw states," the "strangest collection of misfits, Looney Tunes and squalid criminals since the advent of the Third Reich" (Editorial 1991). Libya, North Korea, and Cuba are still on the list, Nicaragua has been dealt with, and Iran must have been removed if it ever was on. As to the relation between the U.S. and Japan, the title, if not the argument, of the 1990 release by George Friedman and Meredith LeBard, *The Coming War With Japan*, is indicative.

REFERENCES

Associated Press. 1991. "U.S. Now Top Arms Broker." *Honolulu Advertiser*. August 12. A6.

Booker, Malcolm. 1991. *Backgrounds to the Gulf War.* Sydney.

Friedman, George, and Meredith LeBard. 1990. *The Coming War With Japan.* New York: St. Martins.

"Editorial." 1991. *The Nation* 252, no. 16 (April 29): 544-45.

Galtung, Johan. 1980. "The Basic Needs Approach." In *Human Needs: A Contribution to the Current Debate.* Eds. Katrin Lederer, Johan Galtung, and David Antal. Konigstein: Hain. 55-125.

_____. *Lessons from the Gulf War.* Forthcoming a.

_____. *Theories of Conflict.* Forthcoming b.

_____. *Theories of Peace.* Forthcoming c.

Galtung, Johan and Sverre Lodgaard, eds. 1970. *Co-operation in Europe.* Oslo: Universitetsforlaget.

Lindgren, Karin, ed. 1991. *States in Armed Conflict 1989.* Report no. 32. Uppsala: Department of Peace and Conflict Research. Chapter 1.

SIPRI (Stockholm International Peace Research Institute). 1990. *SIPRI Yearbook.* Stockholm: Almquist and Wiksell.

Solzhenitsyn, Alexander. 1991. *Rebuilding Russia: Reflections and Tentative Proposals.* New York: Farrar, Straus and Giroux.

Part I

Peace With Security

3

New Conceptions of Security and Their Implications for Means and Methods

CAROLYN M. STEPHENSON

RECONCEPTUALIZING SECURITY

A point of change in the structure or process of a system is the time when it is most vulnerable not only to crisis but to new ideas. Thus it is not surprising that the changes in the international system near the end of the twentieth century have occasioned a new debate over security. The waning of the Cold War, the relatively declining power of both superpowers, the reemerging independence of Eastern Europe, the proliferation of all kinds of weapons systems throughout the world, the debt crisis, the environmental crisis, the increased use of the United Nations for mediation, peacekeeping, and enforcement, and the rise of regional hegemons amid the continued decline of the "third world," are leading to a reconceptualization in security thinking. This is occurring in the fields of international studies, strategic studies, and peace and conflict studies, as well as in the media and the policy community. As any crisis entails both danger and opportunity (as the Chinese character for crisis denotes), this is both a time of danger and an opportunity for new thinking.

The security debate has become much like the proverbial debate over how many angels can stand on the head of a pin. Abstracted from the realities of human and organizational decision making, technological imperfection, and geophysical or environmental circumstances, let alone those of basic human living, the security debate has become increasingly unreal, played out in game rooms and conference rooms, in computer simulations as well as on the backs of envelopes, with little connection to the real world of people living in political communities.

The establishment and preservation of security is much more difficult than people in either military policy organizations or peace movements generally believe. It is more difficult than most military planners think, in that it defies military solutions. It is more difficult than most of those in peace movements believe, in that it cannot be achieved simply by disarmament and diplomatic dialogue.

We all know what security is until we try to define it. Whether we are ordinary citizens or national security analysts or psychologists, it becomes a bit more difficult to agree on what we mean. Why? Because the question of security is a question of values and most of us, whether as individuals or nation-states, are not very clear about our values and thus not very clear about our security.

Security is difficult, if not impossible, to achieve. Neither in international relations nor in our personal lives is there any possibility of being absolutely secure. Nor is absolute security necessarily desirable. Eric Fromm compares the nation-state which seeks absolute national security to a paranoid individual. We can aspire only to relative security, and we must weigh our need for it against the cost of maintaining it. A nation can maintain huge armaments only at the cost of diverting resources from other national goals. Nor is it clear that armaments provide security in most cases.

To understand national security, it may be necessary to first develop an understanding of the concept of security itself. Security, at its most basic level, is knowing that you and your community (whether you conceive of that as your neighborhood, your nation, or your world) will not be hurt or worse off for the foreseeable future than they are today. It is a relative concept, relating how bad things seem today to how bad—or good—you can imagine them to be.

A common dictionary definition of security is simply safety, in the first case meaning both freedom from exposure to danger, or protection, and a feeling of assurance of safety, and in the second, the means of protection or defense. Clearly security has both psychological and mechanical aspects, yet there is a wide gap between psychologists who write about security as a feeling of safety and political scientists who write about security as defense. Certainly the feeling of security is more than defense or protection, but the ability to defend is a necessary part of security when there is danger.

THE INTERPLAY OF SECURITY DISCOURSES

The reopening of the security debate has occasioned new claims on the concept of security by two competing discourses. At first glance, the claims appear to be convergent; both agree that the concept of security must be expanded. But the goals of the proponents of the two discourses are divergent, as are their assumptions about human and international relations, and especially their views of the means and methods by which security is to be achieved. The debate is, in many ways, simply the continuation of the realist-idealist debate in international relations, but that debate itself is changing in response to the changing world scene.

The dominant discourse in security thinking is that of strategic or national security studies, a field which became prominent after World War II, and which through the 1960s concentrated primarily in the area of nuclear deterrence, arms control, and the understanding of a bipolar international system. The field languished through the decade of the 1970s and was regenerated in the period of military buildup during the Reagan era (Nye 1989). Realism has been the primary theoretical base for strategic studies (Nye 1990; Buzan 1990). Due to the centrality of security issues since World War II, realism has also been dominant in the wider field of international studies and the discipline of political science. Conceived by such theorists as Hans Morgenthau, George Kennan, and others as an antidote to the idealism and isolationism they saw as one of the causes of World War II, realism provided the dominant explanatory and prescriptive theory for the East-West conflict. Focusing on struggle in anarchy as the major dynamic of international relations, on military power as the ultimate arbiter of conflict, and on the accretion of power as the primary motivator of states, realists have looked especially at East-West relations and have prescribed and analyzed nuclear deterrence as the primary method of interaction. Within realism, strategic studies have been predominant. This is not the place to critique strategic studies; its own proponents have done that quite well. Deterrence theory and strategic studies have been faulted as static, as oriented to the short-term rather than grounded by historical perspective, as ethnocentric (i.e., U.S.-oriented), as focusing predominantly on nuclear weapons, as missing the linkage between domestic politics and international affairs, as inadequately related to the rest of international relations, as overreliant on the usually unfulfilled conditions of a rational actor model, as lacking both theory and data, and as apolitical (Nye 1989: 26-29; 1990: 234-35, 240-41; Buzan 1983: 8).

A second discourse also emerged in the wake of World War II, in many ways as a reaction to that of strategic studies and to the realist emphasis in international relations. This was the interdisciplinary field of peace and conflict studies, which began as early as the 1930s with the quantitative work of Quincy Wright and Louis Richardson on the causes of war, but which evolved into a field of its own by the late

1950s and early 1960s. While this field began with a narrow focus on war, by the late 1960s or early 1970s, under the influence especially of Johan Galtung and others at the Peace Research Institute in Oslo, it broadened its focus to look at issues of exploitation and justice and what Galtung came to call "structural violence" (Stephenson 1990).

A continuing debate in this field over whether its focus should be on peace as the absence of war—"negative peace"—or peace as the absence of war and the presence of social justice—"positive peace"— had its beginning in the period that centered around the Vietnam War and its international and domestic impacts. Peace studies were widely criticized by strategic studies writers as being value-based and normative; peace studies writers countered that they were value-explicit, and that strategic studies scholars needed to be more explicit about their own very different value preferences.

During the mid-1970s, while the field of strategic studies declined and the "negative peace" side of peace studies took a back seat to some of the "positive peace" issues, the old idealists in international relations, along with radical and Marxist theorists, took up the study of the international economic system. While liberal idealists studied West-West trade relations and the development of international trade and monetary regimes, radical and Marxist theorists turned to develop first a dependency and then a world systems theory in reference to North-South economic relations and the presence or absence of development. International political economy (IPE) was in reality two separate fields with different sets of values and theories dominant in each. One brand of IPE scholars studied the relations of Western-developed nations from a liberal idealist perspective; another brand studied the relations between Western-developed and Southern-less developed nations from a radical or Marxist perspective. Strategic studies scholars studied East-West security relations from a realist perspective, while peace studies scholars first studied East-West relations from a liberal idealist perspective and then North-South relations from a radical Marxist perspective.

As the conditions of world politics changed, beginning in the 1970s with the decline of liberal internationalist economic regimes and the rise of the third world as a bloc, continuing through the waning of the Cold War, the decline of the USSR, and the resurgent independence of Eastern Europe in the late 1980s, together with the rising economic power of Japan, Germany, the European Community, and transnational interests, all three of these fields and/or subfields were thrown into question. None of the theories have proved to have overwhelming explanatory power over the broader range of international relations; many have failed to explain or even predict the changes in their own relatively narrow area of focus, let alone to provide good policy advice in a period of crisis. We are left with the unanswered question of what the relationship is between these parts of the field and whether an overarching theory of international relations is possible. The more immediate question is that of the reconceptualization of security and, in the process, the claiming of that term by the various fields and subfields related to it. A brief look at the historical development of security systems may help to put the new debate in context.

A HISTORICAL LOOK AT SECURITY SYSTEMS

Keohane and Nye (1977) were among the first to talk of the reduced utility of military force in the face of the increasingly "complex interdependence" of international and transnational relations. Among the characteristics of the "complex interdependence" among Western developed states, they identified: (1) the absence of hierarchy among issues (i.e., that military security does not consistently dominate the agenda), (2) the decreased role of military force, and (3) the presence of multiple channels of connection between societies. In the wake of the Cold War, complex interdependence may be said to have spread beyond just the Western-developed nations.

One needs, however, to glance back in history at the evolution of dominant security systems from empires (Pax Romana, and later Pax Britannica) to the great-power balance of power system, through the bipolar system of nuclear deterrence combined with alliances, which has been termed Pax Americana for one part of the world and Pax Sovietica for another. In all these cases, security was conceived of as an order that was maintained by overwhelming military force. This emphasis continues in President Bush's conception of the "new world order" put forth in the context of declining U.S. power, more rapidly declining Soviet power, and the resurgence of U.S. military intervention against aggression, backed up by an international consensus in the UN Security Council. There is nothing new in this conception of security; it could be called the "old world order without the Russians." In many ways, it takes us back to the combination of collective security and U.S. hegemony that characterized the immediate postwar period. There is nothing new about a world order in which the U.S. serves as world policeman.

There is, however, a subordinate discourse in the reconceptualization of security, which began in the early 1980s, but harked back to the idealist "peace plans" of Kant, Grotius, and others, and later, to the creation of the UN. It contains major differences from the notion of security defined narrowly as defense and the protection of national interest maintained ultimately by a preponderance of military threat and force. Nor was this second approach to security simply a theoretical or ideal approach; in practice, nation-states have followed multiple approaches to security, although one has been privileged over the others in terms of being the dominant rhetoric or discourse, in both public policy and academia, and in terms of the proportion of resources devoted to it.

The subordinate theme in the security discourse had as its predecessor the "collective security" approach, nascent in the League of Nations, which became a primary approach in the organization of the United Nations. "Collective security" was an argument for the collective resistance of all nations together against aggression by any one of them against any other. It was, in essence, a mild version of Hobbes's social contract, but used at the international level (in ways Hobbes would not have liked). Thus, nation states agreed, in order to escape "the war of all against all" or, in the language of the UN Charter, "to save succeeding generations from the scourge of war, which twice in our lifetime has brought untold sorrows to man(sic)kind," to create a new social contract, the UN Charter, and to set up a very mild Leviathan, the UN Security Council and the Military Staff Committee. Never mind that this in part was to be the guarantee of the security of the weak and strong by the strong (especially the five permanent members of the Security Council), and never mind that those strong happened to be the victors of the most recent war; nevertheless, this approach to security did represent something of a shift in focus from the national to the international level, based in the notion of a social contract of the full international community (defined at that time as the 51 primarily European and Latin American nation-states who were the initial UN members).

This was not an unprecedented case. It paralleled in many ways the earlier organization of diplomatic relations in the Peace of Westphalia in 1648, after the Thirty Years War, and the development of the first permanent international organizations in 1815 at the Congress of Vienna after the Napoleonic Wars. More directly related to the "collective security" approach was the creation of the Organization of American States in 1945 as the first of a series of regional security arrangements which were accorded a special role under Articles 33 and 52-54 of the UN Charter. The OAS was unique among such regional arrangements as it contained both elements of "collective security" (by which all members agreed to forswear aggression among themselves and to band together to stop any member who violated this commitment) and "collective defense" (by which a group banded together to counter any possible aggression by another group).

Collective defense succeeded collective security as the primary method of maintaining international security even before the failure of collective security in the UN system after Korea. This stands in contrast to national security, in which nuclear deterrence, at least in the U.S., was seen as the primary method. The construction of NATO in 1949, ANZUS in 1951, the Warsaw Pact in 1955, and other alliances which were part of a bipolar world security system, represented a throwback from the idea of a social order based on a universal social contract backed up by military power to a balancing system of deterrence which pitted one part of the system against another.

Only as power began to shift in the international system, beginning with the mid-1970s accretion of economic power by the newly oil rich nations, and of political power, at least in the UN context, by a new third world bloc, did the reconceptualization of security begin. While strategic studies analysts in the U.S. continued to focus on East-West relations as the primary conflict dimension, with Europe as the primary locus and nuclear deterrence and alliance strategy as the primary means, others began to question both the traditional definition of security and the means of achieving it.

In September 1977 in New York, Willy Brandt, at the urging of Robert McNamara (who by then was no longer U.S. Secretary of Defense but President of the World Bank), announced his willingness to form and chair an "Independent Commission on International Development Issues," whose report would eventually be received in 1980 by then UN Secretary-General Kurt Waldheim. While the focus of the Commission was on development issues and questions of the new international economic order, originally raised in UN General Assembly Resolutions 3201 and 3202 of 1974, the title, *North-South: A Programme for Survival*, presaged new thinking linking questions of economic security and security as world survival. While the chair and initiators were from the North and West (half the funding came from the Netherlands), and there were no Eastern bloc members, a majority of the members were from the third world so they could not be outvoted. Among other things, the report stressed that aid was an inadequate approach to development and international restructuring of food, energy, and other economic systems necessary for global survival (Brandt 1986). While the U.S. media and policy community virtually ignored the report and its 1983 sequel, at least 40 governments referred to it during the UN General Assembly Special Session in 1980. The interdependence of world economic security had been given an official stamp of approval.

The Brandt report was followed in rapid succession by a report from the Independent Commission on Disarmament and Security Issues (Palme Commission) in 1982 and the World Commission on Environment and Development (Brundtland Commission) in 1985. Notions of common security articulated by the Palme Commission not only further accented the linkages between economic and traditional political-military security issues, and the interdependence of "first" and "third" worlds, but also suggested that security for states on opposite sides of the Cold War and the nuclear deterrence wall had to be based on their interdependence and common interest in avoiding a war that could lead to a nuclear holocaust. The guns versus butter dilemma, the superiority of defense over offense, the risk-prone nature of arms races, and the contradictions of nuclear deterrence led the Commission to recommend a less militarized approach to security.

"Common Security" continued to refer to the security of nation-states, but the notion that nation-state security could only be achieved in common with other states rather than against them was a radical one, given the context of the dominant discourse of security through nuclear deterrence and alliances. Two primary parts of the argument addressed the security issue from an East-West and a North-South context. First, there could be no victory in nuclear war, therefore we could only survive together; thus reduction of nuclear weapons arsenals, beginning with the U.S. and USSR, would further security (Independent Commission on Disarmament and Security Issues 1982: 6). This argument first surfaced in a December 1981 memo from Egon Bahr at the time of the Commission's meeting and visit to the war memorial in Hiroshima, the site of the dropping of the first nuclear weapon. Second, the costs of the military were contributing to economic insecurity everywhere; thus reduction of such costs could contribute to development (Independent Commission on Disarmament and Security Issues 1982: 71, 172).

Among the principles of common security were a right to security for all nations, the illegitimacy of military force except in self- or collective defense, the fact that security could no longer be attained by military superiority, and the need for quantitative and qualitative arms limitations. Among the methods proposed were certain specific short- and medium-term measures, with particular reference to East-West conflict and to nuclear weapons, especially in the European context, plus procedures for strengthening the United Nations and for regional approaches to security, including regional Conferences on Security and Cooperation, zones of peace, and nuclear-weapon-free zones (Independent Commission on Disarmament and Security Issues 1982: 8-11, 178-81). While the ideas in the Commission report had been put forth before by peace movements in Europe and the U.S., and even by states elsewhere in the world, the codification of such ideas by established statesmen, including those of powerful Western nations, gave them a visibility and legitimacy they had not received before then.

The World Commission on Environment and Development continued the expansion and demilitarization of the concept of security with the publication of its report, *Our Common Future,* in 1987. The Brundtland Commission added the dimension of environmental security to the Brandt Commission's work on economic security and the Palme Commission's on the interdependence of states' political and military security. A secure common global future was now also seen to be dependent on all of the elements of the global environmental infrastructures, which increasingly were being damaged by human activity. As with the Brandt and Palme reports before it, the Brundtland report contained little that was new, as it reiterated much that had come up in the work of the Club of Rome, in the Fate of the Earth Conference, in the Stockholm Conference of 1972, and in the Environment and Development Conference of 1982, but it did again provide a sense of global visibility and legitimacy for these ideas.

Meanwhile, other elements of the security debate were also evolving. Europeans had experienced some measure of security in the period since World War II through two different methods, one distinctly integrative and the other distinctly disintegrative or polarizing. While nuclear deterrence and the NATO alliance were seen as one primary method of keeping the peace between East and West in Europe by deterring potential Soviet aggression (a disintegrative method), the development of the European communities was seen as the primary method by which security between France and Germany had been attained (an integrative method). The neofunctionalist approach to European integration, beginning with the European Coal and Steel Community in 1952 and expanding to the European Economic Community and European Atomic Energy Agency in 1958, had so tied France and Germany together economically that a break in relations would damage each. By this time, public opinion, both mass and elite, reflected improved affective relations between the two populations.[1]

There had also been a degree of integration between Eastern and Western Europe, especially through the UN Economic Commission for Europe, founded in 1947. The decline of detente had not been so obvious between Eastern and Western Europe as between the U.S. and the USSR, and NATO's "dual-track" decision in 1979 both to invest in military defense against the Warsaw Pact and seek constructive engagement with it was taken somewhat more seriously in Europe than in the U.S. The Conference on Security and Cooperation in Europe from 1975 on had shown the effective linkage of the three concerns of security, economic, and human rights issues and even appeared to be having some impact, primarily through Helsinki Watch groups, on human rights in the authoritarian regimes of Eastern Europe.

In this context, the American military buildup under the Reagan Administration (actually beginning with Carter in 1979), and particularly the notion of waging nuclear war if deterrence should fail, was received with mixed feelings in Europe. When it became more and more clear that Reaganite notions about the feasibility of "limited nuclear war" meant war limited to Europe, it spawned the development of a massive peace movement not unlike that of the mid-1950s. It also spawned the development of peace researchers' thinking on alternatives to nuclear deterrence, and particularly the development of the school of nonprovocative or defensive defense. Work by the Alternative Defense Commission around the issue of what policies the UK might adopt if the Labour Party were actually to forswear nuclear weapons, as the party platform proclaimed, led to the publication of two books in 1983 and 1987 which looked at a range of alternative systems and their implications for British membership in NATO.[2] While the dominant debate in the U.S. and Europe centered on only two alternatives—continued nuclear deterrence or the massive strengthening of conventional defenses—proponents of nonprovocative defense began to argue not only that nuclear deterrence, if it should fail, could not then defend, but that conventional defense was no solution either. Alternative defense thinkers in the UK, in Scandinavia (especially Norway and Denmark), and in West Germany, pointing to the risks inherent in the security dilemma and arguing the superiority of defensive defense, began to produce volumes of research promoting European security through a variety of methods emphasizing defense over offense. These methods ranged from nonviolent resistance to restructuring the military toward a "structural inability to attack," that is, methods with lower range, mobility, and destructive force.

The idea of defensive defense eventually spread to the U.S., where only a few isolated researchers had previously worked on it. It was taken up by the peace movement, in the wake of the "freeze," as well as by more conventional defense analysts.

In order to counter the growing European and American peace movements, Reagan moved to incorporate the language, though not the content, of defensive defense. In his Star Wars speech of March 1983, a brilliant defense against the growing popularity of the peace movement, Reagan argued that the nuclear era must come to a close and that the Strategic Defense Initiative could move us away from the dangers of nuclear weapons and toward a viable defense of the U.S. While the technology needed to achieve this was severely questioned by the scientific community, and the strategy of moving from nuclear deterrence to high technology defense was questioned by the conventional military establishment, it was clear that the move had been a brilliant political success, taking the sense of insecurity in nuclear weapons which the peace movement had managed to create in the American public and moving them back to a sense of trust in a high technology military defense. The U.S. public went back to sleep on issues of foreign and security policy.

However, defensive defense ideas also spread to the Soviet Union, where Gorbachev eventually began to make use of them in a new peace initiative. Just as Reagan attempted to use such ideas to diffuse peace movements in the U.S. and Western Europe, so Gorbachev attempted to woo the U.S. and especially the European peace movement (inadvertantly strengthening what little there was of an independent peace movement in the Soviet Union and Eastern Europe). What was different here was that it eventually became clear that the internal condition of the Soviet Union had led Gorbachev to develop serious integrative and de-escalating initiatives toward the West. In February 1986, Gorbachev proclaimed the desirability of yet another security concept, that of "mutual security," which stressed the intertwined nature of the security of the superpowers due to the nuclear threat, and thus the need to move toward nuclear disarmament. A series of speeches suggesting Soviet movement toward defensive defense followed, accompanied by changes in Soviet force structure. The withdrawal of troops and materiel from Eastern Europe, the Spring 1991 end of the Warsaw Pact military alliance, and the restarting of the START and INF negotiations that followed from the new Soviet thinking were representative of this mutual security approach.

However, as with the "new world order," this is only one of the two strands of security discourses. Mutual security and Bush's new world order emphasize the intertwined security of the superpowers, which is indeed new thinking, but also the continued superiority of the large northern powers, which is not. This is once again the model of the U.S. as the world's policeman, backed now by the UN Security Council, with the active or passive military and/or economic support of northern and a few richer southern powers (most of Europe, Japan, the USSR, China, Saudi Arabia, Kuwait, etc.) This is a modification of the original system of collective security with a slightly more hegemonic approach, and is located centrally within the traditional security discourse. While it is clearly different from the we/they bipolar world of the Cold War, it still emphasizes political-military threat and enforcement as the dominant means of guaranteeing security, defined primarily as order. The approach is still disintegrative, we they; the new poles of this system are no longer east and west, but north and south, and they are more clearly unequal.

ENDS AND MEANS

The other strand in the current security debate involves a more integrative approach, with an emphasis on means other than political-military threat and coercion, and with a redefinition of security not only as order, but as the global fulfillment of individual human needs. The common security concept comes much closer to this end of the debate. It involves not only the security of the superpowers and major powers, but security, defined as both protection from attack and as access to sustainable human development, for individuals in all societies. Common security incorporates both economic and ecological security. Both these terms are derived from the Greek *oikos* or "household." It involves the recognition of our living together. This is a different world from the anarchy of supposedly sovereign nation-states each seeking power to protect itself from the others. Common security presupposes a world where there is an increasing realization of interdependence in security and other matters and a realization that security is itself interdependent with development and the better fulfillment of human needs.

This recognition of the need for the common pursuit of security has implications for the means and methods by which security is pursued. Where there is interdependence, as Keohane and Nye have pointed out, the threat and use of force or coercion are less effective and less likely to be used. Coercion has a tendency to produce disintegration. Where lasting integration is the goal, methods based more on fair exchange and the meeting of individual needs work far better. Violence between spouses results in death, divorce, and misery. Civil war most often results in the disintegration of nation-states, accompanied by generations of further mistrust and lack of cooperation. International war or coercion (coercion as defined within the Warsaw Pact, war as in the case of the UN versus Iraq) is also more likely to lead to further division, poverty, and human and environmental degradation.

Perhaps the question of restructuring for peace is not the right question. Karl Deutsch argued that peace exists both in structures where there is and is not integrated political organization. "Security-communities" exist, with or without the presence of state or international organization machinery, where communities are sufficiently rich to meet the basic needs of their members, where exchange among them is reciprocal and fair, and where there is good communication (Deutsch 1957).

Structure may in some ways be regarded as frozen process. The results of attempting to freeze the processes of change, which are always with us, may be like trying to stop an earthquake. Violent means of preventing change, and violent means of change, are likely to be equally unproductive in an interdependent world. Where we freeze the boundaries of nation-states or international organizations, or perhaps world government, and back that up with enforcement by violence, we are not likely to end up with lasting security.

The restructuring that is appropriate for peace, then, is restructuring of our processes of interaction, of the means and methods by which we attempt to maintain peace and security. If security involves both the feeling and the actuality of safety, then the means must be consistent with providing that security. Those means must provide constructive ways of dealing with conflict and change. The more the means provide for the security of all parties, the greater the potential security.

Defining security as defense, especially the defense of the nation-state, implies means which either protect one from the other or which deter. These methods are necessary, but when defense becomes dominant, it ultimately reduces real security. This is particularly true when methods of defense blur into offense. Ultimately, if weapons are the methods, it is difficult to distinguish between offense and defense. Because protection must always be one element of security, there must be methods for defense, but these methods must remain as nonprovocative as possible. The methods of nonprovocative defense, including nonviolent civilian-based defense, are an attempt to move away from the offensive weapons of war. They continue to rely on coercion, but not on direct violence. Nonviolent action can also be used as a means for constructive change as well as a means of protecting against unwanted change. While security here is still the security of one's own unit, there is at least the reduction of one's willingness to hurt others.

If one moves to the concept of common security, then the methods must take into account the welfare of others. Methods of constructive conflict and conflict resolution—direct methods of interaction which are equitable and allow open communication, plus third-party assistance in the form of mediation, conciliation, good offices, facilitation of negotiation, and peacekeeping—are more in keeping with the concept of common security.[3] Negotiation, mediation, nonviolent struggle, including economic and political sanctions, and UN peacekeeping are more likely to lead to a peaceful world than the attempted enforcement of peace by either the United Nations or the United States and its friends and allies.

The choice of definition of security is basic here, and each definition of security currently being discussed has implications for the means and methods of its achievement. The adequacy of each definition can also be judged by the methods it implies. The more those methods provide for the security of all, the better the security they will provide. The more offensive the means, the greater the likelihood of being embroiled in the security dilemma of constant escalation of means. But even defense can lead to the security dilemma, as defense is interpreted as offense. Definitions of security, and the means to provide it, must ultimately move even further toward inclusivity rather than exclusivity, toward meeting the basic needs of all parties, including the environment in which we live. The further development of methods of constructive conflict, based in principles of equity, reciprocity, and good communication, is an essential part of this. Restructuring for security implies a change in balance in the way we prepare for conflict. If we prepare for war, we are more likely to get it. We need to shift our investment toward building an infrastructure of peace. For a peaceful world, security can only be achieved by peaceful methods.

NOTES

1. Franco-German mutual esteem had already risen by 1958, and continued to rise (see Puchala 1970).

2. The Alternative Defence Commission also held a meeting in 1985 bringing together researchers from the U.S. and Western and Eastern Europe (see Alternative Defence Commission 1983, 1987).

3. There is insufficient space here to review the development of alternative methods for providing international security. Stephenson 1982 and 1988: 55-76 contain citations and an analytic review of that development.

REFERENCES

Alternative Defence Commission. 1983. *Defence Without the Bomb*. London: Taylor and Francis.

_____. 1987. *The Politics of Alternative Defence*. London: Paladin/Grafton.

Brandt, Willy. 1986. *Arms and Hunger*. New York: Pantheon.

Buzan, Barry. 1983. *People, States, and Fear*. Chapel Hill, NC: University of North Carolina Press.

_____. 1990. "The Case for a Comprehensive Definition of Security." *Washington Papers* (Center for Peace and Conflict Research) 4: 10.

Deutsch, Karl. 1957. *Political Community and the North Atlantic Area.* Princeton, NJ: Princeton University Press.

Independent Commission on Disarmament and Security Issues. 1982. *Common Security.* New York: Simon and Schuster.

Keohane, Robert and Joseph Nye. 1977. *Power and Interdependence.* Boston: Little Brown.

Nye, Joseph. 1989. "The Contribution of Strategic Studies: Future Challenges." *Adelphi Papers* 235 (Spring): 20-21.

_____. 1990. "International Security Studies." In *American Defense Annual 1988-89.* Ed. Joseph Kruzel. Lexington, MA: Lexington Books. 238-39.

Puchala, Donald. 1970. "Integration and Disintegration in Franco-German Relations, 1954-1965." *International Organization* 24 (Spring).

Stephenson, Carolyn. 1982. *Alternative Methods for International Security.* Washington, D.C: University Press of America.

_____. 1988. "The Need for Alternative Forms of Security: Crises and Opportunities." *Alternatives* 113: 55-76.

_____. 1990. *Peace Studies: The Evolution of Peace Research and Peace Education.* Occasional Paper 1. Honolulu: University of Hawai'i Institute for Peace.

World Commission on Environment and Development. 1987. *Our Common Future.* New York: Oxford University Press.

4

Global Restructuring:
Arms Control and Disarmament

KENNEDY GRAHAM

INTRODUCTION

The international system is in need of a global restructuring for peace. A restructured new world order for the 1990s will require far-reaching measures in arms control and disarmament. What sort of initiatives are desirable in the future? What initiatives are possible? Which are likely? Will such measures amount to "tinkering on the margins," or could they contribute to a major restructuring of security relationships?

The definition of peace in this chapter is a state of global self-governance by humankind which rests on a developed mechanism for the prevention of conflict, or its suppression, in a manner consistent with international law but which countenances the lawful use of force, as necessary, for conflict control. It postulates the concept of global peace in a manner akin to the peace that prevails in a national society, with an emphasis on law and order and justice. In this chapter the mechanism of peace focuses primarily on the military dimension, with full knowledge that the causes of conflict are minimized if more enlightened political, social, economic, and environmental circumstances prevail.

Two further definitions are used here; arms control and disarmament. Disarmament may be either a process or an end state. The process of disarmament is the process, through bilateral or multilateral negotiation or through unilateral action, whereby the number of weapons a state possesses is actually reduced. For example, the first nuclear disarmament agreement concluded was the 1987 INF accord, whereby intermediate range ballistic and cruise missiles already deployed in Europe were dismantled. The START treaty, reaffirmed by the Commonwealth of Independent States, will comprise another nuclear disarmament measure. In contrast, arms control is the process of slowing down and perhaps halting the arms race. The two SALT agreements of the 1970s were arms control agreements. Some measures are quite difficult to categorize. A comprehensive nuclear test ban treaty, for example, would be an arms control measure in that it would curb the continuing weapons modernization programs of the nuclear powers; but it can also be seen as a disarmament measure in that it would prevent continued "reliability testing" and thus slowly erode the basis of confidence in the deterrent effect of the existing nuclear weapons stockpile.

Finally a differentiation in time frames should be drawn, between the medium term, defined here as the 1990s, and the longer term, defined as the first two decades of the 21st century.

ROLE OF DISARMAMENT AND ARMS CONTROL

Can arms control and disarmament lead to political and military change, or are they consequent to it? Are they simply "tinkering at the margin" of the world order, or could they contribute to a major restructuring of security relationships? Past experience will be considered in this section. Future prospects will then be considered after both these questions have been explored.

It is necessary, first, to identify the basic structure of global security relationships of the past 40 years. Following the failure of collective security after an initial 30-year attempt, the international community returned, in the 1950s, to the balance-of-power system that had marked 19th-century security relationships, although this time balanced along bipolar lines and with nuclear alliances in support. Since then the governing security structure has been nuclear deterrence through mutually assured destruction (MAD). The main characteristics of this security system have been an emphasis on retaliatory offense, at high strategic force levels, without significant strategic defense; an asymmetry between nuclear and conventional force levels on each side; no weapons of mass destruction in space; and constraints on the spread of nuclear weapon capability beyond the five permanent members of the Security Council. All arms control treaties to date—at least those between the superpowers—have been prosecuted within the context of that security relationship, designed at the negotiating stage to be compatible with its requirements and often justified, at the stage of ratification, as "enhancing and stabilizing deterrence at lower force levels." They could hardly be said to have contributed to a major restructuring of security relationships, since their express purpose was to make nations safer within the context of existing security relationships. There is a popular maxim among arms control professionals: if it's significant, it's not possible, if it's possible, it's not significant. The experience of the 1950s through the 1980s tended to underscore this.

Some treaties were indeed judged at the time, even by the negotiating powers themselves, to be peripheral to fundamental security relationships—again, "tinkering at the margins." Examples include the Threshold Test Ban and Peaceful Nuclear Explosions treaties, and the Environmental Modification and the Biological Weapons conventions. But these last two conventions, Enmod and Biological Weapons, have subsequently attained a political and military significance beyond anything anticipated in the 1970s at the time of their drafting. Biological weapons factories were suspected in Iraq before the UN enforcement action. Could other states succumb to similar programs in the future? Had Iraq ratified its signature of Enmod, it would have violated that convention by releasing oil into the Gulf and firing oil wells across Kuwait. Indeed, such was the international devastation caused by that act, it might be judged that customary international law was violated.

However, the two global arms control treaties, the Partial Test Ban Treaty and the Non-Proliferation Treaty, were certainly not tinkering at the margin. The regional or zonal treaties concluded to date—Antarctica, Outer Space, Tlatelolco, Rarotonga—also have had an effect on major power policies, judging by the drawn-out agonies the U.S., Britain, and France endured in acceding to them. Finally, the strategic treaties, ABM and SALT, are too fundamentally close to the heart of deterrence theory and planetary survival to be dismissed as tinkering at the margin. But precisely for that reason, those treaties were creatures of the system, seeking not to reshape but rather to reinforce nuclear deterrence.

In contrast with these arms control treaties stand the INF accord of 1987 and the START treaty of 1991, the first two nuclear disarmament treaties concluded, and also the historic CFE Agreement for conventional force reductions signed in Paris in November 1990. These agreements do contribute to a major restructuring of security relationships. A treaty is effective, in an instrumental sense, if at conception it makes the body politic pregnant with positive future change. The best example is in the economic sphere, where the treaties of Rome have made probably irreversible positive changes for European integration. In a similar manner, it is possible that the INF, START, and CFE treaties will portend similar changes in European military relationships during the 1990s. Yet even these disarmament agreements were still concluded within the context of prevailing political and military doctrine.

Thus it can be said that, in the 30 years from the 1950s to the mid-1980s, arms control and disarmament treaties have had a broad effect on international security relationships, both tinkering at the margin in some instances and, on a few occasions, helping to restructure fundamental security relationships. As a general rule, however, they serve the modest but useful job of achieving the "ratchet effect:" securing the military status quo when the political climate is relatively benign, so that if and when relationships turn sour again, certain military options that could make things worse for the nation and the planet are ruled out.

THE FUTURE

What then of the future? Will future treaties tinker at the margin, strengthen global security through the ratchet effect, or contribute to a major restructuring of security relationships? Since 1985, the world has begun to emerge from the era of strategic nuclear deterrence. The Cold War is over, yet bilateral nuclear deterrence continues in the "new era of cooperation" proclaimed at Malta. What sort of arms control/ disarmament initiatives are desirable in the future? Which of these are possible, and which are likely?

Prescription

First, what is desirable? How could the world be restructured for peace? How could global security be strengthened through arms control and disarmament measures? In the most fundamental sense, it is desirable that the world restructure its security relationships for two primary goals: (a) so that the combined force levels of all nation states do not threaten devastation of the planet and its life forms; and (b) so that conflict be prevented or controlled in a rational, lawful, democratic, and equitable manner without the need for such force levels. This is, of course, a longer-term vision. But in a prescriptive sense, what arms control/disarmament initiatives are desirable for this end?

First, and paradoxically, the concept of general and complete disarmament should be dropped from official terminology, as found in UN resolutions and Conference on Disarmament (CD) committee deliberations. The concept is not captured in the UN Charter, which speaks more realistically of plans to be drawn up by the Military Staff Committee "for the regulation of armaments and possible disarmament." The notion of general and complete disarmament is rather the product of the diplomatic corridors of the 1950s, defined in a seminal 1959 UN resolution as "a system of international security in which States will possess armed forces for the purposes only of (1) maintaining internal order and (2) providing agreed personnel for a UN peace force." It is the subject—the end goal—of some desultory discussions in Geneva that pass for negotiations for a Comprehensive Program of Disarmament. But it is as unrealistic to expect the global power structure of our planet to be reduced to agreed levels of personnel as it is to anticipate a disbanding of the New York Police Department. A UN peacekeeping and enforcement capability would indeed be the global equivalent of a local police force. But as the level of force increases in human affairs with the size of the social unit, so it must be expected that the global community will govern itself with more military potency than "agreed personnel for a UN peace force." To postulate otherwise and highlight the concept of general and complete disarmament diminishes the credibility of the United Nations, diverts diplomatic resources from important work, and nourishes misplaced dreams.

A more realistic vision for the future is found in Article 26 of the UN Charter: "the least diversion for armaments of the world's human and economic resources." Like all principles, "least diversion" is a generalized concept, open to interpretation and debate as to what force level is necessary for peace. But it nonetheless should serve as the cardinal principle governing the debate on disarmament, not least because it is a binding legal obligation on all UN member states.

The least diversion principle would thus serve as the binding obligation on the major powers to reduce their weapons of mass destruction to combined levels that do not threaten the planet. The nuclear winter threshold of some hundred megatons, identified by scientists in the mid-1930s, may be otherwise defined as the "threshold of planetary survival." It can reasonably be accepted as consistent with the least diversion principle. Indeed, the two can be postulated as one and the same thing.

Major powers, however, will not easily be persuaded to reduce their nuclear arsenals unless and until the confidence paradigm shifts from nuclear reliance to the only alternative modern security system yet devised—collective security. This will be, at best, a slow process, since the Great Powers are less the beneficiaries than the guarantors of collective security. Their retention of nuclear weapons are due at least equally to their role as major powers. As permanent members of the Security Council, they retain their nuclear "currencies of power" to symbolize great power status as much as to meet intrinsic national security interests. But in a "desirable world," the rationality of the least diversion principle would prove compelling in the longer term, and the combined nuclear arsenals of all states would be reduced to a few score weapons each. Initially, the incentive for Great Power restraint would be the strengthening of nonproliferation. But ultimately, the logic of a country's national interest in sharing in "planetary survival" would prevail. Humanity would then break through the barriers of minimal deterrence, and subsequently, the national control of nuclear arms, ceding nuclear military power to a centralized control of a few weapons only, whose purpose would simply be deterrence of nuclear proliferation in nation-states. The repudiation of nuclear weapons by Belarus and Ukraine reflect a qualitative change in security thinking by nation-states. It is significant that in recent months several leading thinkers have revived the memory of the Baruch Plan of 1946, implying that the times are right to consider anew the notion of internationalized control of nuclear power.

What could this mean in practical terms for disarmament initiatives over the medium and longer term? Of equal significance to INF and START as the first nuclear disarmament agreements ever was the Gulf enforcement action against Iraq, albeit imperfectly prosecuted in terms of UN command and control. The Gulf operation was the first successful act of collective security after 70 years of effort. Coming within four years of INF and START, it constitutes an important complement to disarmament. Nuclear disarmament and collective security go hand in hand, the latter being a precondition of the former.

What is desirable, in the medium term, is that the UN Military Staff Committee be reactivated and the special agreements envisaged in Article 43 of the UN Charter be struck with leading member states for the availability, "on call" to the Security Council, of their armed forces and associated military facilities, including rights of passage across their territories. This would enable the UN in a future crisis to act more coherently as the principal agent under Chapter 7 with enforcement action under the UN flag and command than was the case with Iraq. It is significant that such establishment figures as UN Under-Secretary-General Spiers are now prepared to speak publicly, albeit informally, about the possibility of a standing UN force sometime in the future. A viable UN enforcement capability, however, will probably require some creative change in Security Council membership and procedures, an entirely separate area of inquiry.

The cancerous growth of nuclear weaponry over the past decades makes it difficult, and even hazardous, to bring to life those parts of the Charter that have hitherto been skeletal. Nuclear weapons, even if they were deemed to be legal, do not sit well with the collective security provisions of the Charter. It is one thing for the permanent five, as the sole declared nuclear weapon states, to have the power of veto under Article 27. But what, for example, about a special agreement with Israel governing the number and types of forces, their degree of readiness and general location, and the nature of the facilities and assistance to be provided? Nuclear weapons are normally deemed to be part of a member state's armed forces and could therefore be the subject of the special agreements referred to in Article 43. Are they to be expressly excluded from such agreements—deemed to be extraneous to the Charter and irrelevant to collective security? Or would a polite fiction be entered into such an agreement, with the international community looking silently away from the question of nuclear weapons and UN enforcement?

Desirable in the medium term is the conclusion of a total nuclear test ban and, as a corollary, a broadened and extended nonproliferation regime. The argument advanced by the three Western nuclear powers for continued underground nuclear testing in the 1990s are palpably weak and anachronistic. They rest on two assertions: the reliability argument that existing nuclear arsenals must be kept reliable through the testing of warheads; and the modernization program introducing a third generation of nuclear weapons. Western nuclear testing programs rested on the premise that there was not sufficient trust of the USSR for the Western powers to forego reliance on nuclear deterrence, and that nuclear testing was essential to the continued credibility of nuclear deterrence. The Western powers maintained that this argument held into the indefinite future. Strategic weapons modernization programs were designed to ensure a credible nuclear deterrent force "well into the 21st century." The Stealth bomber, F-22 fighter, and D-5 sea-launched missile are all explicitly justified to this day as containing the "Soviet threat."

Coupled with this "nuclear inertia" is an interest—more pragmatic during the Bush administration than during the Reagan era—in a space-based strategic defense system in a post-Gulf War situation. The concept of "Brilliant Pebbles" for national protection against Third World missiles still threatens the ABM Treaty and portends the introduction of weaponry in space. Although the United States sees its space-based missile defense as serving its national security interest, such a defense system does not serve the broader interest of a stable global security system. A desirable initiative in the medium term, therefore, would be to amend the Outer Space Treaty to ban all weaponry in outer space, thereby endowing the heavens with a more civilized order than the Hobbesian purgatory that exists today in our terrestrial habitat.

Of equal importance, it would be desirable for a chemical weapons convention to be concluded within the next few years, not because it would be central to global strategic relationships, but because it would symbolize in an important way the further emergence of humanity from the "barbaric" stage of international relations.

Thus, a desirable vision for a viable global security system, in the longer term, would include the following characteristics:

> —low combined strategic force levels, within a ceiling of a few score nuclear weapons, below the "threshold of planetary survival," leading ultimately to their centralized command;

> —no national strategic defense systems;

> —a universal nonproliferation regime, including a comprehensive nuclear test ban;

> —a weapon-free zone in outer space, with exceptions agreed to by the Security Council;

> —a ban on the production and possession of chemical weaponry;

> —a strengthened collective security mechanism through the United Nations, and standing arrangements for the provision of national armed forces under the UN flag and command.

Assessment

That is the prescription. Which of these desirable arms control/disarmament measures is possible?

The political environment that prompted and sustained security relationships in the postwar era—an adversarial, bipolar Cold War—no longer applies. Yet the security relationship continues, at least in Western doctrinal thought. Strategic nuclear weapons have become even more remotely connected to day-to-day military realities around the world than they were during the Cold War. The incipient atrophy of the doctrine of nuclear deterrence resembles the way the world economy slowly drifted away from the gold standard in the 1920s. But nuclear weapons still represent the bottom line of global self-governance of the human species—testimony still to the primal state of international society in the late-20th century.

Arms control and disarmament treaties, as noted, are negotiated within the context of the prevailing strategic doctrine, which in turn is determined by the political relationships of the time. The future of arms control and disarmament depends fundamentally on the fate of nuclear deterrence. What is the possible, and the likely, fate of nuclear deterrence in the post-Cold War era? Three broad alternative developments are possible.

It is not impossible, conceptually, that the doctrine of nuclear deterrence as the world has known it for four decades will gradually wither on the vine and that, in the longer term, the bottom line for global self-governance will become collective security through the UN with a few score nuclear weapons to back it. In this event, deep cuts in strategic force levels would necessarily follow, from the combined level of some 20,000 to simply a few score. There would be no need for any strategic defense system. This could be accompanied by substantive arms control measures—a universal nonproliferation regime, a test ban, and possibly a weapon-free zone in outer space. The question remains how the major powers could proceed to these goals.

Could a weakened Russia move unilaterally to close nuclear missile silos for economic or geopolitical reasons? Or will it insist on remaining militarily at par with the United States and laboriously negotiate "mutual balanced force reductions at equal and undiminished security," to use the phraseology of the 1970s and 1980s? Either alternative is possible. Could a dominant United States conclude that with Russia no longer a proclaimed adversary, the targeting of 10,000 strategic warheads on one country is an indulgence and move unilaterally to reduce numbers? Or will it find an ex-post rationale for retaining strategic retaliatory offense against nonnuclear Third World nations? Again each alternative is possible. It is significant that a call has recently been made by a former leading U.S. official for a unilateral cut by the U.S. to 10,000 nuclear weapons. Certainly, the current political and security situation—an unstable and uncertain Russia and a stable and confident United States—calls for a major initiative by the Bush Administration. But there are no indications yet that the President will be prepared to undertake a political risk of this magnitude. If and when political developments in the Commonwealth of Independent States become more stable, presidential policies after the 1992 election may reflect a greater disposition to proceed.

Alternatively, it is possible that the doctrine of nuclear deterrence will remain an article of faith of the powerful, but that it will be redefined and refashioned, no longer as a precision instrument to combat ideological "evil" to the last pound per square inch, but as a global truncheon to intimidate sundry aggressors and to maintain law and order. In this event, far-reaching strategic disarmament measures would be possible, either through unilateral or bilateral force reductions. But a small number of strategic nuclear weapons would be maintained in the national arsenals—perhaps several hundred each— in the context of nuclear deterrence. In that event, if the major powers still saw a need for a nuclear strike force, albeit small in number and with targeting accuracy not a priority, the standard arms control debates would continue over the merits of a test ban, universal nonproliferation, and strategic defense. A test ban would be opposed for the sake of continued modernization, notwithstanding that it would freeze military superiority in favor of the nuclear powers. Nonproliferation would remain bedeviled by the "discrimination problem," but in less compelling form. Strategic defense would be developed for protection against the perceived threat from Third World missiles, thus thwarting the possibility of an outer space weapon-free zone.

A third fate for nuclear deterrence is hard to envisage: a continuation in the post-Cold War era of strategic forces at current levels. This would be possible, however, in the event that the U.S.-Russia relationship turned adversarial once more. The fate of the military relationship between the superpowers is often too readily dismissed today. The present strategic situation still threatens the planet. It is clear that both superpowers are striving to direct their policies and their relationship along parallel and cooperative lines, but each country retains a massive nuclear strike force. Such forces remain under sovereign national discretion and control, and the world remains an unpredictable and turbulent place. It is too easy and too soon for humanity to assume that nuclear weapons are no longer a threat to its survival.

Assuming a continued "era of cooperation" between the superpowers, however, what security futures are possible for Europe? The initial rationale for NATO's policy of nuclear deterrence in Europe was the Lisbon communique of 1952, which judged that West European societies were too war weary and impoverished to match the conventional force buildup of the USSR, and that a primary reliance on the more cost-effective nuclear weaponry was necessary. Forty years later, Western economies are relatively strong while Russian and East European economies are in shambles. The geostrategic circumstance that spawned nuclear deterrence has become a political relic. The trend is clearly towards a Europe free of tactical nuclear weapons, and with the Bush-Gorbachev proposals of September 1991, it is likely that this will be completed in the medium term.

In Europe and surrounding seas, however, British and French strategic nuclear forces will remain targeted on their CSCE partner, Russia. What disarmament initiatives are possible in the smaller nuclear arsenals of China, France, and the UK? With the move away from the British Labour Party's unpopular unilateral disarmament policy, it is scarcely possible that these three nuclear powers will initiate moves to reduce their small forces in the medium term. The possibility of their doing so over the long term depends, according to conventional wisdom, on progress made in bilateral nuclear disarmament between the two superpowers. But it will also be driven by national economic pressures, just as the USSR was driven to politico-military change by economic considerations.

Would these future measures amount to tinkering at the margin? No. Measures as significant as a nuclear test ban and strategic force reductions are central to fundamental security relationships. But it does not necessarily follow that even these far-reaching measures would contribute to a fundamental restructuring of existing security relationships. What is necessary is a clear understanding of the politico-military methodology that underlies arms control negotiations. Such negotiations are designed to serve and strengthen, rather than restructure, prevailing security faiths and paradigms. If conventional doctrine is strong, arms control treaties are contained within its context. It is only when political relationships and judgments among states have fundamentally altered for the better that far-reaching disarmament measures will be concluded. Deep strategic cuts will follow and as a consequence, an improved political climate that will prove to be stable and enduring. Cuts will not be undertaken in an attempt to foster that climate. Nuclear missile silos will have their essential contents removed only after they have become military relics, not while they are seen as a dangerous necessity. The far-reaching treaties that may well come in the medium- and long-term future are not tinkering at the margin. They are central to fundamental security relationships. But they will not cause fundamental change. Rather, once again, they will serve the "ratchet effect," albeit in a more far-reaching way than has been the case in recent decades.

Prediction

Of the three possible courses outlined earlier, which is the most likely to occur in the superpower relationship and attendant strategic doctrine over the medium and long term? I favor a linear course in the medium term, without sudden changes of direction such as the 1989 revolutions. During the 1990s, it is likely that Russia will continue along its path of political and economic reform, irrespective of who retains leadership, since national circumstances require it. Reform has developed its own faltering momentum. The United States is likely to remain the dominant superpower, hewing to a moderate, prudent, but forward-looking strategic policy.

Under these circumstances, the U.S.-Russia relationship will most likely continue along broadly cooperative lines. This should be translated into more forthright initiatives to reform and strengthen the security role of the United Nations, especially in preventive peacekeeping and possibly in enforcement capability. The firm UN response to the Iraqi aggression will set new standards of conduct for all states, both the major powers themselves and any potential aggressors. If these standards are adhered to, the international community will no longer be offended by future Panama, Grenada, Afghanistan, Czechoslovakia, or Suez experiences. Equally, however, it is likely that blatant cross-border aggression by medium powers will be effectively discouraged with UN enforcement unlikely to be called upon. More likely is the continuing use of traditional peacekeeping in more complex situations of internal strife and adversity, as in Nicaragua, Cambodia, and Northern Iraq—less challenging for military than for legal thought. A newly interpreted doctrine of humanitarian intervention should accelerate the erosion of national sovereignty.

In this middle-line, linear future, what are the most likely strategic relationships and arms control/disarmament measures? The second alterative is most likely in the medium term; that is to say, the doctrine of nuclear deterrence will be retained by Western nuclear powers, but refashioned into a broader, less specifically focused strategy. It will not be predicated or justified in adversarial, zero-sum terms vis-a-vis Russia, but rather in terms of the need to keep America preeminently strong in an unpredictable world. Weapons modernization will therefore be driven more by internal factors of economic and technical opportunity and need than by external factors of rival force developments. There are probably even odds that either major power will initiate unilateral strategic force reductions and that a nuclear test ban will be concluded before the 1995 Non-Proliferation Treaty Review Conference. It is unlikely, however, that a new, universal, nonproliferation regime will be concluded in the medium term; more likely is an extended nonproliferation treaty on current terms. Given the developing political and technological drive for "Brilliant Pebbles," a weapon-free zone in outer space is also unlikely. It is likely, however, that a chemical weapons convention will be concluded within this medium-term time frame.

CONCLUSIONS

By the year 2000, then, it is likely that the global security system will be restructured for peace along the following lines:

—a redefined nuclear deterrence doctrine to maintain international order and "keep the peace" rather than to mutually deter major power nuclear strikes;

—smaller strategic force levels between the two superpowers, in the low thousands;

—a nuclear test ban and extended nonproliferation treaty;

—a limited space based, strategic defense system deployed by the United States, with no technology sharing, and with the United States the dominant strategic power;

—a chemical weapons convention;

—a strengthened UN mechanism for both preventive and reactive peacekeeping, and UN Security Council readiness to back it up with enforcement action as appropriate.

Would such an outcome contribute to a major restructuring of security relationships? Certainly, a strong "ratchet effect" would be achieved, particularly by deep strategic cuts. A nuclear test ban and extended NPT would indeed contribute to a restructuring of security relationships on a global basis insofar as, assuming adequate verification, it would thwart the drive for regional nuclear capabilities. Would such restructuring guarantee world peace? No. But it would represent significant progress away from the extraordinary threat to the planet that has existed for three decades towards a safer and saner global security system. Peace, as defined in this chapter, can be attained. But the progress will be rather like that of Bunyan's pilgrims—slow, painstaking, fraught with hazard and setback, and requiring unremitting patience and faith. This time, the goal will not be personal salvation but the collective survival of the species.

5

The Future of the United Nations

ANGELA KNIPPENBERG

THE UN CHARTER AND THE SECURITY COUNCIL

In order to grasp the significance of the developments presently taking place in—and transforming—the United Nations, it is necessary to look at the precepts of the UN Charter and its provisions for maintaining peace and security, as established by its founders in 1945. For an organization entrusted with keeping a global world order, the UN Charter is a remarkably brief document, comprising a preamble and 70 articles, less than half of which are devoted to the Security Council (Chapter V), peaceful settlement of disputes (Chapter VI), and action with regard to threats to the peace, breaches of the peace, and acts of aggression (Chapter VII).

The means given to the Security Council are few. The founders relied on two basic principles: the renunciation of force in international relations, and the peaceful settlement of disputes. If the parties to a dispute cannot settle their differences by "peaceful means of their own choice" (Article 33), the Security Council can determine the existence of any threat to peace and can "make recommendations, or decide what measures shall be taken . . . to maintain or restore international peace and security."

Other than calling upon the parties concerned to comply with any provisional measures to prevent an aggravation of the situation, the council may decide "what measures not involving the use of armed force are to be employed to give effect to its decisions. . . . These may include complete or partial interruption of economic relations and of rail, sea, air, postal, telegraphic, radio, and other means of communication, and the severance of diplomatic relations" (Article 41).

Should these measures be inadequate, the council may take "such action by air, sea or land forces to maintain or restore international peace and security" (Article 42). In this connection, member states are to make available to the Council the necessary armed force, assistance, and facilities. Plans for the use of armed force are to be made by the Security Council with the assistance of a Military Staff Committee, which consists of the chiefs of staff of the permanent members of the Security Council or their representatives, who "shall be responsible for the strategic direction of any armed forces placed at the disposal of the Security Council." The Committee was to have a central role in the Council's enforcement action, as outlined in Article 47.

Overall, Chapter VII of the Charter is a key element of the United Nations' system of collective security. The working of the system is, nevertheless, governed by two factors. One is the determining role assigned to the five permanent members of the Security Council—China, France, the Soviet Union, the United Kingdom, and the United States of America—any of which can block any of the Council's substantive decisions by their veto. The other is the control of the activities of the Military Staff Committee by the permanent members. Under these circumstances, the United Nations collective security system, and especially its provisions concerning the use of armed force, can work only if there is full agreement and cooperation among the permanent members.

FUNCTIONING OF THE COLLECTIVE SECURITY SYSTEM

In the years following World War II, international relations evolved from wartime collaboration to confrontation in peace. Collective security, in the words of former UN Secretary-General Javier Perez de Cuellar, "became a hostage of the cold war." While the Council has remained, in many cases, the court of last resort—the place where states bring their most bitter quarrels only after unsuccessful attempts have been made to settle them—its record in settling these entrenched conflicts was limited for over 40 years, despite the often ingenious use of the capacities given to the Council in the charter.

In response to the Cold War division in the Security Council, which blocked any joint military action, the United Nations began to field military observer missions and, later, lightly armed forces normally provided by medium and small states. Though the term "peacekeeping" only formally came into use in the mid-1960s, the practice had evolved to bridge the gap in the charter between Chapter VI (peaceful settlement of disputes) and Chapter VII, which authorizes the use of force and enforcement action.

A peacekeeping operation is essentially a holding action. It is an operation involving military personnel, but without enforcement powers, undertaken by the organization to maintain or restore international peace and security in areas of conflict. The operation must have the consent of the host government(s) and other parties directly involved, and it is directed by the Secretary-General, who reports periodically to the Security Council .

Peacekeeping operations have been set up to observe situations and report on them to the Secretary-General; investigate incidents and negotiate with the parties to avoid resumptions of fighting; serve as a buffer between hostile elements in a conflict; control movement of armed personnel and weapons in sensitive areas; verify compliance with cease-fire and other agreements; help maintain law and order; help local governments restore normal conditions in areas where fighting has taken place; provide humanitarian assistance to local populations; supervise and control elections; and demobilize irregular forces and dispose of weapons and material.

As no formal definition of peacekeeping has ever been agreed upon, this list of functions shows the flexibility of the concept, which has evolved according to political and operational needs. Between 1948 and 1987, 13 peacekeeping operations were launched by the United Nations. This started to change in the late 1980s. In 1988 and 1989 alone, the Security Council set up five new operations, doubling the number of operations in the field in the span of two years. More operations are currently being mounted.

THE WORLD ORDER RECONSIDERED

In his 1982 report on the work of the organization, Secretary-General Perez de Cuellar focused entirely on its capacity to keep the peace and serve as a forum for negotiations. His proposals were aimed at enhancing the effectiveness of the UN and of the Security Council in particular. He made specific suggestions involving initiative and a more forthright approach to deal with potential conflict situations. He also urged the development of a wider and more systematic fact-finding capacity.

Prophetic though these proposals now seem, the then prevailing global political climate was not conducive to their implementation. It was only by the late 1980s that international relations changed. The dynamics of the political transformation whose epicenter lay in Moscow renewed the interest and confidence of the international community in the UN, and increasing demands were made on it to play a more active role in the maintenance of peace and security.

The impact on the United Nations was dramatic. Within a short span of time, protracted efforts to settle conflicts yielded notably positive results. Examples include peacemaking efforts between Afghanistan and Pakistan, between Iran and Iraq, the far-reaching political mandate given to the UN in Namibia, and the growing involvement in the peace process in Central America. The number and diversity of operations is still growing, and a new watershed was reached in 1991, when the organization, in the aftermath of the Iraqi invasion of Kuwait, was asked to undertake measures that went far beyond any other tasks with which it had ever been entrusted.

PEACEMAKING AND PEACE BUILDING

With these mandates, the UN vocabulary has been expanded to include the terms "peacemaking" and "peace building," yet the distinction from the generic term peacekeeping is not always well understood.

Until about 1988, peacekeeping meant all operations undertaken by the United Nations to help maintain or restore international peace and security. Such operations usually involved military personnel without enforcement powers, though two exceptions were the operation in the Congo (1960-64) and in West Irian (1962-63).

The operation in Namibia (UN Transition Assistance Group, or UNTAG) changed perceptions of the traditional UN role. UNTAG was a complex operation, involving military, police, and civilian personnel, bonded together in the field under a special representative of the Secretary-General, with a view to achieving a structural change in a society by means of a democratic process.

While no firm definition for any of the three terms as yet exists, I would define classical peacekeeping operations as those involving military personnel, established in response to specific conflicts or outbreaks of fighting. They are designed to stop or contain hostilities or to supervise the implementation of an interim or final settlement to a conflict. Peacemaking is the search for peaceful solutions to underlying political problems and involves the Secretary-General's good offices, mediation, conciliation, or other diplomatic efforts. Ideally, peace-keeping should move in step with peacemaking in a combined effort leading to the peaceful resolution of a conflict. In practice, this ideal cannot always be attained as it is easier at times to maintain a cease-fire than to resolve or negotiate away the causes of the original conflict. Peace building encompasses all forms of assistance to fragile state structures. Efforts have focused on electoral processes (Namibia, Nicaragua, Haiti) or a referendum process (such as the one planned for

Western Sahara, in which the people of the territory would choose between independence and integration with Morocco). A significant expansion of the concept occurred when it was decided to include the monitoring and verification of respect for human rights (as in El Salvador).

It is thus increasingly clear that the role of the United Nations is becoming more complex and multifaceted. While the operation in Namibia was based on a plan that had been drawn up a decade before, the involvement and subsequent expansions of UN mandate in Central America happened more swiftly, demanding versatility and constant adaptation to changing needs. This was accompanied by growing confidence in the ability of the UN to discharge the functions entrusted to it. Another important and large-scale operation is pending in Cambodia, where the framework for a comprehensive political settlement is based on an enhanced role for the United Nations, with both military and civilian components.

As with all these operations, the establishment of a durable peace will ultimately depend on genuine national reconciliation among the people themselves, as well as on the full support and cooperation of all the parties involved in the conflict. The United Nations is seen as the facilitator in this process.

FACING AGGRESSION: THE INVASION OF KUWAIT

The swift and united approach adopted by the Security Council to deal with the crisis in the Persian Gulf was without precedent in the history of the United Nations. Only 11 hours after Iraq's invasion of Kuwait, the Security Council adopted Resolution 660, which condemned the invasion and demanded that Iraq "immediately and unconditionally withdraw" all its forces. The Council also called on Iraq and Kuwait "to begin immediately intensive negotiations for the resolution of their differences." Following Iraq's failure to comply, the Council adopted a series of 12 resolutions. These censured Iraq's aggression, declared its annexation of Kuwait null and void, and imposed measures, including economic sanctions. The Council also froze Iraq's assets and held Iraq responsible for the safety and well being of foreign nationals in Iraq and Kuwait.

As Iraq gave no indication of compliance with the resolutions, the Security Council went further, holding Iraq liable for any loss, damage, or injury to Kuwait and third states as a result of Iraq's invasion and illegal occupation of Kuwait. It invited states to collect relevant information regarding their claims for restitution or financial compensation by Iraq. This resolution represented the first time that the Council took such actions to penalize a state's aggression. At the same time the Council highlighted human rights abuses in Iraq and Kuwait and asked states to document such violations.

Following protracted consultations, and in light of Iraq's continuing intransigence, the Security Council on November 29 adopted Resolution 678 in which it authorized "member States co-operating with the Government of Kuwait . . . to use all necessary means to uphold and implement Security Council resolution 660 and all subsequent relevant resolutions and to restore international peace and security in the area." All states were requested to provide appropriate support for "the actions undertaken," and Iraq was given a deadline to withdraw from Kuwait on or before January 15, 1991.

This action was taken without specific reference to the Charter's collective security concept outlined in Chapter VII. There was no basis for the Council to mobilize a United Nations force for military enforcement of its resolutions. The Council did not intend to send UN troops, under a UN commander who reported to the Secretary-General and thus to the Security Council. Instead, the Council turned to member states to act in its behalf through such measures as might be necessary. As Resolution 678 did not spell out any specific course of action, it was left to individual states or group of states to interpret what was meant by "use all necessary means."

The adoption of this resolution was not unanimous. While there was consensus that Iraq's brazen aggression needed to be checked, some council members felt uncomfortable with what they saw as carte blanche being given to states that wanted to move against Iraq without Security Council control. While most members went along with the United States, China decided to abstain, and Cuba and Yemen voted against Resolution 678.

With a membership of only 15, the Security Council cannot represent the whole spectrum of national views on any issue; differences would be even greater if brought to a larger forum such as the General Assembly. In fact, the forceful leadership of the United States on the issue of Iraq occasioned grumbles from many smaller and medium-sized states who felt marginalized in the decision-making process. While agreeing that naked aggression had to be checked, these states felt that the approach taken to enforce the Council's decisions gave too much freedom of action to individual states, without UN supervision and control. Implementing states were simply requested "to keep the Council regularly informed" of their actions.

WAGING WAR: THE COALITION AGAINST IRAQ

Within hours of the January 15 deadline, U.S. President Bush announced the start of hostilities with Iraq. In his speech he described the opportunity for building a new world order "where the rule of law . . . governs the conduct of nations," and "in which a credible United Nations can use its peacekeeping role to fulfill the promise and the vision of the UN's founders."

In reality the coalition was not quite so idealistic. Rather than being motivated by a global sense of community, states had their own, usually domestic, reasons for joining the coalition against Iraq. Only the United Kingdom seemed to share the U.S. view without reservations.

The alliance against Iraq was a U.S.-led achievement. Forces were under an American commander who received his orders from and reported back to Washington. The Security Council and the Secretary-General were totally eclipsed during the fighting in the Persian Gulf and had to stand by as member states took the initiative and authority on the basis of the relevant Council resolutions to contain Saddam Hussein's aggression.

IMPOSING A CEASE-FIRE

It was only after the cessation of hostilities—again announced by President Bush—that the conflict came back to the United Nations. The Security Council on March 2, 1991 adopted a U.S.-sponsored resolution that set the stage for a cease-fire (Resolution 686) by setting out precise steps Iraq had to take. Reflecting a growing unease at seeing the United Nations bypassed in the peace process, China, India, and Yemen abstained in the Council vote, while Cuba voted against the resolution.

The terms for the cease-fire were spelled out in a 10-page resolution (Resolution 687), which imposed stringent conditions and deadlines with a precision unusual in UN parlance. It practically made Iraq a ward of the United Nations and aimed at the complete destruction of its war-making capabilities, as well as the long-term monitoring and verification of its compliance with the terms.

In addition to the military aspect, a procedure for extracting war reparations from Iraq was outlined, and a UN force was set up to monitor a demilitarized zone along the Iraq-Kuwait frontier. Yet another issue was the plight of the Kurds and how best to protect them.

The uniqueness of the UN action in settling the war in the Persian Gulf needs to be recognized. No precedent exists for similar action. Resolution 687 was the first involvement of the Security Council in disarming an entire country, in adjudicating and administering claims for loss and war damage, in deciding a boundary dispute, and in ensuring compliance with the terms. Despite the forceful language and harsh conditions, the resolution was adopted by a vote of 12 in favor to one against (Cuba), with two abstentions (Ecuador, Yemen).

New ground was also broken in Resolution 688, which dealt with the fate of the Kurds in Iraq. The adoption of this resolution was preceded by a long debate, as the Council broke a serious taboo—condemning a country for acts committed in its own territory. The principle of noninterference in the internal affairs of a sovereign state—enshrined in Article 2, paragraph 7, of the Charter—has been one of the pillars of international law, despite well known abuses of the principle. The problem of how best to protect the Kurds brought to the fore the legal conflict between safeguarding human rights and noninterference in states' internal affairs. Arguments to set aside considerations of national sovereignty in this case were based on the 1948 Geneva Genocide Convention and the Security Council's power to intervene if it finds that a threat exists to international peace and security. The latter provision is explicitly invoked in the resolution.

Strong misgivings existed with regard to Resolution 688. Only 10 states voted in its favor (nine votes are needed to ensure adoption); three nonpermanent members voted against it (Cuba, Yemen, and Zimbabwe), and China and India abstained. The encroachment on sovereignty disturbed those states that feared unrest in their own territory and were apprehensive about establishing a legal precedent to permit foreign intrusion, which could later be used against them.

ROLE OF THE UN IN THE NEW WORLD ORDER

There is growing recognition that current and future global issues demand more effective international institutions, and the new world order envisioned by Presidents Bush and Gorbachev gives a preeminent place to the rule of international law and the principle of collective security. The functioning of the UN as conceived in the Charter is central to this vision.

Joint action in the Security Council presupposes a convergence of interest by the five permanent members in upholding the rule of law. While interests coincided in the case of Iraqi aggression, it is by no means certain that other issues will galvanize the Council into similar action. Also, should an issue encounter opposition from any one of the permanent members, the right of veto would automatically block unified action. It is thus too facile to assume smooth functioning of the

Council in the future due to an improved political climate among the major powers.

In addition, without a state or group of states to assume leadership, the international community is not able to function decisively. Iraq provided a catalyst for unified action. Without U.S. leadership, however, the world community would almost certainly have acted in a less resolute manner. While this is not to deprecate U.S. action, I would argue that rather than setting a precedent to be followed within the United Nations, the events in the Persian Gulf, while undeniably demonstrating the power of collective enforcement action by the world community, have glaringly highlighted the discrepancy between the various roles of the United Nations.

Commonality of interest produces joint action; the most persuasive recent example can be found on the European continent. We are, however, far from achieving a global community of interest, and the forceful joint action countering Iraq's aggression should not lull us into thinking otherwise. The harsh terms dictated to a defeated Iraq will certainly act as a deterrent to some states who previously assumed that their unlawful actions would be penalized by verbal denunciation at most. They can no longer be sure that their violation of international law will go unpunished. From now on a reasonable doubt will exist on this point. However, as we are far from the utopia of achieving a global government, we have to struggle on with an imperfect world, and this is mirrored in the UN. Mindful of these flaws, we will have to see how an improved global political climate can be translated into effective international action. While this examination may lead to scrutinizing and restructuring the UN, particularly in the security field, there are a number of caveats.

I mentioned the misgivings of some nonpermanent members of the Security Council with regard to UN action. Secretary-General Perez de Cuellar, in a April 22, 1991 speech at the University of Bordeaux on the functioning of the organization, also warned:

> when the permanent members agree on the course of action to be followed by the Council, they wield enormous power, which can overshadow the role of the other members of the Council and other organs of the United Nations, including that of the Secretary General, and affect the public perception of the UN as an impartial intermediary for peace. It is important that this special power is exercised in such a manner as to avoid creating imbalances in the international community as well as in the United Nations. A disequilibrium in this respect may, I fear, prove dangerous in the future. (SG/SM/4560 24 April 1991)

We have reached a moment of global hinging. A "Pax Americana" under a UN umbrella cannot be a reality; neither can a partnership of two or even three nations. The dynamics of the international situation now favor multilateral action by the United Nations, yet implementation has been hesitant and experimental at best.

REFORM AND RESTRUCTURING OF THE ORGANIZATION

International disputes and conflicts will continue despite East-West detente, progress in arms limitation, and border security. Mediation and conflict resolution will thus continue to make heavy demands on the UN's peacekeeping and peacemaking capabilities.

There are two aspects to reform: one is external, that is, within the purview of member states; the other is internal and involves a restructuring of the UN secretariat, initiated by the Secretary-General.

Peacekeeping: In the case of peacekeeping operations, the two reforms must act together. With the recent expansion of activities, and being particularly mindful of the events in the Persian Gulf, it is imperative that definitions and ground rules be agreed upon. Without wishing to hamper the flexibility of these operations, consensus must be sought on the nature of these activities, a consensus which as yet does not exist. Such a list would include:

1) an operation must have a clear and workable mandate;
2) it must be provisional, without prejudice to the positions of the parties concerned;
3) it must have the prior consent of the parties involved;
4) the principle of the nonuse of arms except in self-defense must be upheld;
5) each operation has to be approved by and enjoy the continued support of one of the organs of the UN, such as the Security Council;
6) the military and support personnel are to be provided by governments on a voluntary basis;
7) the forces must be under the operational command of the Secretary-General, who in turn reports to the Security Council; and
8) the forces should be financed by the member states as an activity of the organization.

A distinction has to be drawn between observer forces (consisting of unarmed officers), deployment in hostile territory after a cease-fire or truce (which acts as a deterrent to the resumption of fighting), and a longer-term presence to establish or guarantee stability in a given region. The latter can in fact include verification and supervision of elections, monitoring of human rights, or some other essentially civilian functions as agreed upon.

Election monitoring: Consensus must also be sought on the principles of UN involvement in election monitoring. A senior officer of long standing in the cabinet of the Secretary-General categorically affirmed in a recent speech that the UN "does not monitor elections." At a symposium on "The Changing Role of the United Nations in Conflict Resolution and Peace-Keeping," held in Singapore from March 13-15, 1991, Alvaro de Soto, personal representative of the Secretary-General for the Central American Peace Process recalled that in his eight years on the 38th floor, "we declined anywhere between twelve and fifteen such requests and we continue to decline them." The cases of Nicaragua and Haiti were "exceptional circumstances" which necessitated UN involvement. It should also be noted that it was the General Assembly, and not the Security Council, which authorized such involvement.

Recognizing that the UN has arrived at a point where the response to requests for electoral assistance needs to be clearly defined, the General Assembly in the fall of 1990 adopted Resolution 45/150, "Enhancing the effectiveness of the principle of periodic and genuine elections," which requests the Secretary-General to seek the views of member states, specialized agencies, other competent bodies of the UN system, and those with specific expertise in this area, concerning suitable approaches that will permit the organization to respond to requests for electoral assistance.

In case it should be thought that this seeking of views is uncontroversial, I should like to add that eight states voted against the resolution, nine abstained, and nine did not participate in the vote. Once criteria are selected, strict enforcement of their application must be upheld to ensure consistency. A principle invoked in a particular situation but disregarded in a similar one is as good as no principle at all, as Perez de Cuellar has pointed out on numerous occasions. Indeed, he said, "its application elicits suspicion and contempt as far as the swelling ranks of law-minded world opinion are concerned" (SG/SM 4560).

Finance: Financing of activities also needs scrutiny. Cobbling together large-scale and diverse operations without the requisite funds is, in the long run, detrimental to their functioning. There are limits to improvisation and cost-saving measures. A case in point is the referendum in Western Sahara, where the initial cost estimate of $350 million was unacceptable to member states. The operation was approved only after costs had been trimmed to some $200 million, yet it is clear that such a huge cost reduction cannot be achieved without taking shortcuts that might ultimately damage the success of the operation.

The costs of large composite operations is irrefutably high when compared to the regular budget of the UN, and this has caused resistance. Namibia had a price tag of nearly $400 million, and Cambodia will undoubtedly cost even more. Yet these amounts have to be contrasted with the exorbitant cost of waging war and continuing hostilities—not to mention the suffering of affected populations.

Staffing: Mounting increasingly complex operations will require staff who are knowledgeable, multilingual, and willing to serve under difficult physical circumstances. Thought should be given to establishing a core group within the secretariat, a pool that could be drawn from whenever the need arose, rather than borrowing personnel from an already depleted secretariat. The slimmed-down United Nations that emerged as a result of the financial cutbacks demanded by member states is not in a position to contribute the large numbers of staff required for the many operations that are currently mandated.

Equally, action should be taken by states to establish core groups of military or civilian contingents ready to serve within hours' notice. They should be trained in peacekeeping "etiquette" and be able to function in English, which for all practical purposes has become the standard means of communication.

Command: The question of command, control, and coordination needs to be addressed as well. It is unclear whether civilian or military personnel should be in charge of a complex operation. It has been the practice to appoint a civilian as special representative of the Secretary-General to be in charge of an integrated operation. This brings into focus the role of the Security Council and whether the Council should continue to be the body responsible for such operations, whether military, civilian, or integrated. Questions of command also revolve around the Council's Military Staff Committee and its responsibilities for these operations, as outlined in the UN Charter.

Future Scenarios: In addition to requirements for existing operations, thought should be given to scenarios that might arise in the future. The implementation of Security Council Resolution 687 is one scenario that had not been anticipated and that left the organization scrambling. While I believe that the Iraq resolution is an exception that will not be repeated in the near future, it is undoubtedly true that purely military operations are increasingly being replaced by multifaceted activities that include a host of other aspects, as we have seen, for example, in Namibia and in Central America. Other scenarios could include what has been called preventive peacekeeping, the stationing of UN forces or observers on one side of a tense border at the request of a state which feels threatened, without the consent of the neighbor.

Obviously more applications of a UN role and presence are imaginable. Yet the new world order and the United Nations deserve better than this haphazard and arbitrary evolution, and I would argue for the considered development of a plan which takes into account different contingencies and situations.

UN Structure: This will also mean scrutinizing the secretariat structure. It is interesting to compare the "yellow pages" of the UN's New York headquarters, which lists the senior officers and organizational arrangements over a 10-year period. What we notice is a spawning of "offices" lumped under the Secretary-General's immediate purview instead of under the traditional "department," for example, the Office of the Secretary-General in Afghanistan and Pakistan, the Office of the Personal Representative of the Secretary-General for the Central American Peace Process, the Mission of Good Offices of the Secretary-General in Cyprus, and the Temporary Office of the Special Representative of the Secretary-General for Western Sahara, to name several variations.

While there are cogent political reasons for this organizational structure, it nevertheless raises the question of whether, to ensure uniform application of criteria and principles, these operations should be under the overall supervision of one person. On a day-to-day basis, this should not be the Secretary-General. Combining responsibility for various peacekeeping activities would have the added advantage of reducing the number of people reporting to the Secretary-General. It should be noted that recently a senior planning and monitoring group for peacekeeping activities has been set up within the secretariat, but this initiative appears aimed at administrative rather than political coordination.

Secretary-General: The role of the Secretary-General is pivotal in all these considerations, and it is from him, as an impartial arbiter and guardian of the UN Charter, that initiatives for reform must stem. The increasing attention that has focused in recent months on the selection process and qualifications for Secretary-General appears to confirm that view, as an increasingly important and visible role is entrusted to him.

Other Aspects: The decades since the end of World War II have seen an increasing codification of international life. Major agreements now govern interstate relations in all spheres of life, whether political, economic, or social. There is an increasing willingness to abide by their provisions and to make sure that those who do not are made to feel the effect of their transgression. Pressure is increasing to make treaties and agreements truly universal. At the same time, the principle of verification has become a sine qua non of agreements—to the point where thought has even been given to adding verification measures to treaties that were adopted without them (such as the Biological Weapons Convention of 1972).

This increasing willingness to conclude and adhere to legal standards should be harnessed to good effect, possibly by giving more weight to the decisions of the International Court of Justice, which until now, despite its important function envisaged in the Charter, has been on the margin of the UN system.

Another aspect that deserves closer examination is the issue of sanctions. Article 41 of the Charter speaks of "complete or partial interruption of economic relations," and while previous UN experience with sanctions (against Southern Rhodesia in 1966 and the arms embargo against South Africa imposed in 1977) was considered a failure, the sanctions against Iraq appeared to have had the desired effect of putting a stranglehold on Iraq's economy. Whether the sanctions would have been successful in causing Iraq to succumb, however, remains a matter of speculation, as the time span in which they were allowed to work was too brief to assess their effectiveness. I would argue, though, that the new international situation warrants a closer look at sanctions, as I believe that their application would be successful if consistently supported by the Security Council.

What lessons the international community has learned from the past few years will become evident in the near future. The nation-state will endure, and it seems that only overwhelming force can resolve a clash of national interests. Whether this force, or threat of force backed by willingness to act, will come from the United Nations depends, in my opinion, on the interests or the state(s) involved. Rather than letting each case be decided by power relationships, bloc activities, or regional considerations, systematic and preventive planning should ensure a somewhat uniform treatment according to previously established criteria.

This seems an entirely rational manner in which to proceed, and the world deserves no less. Let us hope that the lofty words of the Preamble to the Charter—We the peoples of the United Nations, determined to save succeeding generations from the scourge of war—will indeed become reality some 50 years after they were written.

APPENDIX

UN Security Council Resolutions on the Iraqi Situation

S/RES/660 (1990) of 2 August 1990
S/RES/661 (1990) of 6 August 1990
S/RES/662 (1990) of 9 Autust 1990
S/RES/664 (1990) of 18 Augsut 1990
S/RES/665 (1990 of 25 August 1990
S/RES/666 (1990) of 13 September 1990
S/RES/667 (1990) of 16 September 1990
S/RES/669 (1990) of 24 September 1990
S/RES/670 (1990) of 25 September 1990
S/RES/674 (1990) of 29 October 1990
S/RES/677 (1990) of 28 November 1990
S/RES/678 (1990) of 29 November 1990
S/RES/686 (1990) of 2 March 1991
S/RES/687 (1990) of 3 April 1991
S/RES/688 (1991) of 5 April 1991
S/RES/689 (1991) of 9 April 1991

6

Possible Roles
for Social Movements

PAUL SMOKER

ON PEACE AND SECURITY

The four section titles in this volume could suggest that, at least in principle, peace is possible without security, justice, freedom, or community. Alternatively, the titles could be interpreted as a positive affirmation that peace can only be achieved with security, justice, freedom, and community. Before discussing the possible roles for social movements, I would like to clarify my own interpretation of this important issue.

In the early days of peace research, when the paradigms of political scientists based in departments of international relations provided the basis for definitions of peace and security, peace was often seen as the absence of war, while security was conceptually limited to "national security," a holy cow concept based on militarized definitions of alleged reality. Given the assertions that peace is just the absence of war, and that security is just "national security," then peace, it can be argued, could be achieved without security.

But contemporary definitions of peace within the international peace research community do not accept the notion that peace is simply the absence of war. Various definitions of negative and positive peace have emerged, including the early formulations of Wright (1942), the later pathbreaking work of Galtung (1969), and many more recent paradigms such as that of the United Nations University (1986) and of Brock-Utne (1985). There are now many variants of the broad definition of peace, including ideas about both negative and positive peace, but most of these variants accept a peace concept that operates across many levels—global, national, local, and personal—and that includes both direct and indirect, intended and unintended, and organized and unorganized human activity.

The concepts of negative peace and positive peace appeared in the editorial of the very first issue of the *Journal of Peace Research,* (Galtung 1964). Negative peace has often been associated with the absence of war although others have taken a broader view. For example, Wiberg (1987) defines negative peace as "the absence of organized, personal violence, that is approximately the same as non-war," although other forms of organized personal violence do exist.

Brock-Utne (1985), using a feminist analysis, extends the concept of negative peace still further by differentiating between organized and unorganized violence. She argues that the global individual violence by men against individual women is not an organized activity, in the sense of war or gang war, but that it does constitute one aspect of negative peace. In making this assertion she uses Galtung's own words: "when one husband beats his wife, there is a clear case of personal violence, but when one million husbands keep one million wives in ignorance, there is structural violence" (Galtung 1969: 171) to provide a basis for her view that negative violence has both an organized and an unorganized component. Thus she argues:

> What if one million husbands beat their wives? That must also be a clear case of personal violence, even of a collective kind. In a society where this happens, there is an absence of negative peace. . . . Even when one million men beat one million wives that brutality is not organized in the same way as when soldiers are trained to kill (or defend themselves) or police trained to combat riots (though some organized gang rapes may be on the definitional border-line).

As a consequence she takes the view that "Negative peace means the absence of both organized (usually 'war') and unorganized personal violence. War is then defined as organized, collective, personal violence, usually between states but possibly within one nation-state, so called domestic wars." Brock-Utne's broad definition of peace similarly includes both organized and unorganized dimensions in its positive peace component.

It is clear, as Alger (1989) points out, that there has been a transformation in the definition of peace from a "peace limited to 'stopping the violence' to a much broader notion of peace as reflected in the UN Declaration of the Preparation of Societies for Life in Peace." The United Nations University summarizes this definition as:

> The removal of institutional obstacles and the promotion of structural conditions facilitating the growth of socio-cultural, economic and political trends, aiming at and leading to Life in Peace understood as both subjective life styles and objective living conditions congruent with basic peace values such as security, non violence, identity, equity and well being as opposed to insecurity, violence, alienation, inequity and deprivation. (United Nations University 1986)

Alger takes the view that this broader definition has emerged out of a "great global dialogue—in the UN system, nongovernmental organizations, and scholarly debate—that has demonstrated that people in different circumstances experience peacelessness as a result of a variety of conditions, such as sickness, poverty, oppression, war or threat of war, threat to cultural survival, and pollution of water, air and food." Given this broad definition, he argues that peace strategies can only gain global acceptance if they simultaneously attempt to overcome the primary causes of peacelessness worldwide.

Given such a broad conception of peace, it would only be possible to have peace without security, and security without peace, if security were still conceptualized in terms of "national security" rather than in the way suggested by the United Nations University and others who more recently have broadened the security concept in part because of three basic errors that are apparent in the old definitions of national security.

The first error is the overly narrow conception of security involved in traditional notions of "national security" as defense of the state; the second is the militarization of even this narrow political dimension of security; and the third is the failure to realize that narrow nationalistic and militaristic conceptions of security are not compatible with global security concerns. Global security requires a realistic assessment of the interdependent planetary needs we all face and a recognition that our previous "national security" policies are no longer appropriate.

Concerning the first error, it is a question of fact that human beings experience many different types of security and insecurity, yet the dominant ideas on national security focus at best on military defense of the nation and at worst on developing military equipment and strategies that make it possible to fight wars at any place on the Earth's surface. The concept "national security" should take account of the broad range of security concerns that affect citizens of any particular country.

In the United States, military expenditures exceed those for health and education and account for more than 30% of the total world military expenditure. Yet national insecurities include rising street and community violence, deteriorating health care for most citizens, environmental degradation, and increasing poverty.

Russia, a nuclear superpower with a military expenditure second only to the United States, is currently seeking food aid from various countries in the West. The national insecurities inside Russia, such as ranking 45th among all nations in terms of infant mortality, have steadily worsened despite, and probably in part because of, the excessive military expenditures associated with the militarization of the national security concept that has dominated for decades. This militarization of national security is a worldwide phenomena. Sivard (1989) places the problem in context:

> The political obsession with military force which has dominated international priorities since World War II has drained the world's vitality and wealth to a degree that is only now beginning to be understood. The financial costs are reasonably clear: in the span of three decades, expenditures on an unprecedented global arms race have consumed over $17 trillion ($17,000,000,000,000) of the world's resources, valued in 1986 US dollars. These expenditures have grown faster than the world's economic product per capita, denying to a rapidly growing population the earned benefits of an expanding economy.

The third basic error in national security policy, that these narrow nationalistic and militaristic conceptions of security are not compatible with global security concerns, relates to the fact that those concerns recognize that we all live on the same planet. No one nation or person can separate their overall security concerns from those of the whole planet. It has long been understood, through paradigms such as the Prisoner's Dilemma, that strategies designed to maximize self-benefit in an interactive situation will fail unless all parties cooperate. For political, economic, technological, bioenvironmental, and social security this assertion is particularly applicable in an era of increasing global interaction.

Militaristic definitions of security have dominated much of the international relations literature on security for many years. National security has emphasized security through military policies designed to defend the state. In the case of national security policies based on nuclear deterrence, the resulting so-called security dilemma elaborated by strategic analysts demonstrated the fundamental theoretical inadequacy of such a militaristic and state-centered approach. A dictionary definition of deterrence includes the idea "to instill fear and anxiety," which is certainly appropriate for national security policies that are based on nuclear deterrence. In fact, all of us who have lived through the nuclear age should appreciate that the pursuit of national security through nuclear deterrence will inevitably result in widespread fear, anxiety, and insecurity. The security dilemma is a white blackbird because deterrence is not defense as it is based on fear and anxiety.

The original meaning of the word "defense" would not have accommodated intercontinental ballistic missiles capable of incinerating millions of people thousands of miles away. Traditional symbols for the concept defense were the shield and city wall, not the spear or bow and arrow. Defense implied protection from attack, that is, to ward off and make safe. The conceptual perversion associated with the militarization of political concepts of security involved, among other things, the need for governments to rename their Departments of War to Departments of Defense.

Recently the idea of "common security" has gained ground, partly as a result of the disintegration of the East-West conflict and partly as a result of the increasing realization that state-centric definitions of security are less than adequate for the needs of the 21st century. While common security is usually conceptualized in terms of a few common needs of states, it is becoming increasingly obvious, even to decision makers who are a part of national government bureaucracies, that such state-centric definitions of security fail to meet the realities we now face as a result of the interdependent nature of the emerging global system. The realization that global security is by nature common security, security for all, has not yet been adequately grasped.

Sometimes, but not often enough, common security involves national security policies based on what is called "defensive defense:" military strategies that are primarily designed to defend the home country and that make it very difficult or impossible to wage war elsewhere. The term defensive defense, like the term common security, illustrates the degree to which state-centered militaristic thinking has perverted the meanings of basic concepts to better facilitate acceptance of policies that entail neither security nor defense.

In fact, defense is defensive and security is common and the time has come to reclaim these concepts from the militarization process. Alternatively, if defensive defense is to be differentiated from (nondefensive) defense, then perhaps "insecure security," that is, nuclear deterrence, should be distinguished from "secure security," that is, global security in the modern sense of the term.

Elsewhere I have argued that there are at least six major interacting aspects of global security: political, economic, social, technological, bioenvironmental, and personal-cultural (Smoker 1991). These interrelated dimensions have not been adequately conceptualized. In fact, the concept of security has until recently been commandeered by military strategists and political theorists whose perceptions of security are essentially militaristic. Many other peace researchers have suggested similar formulations. For example, Brauch (1991) defines his proposed Collective Security System in Europe in terms of a political pillar which includes a conflict and crisis control center, a military and arms control pillar which includes a verification agency, and economic, ecological, human rights, and cultural and functional pillars.

My view of security reflects the central concerns of peace research. A world in which all these dimensions of security were optimized would be a world of positive peace in Galtung's sense of the term. It would be a world in which global political democracy was operating effectively through a network of global political institutions, namely, a participatory world government; a world in which economic security had been established and poverty had been abolished; and a planet where human rights were universally respected and basic human needs satisfied. The technological and economic systems in this world of global security would be environmentally friendly, would be in tune with the global Gaia, and compatible with positive human lifestyles. Individuals could lead positive and fulfilled lives within the meanings of their own cultures, free from the threat of war, poverty, environmental degradation, and preventable disease.

This is the view of peace and security that underlies this chapter. As a consequence, I interpret the section titles of this book as affirming the interdependence between the concepts of peace and security, both broadly defined.

GLOBAL PEACE MOVEMENTS IN THE INFORMATION AGE

In the same way that concepts of peace and security have been transformed, the theoretical paradigms we use to interpret the concept "global" have also undergone radical change. "Realist" interpretations of global, just in terms of relationships between the governments of states, have for some time been challenged by multiactor formulations in which states, transnational corporations, international governmental organizations, international nongovernmental organizations, and ordinary citizens interact (Smoker 1969, 1974). Peace researchers have been in the forefront of this continual reconceptualization process for decades, as witnessed by pathbreaking articles such as "Entropy and the General Theory of Peace" by Galtung

(1968), the work of Boulding (1985), and global conceptualization efforts such as the World Order Models Project.

The emergence of a global economy and the development of modern transportation and information technologies have accelerated the demise of the state-centric system, even if this fact is not yet recognized in many international relations textbooks (Alger 1984-1985). Recent events in Europe, Asia, and elsewhere have highlighted the power of nonstate actors to determine the parameters of peace and security on our planet.

It is at last becoming clear that social movements and other nonstate actors have played and will increasingly play a central role in restructuring our planet for peace and security. Some of the research on social movements has concentrated on national peace movements (Taylor and Young 1987) and some on social movements and world peace (Mendlovitz and Walker 1987). Katsuya Kodama, convener of the Peace Movements Study Group of the International Peace Research Association, has published an annotated bibliography on global peace movements that includes 287 items (Kodama 1989) and details the broad literature that has evolved.

For the purposes of this chapter I would like to define the global peace movement as that combination of local, national, and international social movements that are working for global peace and security in the broad sense discussed in the first section. The movements may be formal, in the sense that Greenpeace, Amnesty International, Oxfam, or the World Disarmament Campaign are formal organizations, or they may be informal in the broad sense that they are social movements and provide the dynamic for events such as citizens' prodemocracy revolutions in Eastern Europe or consumers' proenvironment ethics in many parts of the world.

A number of formal global peace movements, such as Greenpeace, have become vast global undertakings. Greenpeace, founded in Vancouver in 1971, has a navy with seven boats, two helicopters, and one hot air balloon in its air force, 24 national Greenpeace offices, and a scientific substation in Antarctica. It has its own telecommunications system, diplomatic corps, press office, publications division, mobile pollution laboratories, and the world's second largest environmental photo archive. In the United States alone, "Greenpeace has a membership base of 2.5 million, which is growing by 77,000 a month, and a budget that has doubled every two years for a decade and now stands at fifty eight million dollars" (Ostertag 1991).

Informal global peace movements often involve millions of people, as in the prodemocracy movements in Europe and China. They do not have budgets per se and may be temporary phenomena arising as a result of social injustice or lack of democracy. But as with formal global peace movements, international communications play a vital role in spreading information about tactics and strategy as well as in informing potential sympathizers. In the case of the prodemocracy movement in China and the Tiananmen Square violence, global communications media carried graphic pictures of the events, while Chinese students worldwide continue to organize using Chinanet, a computer network carried on BITNET that links many universities worldwide.

Several authors have stressed the vital role communications can play in influencing local and national publics (Singh 1991) and in linking local and global levels (Varis 1986). As we enter the information age it is reasonable to suggest that a restructuring of social movements to make maximum use of its technology will enhance the local, national, and global performance of the global peace movement. At the same time, research has shown that effective use of information in the local context can contribute significantly to the success of local peace movements (Smoker 1989).

The move has already begun towards creating global peace movements in an information age. Recent advances in information technology have led to a situation where high-speed, inexpensive, international communications, which were formerly used only by governments, international governmental organizations, and multinational corporations, have become available to global peace movements through the emerging Association for Progressive Communications. With more than 10,000 users in 70 countries, the APC Networks and their affiliates are used by nongovernmental advocacy organizations, peace studies programs, and opinion shapers worldwide.

Amnesty International, the Campaign for Nuclear Disarmament, Greenpeace, Oxfam, SANE/Freeze, War Resisters International, and the Women's International League for Peace and Freedom all use the APC networks, as do a number of peace research institutes and associations, including the Spark M. Matsunaga Institute for Peace at the University of Hawai'i, the International Peace Research Association at Antioch, the Peace Research Institute in Oslo, and the Kamome Peace Center in Hiroshima. Not only do nongovernmental groups such as the Rainforest Action Network use APC networks, but central and sympathetic international governmental groups, such as the United Nations Conference on Environment and Development, also subscribe.

Thousands of organizations and individuals and formal and informal global peace movements already use computer networks to exchange communications and information, greatly enhancing their productivity and reducing costs. In the United States the hub of this system is the San Francisco-based Institute for Global Communications

(IGC), home of PeaceNet, the world's only computer communications system dedicated to helping the peace and human rights communities to cooperate more effectively and efficiently. PeaceNet and its sister network EcoNet are connected to partner networks in Australia, Brazil, Canada, Germany, Nicaragua, Russia, Sweden, and the United Kingdom, and to affiliated networks in Bolivia, Uruguay, Costa Rica, Kenya, and Zimbabwe. PeaceNet is linked by electronic "gateways" to 60 other commercial and noncommercial systems, including the worldwide Internet research network. There is virtually no computer user in the world who cannot gain access to PeaceNet, and no PeaceNet user who cannot access these other global information systems (Frederick 1991: 55).

PeaceNet and its partner networks have built a truly global network dedicated to the free and balanced flow of information. The draft APC constitution mandates its partners to serve people working toward "peace, the prevention of warfare, elimination of militarism, protection of the environment, furtherance of human rights and the rights of peoples, achievement of social and economic justice, elimination of poverty, promotion of sustainable and equitable development, advancement of participatory democracy, and nonviolent conflict resolution." Howard Frederick, president of PeaceNet, describes the use of electronic mail:

> Simply put, electronic mail (or 'email') connects two correspondents through a computer and a modem to a "host" computer. One user, let's say a peace researcher in Finland, uses her computer to dial into a local data network (analogous to the telephone network but for data traffic instead of voice). She either types in a message or "uploads" a prepared text, which is then sent to the PeaceNet host computer in California. Later, her correspondent, a university peace studies professor in Hawaii, connects in the same way to the host and "downloads" the message. This miraculous feat, near instantaneous communication across half the globe, costs each user only the price of a local phone call plus a small transmission charge. (Frederick 1991: 55)

Frederick further points out that unlike systems used by the large commercial services, the APC Networks are highly decentralized and preserve local autonomy. One microcomputer serves a limited geographical region and is, in turn, connected with other "nodes." The local node collects the international mail, bundles and compresses it, then sends it to the appropriate messaging system for distribution using a special high-speed connection.

In addition to email, the APC Networks also have more than 600 electronic "conferences," which are basically collective mailboxes which are open to all users or to a specific group of users. It is here that people can publicize events, prepare joint proposals, disseminate vital information, and find the latest data on everything from the arms race to Zimbabwe. In these conferences PeaceNet carries a number of important alternative news sources, including Inter Press Service (the Third World's largest news agency), Environmental News Service, Amnesty International alerts, Greenpeace News, and the United Nations news service.

When asked what people actually do online with their computers and modems, PeaceNet gave a few real-life examples taken from actual online messages:

> Back in the olden days, we had to ride 24 hours on the bus every 2-3 months to San Antonio, where another Mujer a Mujer member lives, to make marathon phone calls. Now we're so excited about the power & possibilities of electronic communication. (Elaine Burns, Mujer a Mujer, Mexico City.)
>
> We're a community-based health project located in the hills of northern Nicaragua. Peacenet has enabled us to maintain contact with our people there even when there was not any reliable mail service. (Cynthia Kruger, Bocay, Nicaragua.)
>
> PeaceNet helps us link elementary and secondary schools so kids can have the opportunity to make a meaningful contribution to the health and welfare of the planet. (Peter Copen, Yorktown Heights, NY.)
>
> The Gulf war proved that PeaceNet is invaluable in gathering news deliberately filtered out by the establishment press. (Larry Bensky, National Affairs Correspondent, Pacifica Radio.)
>
> I use my solar-powered laptop out here in the Australian bush to publish *The Bush Telegraph*. The network has allowed me to inform myself to a degree which would be impossible through the establishment media. (Mike Holland, New South Wales, Australia.)
>
> We are the Center for Information, Documentation and Research Support of the Jesuit-run Central American University of El Salvador (UCA). Our weekly bulletin of news analysis, Proceso, is sent to organizations and individuals on PeaceNet. (Christina Courtright, San Salvador, El Salvador.)

Of course, global peace movements do not utilize information technology as well as they should; there is still considerable, possibly justifiable, resistance to using the new information technology, particularly among peace researchers. Activist groups, as described above, make far more use of the APC networks than do academic groups, although there is some evidence that this situation is now changing. As we enter the 21st century a major component of the restructuring of global peace movements is the need to stress increasing effectiveness in the use of locally controlled, networked information technologies.

GLOBAL PEACE MOVEMENTS: RESTRUCTURING FOR A MULTICULTURAL DEMOCRATIC FUTURE

There is no doubt that more effective communication is an essential component of restructuring the global peace movement. The network structure evolving through the Association for Progressive Communications represents an essential component of this restructuring process. Given the widely differing dimensions of peace that are appropriate in different political, economic, social, and environmental contexts, the democratization of global peace movements, formal and informal, needs to accommodate considerable variability in human cultural contexts.

In this regard a number of currently successful global peace movements require greater sensitivity to the variety inherent in the human condition. Ostertag, for example, raises serious questions concerning the European/North American perceptual base of Greenpeace, citing the Newfoundland harp seal campaign as an example.

> But the campaigns also revealed the problems that arise when a small group of mostly male white people goes charging around the world saving the planet without checking in with the majority of its inhabitants. Angry locals forced Greenpeace to call off some actions in Newfoundland. Appearing on arctic ice with cuddly baby harp seals and French actress Brigitte Bardot did wonders for fundraising, but when the bottom eventually fell out of the seal pelt market, it wasn't Greenpeace that paid the price. "Inuit (Eskimo) communities suffered because they couldn't sell their pelts" admits Greenpeace USA spokesperson Peter Dykstra. "Probably some people went hungry." Winona LaDuke, an Amishinabe activist in northern Ontario, knows who went hungry. "Forty native communities in the Arctic had their economies totally devastated by the seal campaign" she declares. (Ostertag 1991)

Ostertag's article documents a number of problems associated with the existing structure and cultural base of Greenpeace, given its position as a global actor. Restructuring of the global peace movement requires that continual emphasis be placed on peaceful means to achieve peaceful ends, including democratic, multicultural operations. New thinking in peace movements requires greater emphasis on democratic principles and practice not just with regard to political structures within organizations but also to equality between peoples, cultures, and species.

The democratization process in Europe can also be seen as a part of a long-term process Kenneth Boulding has termed the movement for peace. The movement for peace does not involve intentional political activity designed to bring about change by social movements; rather it is the progressive, cumulative, integrative bonding that occurs as a by-product of various interactions between peoples. I have argued elsewhere that the low level of warfare in Europe since World War II is not the result of nuclear deterrence, but of a long-term process of social, political, and economic integration that has been underway for more than 500 years (Smoker 1984). The democratization process might similarly be associated with the progressive integration of a geographic region.

There are, of course, various views on what is meant by democracy. One view of democracy argues that it is characterized by particular forms of political institutions, such as parliamentary democracy. Modern industrial states, such as the United States of America, Japan, or the countries of Western Europe are, according to this viewpoint, examples of democracies where the power of the people is expressed through elections, and the elected political leaders are endowed with the legitimate right to govern. Advocates of this viewpoint have welcomed the recent historic changes in Eastern Europe, often equating peace and the possibilities for disarmament with the newly established political institutions that have replaced the old order.

I would like to challenge this dominant democracy paradigm and in so doing suggest that new thinking is needed by the global peace movement to advance the democracy ideal beyond the currently primitive interpretations inherent in the parliamentary democracy paradigm. The euphoria that has developed over events in Eastern Europe has to some extent masked the irreparable inadequacies that exist in the new state democratic systems that have replaced the old less democratic systems. These inadequacies are not just related to issues such as the role of women and proportional representation, although arguments for proportional representation do carry much weight in discussions of the democratic ideal. Rather they center on the more fundamental proposition that democracy is essentially concerned with participation and egalitarian interactions between people, women and men, and between cultures, and that it is achieved through continuous ongoing process rather than structure.

The establishment of the institutions of parliamentary democracy does not necessarily facilitate egalitarian interactions and the distribution of power evenly throughout a society. In fact, it can and has been argued that most if not all existing state democratic institutions contribute in some way to a reduction in democratic participation in any society. In giving their vote to a politician, citizens can abdicate their right to participate. In such parliamentary democracies it is often the case that significant proportions of the population simply do not vote at all, particularly among the lowest socioeconomic sectors. Those who are powerless do not try to exercise power.

There are thousands of examples of the inadequacy of existing democratic institutions. For example, in the United Kingdom the British government has implemented a nuclear deterrence policy involving the construction of four Trident nuclear submarines despite the fact that the majority of the British people opposed construction of the submarines. Similarly, the British nuclear power program continues despite the fact that the majority of people in the United Kingdom oppose such a program. Similar examples exist in every parliamentary democracy.

Those who support the existing system argue that such examples have to be accepted as the price we pay to establish democratic systems that work; when we vote for political parties we make a choice between whole packages of policies, and some of the individual items might not be to our liking. Parliamentary democrats often deride the idea of constant plebiscites for decision making on every issue, often on the grounds that such a system would not be workable. In so doing, it can be argued, they are asserting either that participatory democracy, real democracy, is unworkable, or that state participatory democracy is unworkable.

In fact, in the information age this is by no means an impossibility. Modern information technology does make new forms of democracy possible. It can be argued that the organizational structures we currently construct to facilitate the process of governance need fundamental change if the positive promises of information technology are to be fulfilled. These include a greater sharing in information and decision-making power as well as increased openness and honesty in the political sphere. The negative aspects, whereby information technology is used to control and manipulate the majority for the benefit of the minority, are well documented.

Peace researchers know that there are many examples of participatory democracy in action worldwide. At the local level, participatory democracy works. A fundamental question then is whether participatory democracy can work not only at the local level but also at the state and global levels. Must we be content with imperfect institutional implementations, which in fact may reduce the level of democratic egalitarian interaction beneath that which is possible?

If we consider small-scale societies, communes, and communities in which participatory democracy has been established, it is clear that democratic interactions in these societies are not simply political. True democracy involves psychological, sociological, economic, technological, cultural, political, and ecological interactions. True democracy is a characteristic of a broad range of human interactions, an integral part of the web and process of everyday life involving an egalitarian ethos of circular complex relationships.

In state parliamentary democracies, democracy is implemented through a vertical, complex, hierarchical political structure. It is a part of the overall society in which complex, vertical hierarchies are dominant. I have summarized this distinction elsewhere (Smoker 1976).

True democracy requires horizontal, complex, circular processes across a broad spectrum of relationships, a condition that is not consistent with parliamentary democracies based on complex, vertical hierarchies. The challenge of democratization requires fundamental changes in psychological, social, political, economic, cultural, technological and human-environmental relationships. It requires new thinking and new practice in peace movements and in our global society.

In the same way that modern conceptions of peace and security embrace relationships across a broad spectrum of phenomena, so too must our definition of democracy. Security, we now recognize, entails political, psychological, social, economic, cultural, technological and bioenvironmental security, and democracy needs to be similarly broadly interpreted.

A distinctive and universal feature of the thousands of small participatory democracies which do exist on the planet is their nonviolent ideology. These small democratic societies are without exception peaceful in the sense that no direct physical violence is used, and a high degree of economic and social equality is present. These societies do not need police forces or weapons. They are disarmed; in fact, they never were armed or used physical force, in part because relationships based on the threat of force are essentially undemocratic. To threaten force is to threaten power over, which is a nonegalitarian relationship clearly incompatible with the process participation view of democracy.

Authors such as Sharp (1973) have detailed democratic nonviolent principles. The idea of a society with all its members engaged in continuous active participation on egalitarian terms is, in fact, the logical extension of the basic theory of nonviolent power. There are, therefore, good empirical and theoretical reasons to suppose that an increase in process democratization is likely to be conducive to disarmament and peace, broadly defined. To the extent that an increase in parliamentary democratization involves an increase in process or participatory democracy, we might anticipate a similar relationship between peace and democratization, both concepts being broadly defined.

There are of course many other factors that contribute negatively and positively to peace in all its manifestations: the degree of social integration, cultural compatibility, economic interdependence, psychological empathy, the sharing of common goals and aspirations, and common political institutions. But it should not be assumed that an increase in the hegemony of parliamentary democracies will necessarily be associated with peace. The widespread global structural violence that currently kills and marginalizes millions, it can be argued, is in part related to the actions of the world's leading parliamentary democracies. The relationships of these democracies to the rest of the world are far from democratic. To the extent that process replaces structure in our discussions of democracy, the prospects for peace will be enhanced.

Global peace movements, as a part of the restructuring process, must strive to maximize democratic practice both within their own structures and in regard to their activities in the world. Particular emphasis must be placed on "the equality of cultures" and the goal of a multicultural and democratic world.

CONCLUSION

Given the globalization process that will continue to influence our political, social, technological, economic, environmental, and personal-cultural states of peace and security, restructuring of the global peace movement requires great flexibility in recognizing the diversity of issues that are relevant to peace and the local and regional variations that exist in different parts of the world. In order to increase our ability to think globally and act locally, three major aspects of restructuring have been stressed as we move towards the 21st century.

To begin with, global peace movements must operate more effectively in the information age. This involves greater sharing of information and better communication between formal and informal parts of the global peace movement. Second, global peace movements must operate more democratically both in their internal and external affairs. Here, democracy, like peace and security, is interpreted in the broad sense of the word, as involving an internal increase in participatory democracy and a stress on equality in relationships with others. Third, the multicultural context of global peace must be incorporated by global peace movements into their long-term strategy as well as their short-term tactics. The different emphasis that is placed on different aspects of peace in different cultures and geographic regions must be respected, as must the integrity of the cultural variety of the planetary human condition. As Alger (1989) comments:

> The broadened notion of peace (including also positive peace) clearly reveals that a diversity of sectors of any society, and a diversity of sectors of relationships between societies, contribute to peacelessness and must be involved in peacemaking. This does not mean that governmental leaders, and a variety of nongovernmental institutions and leaders, no longer have important roles to play in peace building. But it does mean that they cannot attain a strong and lasting peace alone without widespread knowledge, participation and support from the people of the world.

For this reason formal global peace movements in the restructuring process must increasingly facilitate participation by local people without imposition of cultural values external to the situation. In this way the global peace movement and the global movement for peace can each contribute to the global restructuring process.

REFERENCES

Alger, Chadwick. 1984-85. "Bridging the Micro and Macro in International Relations Research." *Alternatives* 10, no. 3 (Winter): 319-44.

_____. 1989. "Creating Global Visions for Peace Movements." In Kodama 1989.

Boulding, Kenneth. 1985. *The World as a Total System*. Beverly Hills, CA: Sage.

Brauch, Hans Gunter. 1991. "From Collective Self-Defense to a Collective Security System in Europe." *Disarmament: A Periodic Review by the United Nations* 14, no. 1: 1-20.

Brock-Utne, Birgit. 1985. *Educating for Peace: A Feminist Perspective.* The Athene Series. New York: Pergamon.

Frederick, Howard. 1991. "Peacetronics: Computer Networking for Peace and Human Rights." *International Peace Research Newsletter* 29, no. 2 (June): 55-56.

Galtung, Johan. 1964. "Editorial." *Journal of Peace Research* 1, no. 1: 1-4.

_____. 1968. "Entropy and the General Theory of Peace." *Proceedings of the 2nd International Peace Research Association.* Ed. International Peace Research Association. Assen, The Netherlands: Van Gorcum. 3-37.

_____. 1969. "Violence, Peace and Peace Research." *Journal of Peace Research* 6, no. 3: 167-92.

Kodama, Katsuya. 1989. *The Future of the Peace Movement.* Lund, Sweden: Lund University Press.

Mendlovitz, Saul and Rob Walker. 1987. *Towards a Just World Peace: Perspectives for Social Movements.* London: Butterworths.

Ostertag, Bob. 1991. "Greenpeace Takes Over the World." *Mother Jones* 16, no. 2 (March/April): 32-34.

Sharp, Gene. 1973. *The Politics of Non-Violent Action.* Boston: Porter Sargent.

Singh, Kusum. 1991. "Mass Communication for Peace: Another Way." In *Peace, Culture and Society: Transnational Research and Dialogue.* Eds. Elise Boulding, Clovis Brigagao, and Kevin Clements. Boulder, CO: Westview.

Sivard, Ruth. 1989. *World Military and Social Expenditures 1989.* Washington, D.C.: World Priorities.

Smoker, Paul. 1969. "Social Research for Social Anticipation." *American Behavioral Scientist* 12, no. 6 (July-August): 7-13.

_____. 1974. "An Action Research Proposal for Global Networks." In *Systems and Management Annual, 1974.* Ed. Russel Ackoff. New York: Petrocelli.

_____. 1976. "Critical Mass and Social Technology." In *Humatriotism: Human Interest in Peace and Survival.* Ed. Theo Lentz. St. Louis: Futures Press.

_____. 1984. "Exploding Nuclear Myths." *Coexistence* 21, no. 1984. The Hague: Martinus Nijhoff.

_____. 1989. "Trident Town: Action Research and the Peace Movement." In Kodama 1989.

_____. 1991. "Towards a New Definition of Peace and Security." Paper presented at the International Studies Association Congress, Vancouver, Canada.

Taylor, Richard and Nigel Young. 1987. *Campaigns for Peace: British Peace Movements in the Twentieth Century*. Manchester, England: Manchester University Press.

United Nations University (Tokyo). 1986. Memo for Panel of UN Experts. "Life in Peace." January.

Varis, Tapio. 1986. *Peace and Communication*. Costa Rica: Universidad para la Paz.

Wiberg, Haken. 1987. *Konfliktteori och Fredsforskning* [Theory of Conflict and Peace Research]. 2d ed. Stockholm: Esselte Studium.

Wright, Quincy. 1942. *A Study of War*. Chicago: University of Chicago Press.

Part II

Peace With Freedom

7

Towards More Effective Protection
of Human Rights

PATRICIA HYNDMAN

> Recognition of the inherent dignity and of the equal
> and inalienable rights of all members of the human
> family is the foundation of freedom, justice and
> peace in the world . . . [and] . . . it is essential, if man is
> not to be compelled to have recourse, as a last resort,
> to rebellion against tyranny and oppression, that
> human rights should be protected by the rule of law.
> —Preamble to the Universal Declaration
> of Human Rights.

INTRODUCTION

International, regional, and domestic human rights promotion and
protection mechanisms all can play an important role in the
restructuring required to achieve the goals of freedom, justice, and
peace. Failure to adequately protect human rights not infrequently
leads to a breakdown of peace. In the Case Study at the end of this
chapter, Sri Lanka is taken as a microcosm of some current human rights
issues which have led, tragically, both in that country and elsewhere
in the Asia-Pacific region, to the breakdown of peace in hitherto
peaceful and democratic places and, in its stead, to a growing ethos of
violence and violent counterreaction that can threaten the very fabric
of society. Although the protection of basic rights, of the independence

111

of the judiciary, and of access to a fair and democratic system are well provided for under the Sri Lankan constitution, as under the constitutions of many states in the Asia-Pacific region and other parts of the world, such protection has frequently failed to prove effective.

The reality is that national guarantees of fundamental rights, however impressive their appearance, are only as effective as those wielding real power allow them to be. When use (and abuse) is made of declarations of states of emergency (and their prolongation) in circumstances not strictly in conformity with the requirements of international human rights law, when opportunity is taken during these periods to increase the power in the hands of the executive body and/or military forces, when minority groups are not afforded protection and respect, and when the independence of the judiciary is not jealously maintained and easy and effective access to both the legal system and the democratic process are not assured, national provisions protecting the rights of individuals (whether in ordinary legislation, the common law, or enshrined in constitutional documents) simply will not work.

Such provisions may look good; they may, to a degree, enable the rulers of the state possessing them to posture on the international stage, but in the final analysis, they will not achieve their purpose—the protection of the rights of the citizens of the country in whose laws they are featured. This is not to say that the enactment of laws or constitutional provisions which aim to achieve this purpose should not be encouraged, but that in themselves they cannot be expected to prove effective in all circumstances. In times of crisis politics tends to override both constitutions and national legal protections.

It was realized with clarity after World War II that domestic protection of basic rights without international guarantees may not always be able to withstand internal political pressures, and that the protection of human rights at the international level is essential. This realization led to the emphasis on the protection of fundamental rights and freedoms for all without discrimination in the UN Charter, to the Universal Declaration of Human Rights, and to the many other human rights instruments that have now been drafted and adopted at the international level.

Despite this growth in international human rights instruments, the development of effective universal enforcement mechanisms (those which achieve both acceptability to large numbers of governments and also offer real protection of fundamental rights) takes time, persistent effort, and a great deal of patience. To date regional implementation systems, specifically the European and Inter-American systems, have offered far more effective protection of human rights than has been achieved at the international level. In this chapter, after looking briefly at the international protection of human rights and at the protection given under European and Inter-American systems, I will examine the initiative currently being taken by the LAWASIA (Law Association for Asia and the Pacific) Human Rights Committee towards the drafting of a Pacific Charter of Rights and the establishment of a human rights promotion and protection mechanism for the Asia-Pacific region. This initiative will serve as one possible means for the promotion of "the recognition of the inherent dignity and of the equal and inalienable rights of all people."

INTERNATIONAL PROTECTION OF HUMAN RIGHTS

The Preamble to the Charter of the United Nations, in its statement of that organization's aims, ranks respect for human rights second only to the need to save later generations from the scourge of war. On joining the United Nations, member states "pledge themselves to take joint and separate action" for the achievement of the UN's goal of the promotion of respect for human rights and fundamental freedoms "for all without distinction as to race, sex, language or religion."

In 1948, the United Nations adopted the Universal Declaration of Human Rights and today the rights it enunciates (encompassing civil, political, economic, social, and cultural rights) are, for the most part, encapsulated in and made legally binding on the states party to them by the two major international covenants on human rights: the International Covenant on Civil and Political Rights and the International Covenant on Economic, Social and Cultural Rights. Undeniably, despite the considerable number of ratifications of these and other important international human rights instruments, the human rights record of some of the signatory states leaves much to be desired. Nonetheless, despite limitations to their effectiveness, the finalization and adoption of international human rights instruments is a significant step forward. They provide an agreed upon, if not always observed, measure which the ratifying governments have accepted as the standard of human rights protection to be afforded to the people within their jurisdictions. No longer can ratifying governments claim with any legitimacy that breaches of these obligations towards the people within their territory are a matter of domestic jurisdiction only. Breaches of the obligations assumed by ratification of, or accession to, these international instruments are breaches of international law for the states party to the instruments and a matter of proper concern to the wider international community.

REGIONAL PROTECTION OF HUMAN RIGHTS

In addition to the development of human rights instruments and systems at the international level, there have been regional initiatives as well. First European states, and then the states of Latin America, developed human rights instruments. Both regions have established regional human rights commissions and courts of human rights. Next, the Organization of African Unity developed a regional charter of human rights and established a commission on human rights in 1987. The Arab region, which has a commission on human rights, has recently produced a draft regional charter of human rights.

The regional settlement of disputes threatening international peace and security is envisaged in Articles 33 and 52 of the United Nations Charter and can, quite legitimately, be extended to disputes concerning human rights violations. In fact, Article 44 of the International Covenant on Civil and Political Rights expressly recognizes this. There are some legitimate concerns, however, over the form regional human rights instruments might take. The whole concept of universal human rights can be threatened if regional instruments stray from the basic norms of the international instruments and, as a consequence, produce one set of human rights for Africa, a different set for the Americas, yet another for Europe, and so on. The United Nations has from time to time expressed reservations about regional arrangements on this score, and care does need to be exercised to ensure that the rights in the universal instruments are strictly maintained in all regional documents.

Despite these cautions, when it comes to implementation there is much to be said for the establishment of regional systems. Many states that have recently shaken off the yoke of colonialism are not happy at conceding part of their newfound independence to any external system, particularly to one located in a remote area of the world, and more particularly if it is the geographical location of their former colonial rulers. Further, the same system of implementation may not be appropriate in different parts of the world; to take just one example, consider the widely differing geographical considerations of size and distance operating in Europe as compared to the Pacific. Also, regional mechanisms have an advantage over international ones in that the nations cooperating within a regional framework are likely to have certain commonalities of culture, language, law, and political and economic institutions, and in such a context, measures adopted for the promotion and implementation of human rights standards are likely to be more realistic and practical than are international counterparts.

Certainly the European and Inter-American systems have developed much more effective implementation procedures than has been possible at the international level. It is too early to know how effective the African Commission will be. The Inter-American system in particular has done a great deal in recent years to encourage the return of democracy to states within that region. Founded and operating as it does in a region which has seen severe breaches of human rights (not unlike those catalogued in the Case Study of Sri Lanka), the system established an individual petition system, scrutinized states in its region that had not ratified the Inter-American Convention on Human Rights, reported on country situations, sent on-site missions, and constantly emphasized the need for democratic systems of government and the observance of the rule of law.

Notably absent from concrete regional arrangements are the Asian and Pacific states. During the last decade a regional body, LAWASIA, has taken steps aimed at encouraging wide-ranging discussion of possible regional and subregional arrangements for this part of the world.

STEPS TAKEN BY THE LAWASIA HUMAN RIGHTS COMMITTEE

The LAWASIA Human Rights Committee has had a continuing interest in the establishment of human rights protection mechanisms in the region since it first came into being at the Sixth LAWASIA Conference held in Colombo in 1979. From the outset, one of the committee's terms of reference has been to initiate steps towards the ultimate establishment of an Asian Commission on Human Rights and/or a Court of Human Rights.

Unlike Europe, Africa, and the Americas, the Asia-Pacific region has no presently existing intergovernmental structure with which a regional human rights commission could be associated. For this and other reasons, the committee has seen the establishment of such a commission as most likely a long-term project and has approached the task in stages. The committee therefore has sought to assist in the promotion of the protection of human rights in the region in several different ways: first, through its dissemination of information concerning human rights issues; second, through its services in setting in motion meetings to establish a regional coalition of nongovernmental human rights organizations; and third, through specific steps ultimately leading to the establishment of subregional, and eventually regional, commissions.

Dissemination

To promote dissemination the committee, like many other human rights nongovernmental organizations (NGO), has produced and distributed various publications. It commissioned the translation of the Universal Declaration on Human Rights, the International Covenant on Political and Civil Rights, and the International Covenant on Economic, Cultural and Social Rights into several important Asian languages (Thai, Filipino, Hindi, Malay, and Burmese). The committee has produced and published several reports covering human rights issues of importance in the region, including annual bulletins on human rights and specific reports on issues such as militarization in the Pacific, the status of women, indigenous populations, and the situations in Burma and Tibet. In addition it has convened a number of conferences on matters of regional human rights concern, including the status of women, the independence of the judiciary and the legal profession, and the exploitation of children. Since governments in Asia and the Pacific have a poor record of accessions to and ratifications of international human rights instruments, the committee has actively urged them to ratify the major international human rights instruments. The committee sends observer missions to contentious human rights trials and to situations raising serious human rights issues, and it publishes reports of these missions (for example, to Pakistan, Sri Lanka, mainland Malaysia, and Sarawak).

Regional Human Rights NGOs

The LAWASIA Human Rights Standing Committee took the initiative in its early years and played the role of catalyst in the formation of a regional coalition of nongovernmental human rights organizations. The lack of intergovernmental structures to protect human rights in the Asia-Pacific region has meant that the activities of nongovernmental organizations have assumed greater significance in the protection and promotion of human rights than might otherwise have been the case. Cooperation and contact between active nongovernmental human rights organizations have the potential to fulfill a variety of useful purposes: to enable more effective pursuit of common goals; to provide contact, information, and support, and the opportunity to avoid duplication of efforts; and also to provide assistance in the protection of members, who are from time to time subject to harassment because of their activities.

Accordingly, in the early 1980s, the LAWASIA Human Rights Committee organized and addressed a series of meetings of nongovernmental human rights bodies to explore potentially useful types of cooperation. The NGOs attending the first meeting in Bangkok in 1981 were very much in favor of establishing some loose form of organization of similar bodies, and the committee undertook to perform a coordinating role. Subsequently, NGO meetings were held in Colombo in June 1982, New Delhi in October 1982, and Manila in September 1983. At the 1983 meeting (attended by 37 organizations from 12 countries), the Asian Coalition of Human Rights Organizations was formed. Established in Manila, this body is separate from and independent of LAWASIA and since that time has pursued its own vigorous program of activities.

Regional and Subregional Human Rights Commission

At the Sixth LAWASIA Conference, P. J. Downey (later to become the co-chairman, with F. S. Nariman of India, of the LAWASIA Human Rights Committee), presented a paper advocating the setting up of a Human Rights Commission for the South Pacific region, urging that such a move would be a viable first step towards the eventual establishment of a Commission of Human Rights for the entire Asia-Pacific region.

Shortly afterwards D. H. Geddes, then secretary-general for LAWASIA, prepared a background paper for the UN-convened Seminar on National, Local and Regional Arrangements for the Promotion and Protection of Human Rights in the Asian Region, held in Colombo in June 1982. In this paper Geddes canvassed the desirabilities and difficulties of setting up a regional human rights commission. He examined the history of the establishment of the European, African, American, and Arab commissions, and based on this pointed out that it should be possible, allowing for the differences appropriate to the context of this region, to set up such a body in Asia. He concluded, however, that since there was no intergovernmental structure for the region as a whole, it would be wise to approach the task in stages, with the establishment of a regional Human Rights Commission as the ultimate aim. Indeed, the UN Colombo seminar did not establish such a commission, as they too saw it as a very long-term project indeed.

Among other approaches Geddes recommended the setting up of subregional commissions as a preliminary step to setting up an overall regional human rights commission. For this purpose he divided the area into four subregions: the western region (Iran, Afghanistan, India, Pakistan, Bangladesh, and Sri Lanka); the central or expanded ASEAN region (Burma, Thailand, Laos, Kampuchea, Vietnam, Malaysia, Singapore, Indonesia, and the Philippines); the south and western region (Australia, New Zealand, Papua New Guinea, Fiji, and the Pacific Island communities); and the north and northeastern region (China, Hong Kong, North Korea, South Korea, and Japan).

In many ways it seemed that the Pacific region would be the easiest to tackle first for the reasons outlined in Downey's paper at the Sixth LAWASIA Conference: cultural affinity, a good degree of political understanding, a certain historical involvement, relationships of trade, and the continual movements of people in and around the region. There is a generally good human rights record in this part of the world—a promising sign in that it indicates a climate favorable to, and respectful of, human rights. In addition there are existing structural groupings, such as the South Pacific Forum and the South Pacific Commission. Judicial conferences are held regularly. Such structures could well provide a base of cooperation from which to begin to build.

In April 1985 in Fiji, the LAWASIA Human Rights Standing Committee convened a seminar to begin the consideration of prospects for the establishment of a Pacific Human Rights Commission. Sixty-three participants attended from Australia, Belau, the Cook Islands, Eastern Caroline Islands, Fiji, France, French Polynesia, Hawai'i, Korea, Malaysia, the Philippines, Nauru, New Caledonia, New Zealand, the Solomon Islands, Sri Lanka, and Western Samoa. They included lawyers, nongovernmental representatives, social workers, judges, church workers, academics, and representatives of minority (including indigenous) groups. Included among the speakers were a senior lawyer from the European Commission of Human Rights; the minister for foreign affairs of the Provisional Government of Kanaky; the vice president of the World Council of Indigenous Peoples; an antinuclear lawyer from the Republic of Belau; the chairman of the New Zealand Human Rights Commission; and the deputy chairman of the Australian Human Rights Commission. The conference was opened by the Fijian minister of justice and attorney-general. Government observers from Fiji, Papua New Guinea, Australia, New Zealand, Hong Kong, Guam, Western Samoa, Kiribati, India, and Malaysia were also in attendance.

Among the topics discussed at the conference were decolonization movements in New Caledonia and French Polynesia, nuclear issues affecting the Pacific, the position of women, the rights of indigenous populations, and issues of development. It was the first time people from or interested in the Pacific area had come together to discuss human rights issues in this way. A report of the proceedings of the conference and all its papers were prepared and distributed to heads of government in the region. At the same time governments were again urged to ratify the major human rights conventions, invited to promote greater awareness of human rights among their people, and encouraged to give consideration to the early establishment of an inter-governmental treaty-based human rights body.

In its Recommendation No.10, the meeting urged the LAWASIA Human Rights Committee to conduct a research project to investigate whether or not a human rights commission for the area might be feasible. In accordance with this recommendation, the committee established first a Drafting Committee, and then a Working Party whose members all possessed considerable experience and expertise within the Pacific area. A fruitful and worthwhile brain-storming session of the Drafting Committee was held in Sydney in late June 1986. Draft proposals were then drawn up. After this first meeting, a Working Party was constituted. It met in Apia in Western Samoa during the first South Pacific Law Conference (August 1986), and the draft which emerged from the Sydney meeting was considered further. The law ministers in Western Samoa for the concurrent South Pacific Law Conference were told of the project and expressed interest in it. After this meeting the members of the Working Party remained in contact and continued to work together.

In May 1987, a regional UNESCO Conference was held at the University of New South Wales Human Rights Centre in Sydney, Australia, on the subject "Human Rights Teaching, Documentation and the Dissemination of Information." In Session 13, "What is to be Done: The Need for a Regional Impetus," the current LAWASIA initiative towards a Human Rights Commission for the Pacific area was the subject of discussion. The Papua New Guinea representative in the LAWASIA Working Party (also a LAWASIA Human Rights Committee member) wrote the paper for this session.

The UNESCO seminar participants, in commenting on the paper, noted that Pacific participants throughout the seminar had expressed a concern about the adoption of human rights instruments from outside the region. The point was made that often what is important is not how human rights are phrased in charters, but how they are interpreted and applied. At the present time the European application of the European Convention constitutes a large proportion of the available jurisprudence. Through a regional charter and commission it was felt that the Pacific region would be able to develop its own distinct jurisprudence. This would assist in avoiding "Eurocentric" interpretations of human rights. The participants saw immense benefit flowing from this concept to the whole international human rights movement. They expressed support for the project and urged LAWASIA to continue, suggesting that perhaps UNESCO might also become involved.

Turning to a larger forum, in August 1988 in Manila the LAWASIA Human Rights Committee organized a seminar entitled "Human Rights Today and Tomorrow: National Human Rights Commissions and Other Organs." A delegate from the Geneva-based

UN Centre for Human Rights joined 37 delegates from 12 countries. The program dealt with human rights and the role of international, regional, and national governmental human rights commissions; the protection of human rights in national constitutions; the dissemination of human rights; education; and issues of implementation.

Returning more specifically to its promotion of a Pacific human rights mechanism, the LAWASIA Human Rights Committee convened another seminar in Apia in May 1989. The Drafting Committee had produced a report which raised the issues to be considered in relation to the establishment of a regional human rights body, and had also developed a draft charter, which had taken as its model the African Charter of Human and People's Rights. The draft Pacific Charter set down civil, political, economic, social, cultural, and people's rights and suggested that a body be established not only to supervise compliance with those rights, but also to assist governments with activities related to human rights issues generally. It was envisioned that this would involve providing assistance to governments in meeting their reporting and other obligations incurred under regional and international human rights treaties, often difficult tasks for small states with limited resources. This draft of the Working Party was the subject of discussion at the Apia seminar and, as a consequence, further amendments were made.

LAWASIA has now forwarded copies of the amended version of the draft Pacific Charter and its explanatory memoranda to all governments in the Pacific region, requesting comments and suggestions. It is expected that the next movement will involve Pacific government representatives in active discussion about the proposed charter, a possible commission, and the whole issue of the protection and promotion of human rights.

CONCLUSION

Although the ultimate aim must be effective universal implementation arrangements, current experience suggests that in the short term, and as a step along the way, it may be beneficial to first establish such arrangements first at regional and subregional levels. Accordingly, these moves by the LAWASIA Human Rights Committee are put forward for consideration as one possible approach to further the promotion of human rights and thus the protection of the "inherent dignity and . . . equal and inalienable rights of all members of the human family." These protections, as acknowledged in the preamble to the Universal Declaration of Human Rights, are essential prerequisites if a firm foundation is to be established for freedom, justice, and peace in the world.

CASE STUDY

Sri Lanka:
Regional Problems and Effective
Protection of Human Rights

Sri Lanka, like many other countries, has recently experienced a deteriorating economy and a consequent serious decline in standards of living, a state of affairs exacerbated (again, as in many other places) by the deflection of government expenditure to military purposes and away from programs of education, research, health, and welfare. Recent events in Sri Lanka can be taken as a study in microcosm of some human rights issues in the Asia-Pacific region, illustrating the need for development of more effective protection of human rights within that region as one necessary part of a wider strategy for the promotion and enhancement of peace.

During the last decade incidents of violence in Sri Lanka—violence with ethnic, religious, and political overtones—have rapidly escalated. In many of these incidents police and security forces have at best stood by ineffectively, or at worst have themselves participated in attacks on unarmed minority groups, peaceful strikers, and demonstrators. Vigilante groups have sprung up in different parts of the country. Torture, arbitrary arrests, murder, and disappearances are widespread, and political detainees have been brutally murdered while held in custody in state prisons. Meanwhile the government has repeatedly failed to mount impartial investigations to identify and bring to justice the perpetrators of these breaches of human rights.

In a different arena, government-sponsored transmigration schemes have exacerbated ethnic tensions, particularly in the eastern parts of the country. Elsewhere, Sri Lanka's indigenous peoples, the Veddhas, have been pushed off the lands they traditionally occupied, and different kinds of discrimination have been practiced against other minority groups. Added to this there have been incidents calculated to undermine the independence of the judiciary and of lawyers. Human rights lawyers have been threatened and attacked, and some have been murdered, as a direct consequence of their involvement in the defense of particular accuseds.

Successive and, in some instances, long continuing states of emergency have been declared and wide powers have been vested in the executive arm of government. This trend has been accompanied by an increasing unaccountability by military and police forces. Emergency powers have been used to disadvantage political opponents of the party in power (and those assumed to be its opponents) through the proscription of opposition parties, the imprisonment of their leaders, and the taking of other measures to silence them and their campaigns in the periods prior to elections. In addition, there has been unnecessarily severe press censorship and extensive government control (both direct and indirect) over the media. Despite such measures, during the last decade there have also been serious irregularities in the conduct of elections, some of which later received sanction in legislation. Overall, during the last decade in Sri Lanka there has been a steady escalation of violence, an erosion of democratic principles and of the rule of law, serious breaches of human rights, the creation of situations of severe deprivation, and an increasing brutalization of society.

As in all communities, the violence and hardship has impacted most severely on those groups least able to protect themselves—the elderly, the sick or injured, the less strong, and children. Sri Lanka has become a major producer of asylum seekers, thereby adding to the strains and stresses currently experienced worldwide by the international system for the protection of refugees.

The tragedy of the catalogue of events just recited is all the more disturbing when viewed against the context in which it occurred. Until the early 1980s, Sri Lanka was widely regarded as a country with an excellent reputation for upholding democratic principles, where human rights were respected, and where the rule of law prevailed. Moreover the present situation of the erosion of democratic values, weakening of the rule of law, perpetration of violence, and provocation of racial antagonism has occurred against the background of a country with considerable assets.

Statistics from the early 1980s show the population to be highly literate, with a literacy rate among adults of more than 85%. Life expectancy was 69 years at birth and there was a low infant mortality rate (37.7 per thousand). While the per capita income of the country has never been high, Sri Lanka possesses the essential resources to be successful. The island is not overpopulated, it enjoys a good climate and possesses large areas of forests, fertile lands, abundant farming and fishing, and productive plantations. Physically Sri Lanka is remarkably beautiful. It has a long-established civilization, many historical monuments of great interest and antiquity, a rich and varied culture, and present problems notwithstanding, a charming, friendly, and overwhelmingly hospitable people.

Yet escalating violence of the kind described above has occurred and must, eventually, reach the stage where it causes total collapse of normal civilized society. In parts of Sri Lanka it would seem that, sadly, that is precisely what has now come about.

Perhaps this current situation of violence and ethnic tensions is one which wise statesmanship could have avoided. Unfortunately, as is so often the case, steps were instead taken simply to secure short-term political advantages, while the rights of many of the people of Sri Lanka, or of particular groups of them, were ignored. Succeeding governments, political parties in opposition, and other powerful factions, militant groups included, have all contributed to this state of affairs.

Once violence erupts, the taking of violent measures to control its perpetrators is an instinctive response leading to a circular pattern. This is precisely the type of instinctive "eye for an eye, tooth for a tooth" response that civilized society, in its establishment of legal systems, has sought to transcend. Long-term solutions will be achieved only through negotiation and removal of the grievances underlying militant movements. There is ample evidence, both in Sri Lanka and elsewhere, that strong legislative, administrative, and military measures by governments to deal with dissatisfied movements do not work and that victory, at any level of society, achieved as a result of coercion merely sets the stage for later retaliation.

The protection of basic rights, of the independence of the judiciary, and of access to a fair and democratic system is well provided for under the Sri Lankan constitution, but this protection has not proved effective. The recent occurrences in this country demonstrate that domestic protections of basic rights may not always be sufficient to withstand internal political pressures, and that the protection of human rights at an international level is essential.

8

Redressing Human Rights Abuses

JON M. VAN DYKE AND GERALD W. BERKLEY

When an authoritarian regime that has engaged in gross violations of fundamental human rights is replaced by a freely elected government committed to the rule of law and fair procedures, how should those newly in power handle thc violations of the previous regime? This question has challenged the new governments in Argentina, Chile, Uruguay, Greece, and Spain directly, and has been an issue recently in a number of other countries in Latin America, Asia, Europe, and, to a lesser extent, Africa.[1]

THE RANGE OF NATIONAL RESPONSES

Argentina

Several different military juntas dominated the Argentine government between 1976 and 1983. Arguing that they were waging a "war against subversion," they forcibly abducted somewhere between 9,000 and 30,000 Argentine citizens. Many of the military personnel who orchestrated this strategy also participated in the torture sessions that frequently followed the kidnappings. The loss of the Malvinas (Falklands) war in 1982 caused the military in Argentina to lose popular support, and civilian rule was restored with the election of Raul Alfonsin as president at the end of 1983. Alfonsin established a special investigatory committee to facilitate the prosecution of those most responsible for the numerous instances of forced disappearances, torture, and executions carried out between 1976 and 1983. The resulting trials were applauded by the general population, but increased the military's sense of persecution and alienation. Subsequent insurrections by the army caused both Alfonsin and his successor, Carlos Menem, to end the prosecutions and to pardon all those who had been convicted.[2]

Chile

In Chile the 16-year rule of General Augusto Pinochet was marked by numerous gross human rights abuses. On March 11, 1989, Patricio

Aylwin became Chile's first freely elected president since 1971. Aylwin found himself in a very difficult position with regard to redressing the human rights violations of the Pinochet period, because General Pinochet retained substantial power as chief of the army. President Aylwin nonetheless courageously appointed an independent Commission of Truth and Reconciliation to investigate and disclose the details of Pinochet's human rights transgressions. In early March 1991, an extensive report, made public both on national television and in the print media, did just that. The report described more than 2,000 gross human rights abuses, including forced exile, imprisonment, disappearance, torture, and execution, and it proposed various forms of reparation and vindication to the victims or their families (Wicker 1990; Reuters Library Report 1990b; Dorfman 1991; BBC Summary of World Broadcasts 1991; "Chile's Litany of Torture" 1991; Coad 1991). Prosecution of the abusers was, however, excluded from the list of suggestions.

Uruguay

In contrast to many of its neighbors, Uruguay was profoundly committed to a pluralist democracy during the first half of this century. In the 1960s this changed. The civilian government proved incapable of handling a deepening economic crisis, and an urban-based guerrilla movement emerged. In 1973, the military took over. Congress was disbanded, and the nation's long-cherished human rights were suspended. During the next 10 years, Uruguay acquired the dubious distinction of having the world's highest per capita rate of political incarceration. Although disappearances and executions were limited, torture was pervasive. Finally, in March 1983, after prolonged negotiations, the military relinquished power. Julio Sanguinetti was elected president on a platform that included a commitment to bring those responsible for the past human rights abuses to justice. When he actually assumed power, however, Sanguinetti opted for a total amnesty, arguing that the experience of Argentina had proven that attempts at prosecution would be more divisive than beneficial. The resulting public outcry was substantial, but in a national referendum, Sanguinetti's decision prevailed (Weschler 1989; International Commission of Jurists 1985; Jones 1984; Zumuran 1985; Varela 1989).

Greece

In 1967, George Papadopoulos established a military dictatorship in Greece, generally referred to as the period of "the Colonels." Maladministration, scandal, corruption, and human rights abuses, including the systematic use of torture, became hallmarks of this era. An ill-conceived military adventure in Cyprus in 1974 caused the

Colonels to lose power. The new government under the leadership of exiled former premier Constantine Karamanlis immediately moved to redress past abuses by means of purges and trials. Over 100,000 civil servants who had served under the Colonels were either disciplined, transferred, or dismissed. Eighteen military leaders were tried and convicted, with sentences ranging from death to substantial time in prison. To avoid any possibility of creating martyrs, the death sentences were commuted to life imprisonment (Tsoucalas 1969; Kourvetaria 1971; Clogg and Yannopoulos 1972; Psomiades 1982; Hadjiyannis 1990; Amnesty International 1977).

Spain

The most severe of the human rights abuses in modern Spain occurred in the years immediately following General Francisco Franco's establishment of his fascist military dictatorship in 1939. Around 1960, however, a more moderate phase began. Opposition groups from the Catholic church, labor, and higher education succeeded in gaining some concessions. The press and the media began to enjoy more freedom, and democracy began to be openly promoted in the universities. The arrest and prosecution of labor and student leaders continued, but more sporadically. When Franco died in 1975, enlightened leaders such as King Juan Carlos and Prime Minister Adolfo Suarez deftly directed the transition to democracy. In July 1976 and March 1977, all political prisoners were released. Memories of past brutalities had sufficiently faded so that redress never became a major issue. The people of Spain appeared content with utterly repudiating the Francoist past at the polls (Thomas 1986; Lancaster and Prevost 1985; Carr and Fusi 1979; Coverdale 1979; Preston 1976; Malefakis 1982; Lopez 1990).

THE OBLIGATION TO PROVIDE REDRESS FOR GROSS ABUSES

Each of these nations considered the problem of how to handle past human rights abuses in the context of its own unique situation. Their actions were affected by the extent to which the new government was stable and secure, the extent to which members of the previous government retained positions of power, and the "passage of time." The responses ran the gamut from total disregard, as in Spain, to investigation and "truth-telling," as in Chile, to prosecution of all those primarily responsible, as in Greece.

A number of human rights scholars and activists have recently written on these diverse approaches, and they have, for the most part, concluded that each nation has an obligation under international law to prosecute members of a previous government who have committed serious violations of the right of each citizen to physical integrity through torture, murder, or "disappearance" (Meron 1989; Garro and Dahl 1987; Lutz 1989; Rogers 1989; Malamud-Goti 1990; Crawford 1990; Roht-Arriaza 1990; Latcham 1990; American University Symposium 1990; Rodley 1990; Orentlicher 1990, 1991; Mendez 1990; Weschler 1990; Hannum 1990). They argue that this obligation arises from the responsibility of each nation:

> —to deter future violations of fundamental human rights (Malamud-Goti 1990: 11-12; Orentlicher 1991: 4);
> —to reassert the central role of law in civilized society, foster respect for democratic institutions and advance the nation's transition (or return) to democracy, and distinguish clearly between the previous regime and the new government (Orentlicher, 1991: 5-6; Malamud-Goti 1990: 11-12; Rogers 1989: 300-304);
> —to reassert the inherent dignity of each individual by providing the victims and their families their day in court (Orentlicher 1991: 5, 6 n. 22);
> —to provide a complete and irrefutable record of what happened, so that no one can convincingly argue the abuses did not occur (Malamud-Goti 1990: 11; Orentlicher 1991: 9 n. 32); and
> —to comply with obligations of international law.

The position that international law requires prosecutions is developed in detail in several recent articles (Roht-Arriaza 1990; Orentlicher 1991; Meron 1989; Crawford 1990; Rogers 1989; Rodley 1990).[3] These commentators identify several specific human rights treaties that contain an explicit duty to prosecute violators.[4] They also contend that other comprehensive human rights treaties[5] establish an affirmative duty to protect human rights that includes investigating abuses and punishing wrongdoers. For instance, one commentator states:

> Authoritative interpretations make clear . . . that these treaties require States Parties generally to investigate serious violations of physical integrity—in particular, torture, extra-legal executions and forced disappearances—and to bring to justice those who are responsible. The rationale behind these duties is straightforward: Prosecution and punishment are the most effective—and therefore only adequate—means of ensuring a narrow class of rights that merit special protection by the state. (Orentlicher 1991: 30)

The recent decision of the Inter-American Court of Human Rights in the *Velasquez Rodriguez Case* is cited in support of this conclusion.

The case involved an unresolved disappearance in Honduras, and the court said that the American Convention on Human Rights imposed on each state party a "legal duty to take reasonable steps to prevent human rights violations and to use the means at its disposal to carry out a serious investigation of violations committed within its jurisdiction, to identify those responsible, to impose the appropriate punishment and to ensure the victim adequate compensation" (judgment of July 29, 1988, Inter-American Court of Human Rights).

Customary international law—as exemplified by the prosecutions after World War II at Nuremberg and Tokyo—can also be cited to support the proposition that prosecutions are required in cases of serious violations of the right to physical integrity (Orentlicher 1991: 48-57). As persuasive as these arguments are, it is also possible to identify substantial arguments against prosecutions:

> —fragile democracies may not be able to survive the destabilizing effects of politically charged trials;[6]
> —even in more stable countries, protracted trials may make it harder to heal the wounds that have divided a country; protracted trials will promote the psychology of vengeance and hatred, which will divide rather than unite a people and will interfere with nation-building and economic development (Orentlicher 1991: 12-13); and
> —authoritarian regimes that face a virtual certainty of punishment will resist voluntarily relinquishing power (Orentlicher 1991: 11).

Some commentators who argue that prosecutions are not always warranted contend that many of the goals of prosecutions can be achieved by a thorough investigation that lays out the facts but does not take the additional step of punishing the wrongdoers (Orentlicher 1991: 8-9 n. 32; Roht-Arriaza 1990: 508-09). It has also been pointed out that punishment need not always take the form of criminal prosecution and incarceration, but can also include loss of rank, job, or pension rights, and monetary fines which can be used to compensate victims and their families (Roht-Arriaza 1990: 509).

"UNIVERSAL" FORUMS FOR REDRESSING ABUSES

The mixed pattern of national responses to human rights abuses indicates that some backup or fail-safe systems are needed to buttress each nation's ability to redress the abuses that occurred during a previous authoritarian regime. If international law does indeed require that all serious violations of physical integrity be punished, then the mechanisms of international law should be called upon to assist this process. Although these mechanisms are still in a primitive and evolving state, they can serve to reinforce national resolve and assist where the nation may feel inadequate to address the task.

The Global Forum: The Human Rights Committee, Geneva

More than 50 nations have now ratified the Optional Protocol to the 1967 International Covenant of Civil and Political Rights (ICCPR), which allows citizens to bring complaints against their own governments. The Human Rights Committee consists of 18 experts elected by those nations that have ratified the covenant, and they are now actively evaluating complaints and issuing opinions concerning alleged human rights abuses. Some of their opinions have addressed major human rights abuses, and they have already established interpretive norms on the meaning of many of the provisions of the covenant.

One of the first decisions of the committee in 1979, for instance, dealt with torture in Uruguay. The committee concluded that torture and other inhumane treatment had occurred.[7] During this early period, the committee established the rule that if a nation did not respond to the committee's request for information about a complaint, "the Committee may consider such allegations as substantiated in the absence of satisfactory evidence and explanations to the contrary submitted by the State party" (*Hiber Conteris Case* 1985). Once a complaint is received, therefore, the burden shifts to the government to respond to it, and if the government provides only vague or inconclusive comments the committee will accept the allegations as true.

Another early case involved the summary execution of 15 prominent citizens by the Surinam government in 1982. The committee ruled that this action had violated their right to life and that the government had a duty to compensate the families of the victims (Communications nos. 146/1983 and 148-54/1983; CCPR/C/24/D/146/ 148-154/1983 [April 4, 1985]). Although the committee does not have the power to enforce its rulings, it is expected that the courts of each contracting party will enforce them.

These and the many similar opinions that the Human Rights Committee is issuing should provide a strong framework for obtaining redress for human rights abuses, and reinforce the obligation of each nation to affirmatively protect human rights.

Regional Forms

Three regional human rights conventions are now operational in Europe, the Western Hemisphere, and Africa.[8] Each allows individuals to bring complaints, and in some circumstances nations can also bring complaints against other nations. The most dramatic case relevant to redressing human rights abuses was the case brought by Denmark, the Netherlands, Norway, and Sweden against Greece during the period of the Colonels.[9] The European Human Rights Commission established a subcommission to examine the merits of the case, but after some initial cooperation the Colonels refused to allow the subcommission members to visit certain notorious prisons. The subcommission and then the full commission prepared a report condemning Greece. The Committee of Ministers was prepared to vote on a proposal to suspend Greece from the Council of Europe in December 1969, when Greece walked out of the meeting and then withdrew from the Council and the European Convention. European banks withdrew financing from Greece and due to economic hardships and the invasion of Cyprus, the Colonels were overthrown and democracy returned (Newman and Weissbrodt 1990: 478-79). The new government then prosecuted the abusive military leaders in the most successful example of a full redress.

In the Inter-American system, the *Velasquez Rodriguez Case* states that affirmative obligations exist to investigate human rights abuses and make a full accounting. This decision establishes a strong precedent and indicates that the Inter-American Human Rights Commission and Court will be vigilant in trying to ensure that human rights abuses are properly redressed.

Domestic Forums of Other Nations

Another useful way to redress human rights abuses is to bring civil suits against the abusers if they should seek asylum or a safe haven in another country. In the United States, these actions have been successful in recent years under the Alien Tort Claims Act (28 U.S.C. sec. 1350), which provides jurisdiction for aliens suing for torts committed in violation of international law. Suits brought by victims of torture and murder and their families against human rights abusers from Paraguay, Argentina, and the Philippines,[10] for abuses that occurred in those countries, have led to verdicts in favor of the victims and their families. Collecting judgments remains a challenge, but the principle appears to have been firmly established that U.S. courts will provide forums for human rights cases if personal jurisdiction can be obtained over alleged abusers.

Other Remedies

Extralegal remedies are also possible, although they present risks of destabilizing the legal system. Kidnappings have occurred (Downing 1990), as in the Eichmann situation, where Israeli agents entered Argentina and spirited the administrator of the death camps back to

Israel for trial (*Attorney General of Israel v. Eichmann,* Israel Supreme Court 1962). Although Israel was scolded for this act by the UN Security Council, Argentina did not object with any vigor, and Israel's assertion of universal jurisdiction over Eichmann's heinous crimes has been accepted. The U.S. actions in Panama in December 1989, which led to the seizure of General Manuel Noriega, are similar in some respects. The United States justified its entry as necessary to protect vital national interests and to free Panama from the burdens of an authoritarian dictator.

The concept of "humanitarian intervention" has become increasingly recognized, although it remains highly controversial. When, if ever, do human rights abuses become so bad that they justify intervention by one or more countries into another to free the citizens of that country? Although few commentators are willing to give a green light to this type of activity because of its susceptibility to abuse, examples can be found of this type of intervention and it is frequently met with general approval.

SUMMARY AND CONCLUSION

The momentum toward freedom and the protection of individual and group rights steadily increased in recent years, and it appears we may be on the threshold of an era in which the goal of universal respect for human rights is at hand. To hasten the movement toward this important goal and to secure the gains that have already been made, it is useful to identify and punish in a full and formal manner those government officials who have abused their positions of power by seriously violating the physical integrity of their citizens. A strong argument can be made that international law already requires such an accounting and, even if it does not, such prosecutions can be justified as necessary to deter future misconduct and ensure that the historical record of past misconduct is accurate.

Most new democracies, however, have been unwilling or unable to embark on this path. Except for Greece, the efforts to redress human rights abuses have been disappointing. It is necessary for the international community to assist newly emerging democracies so that they do not have to shoulder the entire burden of punishing the members of the authoritarian regime that previously governed. International and regional human rights bodies can assist greatly by adjudicating disputes and clearly articulating the rules that govern these situations. National courts of other nations should also be receptive to providing jurisdiction for civil suits.

Redressing human rights abuses is not a matter of vengeance, but of simple justice. The victims deserve the dignity of a full redress, and the commitment to a rule of law and democratic principles can be greatly strengthened by this process. The process of developing and strengthening international and regional human rights mechanisms should greatly assist in the achievement of this goal.

NOTES

1. For example, in Paraguay, the reign of the Western Hemisphere's most durable dictator ended in February 1989. General Alfredo Stroessner was ousted in a fierce military coup led by General Andres Rodriques. Stroessner had utilized repression to cling to power for over 34 years. Rodriques, while promising to respect human rights and eventually bring democracy to Paraguay, ominously observed that political change would be neither sudden nor profound (Reuters 1986, 1989; United Press International 1989).

In Panama, U.S. forces finally dislodged General Manual Antonio Noriega in December 1989. Unfortunately, one of the leaders of the three-party coalition that replaced Noriega, Ricardo Arias Calderon, has begun rebuilding the military with many of the same officers and men who made up Noriega's corrupt and brutal Panama Defense Forces (Dewar and Kenworthy 1989; Freed 1990).

Communist rule in East Germany collapsed in 1989. The new united German government has arrested a few of the former East German leaders, but according to the newspaper *Der Morgen:* "There is only a vague hope of more trials against those who ruled East Germany close to bankruptcy, ignored human rights and almost succeeded in robbing the 17-million-strong population of its dignity" (Reuters Library Report 1990a; see also Tagliabue 1991).

In South Korea, Roh Tae Woo's 1987 election to the presidency was that country's first free election. Roh's government has acted to redress some past human rights violations, but with a rather obvious attempt to balance the punishment of past misdeeds with a desire to counter demonstrations aimed at ending his rule (Hiatt 1990; Sanger 1990).

Both Amnesty International and the U.S. State Department issue annual reports on human rights in various countries. The UN Human Rights Committee also evaluates complaints and issues opinions concerning human rights abuses, and Asia Watch monitors and reports on human rights concerns in Asia.

2. The exact number of the "disappeared" (a euphemism for the forced and unacknowledged abduction of persons by the state military, security, or police forces, or by other state-sanctioned groups) is disputed. The National Commission on the Disappearance of Persons (1986: 479-81) gives a figure of 8,960. Others, however, insist that the number is much higher (Osiel 1986; Migone, Estlund, and Issacharoff 1984; Nino 1985; United Press International 1991; and BBC Summary of World Broadcasts/The Monitoring Report, 1991).

3. One dissenting perspective has been offered by Hannum, who said in 1990 that he thought the "conclusion that punishment of human rights violators was required under international law . . . cannot be sustained at the present time." Hannum also said that he was "quite attracted to Diane Orentlicher's suggestion that 'wholesale impunity' . . . might be an illegal abdication of international responsibility, but I think we are far from having achieved customary international law that any foreign ministry in any country in the world would consider itself bound by"'' (Hannum 1990).

4. See, for example, the Convention on the Prevention and Punishment of Genocide, UN General Assembly Resolution 260 A (III) of December 9, 1948, and the Convention Against Torture and Other Cruel, Inhuman or Degrading Treatment or Punishment, opened for signature on February 4, 1985, entered into force June 26, 1987.

5. These include the International Covenant on Civil and Political Rights (ICCPR), done at New York, December 16, 1966, and entered into force March 23, 1976, UN General Assembly Resolution 2200 (XXI); the European Convention for the Protection of Human Rights and Fundamental Freedoms, done at Rome, November 4, 1950, and entered into force, September 3, 1953 and the American Convention on Human Rights, done at San Jose, November 22, 1969, and entered into force July 18, 1978.

6. This argument has been used, for instance, in Uruguay and the Philippines, as noted in the section on Uruguay.

7. *Uruguay Human Rights Case;* see also, for example, the *Case of Hiber Conteris,* concluding that Uruguay had violated the complainant's human rights through extreme ill-treatment during periods of confinement.

8. The European Convention for the Protection of Human Rights and Fundamental Freedoms was done at Rome, November 4, 1950, and entered into force, September 3, 1953, the American Convention on Human Rights was done at San Jose, November 22, 1969, and entered into force July 18, 1978); and the Africa Charter on Human and Peoples' Rights was done at Banjul, June 26, 1981, and entered into force October 21, 1986,.

9. The Greek Case, European Commission on Human Rights, is found in Becket 1970.

10. The Paraguay case is *Filartiga v. Pena-Irala,* 630 F.2d 876 (2d Cir. 1980); the Argentina case is *Forti v. Suarez-Mason,* 672 F. Supp. 1531 (N.D. Cal. 1987) and 694 F. Supp. 707 (N.D. Cal. 1988); and the case from the Philippines is *Trajano v. Marcos,* Civ. No. 86-0207 (May 13, 1991), in which an award of $4.5 million against Imee Marcos was made to the family of a young man tortured and killed.

REFERENCES

American University Symposium. 1990. "Transitions to Democracy and the Rule of Law." *American University Journal of International Law Policy* 5, no. 4 (Summer): 965-1086.

Amnesty International. 1977. *Torture in Greece: The First Torturers' Trial, 1975.* London: Amnesty International.

BBC Summary of World Broadcasts. 1991. "Chilean President's Address and Comments on Human Rights Violations Report." March 6.

BBC Summary of World Broadcasts/The Monitoring Report. 1991. "Argentina Decrees Explain Why Former Military Leaders Were Pardoned." January 1.

Becket. 1970. "The Greek Case Before the European Human Rights Commission." *Human Rights Journal* 1: 91 ff.

Carr, Raymond and Juan Gizpurua Fusi. 1979. *Spain: Dictatorship to Democracy.* London: George Allen and Unwin.

"Chile's Litany of Torture Becomes Contested History." *Financial Times.* March 21. 8, section 1

Clogg, Richard. 1979. *A Short History of Modern Greece.* Cambridge: Cambridge University Press.

Clogg, Richard and George Yannopoulos. 1972. *Greece Under Military Rule.* New York: Basic Books.

Coad, Malcolm. 1991. "Chile to Press Rights Probes Despite Pinochet's Criticism." *Washington Post.* March 29. A17.

Coverdale, John F. 1979. *The Political Transformation of Spain After Franco.* New York: Praeger.

Crawford, Kathryn Lee. 1990. "Due Obedience and the Rights of Victims: Argentina's Transition to Democracy." *Human Rights Quarterly* 12, no. 1 (February): 17-52.

Dewar, Helen and Tom Kenworthy. 1989. "Decision Was Made Necessary by the Reckless Actions of General Noriega." *Washington Post.* December 21. A35.

Dorfman, Ariel. 1991. "Perspectives on Chile." *Los Angeles Times.* March 26. B9.

Downing, Richard. 1990. "The Domestic and International Legal Implications of the Abduction of Criminals from Foreign Soil." *Stanford Journal of International Law* 26, no. 2 (Spring): 573-599.

Freed, Kenneth. 1990. "Noriega Officers Resurface: Panama Coalition Strained." *Los Angeles Times.* June 25. A1.

Garro, Alejandro and Enrique Dahl. 1987. "Legal Accountability for Human Rights Violations in Argentina: One Step Forward and Two Steps Backward." *Human Rights Law Journal* 8, no. 2-4: 283-344.

Hadjiyannis, Stylianos I. 1990. "Democratization and the Greek State." In *Transitions from Dictatorship to Democracy*. Eds. Ronald H. Chilcote et al. New York: Crane Russak.

Hiatt, Fred. 1990. "S. Koreans Reflect on Changes." *Washington Post*. June 29. A29.

Hannum, Hurst. 1990. "Remarks." In American University Symposium 1990: 1080-83.

International Commission of Jurists. 1985. "Uruguay: Encouraging Return to Democracy." *International Commission of Jurists* 20.

Jones, Camille. 1984. "Human Rights: Rights of Relatives of Victims (Uruguay)." *Harvard International Law Journal* 25, no. 2 (Spring): 470-77.

Kourvetaria. 1971. "The Role of the Military in Greek Politics." *International Review of History and Political Science* 8, no. 3 (August): 91-111.

Lancaster, Thomas and Gary Prevost. 1985. *Politics and Change in Spain*. New York: Praeger.

Latcham, Anne Marie. 1990. "Duty to Punish: International Law and Human Rights Policy of Argentina." *Boston University International Law Journal* 7, no. 2 (Fall): 355-78.

Lopez, F. 1990. "Bourgeois State and the Rise of Social Democracy in Spain." In *Transitions from Dictatorship to Democracy*. Eds. Ronald H. Chilcote et al. New York: Crane Russak.

Lutz, Ellen L. 1989. "After the Elections: Compensating Victims of Human Rights Abuses." In *New Directions in Human Rights*. Eds. Ellen L. Lutz, Hurst Hannum, and Kathryn J. Burke. Philadelphia: University of Pennsylvania Press.

Malamud-Goti, Jaime. 1990. "Transitional Governments in the Breach: Why Punish State Criminals." *Human Rights Quarterly* 12, no. 1 (February): 1-16.

Malefakis, Edward. 1982. "Spain and Its Francoist Heritage." In *From Dictatorship to Democracy: Coping With the Legacies of Authoritarianism and Totalitarianism*. Ed. John H. Herz. Westport, CT: Greenwood.

Mendez, Juan. 1990. "Remarks." In American University Symposium 1990: 1058-61.

Meron, Theodor. 1989. *Human Rights and Humanitarian Norms as Customary Law*. Oxford: Clarendon Press.

Migone, Emilio Fermin, Cynthia Estlund, and Samuel Issacharoff. 1984. "Dictatorship on Trial: Prosecution of Human Rights Violations in Argentina." *Yale Journal of International Law* 10, no. 1 (Fall): 118-150.

National Commission on the Disappearance of Persons. 1986. NUNCA MAS. London: Faber.

Newman, Frank C. and David S. Weissbrodt. 1990. *International Human Rights*. Cincinnati:, OH Anderson.

Nino, Carlos Santiago. 1985. "The Human Rights Policy of the Argentine Constitutional Government: A Reply." *Yale Journal of International Law* 11, no. 1 (Fall): 217-250.

Orentlicher, Diana. 1990. "Remarks." In American University Symposium 1990: 1049-58.

_____. 1991. "Settling Accounts: The Obligation Under International Law to Prosecute a Prior Regime's Human Rights Violations." *Yale Law Journal*. 100, no. 8: 26-75.

Osiel, Mark. 1986. "The Making of Human Rights Policy in Argentina: The Impact of Ideas and Interests on a Legal Conflict." *Journal of Latin American Studies* 18, no. 1 (May): 135-180.

Preston, Paul. 1976. *Spain in Crisis*. Hassochs, England: Harvester.

Psomiades, Harry J. 1982. "Greece: From the Colonels' Rule to Democracy." In *From Dictatorship to Democracy: Coping with the Legacies of Authoritarianism and Totalitarianism*. Ed. John H. Herz. Westport, CT: Greenwood.

Reuters. 1986. "Stroessner Shows Force That Has Kept Him in Power 32 Years." June 25.

_____. 1989. "Thousands of Paraguayans March to Mark Stroessner's Downfall." February 11.

Reuters Library Report. 1990a. "First Former East German Leader Goes on Trial." January 19.

_____. 1990b. "Chile's Government Seeks to Heal Scars of Military Rule." April 23.

Rodley, Nigel S. 1990. "Remarks." In American University Symposium 1990: 1044-48.

Rogers, George C. 1989. "Argentina's Obligation to Prosecute Military Officials for Torture." *Columbia Human Rights Law Review* 20, no. 2: 259-308.

Roht-Arriaza, Naomi. 1990. "State Responsibility to Investigate and Prosecute Grave Human Rights Violations in International Law." *California Law Review* 78, no. 2 (March): 449-514.

Roufas, R. 1972. *Inside the Colonels' Greece*. New York: Norton.

Sanger, David E. 1990. "Crackdown in a 'Freer' Korea Puzzles Opposition." *New York Times*. August 3. A2.

Tagliabue, John. 1991. "4 Ex-Officials of East Germany Arrested." *New York Times*. May 22. A3.

Thomas, Hugh. 1986. *The Spanish Civil War*. 3d ed. London: Hamilton.

Tsoucalas, Constantine. 1969. *The Greek Tragedy*. Hammondsworth, England: Penguin.

United Press International. 1989. "Paraguayans Await Changes in Wake of Coup." February 4.

_____. 1991. "Menem Pardons: A Bid for Military Support." January 1.

Varela, Carlos. 1989. "The Referendum Campaign in Uruguay: An Unprecedented Challenge to Impunity." *Human Rights Internet Reporter* 13, no. 1 (Spring): 16-18.

Weschler, Lawrence. 1989. "A Reporter at Large: The Great Exception." Parts 1 and 2. *New Yorker*. April 3: 43-89 and April 10: 85-108.

_____. 1990. "Remarks." In American University Symposium 1990: 1004-08, 1061-63.

Wicker, Tom. 1990. "'Middle Way' in Chile.'"*New York Times*. August 16. A25.

Zumaran, Alberto. 1985. "Statement by Senator Dr. Alberto Zumaran, Special Representative of His Government of Uruguay to the United Nations Commission of Human Rights." Transcript. March 8, 1985. *Human Rights Quarterly* 7, no. 4 (November): 574-81.

9

Humanitarian Intervention

VED NANDA

INTRODUCTION

Any attempt at creating a new world order, with emphases on peace, security, freedom, and justice, among other goals, must address the ambiguous norm of "humanitarian intervention" (Teson 1988; Walzer 1977; Lillich 1973; Behuniak 1978; Brownlie 1974; Farley 1980; Fonteyne 1974; Nanda 1978; Suzuki 1980). The recent poignant situation of the Iraqi Kurds has again challenged the traditional rules of international law, under which Iraq invoked sovereignty and territorial integrity, claiming that the world community was not entitled to intervene in its internal affairs (Ibrahim 1991). Is there an emerging right, and perhaps even a duty, on the part of the world community to intervene in the internal affairs of a state when egregious violations of basic human rights occur there?

This chapter examines the pertinent issues involved in a determination of the validity, under international law, of claims to humanitarian intervention. The recent foreign intervention in Iraq—the presence of U.S. and allied forces to establish safe havens, and the stationing of United Nations guards in northern Iraq to protect the Kurds from the forces of Saddam Hussein—occurred pursuant to UN Security Council action under Chapter VII of the UN Charter. I will argue, however, that a right to intervene exists even in those situations in which Chapter VII is not invoked, suggesting that the doctrine of nonintervention should be interpreted in light of the equally strong and complementary norms of international human rights law. Thus, when egregious violations of human rights occur, including those situations in which a government might wish to prevent foreign humanitarian aid from reaching starving people in rebel areas, the world community need not helplessly watch, for the right to provide humanitarian assistance can be balanced against the duty of nonintervention. The choice between these complementary norms, the former reflecting developments in international human rights law, and the latter reflecting state sovereignty, with its attributes of territorial integrity and political independence, must be based on specific criteria, which I will enunciate.

First, this chapter discusses the doctrine of nonintervention. Then I will analyze humanitarian intervention as an exception to nonintervention. The next section applies the doctrine to the Kurdish situation. Finally, the chapter concludes with an appraisal and some recommendations.

NONINTERVENTION AS CUSTOMARY INTERNATIONAL LAW

Normative ambiguity is inherent in intervention, for the concept may refer to events, legal consequences of assumed, asserted, or ascertained facts, responses of decision makers to the claims made, or a combination of these. Any determination of the permissibility or impermissibility of an "interventionary" coercive activity must be based on a contextual analysis. This involves an examination of the nature and intensity of the coercive measures involved, the participants undertaking these measures, their motives, the strategies they use, and the outcomes of these measures.

States have widely accepted nonintervention as a governing principle of international law. This principle is premised on respect for sovereignty, territorial integrity, and political independence, and is an adjunct to the principle of the nonuse of force embodied in Article 2, section 4, of the UN Charter, which reads: "All members shall refrain in their international relations from the threat or use of force against the territorial integrity or political independence of any State, or in any other manner inconsistent with the Purpose of the United Nations." Numerous resolutions, declarations, and conventions adopted by international organizations and conferences reflect state acceptance of the principle of nonintervention as customary international law. To illustrate, the 1928 Convention on the Duties and Rights of States in the Event of Civil Strife prohibited intervention even by nationals of one state in the affairs of another state (46 Stat. 2749, T.S. No. 814, 134 L.N.T.S. 45, art. 1). In 1933, the Montevideo Convention on Rights and Duties of States explicitly asserted that no state "has the right to intervene in the internal or external affairs of another" (49 Stat. 3097, T.S. No. 881, 165 L.N.T.S. 19, art. 8). Three years later, the Buenos Aires Additional Protocol Relative to Non-Intervention affirmed that the parties "declare inadmissible the intervention of any one of them, directly or indirectly, and for whatever reason in the internal or external affairs of any of the contracting parties" (51 Stat. 41, T.S. No. 923, 188 L.N.T.S. 31, art. 1). Following the Second World War, the 1947 Inter-American Treaty of Reciprocal Assistance (Rio Treaty) reaffirmed the inviolability of the territorial integrity, sovereignty, and political independence of each member state (62 Stat. 1681, T.I.A.S. No. 1838, 21 U.N.T.S 77, art. 1, 6). The following year, the Charter of the Organization of American States (OAS) stated in Article 18 (2 U.S.T. 2394, T.I.A.S. No. 2361, 119 U.N.T.S. 3, as amended by the Protocol of Buenos Aires, February 27, 1967, 21 U.S.T. 607, T.I.A.S. No. 68476): "No State or group of States has the right to intervene, directly or indirectly, for any reason whatever, in the internal or external affairs of any other State." The foregoing principle prohibits not only armed force but also any other form of interference or attempted threat against the personality of the State or against its political, economic, and cultural elements. Article 20 of the OAS Charter is unequivocal in its prohibition on intervention: "The Territory of a State is inviolable; it may not be the object, even temporarily, of military occupation or of other measures of force taken by another State, directly or indirectly, on any grounds whatever." Charters of other regional organizations, including the Organization of African Unity, Pact of the League of Arab States, and Treaty of Friendship, Co-operation and Mutual Assistance (the now defunct Warsaw Pact), also contain similar prohibitions.[1]

The pertinent United Nations declarations include the 1965 Declaration on the Inadmissibility of Intervention in the Domestic Affairs of States and the Protection of Their Independence and Sovereignty, which states that "no State may use or encourage the use of economic, political, or any other type of measures to coerce another State in order to obtain from it the subordination of the exercise of its sovereign right or to secure from it advantages of any kind" (General Assembly Resolution 2131, 1965, UN GAOR Supp. (No. 14) at 12, UN Doc A/6620). Five years later, the General Assembly adopted a Declaration on Principles of Law Concerning Friendly Relations and Cooperation Among States (General Assembly Resolution 2625 (XXV), 1970), which approved the principles enunciated in the 1965 Declaration as the "basic principles" of international law.[2] As to the content of the principle of nonintervention, the International Court of Justice noted in its decision on the merits in the case of *Nicaragua v. U.S.*: "In view of the generally accepted formulations, the principle forbids all States or groups of States to intervene, directly or indirectly, in internal or external affairs of other States" (International Court of Justice 1986: 108). Earlier, in the 1949 *Corfu Channel* case, the International Court of Justice stated: "[T]he alleged right of intervention has the manifestation of the policy of force, such as has, in the past, given rise to most serious abuses and such as cannot . . . find a place in international law, [especially when] it will be reserved for the most powerful States, and might easily lead to perverting the administration of international justice itself" (International Court of Justice 1949: 34-35).

This is not to say that states have faithfully complied with the principle of nonintervention, for history is replete with instances of state interventions. In the post-UN era, superpowers have often used coercive measures, directly or indirectly, against other states in flagrant violation of this principle. Examples abound: U.S. interventions in the Dominican Republic, Vietnam, Grenada, and Nicaragua; Soviet interventions in Hungary, Poland, Czechoslovakia, and Afghanistan. Similar instances can be cited in Angola, Mozambique, and Central America. But the point is that states justify their interventionary activities by invoking complementary norms of international law, such as self-defense and collective self-defense. If one accepts a simple definition of intervention as "interference by a State in the domestic or foreign affairs of others in opposition to its will and serving by its design or implication to impair its political independence" (Hyde 1945),[3] one has to conclude that intervention is prohibited under customary international law.

HUMANITARIAN INTERVENTION

As an exception to the general prohibition on intervention, states have traditionally asserted their right to intervene on humanitarian grounds to protect their own nationals or a third state's nationals in another state, or even the nationals of the state against which coercive measures are undertaken. Most publicists writing in the late 19th and at the turn of the 20th century supported this assertion on the assumption that if a state denied certain minimum basic rights to the people within its territory, any other state could remedy the situation by intervention.[4] Such intervention was justified, however, only "in extreme cases . . . where great evils existed, great crimes were being perpetrated, or where there was danger of race extermination" (Hershey 1927: 239). In the words of another commentator, intervention was permissible on the grounds of "tyrannical conduct of a government towards its subjects, massacres and brutality in a civil war, or religious persecution" (Hall 1895: 302).

A major criticism of the doctrine is that since only powerful states are able to exercise the alleged right, it is subject to abuse, especially in the absence of effective safeguards. Brownlie contends that humanitarian intervention was occasionally abused during the 19th century, and had fallen into disuse by 1945 (Brownlie 1974: 338-42). Another observer, however, concluded after his study of state practice, that while divergences certainly existed as to the circumstances in which a country could resort to the institution of humanitarian intervention, as well as to the manner in which such operations were to be conducted, the principle itself was widely, if not unanimously, accepted as an integral part of customary international law (Fonteyne 1974: 235). Opponents of humanitarian intervention claim that the prohibition of the use of force embodied in Article 2, section 4, of the UN Charter should be interpreted broadly, in a manner consistent with its plain language. Consequently, they argue, there is no scope for considering humanitarian intervention permissible as an exception to the Article 2, section 4, norm (Brownlie 1963; Franck and Rodley 1973; Rodley 1989).[5]

Proponents argue that the proper interpretation of Article 2, section 4, would be to prohibit the use of force when it is directed at the territorial integrity or political independence of a state; humanitarian intervention, by definition, does not seek to challenge these attributes of a state. Rather, they focus on the promotion and protection of human rights as constituting an important obligation under the UN Charter, as shown in the Preamble and Articles 1, 55, and 56, among others. They also point to the broad acceptance of the doctrine by states and publicists alike under traditional international law (Fonteyne 1974).

An observer must conclude that a general consensus is lacking on the definition of humanitarian intervention, the set of criteria to judge its permissibility or impermissibility under international law, and the safeguards necessary to prevent its abuse. Claims to rescue one's own or a third state's nationals are generally regarded as permissible under international law, even though they cause a temporary breach of a state's territorial integrity.[6] After examining six cases of unilateral state intervention, which could conceivably be considered humanitarian or in which a claim was made that the intervention was in part on humanitarian grounds—the US interventions in 1965 in the Dominican Republic, in 1983 in Grenada, and in 1989 in Panama; India's intervention in East Pakistan in 1972; Tanzania's intervention in Uganda in 1979; and Vietnam's intervention in Cambodia in 1978[7]—I offer the following criteria to judge the permissibility or impermissibility of intervention on humanitarian grounds:

1. The Nature of the Rights Violations
     a. Genocide

       b. Gross, Persistent, and Systematic Violations of Basic
         Human Rights
  2. The Nature of the Intervention
       a. Does the force meet the test of proportionality: is it
         proper or excessive?
       b. Duration
  3. The Purpose of the Intervention
       a. Motives: Humanitarian Concern? Self-interest? Mixed?
  4. Was the Action Collective or Unilateral?
  5. Balancing Alternatives and Outcomes

APPLICATION OF THE DOCTRINE TO THE KURDISH SITUATION

The Kurdish Crisis

Does the intervention maximize the best outcomes? (Macintyre 1984: 62-66) The crisis began with the Kurdish insurrection in the aftermath of the Gulf War. After the Iraqi forces, especially the Republican Guard, suppressed the uprising, approximately 2 million Kurds fled Saddam Hussein's terror. Turkey and Iran opened their borders to the fleeing refugees. Iraq's protest against interference in its internal affairs notwithstanding, the United States, Great Britain, and France initially provided relief operations and later sent their armed forces to carve out "safe havens" for displaced Kurds in northern Iraq. As the Kurds were unwilling to return to their homes without a foreign presence to ensure their protection, Iraq consented to the stationing of United Nations guards in northern Iraq. Earlier, the UN Security Council adopted Resolution 688 demanding that Iraq "immediately end [the] repression" of the Kurds, and insisting that Iraq "allow immediate access by international humanitarian organizations to all those in need of assistance in all parts of Iraq."

    Informal "safe havens" were established where aid and refuge could be given to the Kurds. The enclave developed through the initial warning by the U.S. prohibiting Iraqi military maneuvers in the Kurdish areas north of the 36th parallel, followed by the movement of U.S. and other coalition forces in the region, and the establishment of refugee camps for the Kurds. The design was to provide assurance to the Kurds that the refugee camps were secure so that they would return to their homes.

Application of the Suggested Criteria

The foreign intervention in Iraq meets the criteria suggested here for judging the validity of humanitarian intervention. The sole purpose was to provide relief to the Kurds and to protect them from the Iraqi army, and consequently to ensure that relief operations were not at risk (Sciolino 1991c). President Bush expressly stated that the effort was purely "humanitarian" and the operation would consist of temporary relief stations to encourage the Kurds to move to areas where they could be provided with food, clothing, and medicine. Bush further stated that the move by the allied forces was not the initial step toward an occupation of Iraqi territory. The United Nations was to monitor the entire process to ensure that relief efforts would be undertaken in conformity with the purpose and spirit of Security Council Resolution 688 (Sciolino 1991a). Hundreds of thousands of Kurds had already fled into Turkey and Iraq, with predictions that over 2 million would eventually leave Iraq, when the initiative was taken by Europeans urging an enclave for the Kurds (Riding 1991). The Kurds fled in such large numbers because of their prior experience with the brutal use of chemical weapons on their villages by the Iraqi army and because of their history of oppression as an ethnic group by the Iraqi government, especially by the Saddam Hussein regime (Sudetic 1991). This history of inhumane treatment and suppression, compounded by reports of chemical weapons again being used against civilians, created terror among the Kurds which further incited their flight out of Iraq (Cowell 1991). According to some estimates, starvation and exposure were claiming the lives of over 1,000 Kurdish refugees daily (Tyler 1991b). The world community was shocked; consequently, there was consensus on the need for urgent action to aid and protect the refugees. In view of the pattern of gross and persistent violation of the Kurds' human rights in Iraq, the claim for humanitarian intervention on their behalf meets the first criterion set out above, that is, severity of the deprivation of human rights. Urgent action was therefore needed to save lives. The UN Security Council Resolution 688 insisted that Iraq allow immediate humanitarian access for relief purposes and condemned the Iraqi repression of the Kurds, the consequences of which it said threatened international peace and security.

As to the second criterion, the nature of the intervention, Britain's Ambassador to the United Nations, David Hannay, explicitly stated that the proposed safe havens were a humanitarian concept (P. Lewis 1991). The intervention lasted until July 15, 1991. As efforts were underway from the beginning to seek UN replacements, the coalition force was indeed proportionate to ward off the risk to the lives of hundreds of thousands of Kurds.

As to the third criterion, the purpose of intervention, the plans specifically embodied a limited purpose of securing a safe region for the Kurds so that they could receive humanitarian aid and return to their homes. The coalition forces did not intend to affect Iraq's territorial integrity, nor even Saddam Hussein's regime (Hoffman 1991). They had planned for an early withdrawal date, and accordingly withdrew on July 15. At the outset of the intervention, the allied leaders agreed to provide protection to the relief workers as authorized by Security Council Resolution 688, paragraphs 1 through 5 (N. Lewis 1991). Another goal was to protect the Kurds. Consequently allied leaders felt it necessary to station troops to curtail the movement of Iraqi forces north of the 36th parallel. Iraq was warned not to use ground or air forces anywhere near the Kurdish refugees (Sciolino 1991b).

As to the fourth criterion, whether the action is unilateral or collective, the initiative came from the British Prime Minister, John Major, but intervention took a collective form after consultations among the Security Council members. A European Community delegation met with President Bush in efforts to gain further support for the plan as a collective action. The decision was made to establish a multinational force to provide the needed relief.

At the United Nations, Security Council Resolution 688 expressed grave concern at the repression of the Iraqi civilian population, and the massive flow of refugees "threaten[ing] international peace and security in the region" (Resolution 688 preamble), and authorized humanitarian access and assistance to the refugees and displaced Iraqi people. Although the intervening force was not under UN auspices, there were consultations at the United Nations and considerable international support for the operation, which drew over 20,000 troops from over 13 countries. Subsequently, the United Nations and Iraq signed an agreement under which UN security guards would move into northern Iraq, allowing the U.S. and allied soldiers to withdraw. ("Security-Force Pact is Settled with Iraq" 1991).

Finally, on balancing alternatives and outcomes, one has to conclude that the intervention was a justified response, for without the presence of the allied forces the Kurds were not willing to return to their villages and homes. After the Kurds' return and the withdrawal of the allied forces, a residual coalition force is to be stationed in Turkey to deter future Iraqi aggression against the Kurds. The head of the coalition forces, U.S. General Shalikashvali, said that the allied forces retained the right to conduct reconnaissance flights north of the 36th parallel, where Iraq is banned from flying fixed-wing aircraft and helicopters. The intervention gave the Kurds a breathing space to negotiate an agreement for autonomy in their region with the Iraqi government (Reuters 1991).

APPRAISAL AND RECOMMENDATIONS

Assuming that the intervention in Iraq meets the criteria set out above to determine the validity of "humanitarian intervention" under customary international law, this interventionary action has serious implications. For example, could the world community take action to provide food and humanitarian assistance to a starving population in a state in opposition to that state's policy? Recent developments with a bearing on the subject include a General Assembly resolution adopted in December 1990 which calls for international relief corridors (General Assembly Resolution 45/100, 14 December 1990). In the United States Congress, Rep. Tony Hall introduced a bill asking the United States government to take the initiative for the drafting and negotiation of an international convention on the right to food (Moffett III 1991). The following statement of the International Court of Justice in *Nicaragua v. United States* is pertinent: "There can be no doubt that the provision of strictly humanitarian aid to persons or forces in another country, whatever their political affiliations or objectives, cannot be regarded as unlawful intervention, or as in any other way contrary to international law" (International Court of Justice 1986: 124).

Could a single state provide aid? Could force be justified to provide food to a starving population under the rubric of "humanitarian intervention"? It is recommended here that, as a last resort, such use of force should be considered justified. The allied forces' response to the Kurdish crisis has demonstrated that in the post-Cold War era "humanitarian intervention" remains a viable alternative. That it should be used sparingly is appropriate. But that it can be used should prove a powerful deterrent to oppressive regimes.

NOTES

1. For the Charter of the Organization of African Unity, see 2 I.L.M. 766, art. III, 1963; for the Pact of the League of Arab States, see 70 U.N.T.S. 237, art. 8, 1945; and for the Treaty of Friendship, Co-operation and Mutual Assistance, see 219 U.N.T.S. 3, art. 8, 1955.

2. For a discussion of this declaration, see International Court of Justice 1986: 100, 107.

3. Oppenheim defines intervention as dictatorial interference in the affairs of a state by another state (Oppenheim 1955:305).

4. For citations to the works of these publicists, see, for example, Brownlie 1963: 338, nos. 1-5; see also Stowell 1921: 53 and 1931: 349.

5. Rodley (1989: 327-28) concludes: "The burden of the [International Court of Justice's] message [in *Nicaragua v. U.S.*] is that the United States could not [justify its military activities]; and, in the process, it has confirmed the view of those of us who argue that the doctrine of unilateral armed humanitarian intervention has no justification at law."

6. Consider the statement by the U.S. representative during the 1976 Security Council debate on the Entebbe rescue mission by Israel, in which he justified Israel's action: "There is a well established right to use limited force for the protection of one's own nationals from the imminent threat of injury or death in a situation where the States in whose territory they are located is either unwilling or unable to protect them. The right . . . is limited to such use of force as is necessary and appropriate to protect threatened nationals from injury."

7. For the Dominican Republic see Nanda 1966 and 1967; for Grenada, see Nanda 1984: 405-11; for Panama, see Nanda 1990: 494, 496-97; for East Pakistan, see Franck and Rodley 1973: 275 and Nanda 1972a and b; for Uganda, see Burrows 1979 and Wani 1980; and generally see Ronzitti 1985: 98-99.

REFERENCES

Behuniak. 1978. "The Law of Unilateral Humanitarian Intervention by Armed Force: A Legal Survey." *Milwaukee Law Review* 79: 157.

Brown, John Murray. 1991. "Last Allies Pull Out of North Iraq." *Financial Times*. July 16. 6.

Brownlie, Ian. 1974. "Humanitarian Intervention." In *Law and the Civil War in the Modern World*. Ed. John N. Moore. Baltimore and London: Johns Hopkins University Press.

_____. 1986. *International Law and the Use of Force by States*. Oxford: Clarendon.

Burrows, Noreen. 1979. "Tanzania's Intervention in Uganda: Some Aspects." *World Today* 35, no. 7 (July): 306-313.

Cowell, Alan. 1991. "Kurdish Refugees, by Thousands, Flee Vengeance of the Iraq Army." *New York Times*. April 4. A1.

Farley. 1980. "State Actors, Humanitarian Intervention, and International Law: Reopening Pandora's Box." *Georgia Journal of International and Comparative Law* 10: 29.

Fonteyne, Jean-Pierre L. 1974. "The Customary International Law Doctrine of Humanitarian Intervention: Its Current Validity Under the U. N. Charter." *California Western International Law Journal* 4, no. 2 (Spring): 203-220.

Franck, Thomas M. and Nigel S. Rodley. 1973. "After Bangladesh: The Law of Humanitarian Intervention by Military Force." *American Journal of International Law* 67, no. 2 (April): 275-427.

Hall, W. E. 1895. *A Treatise on International Law.* 4th ed. Oxford: Clarendon.

Hershey, Amos Shartl. 1927. *Essentials of International Public Law and Organization.* Rev. ed. New York: Macmillan.

Hoffman, David. 1991. "Allied Mission Among Kurds Unsettled as Northern Iraq Safe Zones Expand." *Washington Post.* May 5. A39.

Hyde, Charles Cheney. 1945. *International Law Chiefly as Interpreted and Applied by the United States.* Boston: Little, Brown.

Ibrahim, Moustef. 1991. "Iraq Rejects European Plan for Kurdish Haven in North." *New York Times.* April 10. A12.

International Court of Justice. 1949. *Corfu Channel Case.* 34.

_____. 1986. "Military and Paramilitary Activities in and Against Nicaragua." *International Court of Justice Report* 14.

Lewis, Neil A. 1991. "Legal Scholars Debate Refugee Plan, Generally Backing U.S. Stand." *New York Times.* April 19. A3.

Lewis, Phil. "Europeans Back Off Plan to Help Kurds." 1991. *New York Times.* April 10. A12.

Lillich, Richard, ed. 1973. *Humanitarian Intervention and the United Nations.* Charlottesville, VA: University Press of Virginia.

Macintyre, Alasdair. 1984. *After Virtue.* 2d ed. Notre Dame, IN: University of Notre Dame Press.

Moffett III, George. 1991. "US Congressmen Pressure UN to Outlaw Denial of Food." *Christian Science Monitor.* July 5. 6.

Nanda, Ved. 1966. "The United States Action in the 1965 Dominican Crisis: Impact on World Order." *Denver Law Journal* 43, no. 4 (Fall): 439-79.

_____. 1967. "The United States Action in the 1965 Dominican Crisis: Impact on World Order.'"*Denver Law Journal.* 44, no. 2 (Spring): 225-274.

_____. 1972a. "A Critique of the U.N. Inaction in the Bangladesh Crisis. *Denver Law Journal*. 49, no. 1 (Winter): 53-67.

_____. 1972b. " Self-Determination Under International Law." *American Journal of International Law* 66, no. 2 (April): 321-36.

_____. 1978. "Humanitarian Military Intervention." *World View* 10 (October): 23.

_____. 1984. "The United States Armed Intervention in Grenada—Impact on World Order." *California Western nternational Law Journal* 14, no. 3 (Summer): 395-424..

_____. 1990. "The Validity of United States Intervention in Panama Under International Law." *American Journal of International Law* 84, no. 2 (April): 494-502.

Oppenheim, Lassa L. 1955. *International Law*. 8th ed. London: Longmans, Green.

Reuters. 1991. "Iraqi Kurds Bargain Hard as Allies Leave." *Christian Science Monitor*. July 15. 4.

Riding, Alan. 1991. "Europeans Urging Enclave for Kurds in Northern Iraq." *New York Times*. April 9. A1.

Rodley, Nigel S. 1989. "Human Rights and Humanitarian Intervention: The Case Law of the World Court." *International and Comparative Law Quarterly* 38, no. 2 (April): 321-33).

Ronzitti, Natalino. 1985. *Rescuing Nationals Abroad Through Military Coercion and Intervention on Grounds of Humanity*. Dordrecht: Martinus Nijhoff.

Sciolino, Elaine. 1991a. "Kurds Will Die in Vast Numbers Without Swift Aid, Agencies Say." *New York Times*. April 10. A1.

_____. 1991b. "U.S. Warns Against Attack by Iraq on Kurdish Refugees." *New York Times*. April 11. A10.

_____. 1991c. "New Activity by Military Purely Humanitarian President Says." *New York Times*. April 17. A1.

"Security Force Pact is Settled with Iraq, Official at U.N. Says." 1991. *New York Times*. May 24. A8.

Stowell, Ellery. 1921. *Intervention in International Law*. Washington, DC: J. Byrne.

_____. 1931. *International Law: A Restatement of Principles in Conformity with Actual Practice*. New York: H. Holt.

Sudetic, Chuck. 1991. "As Kurds Limp Back in, Ghost Town Relives '88." *New York Times*. April 9.

Suzuki, Eisuke. 1980. "A State's Provisional Competence to Protect Human Rights in a Foreign State." *Texas International Law Journal* 15, no. 2 (Spring): 231-260.

Teson, Fernando R. 1988. *Humanitarian Intervention—An Inquiry into Law and Morality*. Dobbs Ferry, NY: Transnational.

Tyler, Patrick. 1991a. "Bush Sees Accord on 'Safe Havens' for Kurds." *New York Times*. April 12. A1.

_____. 1991b. "U.S. Scouting Sites for Refugees Well Inside Iraq." *New York Times*. April 18. A1.

Walzer, Michael. 1977. *Just and Unjust Wars*. New York: Basic Books.

Wani. 1980. "Humanitarian Intervention and the Tanzanian-Uganda War." *Horn of Africa* 3.

10

Redress for Violations of
International Law:
The Gulf War

FRANK C. NEWMAN

Speaking to a Honolulu audience in October 1990, President Bush stated, "Two weeks ago, I mentioned the Nuremberg Trials." He pronounced that "Saddam Hussein . . . will be held accountable for his 'outrageous' behavior. . . . [He] must know [that the] stakes are high." Addressing the UN General Assembly a month earlier, the president had declared that Iraq and its leaders must be held liable for their "crimes of abuse and destruction. But this outrageous disregard for basic human rights does not come as a total surprise. Thousands of Iraqis have been executed on political and religious grounds and even more through a genocidal, poison-gas war waged against Iraq's own Kurdish villagers."

Who still, I wonder, is looking to Nuremberg law? Will Hussein and his ruling clique really be "held liable"? As yet, we do not know. We do know, though, that the Iraqi government has been proclaimed accountable and that, via a set of UN Security Council resolutions, severe penalties have been prescribed.

The most important question we confront, I suggest, is how the United Nations, the U.S., and other nations will continue to deal with Iraq's victims as well as its vanquished, recognizing that the stakes are high not only because of wrongdoings, but also because people's legal rights (notably including, as President Bush said, "basic human rights") have been violated and, in UN parlance, grossly violated.[1]

My inquiries here concern (a) whether those who manage the affairs of the United Nations and its member nations really do respect the rule of law, and (b) whether they have the sagacity—while some of them seek to restructure the world order—to honor international law and, especially, the mandates of the UN Charter that concern "human rights and fundamental freedoms," as well as "universal peace."

RESOLUTION 687: APRIL 5, 1991

"[A]cting under Chapter VII of the Charter" (i.e., "to maintain or restore international peace and security") the UN Security Council in Resolution 687 declared a cease-fire "effective between Iraq and Kuwait and the Member States cooperating with Kuwait in accordance with resolution 678." Resolution 678 and 12 others were affirmed, "except as expressly changed to achieve the goals" of Resolution 687.

As of July 1991, media representatives still seemed to hold the view that civilians in Iraq suffered more than those in Kuwait, Jordan, and Iran, and also that U.S. leaders (and, thus, the UN) were focused primarily on the needs of the Kurds and on nuclear and other weapons controls, plus oil slicks and wells that continued to burn. There was at least an awareness, but little news about either the Security Council's "prohibitions against the sale or supply to Iraq of commodities or products" and other embargo rules, or the modifications of those rules that were forthcoming because of "humanitarian needs," as well as Iraq's desire for income sufficient to meet its obligations regarding burning wells and the other gigantic costs of the war.

That too brief summary, accurate or not, must next be tested by careful examination of the terms of Resolution 687:

1. Kuwaiti Property. The Security Council requested a secretary-general's report on "steps taken to facilitate the return of all Kuwaiti property seized by Iraq, including a list of any property that Kuwait claims has not been returned or which has not been returned intact."

2. Losses, Damages, Debts. The Council reaffirmed "that Iraq, without prejudice to the debts and obligations of Iraq arising prior to 2 August 1990, . . . is liable under international law for any direct loss, damage, including environmental damage and the depletion of natural resources, or injury to foreign Governments, nationals and corporations, as a result of Iraq's unlawful invasion and occupation of Kuwait," and decided "to create a fund to pay compensation for claims . . . and to establish a Commission that will administer the fund." Those words in Resolution 687 restate Paragraph 8 of Resolution 674 (October 29, 1990), which warned Iraq that, "under international law, it is liable for any loss, damage or injury arising in regard to Kuwait and third states, and their nationals and corporations, as a result of the invasion and illegal occupation of Kuwait by Iraq."

Further, all Iraqi statements made since August 2, 1990 repudiating its foreign debt are null and void, and "Iraq must adhere scrupulously to all of its obligations concerning servicing and repayment of its foreign debt."[2]

REDRESS, REPARATIONS, AND INTERNATIONAL LAW

The 1990-91 Security Council resolutions as a whole are precedent shattering and respect often ignored requirements of the UN Charter. Regardless of how or whether they continue to be enforced, they are destined to have an immense impact on the international laws of armed conflict, both external and internal.

Here I will not discuss national law—constitutional powers of the President vs. Congress; federations vs. "republics;" civilian uprisings; and so on—nor will I propose any amendments or revisions of law, because I want to stress how the implementation and enforcement of existing law might be made more effective. I will also reserve for future study some obviously troubling questions regarding criminal punishment. My focus instead is on civil redress and critical issues of how best we can help people whose human rights are being or have been violated.

My hope is that ideas such as these may be of aid to the many dedicated UN leaders—official and unofficial—who believe (a) that "to blame" is merely one entry way among many to the corridors labeled "to help," and (b) that the victims of a war "that has been won" merit much more attention than do violators of laws that clearly should have governed. Since 1989 Theodoor van Boven of The Netherlands has been entrusted with the undertaking of "a study concerning the right to compensation and rehabilitation for victims of gross violations of human rights . . . taking into account relevant existing international human rights norms on compensation and relevant decisions and views of international human rights organs, with a view to exploring the possibility of developing some basic principles and guidelines in this respect." His progress report was presented to the UN Human Rights Sub-Commission in August 1991.

What About Nuremberg Law?

A powerful fact is that the post-WW II Nuremberg trials enlightened us regarding not only criminal but also civil law. A brief analysis recently filed with a U.S. court reads, in part:

It is true that many torturers and others . . . should be punished as criminals. Yet it is not always true that seeking criminal punishment is an effective means of helping people whose human rights have been violated.

[T]he forms of redress that most often help victims of human rights violations are not penal fines and/or imprisonment. So what are they? The list includes restitution, damages (including punitive damages), injunctions (from courts) and cease and desist orders (from administrative tribunals), declaratory judgments (judicial) and declaratory orders (administrative), as well as the imposition of varied types of civil discipline (e.g., rebuke, demotion, and discharge of military personnel and other government officials; suspension and revocation of licenses and permits; etc.). . . .

[M]ost people whose international human rights have been violated will be aided more by non-criminal than by criminal sanctions. The main contribution of international criminal law will be the proscription of conduct regarded as wrongful. If the wrongs are provable, jurists and activists then can design forms of redress that will be far more constructive than are fines and imprisonment. (*Fatimeh Ali Aidi v. Yaron*, Civil 87-1216, District of Columbia District Court)

A related point is made by Vasak and Alston (1982).

Here there is no room for a summary or precis of the case law and practice of international criminal law. There is room, however, for a warning that repeatedly seems to be unheeded.

This is the warning: Human rights activists must remember that a main contribution of the relevant criminal law is its proscribing of illegal conduct. . . .

Why is that important? For many reasons. A crucial fact is that too many people, once the word "Nuremberg" is mentioned for example, immediately begin discussing criminal intent, proof beyond a reasonable doubt and related concepts of penal law. Because those topics are labyrinthine, we tend to forget that governments and government officials may well have committed illegal acts whether or not the acts also were criminal.

That is exactly what happened, for example, in numerous discussions of "Nuremberg and Vietnam." The cost to human rights law was not that possibly guilty individuals escaped prosecution. The greater cost was that, too often, all the talk of criminality left undiscussed and unsettled the basic issues as to whether the new and brutal techniques of warfare that were used in Vietnam were illegal or not. (1982: 166)

These paragraphs suggest the following conclusions: first, that a variety of noncriminal forms of redress may often be enforceable against some participants in wars, armed conflicts, or related confrontations; and second, that the patent needs of many victims for such redress can be bolstered by pertinent provisions of international criminal law.

Several of the UN's Gulf War resolutions refer to "international law" and "international humanitarian law;" and Security Council Resolution 674 of October 29, 1990, adds "general principles of international law." Those phrases include treaties and also customary law that not all nations have "ratified." (A widely endorsed restatement of that phenomenon is found in Article 39 (section 1) b and c of the Statute of the International Court of Justice.)

Because Iraq, like most nations, arguably has not ratified any treaty that defines the Nuremberg crimes of aggression, war crimes, or crimes against humanity, those three proscriptions illustrate here the full sweep of customary law. Sometimes it incorporates words of treaties that have not quite been universally ratified, such as most clauses of the 1949 Geneva conventions and much of the UN Charter. Sometimes only a few nations have inaugurated it, as with the 1945 Allied Victors' Charter for the International Military Tribunal at Nuremberg. Sometimes every nation is bound even when the inaugurating lawmakers are unidentified, as, for example, with piracy, the slave trade, torture, and so on. The most authoritative pronouncements of "customary" Nuremberg wrongs, I believe, are in Allied Control Council Law No. 10:

> (a) Crimes against Peace: Planning, preparation, initiation, or waging of a war of aggression, or a war in violation of international treaties, agreements, or assurances, or participation in a common plan or conspiracy for the accomplishment of any of the foregoing.
> (b) War Crimes: Violations of the laws or customs of war. Such violations shall include, but not be limited to, murder, ill-treatment, or deportation to slave labor or for any other purpose of civilian population of or in occupied territory, murder or ill-treatment of prisoners of war or persons on the seas, killing of hostages, plunder of public or private property, wanton destruction of cities, towns, or villages, or devastation not justified by military necessity.
> (c) Crimes against Humanity: Atrocities and offenses, including but not limited to murder, extermination, enslavement, deportation, imprisonment, torture, rape, or OTHER INHUMANE ACTS COMMITTED AGAINST ANY CIVILIAN POPULATION, or persecutions on political, racial or religious grounds. . . .

What About Saddam Hussein and His Cohorts?

> "This conflict [may] reinvigorate the arcane 'law of war' and
> further advance it from its genesis as an oxymoron to an
> increasingly operative rule of law. Perhaps most sensitive . . .
> is the extent to which war crimes may have been committed
> and, if so, whether those who committed them will be held to
> account, and how " (Moyer 1991: 2).

From 1950 to 1990 innumerable Nuremberg wrongdoers were not punished. Should we nonetheless now reinvigorate the punishment process? The only tolerable answer is yes. If the question involved wrongs such as piracy and the slave trade, or drug barons and other terrorists, there would be few objections. Are unpenalized crimes against peace, war crimes, and crimes against humanity for any reason more tolerable?

In future years the world will need international courts and prosecutors, as well as processes that assure fairness and adjudications that respect due process. Yet while we strive for those goals we need not abjure the assessment of blame. By utilizing both national tribunals, as can be done for grave breaches of the 1949 Geneva conventions and many other international violations, and international "civil" penalties, as has been done via the Security Council's Gulf War resolutions and countless resolutions of other UN bodies concerning gross violations of human rights, we certainly can penalize wrongdoing and also aid victims.

Since 1950 have tyrants sometimes been penalized in ways that help their victims? Yes, often; and progress is being made, gradually. That it has been "modest" suggests that we contemplate "modest victories," such as those that analogously have marked for decades the hesitant use of penalties and remedies other than injunctions in so many civil liberties and civil rights conflicts in the U.S.

What About the Kurds and Other Ill-Treated Groups?

On April 5, 1991, the Security Council in Resolution 688 condemned "the repression of the Iraqi civilian population in many parts of Iraq, including most recently in Kurdish populated areas." The Resolution demanded that Iraq "immediately end this repression" and expressed "the hope that an open dialogue will take place to ensure that the human and political rights of all Iraqi citizens are respected." The secretary-general was asked to report and also "to address urgently the critical needs of the refugees and displaced Iraqi population," and the council decided "to remain seized of the matter."

The media have not focused on the fact that Resolution 688 should protect many more populations than Kurds. Far too little attention has been given to phrases in the Resolution such as "the Iraqi civilian population" and "the human . . . rights of all Iraqi citizens." Note too that the secretary-general must "use all the resources at his disposal . . . to address urgently the critical needs of the refugees and displaced Iraqi population."

Writing in *The Humanist*, O'Sullivan (1991) has predicted that "[w]ith the war now officially declared over, the United Nations will again be about as newsworthy as a cat up a tree." While the media recently may have improved the "prepeace" coverage of UN news, I suggest that, overall, no more than a B-minus is merited. To illustrate: Could many reporters, media analysts, and pundits answer questions like these?

1. How many coalition allies did the U.S. muster, and which sent military aid and in what quantity? Who now are "active" UN allies?

2. Of the numerous UN bodies other than UNICEF and the Office of the High Commissioner for Refugees, which have participated?

3. Has the U.S. at last paid to the UN all dues and other moneys and services it owes?

4. Has the UN estimated its Gulf War costs and published the figures?

5. Do U.S. citizens have access to reasonable estimates of how many dollars we "spent" during the past 12 months?

6. Have UN bodies, the ICRC, and other organizations supplied reasonable estimates of war deaths—military and civilian? Of other casualties? Of refugees (from August 1990 through July 1991)?

7. Have friends in the UN become less satisfied or more satisfied about the good faith and performance of U.S. representatives in UN forums?

8. Most significantly, on whom do we rely for information that citizens in the U.S. and elsewhere need concerning all who have suffered or are suffering "direct loss, damage . . . or injury" (the Security Council's words) and/or analogous harm?

THE POSTWAR MEDIA

On the morning of July 15, 1991, two newspapers delivered to my home reported the following stories:

Iraq Gives U.N. List Citing More Nuclear Plants

("Inspector remains skeptical that Baghdad has
revealed all sites for enriching uranium.")

Iraqi Atom Effort Exposes Weakness in World Controls

Iraq's Nuclear Skills Surprise the West

Bush, Mitterand Agree on Force If Iraq Pursues Nuclear Weapons
("Repression of Kurds also a Consideration")

Iraqi Officers Reportedly Executed
("They thought they were going to get medals. . . .
Instead, they were hanged.")

Suspected Terrorists Slain As Bush Prepares to Visit
("Turkish police kill 10")

Kuwait Punishes Students Of Iraqi-Run Schools
("[O]f 136,000 non-Kuwaiti students . . . before the
invasion, only 46,000 stayed in the country. Al-Badr
did not say how many students will be barred from
enrolling next month.")

Reuters dispatch: "Eighteen people were killed . . . in battles
between Kurdish rebels and security forces in southeast
Turkey."

AP dispatch: "China signed a contract . . . to join American
and Canadian companies in dousing oil well fires started by
Iraqi soldiers."

San Francisco soldiers: "Two . . . Marine Corps reservists who
filed for conscientious objector discharges during the war and
now face a possible court-martial for desertion are no longer
threatened with the death penalty, members of their family said."

On the editorial pages, the editors and columnists of the *New
York Times* mentioned neither the Middle East nor the UN, but one
letter did refer to a July 1 editorial that proposed "to let Iraq export oil
but turn the proceeds over to the United Nations." In the *San Francisco
Chronicle* the only pertinent pundit was A. M. Rosenthal, who
concluded: "We should now recognize a whole series of coalition
mistakes, misjudgments and delusions. They add up to one huge, historic
error, uncorrectable until understood, acknowledged and rectified:
allowing a beaten dictator to stay in power, slaughter his domestic
enemies and prepare for renewed struggle with foreign enemies." The
lead *Chronicle* editorial, concerning the London session of the G-7
leaders, predicted that "global arms trade . . . and other items will
crowd the agenda—environmental issues, Third World debt, the

Middle East and Yugoslavia, among others—and none should be shortchanged."

The morning's sole report on victims is Jean Mayer's column, "Iraq's Malnourished Children." But what about the many "foreign Governments, nationals and corporations" that also were promised redress by the UN Security Council's resolutions? Indeed, what has happened to them; and who among those who may know now seek to keep us informed?

Of course, not all has been lost, by any accounting. For instance, Reuters reports that "George Bush remains the most popular U.S. President in modern times. . . . [H]is over-all approval rating remains sky-high more than four months after the gulf war." And the UN Security Council is, thank God, still in business.

Yet hauntingly relevant is this metaphor (unwitting I think) supplied by columnist Herb Caen: "Don't miss Steinhart Aquarium's finest sign—the one above the shark tank that reads 'If you are in the water with a dangerous shark, swim normally, not excitedly, and try not to bleed.'"

For me, the uniquely thoughtful and poignant piece is Arthur Hoppe's "Suffer Little Children."

> Another waif was at the door [and] said he was from Iraq. "Go away," I said testily. "I'm already supporting 10 Bangladeshi, six Eritreans and my lazy brother-in-law."
>
> "Oh, please, sir . . ." he said. "I was hoping you might see your way clear to releasing some of those frozen Iraqi assets so that I could buy a little food and medicine."
>
> "Well, I'd like to," I said, "but we froze those assets to punish you for invading Kuwait."
>
> . . . "Excuse me, sir," he said, "But a Harvard research team said . . . that 170,000 Iraqi children would succumb to malnutrition and disease unless you lifted your sanctions. And 6,000 have already died."
>
> "Lift our sanctions?" I cried. "I can see you don't understand a thing about our foreign policy, young man.". . . I [then] said patiently, "our president has made it quite clear that we can't lift those sanctions until you get rid of that monster Saddam Hussein. . . . We licked him fair and square [and] now we're going keep those sanctions on to teach him a lesson. . . . The man's a selfish, lying, power-mad, corrupt dictator. Our plan is to make him suffer by starving you. . . . Don't you worry, son. . . . We'll save you from that rotten tyrant. Our policy never fails. Look at all the Nicaraguans and Vietnamese we saved from communism through our starve-the-kids policy."

"But I thought millions of Vietnamese children survived to live under communism," he said.

"I'm speaking of the ones who didn't," I explained.

The scrawny tyke sighed. "Well, I'll do my best to go along [but] my hunger pangs are getting just awful, and I think I'm coming down with a fever.""

I couldn't help but pat him on the head. "Keep up the good work, son," I said encouragingly. "We'll get that S.O.B. yet."

NOTES

1. I use the adjective "gross" because it is now a UN word-of-art. The Geneva conventions favor "grave." Also the ICRC, when it seeks to implement the Red Cross treaties, generally employs "discreet indignation" rather than condemnation and sanctions á la UN bodies.

2. Eric Yamamoto, in Chapter 12 of this volume, focuses on the $1.2 billion and the U.S. apology for redress for Japanese-Americans. My paragraphs on property, losses, damages, and debt disclose that even without reference to other paragraphs of Resolution 687, Iraq's obligations are immeasurably larger than those belatedly assumed by the U.S. government toward Japanese-Americans.

REFERENCES

Moyer, Homer. 1991. "Legal Issues of the Gulf War and Policy." *American Bar Association International Law News* 20, no. 1 (winter): 2.

O'Sullivan, Gerry. 1991. "Against the Grain." *The Humanist* 51, no. 3 (May/June): 39-42.

Vasak, Karel and Philip Alston. 1982. *The International Dimensions of Human Rights*. Westport, CT: Greenwood.

11

Redress for Indigenous Peoples' Rights: The Case of Native Hawaiians

DAVIANNA PŌMAIKA'I MCGREGOR

Peace with freedom can only be attained through the realization of peace with justice. Before a people who have been historically suppressed can enjoy freedom, their just claims of redress must be recognized and resolved. Overcoming social, political, economic, and cultural discrimination, exploitation, deprivation, and repression is the essence of freedom.

The historical oppression and just claims of Ka Po'e Hawai'i/The Hawaiian People is most appropriately addressed within the framework of the claims and rights of indigenous peoples. Indigenous peoples throughout the world are attempting to restructure the settler nations which surrounded, intruded upon, and fragmented their original traditional communities. They seek sovereign control over ancestral lands and natural resources to enable them to exist in their own territories free of interference, intrusion, or economic exploitation.

The United Nations Subcommission on the Prevention of Discrimination and Protection of Minorities commissioned the Martinez Cobo *Study of the Problem of Discrimination Against Indigenous Populations* to make a complete and comprehensive study of discrimination against indigenous populations and to suggest the necessary national and international measures for eliminating such discrimination. Cobo surveyed the conditions of indigenous peoples in 37 different countries throughout the world from 1971 through 1984. The report defined indigenous populations as follows:

Indigenous communities, peoples and nations are those which, having a historical continuity with pre-invasion and pre-colonial societies that developed their territories, consider themselves distinct from other sectors of the societies now prevailing in those territories, or part of them. They form at present non-dominant sectors of society and are determined to preserve, develop and transmit to future generations their ancestral territories, and their ethnic identity, as the basis of their continued existences as peoples, in accordance with their own cultural patterns, social institutions and legal systems.

The historical continuity may consist of the continuation, for an extended period reaching into the present, of one or more of the following factors: (a) Occupation of ancestral lands, or at least part of them; (b) Common ancestry with the original occupants of these lands; (c) Culture in general, or in specific manifestations . . . (d) Language . . . (e) residence in certain parts of the country, or in certain regions of the world; (f) other relevant factors (Cobo 1987: 29, points 379-380).

One of the most important findings of the report, with significance for Ka Po'e Hawai'i, is the assertion that restitution of ancestral lands is at the heart of providing redress to indigenous peoples. The report stated:

It is essential to know and understand the deeply spiritual special relationship between indigenous peoples and their land as basic to their existence as such and to all their beliefs, customs, traditions and culture.

For such peoples, the land is not merely a possession and a means of production. The entire relationship between the spiritual life of indigenous peoples and Mother Earth, and their land, has a great many deep-seated implications. Their land is not a commodity which can be acquired, but a material element to be enjoyed freely.

Indigenous peoples have a natural and inalienable right to keep the territories they possess and to claim the land of which they have been deprived. In other words, they have the right to the natural cultural heritage contained in the territory and freely to determine the use to be made of it (Cobo, 1987: 16, points 196-198).

This chapter will review the current conditions of Ka Po'e Hawai'i and the foundation for their claims for sovereignty and redress.

CURRENT CONDITIONS OF KA PO'E HAWAI'I

In 1980, approximately 175,000 Ka Po'e Hawai'i comprised 19% of the overall Hawai'i population. Of that number, only 10,000 were pure Hawaiian and another 70,000 were estimated to be of at least half Hawaiian ancestry. Thirty-one percent still lived outside of O'ahu (Kanahele 1982).[1]

In 1980, Hawaiians earned low incomes, comparable to the most recently arrived immigrant groups, held low-status jobs, and had the highest rate of unemployment of all the ethnic groups in the islands. By contrast, the descendants of Caucasian, Japanese, and Chinese immigrants earned high incomes and held a greater portion of the managerial and professional jobs in Hawai'i. Moreover, a significant portion of the native Hawaiians (35%) earned incomes that were insufficient to provide for their families and thus received public assistance to supplement their incomes. Some depended entirely upon welfare support to meet their day-to-day needs. Thus, Hawaiians made up 40% of all the welfare recipients in Hawai'i, although they comprised only 19% of the population (Kanahele 1982).[2]

Hawaiians had the lowest life expectancy among ethnic groups in Hawai'i, at 67.6 years compared to 73 for Caucasians, 77 for Japanese, 72 for Filipinos, and 76 for Chinese. In 1980, 12% of Hawaiian youth between 18 and 24 did not complete high school and overall, half of the Hawaiian adults over 25 did not graduate from high school. Thirty-nine percent of the adult inmate population and 60% of the youth in correctional facilities were of Hawaiian ancestry (Kanahele 1982: 8, 18, 27-28).

These socioeconomic statistics reflect a disparity in the standard of living between native Hawaiians and Caucasians, Japanese, and Chinese in Hawai'i. They also indicate a high degree of alienation from the social system and the political power structure of modern Hawai'i. On the one hand, they represent the effect of institutionalized cultural barriers which prevent equal access to opportunities in the educational system, health care delivery systems, and adequate representation in the judicial system (Alu Like 1976, 1985). On the other hand, they are the result of the historical failure of rural-based Hawaiians to fully assimilate into Westernized Hawai'i society.

Much of the socioeconomic disorientation suffered by Ka Po'e Hawai'i today can be attributed to dislocation from ancestral homelands and related disruptions to the traditional family and social order. A survey of the needs of Ka Po'e Hawai'i conducted in 1976 by the non-profit Hawaiian corporation Alu Like, Inc., concluded:

Different categories of the population have different problems. The urban higher-income group, both men and women, lack adequate educational preparation for the better jobs they want. One-third report a desire for housing that they cannot afford. The lower-income urban group suffers from joblessness and insufficient supply of low-cost housing in urban areas, and consequent doubling-up of families. The rural group suffers from lack of job opportunities, a limited range of job choices, and, particularly on O'ahu, a steady loss of access to natural resources.

Hawaiians in all groups frequently report loss of pride and bitterness resulting from historic loss of their family lands and their homeland (Alu Like 1976).

These statistics reflect the individual and collective pain, bitterness, and trauma of a people whose sovereignty has been and remains suppressed, who are dispossessed in their own homeland, and who lack control over the resources of their ancestral lands to provide for the welfare of their people.

HISTORICAL FOUNDATION OF HAWAIIAN SOVEREIGNTY

Ka Po'e Hawai'i were forged as a self-sufficient, sovereign, and distinct people sharing a common ancestry, language, cultural and spiritual customs, beliefs, practices, territory, and subsistence social system through an extended period of migrations and settlements long before the 12th century. Aloha 'āina/love the land, aloha in na akua/love the gods, aloha kekahi i kekahi/love one another are the three precepts which formed the core of the Hawaiian people's philosophy, worldview, and belief system. It was important for Hawaiians to sustain supportive, nurturing, and harmonious relations with the land, the gods, and each other, particularly with their 'ohana or extended family. Moreover, the Hawaiians, the land, and the gods were also spiritually, culturally, and biologically united as one—lōkāhi—by lineal descent. In their mo'o ku'auhau/family genealogy chants, Hawaiians traced their lineal ancestry to historical figures and ultimately, through them, to various deities and gods of the land, ocean, forest, and nature (Handy and Pukui 1976; Johnson 1981).

The land and all of nature was the source of existence for the Hawaiians—not only as the origin of humanity, but also as the source of natural resources for day-to-day subsistence. The Hawaiian related to the land as an ancestor and dear friend. They honored and worshipped the life forces of nature as gods. They did not possess or own the land or its abundant resources. This was inconceivable. Instead, they maintained stewardship over it—planting and fishing according to the phases of the moon and changes from rainy to dry seasons.

The traditional Hawaiian land system evolved to provide Hawaiians access to the resources they would need for subsistence and to allow for stewardship over the land by the lineal descendants associated with particular ancestral 'aumākua/deities and akua/gods. The basic unit was an ahupua'a, which usually coincided with a valley system. Within the ahupua'a, 'ohana or extended families of maka'āinana/commoners were responsible for cultivation and stewardship of 'ili, parcels of land which usually ran from the mountain to the sea and afforded access to all of the natural resource zones. There was no need for individual accumulation of wealth, for the land provided all of the necessities of life and the 'ohana collectively performed work projects as necessary (Handy and Pukui 1976; Handy, Handy, and Pukui 1972).

Between 1100 and 1600 a class of ali'i, ruling chiefs, emerged and imposed their control over the land and the people. Ultimately all of the lands of Hawai'i, together with the people living on them, were divided up among the chiefs. While the tenure of a chief over the land was subject to his ability to defend his control over it, the various 'ohana of common people remained stable on their designated ancestral lands. The Hawaiians had a saying which referred to the stability of the common people on their lands, "Kō luna pōhaku no ke ka'a ilalo, 'a'ole hiki i ko lalo pōhaku ke ka'a/A stone that is high up can roll down, but a stone that is down cannot roll." In other words, a chief could be overthrown in battle or lose tenure over the land upon the death of his patron chief. However, the common people who lived on the land from the days of their ancestors would not be displaced (Handy and Pukui 1976; Handy, Handy, and Pukui 1972; Pukui 1983: 198; Kirch 1985; Kamakau 1961).

To the extent that Hawaiian society evolved into a socially and economically stratified system by 1600, the responses of the Hawaiian people to contact and change after 1778 were divergent and largely influenced by the individual social and economic role they played in the society. The acceptance or rejection of Western culture was largely the prerogative of the ruling class of ali'i. The common people did not play a major role in determining the political and economic future of Hawai'i. Those factions among the ali'i who opposed Western influence were defeated by Kamehameha I in his wars of conquest, or by Kamehameha's Council of Chiefs under the leadership of Mō'i Kamehameha II, Kuhina Nui Ka'ahumanu, and High Chief Kalanimoku, when they instituted the 'Ai Noa or abolition of the state religion (Kamakau 1961: 219-28; Kalakaua 1888: 429-46; Sahlins 1981: 55-64; Davenport 1969: 1-20; Kroeber 1948).

CHANGES UNDER THE HAWAIIAN MONARCHY

The common people let the ali'i take the lead, while they were struggling to survive the burden of contact. Plagued by foreign diseases, the common people were killed on a massive scale. For example, in the year 1804 alone, half of the Hawaiian population died of ma'i ōku'u, a disease that was either cholera or bubonic plague. When the first census was conducted by missionaries in 1823, it was found that only 135,000 Hawaiians had survived the first 45 years of contact (Schmitt 1971: 237-43; Malo 1839). The survivors were left to bury their dead and struggle to carry on with life on a subsistence basis (Handy and Pukui 1976: 234-35).

Beginning in 1820, the foreign resident population steadily increased with the settling of missionaries, sailors, and businessmen in the islands. They, together with the gunboats of their national governments, placed increasing demands upon the monarchy of the Hawaiian Kingdom to grant them the rights of citizenship and to allow them to own land on a private basis. Ultimately they persuaded the Kamehameha dynasty to transform the traditional Hawaiian subsistence social system by instituting a constitutional monarchy, establishing a system of private land ownership, permitting foreigners to naturalize, setting up a capitalist economy based upon plantation agribusiness, introducing a system of wage labor, and importing immigrant laborers on a large scale. The result was the alienation, dispossession, and impoverishment of Ka Po'e Hawai'i in a multiethnic society in which they were reduced to a minority. Western domination of Hawai'i culminated with the overthrow of the monarchy of the Hawaiian Kingdom on January 17, 1893 by American businessmen backed by U.S. marines.

The clearest indictment of the illegal role of the U.S. military in overthrowing the monarchy of the Hawaiian Kingdom are the words of President Grover Cleveland in his report to the U.S. Congress on December 18, 1893:

> The lawful Government of Hawaii was overthrown without the drawing of a sword or the firing of a shot by a process every step of which, it may safely be asserted, is directly traceable to and dependent for its success upon the agency of the United States acting through its diplomatic and naval representatives. . . .
>
> But for the landing of the United States forces upon false pretexts respecting the danger to life and property the committee would never have exposed themselves to the pains and penalties of treason by undertaking the subversion of the Queen's Government. . . .

Believing, therefore, that the United States could not, under the circumstances disclosed, annex the islands without justly incurring the imputation of acquiring them by unjustifiable methods, I shall not again submit the treaty of annexation to the Senate for its consideration . . .

By an act of war, committed with the participation of a diplomatic representative of the United States and without authority of Congress, the Government of a feeble but friendly and confiding people has been overthrown. A substantial wrong has thus been done which a due regard for our national character as well as the rights of the injured people requires we should endeavor to repair. . .

I instructed Minister Willis to advise the Queen and her supporters of my desire to aid in the restoration of the status existing before the lawless landing of the United States forces at Honolulu on the 16th of January last, if such restoration could be effected upon terms providing for clemency as well as justice to all parties concerned. (US. House of Representatives, 53rd Congress, 2nd Session, December 21, 1893, pp. 13-14)

American business interests in Hawai'i rejected the position and the diplomatic efforts of President Cleveland to restore Queen Lili'uokalani to the throne. Their Provisional Government and its successor, the Republic of Hawai'i, continued to usurp the power of the monarchy and suppress Hawaiian sovereignty. In 1898 the Republic of Hawai'i annexed itself to the United States government. Ka Po'e Hawai'i, however, never directly relinquished or surrendered their claims to sovereignty as a people or to their national lands, either through the monarchy or through a plebiscite or referendum. Therefore, the sovereign claims of Ka Po'e Hawai'i persist today and are exercised to various degrees, even though they do not enjoy the benefit of formal recognition or settlement.

NATIVE HAWAIIAN PUBLIC LAND BASES

Partial recognition of the rights of Ka Po'e Hawai'i to the Crown and kingdom lands of the Hawaiian Kingdom was acknowledged by the U.S. government in the creation of two public land bases set aside for Hawaiians of half-Hawaiian ancestry or more: 200,000 acres of Hawaiian Home Lands, and at least one-fifth of the 1.75 million acres of ceded public lands. However, the Hawaiian people do not exercise sovereign control over these land bases, as control was vested in the State of Hawai'i under the 1959 Admissions Act. Both land bases continue to be reduced and damaged through land exchanges, non-

Hawaiian leases for commercial and industrial uses, and military training and storage usage.

The Hawaiian Home Lands is administered as a regular department of the State of Hawai'i, having to conform to state budget policies and economic planning priorities. In 1980, 21,000 persons of half-Hawaiian ancestry were on the waiting list for an allotment of land. Some of the applicants had been on the waiting list for 20 to 30 years. Despite such a long waiting list, a significant portion of the Hawaiian Home Lands is leased to non-Hawaiian ranches and commercial enterprises to generate revenues for the department. The State of Hawai'i has periodically utilized Hawaiian Home Lands for public facilities such as airports, schools, rubbish dumps, small boat harbors, and parks without compensating the trust with money or with land (Federal-State Task Force on the Hawaiian Homes Commission Act 1983). The homesteaders on Hawaiian Home Lands still lack an adequate infrastructure for irrigation, soil conservation, and the marketing of crops.

The unique and special rights of native Hawaiians to the remaining Crown and Kingdom lands ceded to the United States were recognized by the U.S. government in the 1959 Admissions Act under which Hawai'i became a state. These lands were turned over to the State of Hawai'i to manage as a public lands trust on behalf of the general public and the native Hawaiians: For the support of public schools and other public educational institutions; for the betterment of the conditions of native Hawaiians, as defined in the Hawaiian Homes Commission Act, 1920, as amended; for the development of farm and home ownership on as widespread a basis as possible for the making of public improvements; and for the provision of lands for public use (Admission Act 1985 vol. 1: 88).

Further recognition of native Hawaiian rights to the ceded public lands trust was provided by the 1978 Constitutional Convention in Article 12, section 4 of the Hawai'i State Constitution: The lands granted to the State of Hawaii by Section 5 (b) of the Admission Act and pursuant to Article 16, Section 7, of the State Constitution, excluding therefrom lands defined as "available land" by Section 203 of the Hawaiian Homes Commission Act, 1920, as amended, shall be held by the State as a public trust for native Hawaiians and the general public.

The 1978 Hawai'i State Constitutional Convention acknowledged the special interest of native Hawaiians in the ceded public lands trust by designating one-fifth of the annual revenues generated from the ceded lands to be set aside to fund programs for native Hawaiians of half-Hawaiian ancestry or more. It should be noted that the convention could have used Article 12, section 4, which identifies only two beneficiaries of the ceded public lands, as the basis upon which to determine the interest of Ka Po'e Hawai'i. In that case, it might have designated one-half of the annual revenues to be set aside for Ka Po'e Hawai'i. Instead, it used section 5 (f) of the Admissions Act, which defined five purposes for the ceded public lands, as the basis upon which to determine native Hawaiian interest in the trust. Groups advocating the sovereignty of Ka Po'e Hawai'i seek sovereign control over at least one-half of the "ceded public lands trust" on the basis of Article 12, section 4 of the Hawai'i State Constitution.

The 1978 Constitutional Convention also created an Office of Hawaiian Affairs to administer one-fifth of the revenues from the ceded lands and to advocate for the interests of Ka Po'e Hawai'i. The operations of that office are funded by the legislature on an annual basis. A board of trustees, chosen in a special election in which only Hawaiians vote, sets the policies and hires the administrator for the Office of Hawaiian Affairs. However, the former Crown and Kingdom lands as a whole are managed by the Department of Land and Natural Resources of the State of Hawai'i. The department has allowed this land base to be used and, in certain cases, undermined by private enterprise.[3]

Unless and until Ka Po'e Hawai'i have sovereign control over these land bases, they will not be able to enjoy the full benefit of the resources of those lands and be able to utilize them for the betterment of their people. In addition, no land base has ever been set aside for Hawaiians of less than 50% Hawaiian ancestry. These land claims should also be addressed.

SOVEREIGN INITIATIVES

In the field of Hawaiian language, vigorous efforts are being made to train a new generation of native speakers through Hawaiian language immersion education in Hawaiian language preschools and special Hawaiian language immersion elementary classes in the state public schools. Between 1984 and 1989, the number of native speakers under age 10 increased from 30 to 180.[4]

Prior to statehood (1959), as much as half of the population of Ka Po'e Hawai'i lived in rural areas and still relied upon traditional and customary subsistence fishing, planting, gathering, and hunting. Beginning with statehood and jet service to Hawai'i, the pace of development intensified at an unprecedented rate. Many rural subsistence communities were displaced and dispersed to make way for tourist, resort, industrial, and other commercial development. Fishing grounds were destroyed by pollution from golf courses, sewage, and increased soil runoff or dredging for small and large boat harbors. Subsistence hunting areas diminished and access to forest and mountain areas for gathering native plants for medicine was cut off. On many islands Hawaiian farmers, especially those planting taro, were deprived of their traditional water rights from streams as this precious source of water was diverted for hotels, golf courses, and subdivisions. Property taxes for small plots of land abutting large-scale developments soared, thus forcing small landowners of Hawaiian ancestry to sell their property. Habitats for native plants used for healing, spiritual, and cultural practices were destroyed by development.

The loss of subsistence gathering opportunities disrupted the mutual sharing and exchange that is an integral part of extended family 'ohana networks in the rural communities. New owners from outside Hawai'i with commercial, industrial, or resort plans threatened customary management and stewardship over the natural, cultural, and economic resources in these rural areas. This contributed to demoralization, fragmentation, and polarization in these formerly cohesive cultural enclaves.

Only a handful of rural Hawaiian communities have survived the onslaught of post-statehood development: the islands of Moloka'i and Ni'ihau; the districts of Hāna and Kahakuloa on Maui; Kahana, Hau'ula, Lā'ie, and sections of the Wai'anae Coast on O'ahu; the districts of Ka'u, Puna, and small communities in Kona, excluding Kailua, on Hawai'i; and Kekaha and Anahola on Kaua'i. These last remaining rural Hawaiian communities provide a continuity for Ka Po'e Hawai'i with traditional spiritual and cultural customs, beliefs, and practices. Their protection is essential to the survival of the native Hawaiian culture.

Historically, these districts were bypassed by early trading activity as well as plantation development due to the severe character of the landscape or the marginal nature of the soils. These enclaves were relatively isolated from the changes which swept through Hawai'i. Thus, traditional Hawaiian values and activities have persisted to a greater degree in these areas (McGregor 1989).

Many of these districts still lack a developed infrastructure of roads, electricity, or running water. Rural Hawaiians who live in these districts still acquire basic necessities for their families through subsistence activities on the land where they employ traditional knowledge and practices passed down to them from their kupuna. Family knowledge about prime fishing grounds and the types of fish which frequent the ocean in their district at different times of the year usually assure them of successful fishing expeditions. Many families continue to plant taro, sweet potato, or other food crops by the lunar phase. They also take advantage of seasonal fruits and marine life for their regular diet. They hunt pigs, deer, and goats. Native plants and marine foods are utilized for healing illnesses by traditional methods. Cultural knowledge attached to the traditional names of places, winds, and rains of their district inform rural Hawaiians about how best to use the natural resources of their ancestral lands. Hawaiian custom, belief, and practice is part of the day-to-day life of the people.

Botanists who study the volcanic rain forest have observed that eruptions which destroy large areas of forest land leave oases of native trees and plants, called kipuka. From these natural kipuka come the seeds and spores for the eventual regeneration of the native flora on top of the fresh lava. For contemporary Hawaiians, the rural Hawaiian community enclaves are cultural kipuka from which native Hawaiian culture can be regenerated and revitalized in the contemporary setting. Protection of the natural resources and the integrity of the lifestyle and livelihood of the Hawaiians in these rural districts is essential to the perpetuation of native Hawaiian culture today and for future generations. The people, businesses, and government of Hawai'i face a unique historical opportunity and responsibility to safeguard the native Hawaiian culture for future generations by protecting these "cultural kipuka."[5]

A number of these rural Hawaiian communities threatened with development have organized to protect their landholdings and the surrounding natural resources in their districts from the assault of proposed tourist, commercial, and industrial development. On the island of Hawai'i, Ka'u Hawaiians formed the Ka 'Ohana O Ka Lae to protect the natural and cultural resources of their district from a planned spaceport to launch missiles. Mālama Ka 'Āina Hana Ka 'Āina are Hawaiians who settled on Hawaiian Home Lands at King's Landing, outside of Hilo, Hawai'i. They seek to have the area designated for subsistence homesteading and to be granted leases under such a program. The Pele Defense Fund is working to stop the development of geothermal energy wells and electric plants which will violate the god Pele, destroy the unique Puna rain forest, and ruin the natural resources that the Puna residents have utilized for subsistence livelihoods. On Moloka'i, the Hui Ala Loa, Ka Leo O Mana'e, and Hui Ho'opākela 'Āina are community groups formed to protect the natural and cultural resources of Moloka'i for farming and fishing rather than for tourist resort development. On Maui, the Hui Ala Nui O Mākena works to keep access to the ocean open for traditional fishing and gathering as well as recreation; Hāna Pōhaku is developing community-based economic development on their kuleana lands; and the Ke'anae Community Association works to keep the water flowing to their taro patches rather than being diverted for development in Kula and Kihei or for hydroelectric plants. The Hawaiian Farmers of Hanalei have community-based projects at Waipā, Kaua'i, and Ka Wai Ola seeks to protect the shoreline of Hanalei from ruin by numerous tour boat operations. On O'ahu, community-based economic development projects are being pursued on the Wai'anae Coast by Ka'ala Farms, the Ōpelu Project, and Na Hoa'āina O Mākaha. The Protect Kaho'olawe 'Ohana, with members from every island, continues its work to permanently stop U.S. military use of Kaho'olawe so that the religious, cultural, and natural resources of the island can be restored, and the island can become a Hawaiian cultural learning center. Mālama I Na Kupuna O Hawai'i Nei, a statewide group, seeks to prevent the disturbance of traditional Hawaiian burials.

A number of Hawaiian organizations are focusing their efforts on attaining sovereign control over the native Hawaiian land base. The Sovereign Kingdom of Hawai'i, originally 'Ohana O Hawai'i, called for the independence of Hawai'i in 1974 and has presented claims to the World Court toward that end. The Sovereignty for Hawai'i Committee and Na 'Ōiwi O Hawai'i/Natives of Hawai'i also seek the total independence of Hawai'i from the United States. Ka Lāhui Hawai'i/The Nation of Hawai'i has drafted a constitution and formed a legislature to create a political entity to represent the Hawaiian people as a nation. On behalf of the Hawaiian people, the organization seeks recognition of native Hawaiian sovereignty from the United States Congress, as has been granted to over 300 Native American, Eskimo, and Aleut nations, tribes, and bands.[6] The Office of Hawaiian Affairs (1986) has developed a "blueprint" which lays out a process for receiving formal statutory recognition of Hawaiian sovereignty from the Hawai'i State Legislature by 1993, the 100th anniversary of the overthrow of the Hawaiian monarchy. They intend to call for a constitutional convention to begin the process of establishing a new sovereign entity for the Hawaiian nation.

All of these efforts, combined, are contributing to the perpetuation of the Hawaiian people, land, cultural base, language, and spiritual beliefs. There is a sense of urgency to these endeavors and a conviction to persevere despite the opposition and obstacles placed before them. There is a general consensus among Ka Po'e Hawai'i that:

>—if they are able to reestablish cultural, social, economic, and political self-governance over their affairs and common (trust) assets as a native people;
>—if they are able to get back all or a portion of the 1.75 million acres of land and related natural resource entitlements that were taken away;

—if they are able to get fair compensation for all or a portion
of the value of the uncompensated use of these lands for
nearly a century by the federal and state governments; and
—if they are able to get restitution for the denial of the
exercise of sovereign rights;
—then they could begin to lay the foundation for reinstating
the sovereignty and self-determination of Ka Po'e Hawai'i.

Self-governance and control over their trust assets and resources would
provide the means whereby Ka Po'e Hawai'i could begin to address and
heal their serious social problems (Hui Na'auao 1991: 6-7).

The year of the overthrow of the Hawaiian monarchy, 1893,
marked the year in which the sovereignty of the Ka Po'e Hawai'i was
completely suppressed. The centennial of that tragic event, 1993, is
looked to as the year in which the sovereignty of the Hawaiian people
will be restored and regenerated. Individual organizations such as the
Office of Hawaiian Affairs, Ka Lāhui Hawai'i, and the Pro-
Hawaiian Sovereignty Working Group are focusing their efforts for
recognition and reestablishment of the sovereignty of Ka Po'e Hawai'i
by 1993. In addition, diverse Hawaiian organizations, from the
conservative Hawaiian Civic Clubs to agencies such as the Hawaiian
Homes Commission and the Office of Hawaiian Affairs, and those
organizations seeking formal recognition of Hawaiian political
sovereignty and self-determination, have formed a new coalition, the
Hui Na'auao/Hawaiian Education Organization. It will hold
workshops and gatherings on all of the islands to educate Ka Po'e
Hawai'i and the general public about Hawaiian sovereignty. It hopes
to create an appreciation of the aspirations of Ka Po'e Hawai'i to
thrive as a distinct people with the flourishing of traditional spiritual
and cultural Hawaiian beliefs, customs, and practices, the Hawaiian
language, and traditional relationships of aloha 'āina in conjunction
with subsistence activities and practices and sovereign control over
ancestral lands. They also want to provide a larger context for
understanding sovereignty and self-determination pertaining to
entitlements, rights, and responsibilities of all sovereign powers
(indigenous, national, international) and how each exercises these
rights in today's world—by Hawaiian and non-Hawaiian alike (Hui
Na'auao 1991: 5).

One question that arises out of this wide range of organizing
activities is whether modern Hawaiian society can be restructured to
tolerate the existence of small subsistence rural communities, or if the
existing social structure will continue to destroy and absorb these rural
areas for commercial and industrial development. Rural Hawaiians are
not demanding that everyone should give up modern conveniences and

live a subsistence lifestyle. They are saying that Hawaiians should be given the right to continue to pursue a way of life passed on to them by generations before and which is crucial to the survival of Hawaiian culture. Those people who want to pursue a modern, Western way of life should not interfere with or infringe upon the Hawaiian way of life, which was established on the lands of these rural districts for centuries. Those who are residents of the districts and want to live in accordance with a more modern Western lifestyle should move away. Those who are not residents should not be allowed to destroy the natural resources essential to the survival and subsistence of the resident Hawaiians of these districts.

Hawaiian tradition, custom, language, religion, and culture— will they persist? It is up to the present generation of Hawaiians and non-Hawaiians in Hawai'i to determine if Hawai'i's cultural and natural resources, particularly in the rural communities, will be protected so that the Hawaiian culture can be perpetuated for future generations.

CASE STUDY

The Return of Kaho'olawe

Kaho'olawe—Kohemālamalama O Kanaloa—is a microcosm of Hawaiian history that reflects the many problems and issues concerning the Hawaiian people. The island continues to be a focus for native Hawaiian political action to restore control of Hawai'i's native resources to the indigenous Hawaiians. Kaho'olawe is one of the eight major islands in the Hawaiian archipelago, located eight miles south of Maui island. It encompasses 45 square miles of varied terrain, including hills and plateaus rising to 1,500 feet, valleys, beaches, and reefs.

Ancient chants and archaeological evidence indicate that Kaho'olawe was inhabited for over a thousand years. Hawaiians fished, farmed, and lived in coastal and interior settlements across the entire island. It is a place where kahuna/priests were trained to read the currents, winds, clouds, earth, and sky. It was a navigational center for early Pacific migrations. The westernmost tip of the island, Lae O Kealaikahiki, was said to be a key directional point in starting voyages to Tahiti. At Pu'u Mõiwi is the second largest adze production quarry in the Hawaiian Islands. Basaltic glass cutting tools were also crafted on Kaho'olawe, where 20,000 tools and fragments of such tools were found in one single site. Thousands of archaeological features including petroglyph clusters, fishing shrines, temples, dwelling and camp sites, and burial sites illustrate a detailed and complex record of habitation by the Hawaiian people.

The island was continuously inhabited from approximately 1,000 A.D. to 1941. In 1832, the Hawaiian Kingdom banished several political rivals as prisoners to the island, but the local residents refused to leave because of their attachment to the place. The first of many ranch leases started in 1858. Unfortunately, due to the introduction of European herbivores and overstocking during the ranch period, much of the island became severely eroded.

On December 8, 1941, Kaho'olawe was seized by the U.S. military to be used as a practice bombing target during World War II. While first promising to return the island after the war, the military kept delaying until President Eisenhower issued Executive Order 10436 in 1952, officially taking Kaho'olawe for naval operations until such time as they no longer needed it. The Navy's abusive bombing and shelling, coupled with its neglect of the natural and cultural resources of the island and the grazing of goats and sheep left the island in an eroded and degraded condition.

In 1976, native Hawaiians on the neighboring island of Moloka'i looked across at Kaho'olawe and decided to go rediscover part of their native land. The resulting awareness of the island's beauty and cultural/spiritual significance and abuse at the hands of the Navy led to direct action by hundreds of native Hawaiians and a civil suit against the government to stop the bombing and return the island. The suit accused the Navy of violating environmental protection and historic preservation laws and invoked the Native American Religious Freedom Act. An out-of-court settlement, called the Consent Decree, was agreed to in 1980. The Consent Decree mandated the Navy to survey and protect historic sites on the island, begin soil conservation and revegetation programs, and allow regular religious and educational access to the island. A complete archaeological survey revealed the importance of the island, and the entire island was placed on the National Register of Historic Places as a National Historic District in 1981.

Over the years since the Protect Kaho'olawe 'Ohana assumed stewardship of the island, it has become a center for the perpetuation of native Hawaiian spiritual beliefs and practices. The 'Ohana has taken over 3,000 visitors to the island for educational, religious, cultural, and scientific activities. Annual Makahiki ceremonies have been conducted to Lono, Hawaiian god of agriculture, at reestablished heiau/temples on the island. Other religious customs and practices to

Kanaloa, Hawaiian god of the ocean and navigation, and patron deities of fishing are regularly carried out on a personal basis by 'Ohana members. A traditional Hawaiian hula mound has been constructed for visiting hula hālau. Trails to major cultural sites on the island are maintained. Water catchments to irrigate planting sites have been constructed and revegetation of the island with native species of plants has begun. An 'Ohana water study has revealed a ground water source of over 13 square miles and rainfall of approximately 24 billion gallons a year. Under 'Ohana monitoring, the Navy has gotten rid of almost all the goats on the island. More than 6,500 acres on the island have been cleared of surface ordnance under the Consent Decree between the 'Ohana and the Navy.

On October 22, 1990, President Bush directed the Secretary of the Navy to "discontinue use of Kaho'olawe as a weapons range effective immediately." On November 5, 1990, Congress, with President Bush's signature, enacted Senate Bill 3088, which stated that Kaho'olawe "may not be used for bombing training, gunnery training, or similar munitions delivery training" from November 5, 1990, until 120 days after the date on which a final report by the Kaho'olawe Island Conveyance Commission is submitted to Congress, April 4, 1993.

The entire island of Kaho'olawe, as land that was taken away from the government of the Hawaiian Kingdom, is part of the ceded public lands. Under the terms and language of the Presidential Executive Order 10436 and the Admissions Act of 1959, the island is to be returned to the state government in a condition reasonably safe for human habitation. The Protect Kaho'olawe 'Ohana proposes that the island become part of the Hawaiian land base under the sovereign control of the Hawaiian nation. The Office of Hawaiian Affairs, Ka Lāhui Hawai'i, and the Hawaiian Home Lands Program are existing entities for self-determination and sovereignty. Jurisdiction of the ceded lands, including Kaho'olawe and the Hawaiian Home Lands may pass to one, all, or some new combination of these groups. In the meantime, while this is being worked out, Kaho'olawe should be held in trust for the nation. It can be landbanked by the federal government, the state government, or a private trust. The 'Ohana would like a survey of the various forms of jurisdiction and title enjoyed by Native Americans which could serve as optional models for Kaho'olawe: federal trust title (most Native American reservations), federally restricted title (some Native American lands), federally protected title (Alaska Native corporation lands), state trust title (some Native American reservations), or a private land trust.

No matter who assumes jurisdiction over Kaho'olawe—the federal government, the state, or the Hawaiian Nation—the Protect Kaho'olawe 'Ohana has demonstrated the commitment, perseverance, and expertise to manage the resources of the island as steward. Hearings conducted by the Kaho'olawe Island Conveyance Commission on the six major islands has reaffirmed that the Protect Kaho'olawe 'Ohana has gained the confidence of the State of Hawai'i, congressional leaders, Hawaiian organizations, and the general public to continue to provide stewardship over the cultural and natural resources of the island and the ocean surrounding it.

What is the vision for the future of Kaho'olawe? The priority of the 'Ohana is to heal the island. The ordnance has to be removed, the cultural sites have to be stabilized, soil erosion has to be stopped, ground cover and trees need to be planted, native birds need to be attracted back to the island, and the surrounding marine life needs to be protected.

All commercial use of the island and surrounding ocean must be banned. The 'Ohana envisions use in the following ways:

—Wahi Pana—a traditional sacred place of Ka Po'e Hawai'i.
—Pu'uhonua—a place of refuge for Hawaiians from all walks of life to visit and experience the warmth and comfort of the land, practice aloha 'āina and get back in touch with their spirituality as Hawaiians.
—Natural Land and Marine Reserve With Guaranteed Hawaiian Access—restore and reestablish the natural resources of the land with native species of flora and fauna. Establish a marine sanctuary around the island. Recognize native Hawaiian access and gathering rights on and around Kaho'olawe.
—Cultural Learning Center—where traditional cultural and spiritual customs, beliefs, and practices can be freely exercised and thereby flourish.

The Kaho'olawe Island Conveyance Commission, in cooperation with the Protect Kaho'olawe 'Ohana, the U.S. Navy, and the State of Hawai'i, will conduct additional studies to recommend future uses of the island, the extent to which ordnance will have to be cleared from the surface and subsurface of the island and the surrounding reefs, and how to best manage the cultural and natural resources of the island.

The possible return of Kaho'olawe to Hawai'i by the end of 1992 provides new incentive and immediacy to the pursuit of sovereignty by Ka Po'e Hawai'i. A newly recognized sovereign entity of Ka Po'e Hawai'i should ultimately maintain jurisdiction over the island. The sooner that entity is reestablished and recognized, the sooner Kaho'olawe can become part of the sovereign land base of the Hawaiian people.

NOTES

1. These figures are based on the Hawai'i Health Surveillance Program, rather than the census. The following table shows the comparison with other ethnic groups.

Hawai'i's Population By Ethnic Group, 1980

Ethnic Group	Census Figure	Census Percentage	Health Figure	Health Percentage
Hawaiian	115,500	11.9	175,453	18.9
White	318,770	33.0	244,832	26.3
Chinese	56,285	5.8	47,275	5.0
Japanese	239,748	24.8	218,176	23.5
Filipino	133,940	13.8	104,547	11.2

The difference in the two sources is due to the difference in handling persons of mixed parentage. The census did not have a mixed category and assigned persons of mixed ancestry to one of the categories on the basis of self-identification or the race of the father. The Health Surveillance Program bases it on birth statistics. The figure of 70,000 is from the Office of Hawaiian Affairs 1986. In a study of the Health Surveillance Program data, the Office of Hawaiian Affairs estimated that there were 208,476 Hawaiians in Hawai'i in 1984, out of which 72,709 had 50% to 99% Hawaiian ancestry and 8,244 had 100% Hawaiian ancestry.

2. The median family income for Hawaiians and part-Hawaiians was $14,221; for Caucasians $20,823; for Chinese $23,859; for Japanese $23,209; and for Filipinos $16,361. The unemployment rate is cited in Kamehameha Schools/Bishop Estate 1983: 28.

3. For example, the State of Hawai'i recently exchanged 27,785 acres of ceded lands on the island of Hawai'i for 25,807 acres of land owned by a private estate to enable it to develop geothermal energy wells in Puna. Not only did the public land trust lose 2,000 acres in the exchange, but the land which the state received in return for the pristine natural rain forest that it gave away included 1,200 acres that had been logged for wood chips and 12,000 acres of land covered over by recent lava flows. Moreover, geothermal energy development will tap into the body and life force of the Hawaiian deity of the volcano, Pele, violating the spiritual beliefs of native Hawaiian religious practitioners. In addition, native Hawaiians who exercised their traditional gathering rights in the public forest were denied access to the forest when the land came under private ownership. See *Kaolelo Lambert John Ulaleo et al. vs. William Paty et al.*, Civil No. 88-00320 ACK, U.S. District Circuit for the District of Hawai'i.

4. The Punana Leo Hawaiian language immersion preschools are established on Kaua'i, O'ahu, Maui, and Hawai'i. Each school enrolls 30 students. In addition, the State Department of Education has initiated kindergarten through third grade Hawaiian language classes on O'ahu, Hawai'i, and Kaua'i.

5. Among the natural resources important to traditional Hawaiian customs, beliefs, and practices for cultural, religious, and subsistence purposes in these areas are: (1) wahi pana/sacred sites, and historical sites—heiau, shrines, burials, terraces, house sites, and so on; (2) streams for taro cultivation, marine resources, and domestic water; (3) shorelines, reefs, and ocean for gathering of foods, medicine, and spiritual customs; (4) forests for hunting, gathering of medicines, foods, ceremonial uses for hula adornment and ritual offerings, and spiritual customs; (5) habitats for endangered native species of plants and animals; and (6) natural and cultural areas as traditional domains of ancestral spirits and Hawaiian deities, where Hawaiians renew their ties to ancestors through experiencing natural phenomena and witnessing ho'ailona/signs (McGregor 1991).

6. The Sovereign Kingdom of Hawai'i has written up its position in the form of a declaration. Na 'Ōiwi o Hawai'i and Ka Lāhui Hawai'i wrote up their positions and presented them at the Native Hawaiian Sovereignty Conference, December 3-4, 1988. Ka Lāhui Hawai'i has also presented its position to the Select Committee on Indian Affairs of the U.S. Senate (Ka Lāhui Hawai'i 1989). Many groups made presentations at August 1989 hearings of the Senate Select Committee on Indian Affairs for oversight of the Hawaiian Home Lands.

REFERENCES

Alu Like. 1976. *Summary of the Analysis of the Needs Assessment Survey and Related Data*. Honolulu: Alu Like.

_____. 1985. *E Ola Mau: Native Hawaiian Health Needs Study; Mental Health Task Force Final Report*. Honolulu: Native Hawaiian Health Research Consortium, Alu Like.

Cobo, Jose R. Martinez. 1987. *Study of the Problem of Discrimination Against Indigenous Populations*. 4 vol. United Nations Subcommission on the Prevention of Discrimination and Protection of Minorities Working Group on Indigenous Populations. New York: United Nations.

Davenport, William. 1969. "The Hawaiian 'Cultural Revolution': Some Economic and Political Considerations." *American Anthropologist* 71, no. 1 (February): 1-20.

Federal-State Task Force on the Hawaiian Homes Commission Act. 1983. *Report to the United States Secretary of the Interior and the Governor of the State of Hawaii*. Honolulu.

Handy, E. S. Craighill and Mary Kawena Pukui. 1976 [1958]. *The   Polynesian Family System in Ka'u, Hawai'i.* Tokyo: Charles E. Tuttle.

Handy, E. S. Craighill, Elizabeth Green Handy, with Mary Kawena Pukui. 1972. *Native Planters in Old Hawaii. Their Life, Lore and Environment.* Bernice P. Bishop Museum Bulletin 233. Honolulu: Bishop Museum Press.

Hui Na'auao. 1991. "A Proposal Submitted to the Administration for Native Americans." Honolulu: Hui   Na'auao   Sovereignty   and   Self-Determination Community Education Project. May 24.

Johnson, Rubellite Kawena. 1981. *Kumulipo: The Hawaiian Hymn of Creation* vol. 1. Honolulu: Topgallant.

Ka Lāhui Hawai'i. 1989. *Native   Hawaiian   Reparations   Community Based Mental   Health   Initiative,   Oversight   Hearing   on   Native   Hawaiian Reparations, Mental Health Care Needs for Native People, August 26-31, 1988, Honolulu.* 100th Congress, 2d Session.   Washington, DC: Government Printing Office.

Kalakaua, David, King of Hawaii. 1888. *The Legends and Myths of Hawaii: The Fables and Folklore of a Strange People.* New York: Charles L. Webster. Rep. Tokyo: Charles E. Tuttle, 1983.

Kamakau, Samuel. 1961. *Ruling Chiefs of Hawaii.* Honolulu: Kamehameha Schools Press.

Kamehameha Schools/Bishop Estate.   1984.   *Native Hawaiian Educational Assessment Project.* Honolulu: Kamehameha Schools/Bishop Estate.

Kanahele, George S.   1982.   *Current Facts and Figures About   Hawaiians.* Honolulu: Project WAIAHA.

Kirch, Patrick V. 1985. *Feathered Gods and Fishhooks: An Introduction to Hawaiian   Archaeology and Prehistory.* Honolulu: University of Hawaii Press.

Kroeber, A. L. 1948. *Anthropology.* New York: Harcourt, Brace.

Malo, David.   1839.   "On the Decrease of Population of the Hawaiian Islands." Tr. L. Andrews. *Hawaiian Spectator* 2, no. 2.

McGregor, Davianna. 1989. "Ku pa'a I Ka Aina: Persistence on the Land." Ph.D. diss. University of Hawai'i.

_____. 1991. "Testimony of the Pele Defense Funds before the Public Utilities Commission of the State of Hawai'i in the Matter of Instituting a Proceeding to Require Energy Utilities in Hawai'i to Implement Integrated Resource Planning." Docket No. 6617. April 8.

Office of Hawaiian Affairs. 1986. "Population Survey/Needs Assessment, Final Report." Honolulu: Office of Hawaiian Affairs.

Pukui, Mary Kawena. 1983. 'Ōlelo No'eau: Hawaiian Proverbs andPoetical Sayings. Bernice P. Bishop Museum Special Publication No. 71. Honolulu: Bishop Museum Press.

Sahlins, Marshall. 1981. Historical Metaphors and Mythical Realities: Structure in the Early History of the Sandwich Islands Kingdom. Ann Arbor:,MI: University of Michigan Press.

Schmitt, Robert. 1971. "New Estimates of the Pre-Censal Population of Hawaii." Journal of the Polynesian Society 80, no. 2 (June): 237-43.

12

Redress of Past Wrongs: The Case of World War II Japanese-American Internees

ERIC YAMAMOTO

Reparations by the United States government for 60,000 surviving Americans of Japanese ancestry imprisoned during World War II without charges, trial, or evidence of necessity; redress for lost homes, families, and freedom; and for serious harm inflicted by a government on its own people because of their race, amounted to $1.2 billion[1] and an apology.

Who has benefited from redress and reparations; who has been ignored? What freedoms have been protected; what obligations forsaken? How have institutions restructured to diminish oppression; how have changes fostered illusions? To put this another way: how have redress and reparations contributed to restructuring societal institutions and attitudes to assure protection of the freedoms of unpopular minorities during times of national stress? What early lessons might be learned from redress and reparations for WW II Japanese-American internees?

Some of the lessons are salutary. Former internees have benefited in myriad ways, financially, culturally, and emotionally. Some also say government and all of society have benefited, that the reparations are proof that a democratic constitution works, that government is self-correcting, and that the American legal and political systems in particular value freedom and are essentially just. Still others say the United States has bolstered its moral foundation to command international allegiance to human rights. Its reparations program may be a model for other countries concerned about redemption for past wrongs.

But are these salutary views overstated or misguided? Might redress and reparations ultimately aid in the perpetuation of power structures and attitudes that suppress freedom for those whom society views as different and vulnerable? Could all this happen again? This chapter examines the early lessons of redress and reparations, first by inquiring into conflicting views of redress and reparations for WW II Japanese-American internees. It then offers a view of the political/legal process of striving for redress and suggests that the principal lesson of the reparations—their salient social value—may lie in the potential of the intergroup linkages and political commitments for institutional restructuring emerging from that process.

REPARATIONS FOR JAPANESE AMERICAN WWII INTERNEES

The Japanese-American redress movement provided more than reparations for former internees (Hohri 1988; Irons 1988).[2] It also provided political and legal insights into the breakdown of a democratic system of checks and balances during a time of national stress. Toward the end of WW II the United States Supreme Court ruled in the infamous *Korematsu* case that the internment was legal and that "military necessity" justified it (*Korematsu v. United States*, 323 U.S. 214, 1944) That same *Korematsu* case was reopened in 1983 on the basis of newly discovered, now declassified government documents from WW II which revealed two extraordinary facts: first, before the internment, all government intelligence services involved unequivocally informed the highest officials of the military and the War and Justice Departments that the West Coast Japanese as a group posed no serious danger and that no need for mass internment existed; and second, in 1944 when it was considering the *Korematsu* case, the military and the War and Justice Departments deliberately misled the Supreme Court about the asserted military necessity justifying the internment.

The Supreme Court in 1944 accepted as true the government's false statements about military necessity without close scrutiny—and with tragic consequences. The Court's unquestioning acceptance "not only legitimized the dislocation and imprisonment of loyal citizens without trial solely on account of race, but it also weakened a fundamental tenet of American democracy—government accountability for military control over civilians" (Yamamoto 1986; Irons 1985). Justice Jackson, in his scathing dissent, pinpointed the dangerous latent legal principle of the 1944 *Korematsu* decision. "What the Court appears to be doing, whether consciously or not . . . [is] to distort the Constitution to approve all the military may deem expedient" (Yamamoto 1986).

The recent reopening of the *Korematsu* case, with its revelations, highlighted the danger to citizens, and minorities particularly, of unscrutinized government national security power (*Korematsu v. United States*, 584 F. Supp. 1406 [N.D. Cal. 1984]). That danger led the federal court hearing the case in 1984 to observe:

> As historical precedent [Korematsu] stands . . . as a caution that in times of distress the shield of military necessity and national security must not be used to protect governmental actions from close scrutiny and accountability. It stands as a caution that in times of international hostility and antagonisms our institutions, legislative, executive and judicial, must be prepared to exercise their authority [to enforce constitutional guarantees] to protect all citizens from the petty fears and prejudices that are so easily aroused. (*Korematsu v. United States*, 518 F. Supp)

The judicial decisions in the reopened *Korematsu* and related *Hirabayashi* cases and the investigation and report in 1983 by the Congressional Commission on Wartime Relocation and Internment of Civilians provided firm legal and factual bases for legislative reparations in 1988 (Congressional Commission 1983).

CONFLICTING VIEWS OF REDRESS AND REPARATIONS

What are the social values of governmental redress and reparations? Or more particularly, how have redress and reparations for WW II Japanese-American internees contributed, if at all, to the restructuring of institutions, laws and attitudes to assure freedom for unpopular minorities during times of national stress and fear? Multiple and sometimes colliding views of the value and effect of reparations have emerged.

Salutary Views

Many of the views are positive. One message is that the Constitution works. Wrongs against a racial group can be made right. Government, if pushed, eventually will do the right thing. This message implies that redress and reparations for WW II Japanese-American internees are a symbolic victory for everyone. Government war and national security powers were ultimately brought within bounds. The system of checks and balances, over time, worked. Government reaffirmed the significance of fundamental freedoms (Hohri 1988: 225). A second salutary message is atonement and abrogation of societal guilt. The past has now passed. Forgive and forget. The slate is wiped clean. Society is finally free to move forward—or even backward. Implicit in this message is a notion peculiarly linked to American culture: money discharges moral obligation. Once you "pay off," you are morally freed. The collective message of these salutary views is that a democratic constitution and its political and legal systems are ultimately responsive to peoples' rights, including the freedoms of minorities. Societal mistakes can be transformed, however belatedly, into social progress.

Critical Views

Salutary views, however, collide with critical ones. A principal criticism is that this salutary message is conveyed from an unstated vantage point—mainstream America. What may further the general interests and serve the values of mainstream America, and the governmental structure that supports it, may undermine the struggles and dreams of those outside the cultural mainstream (Matsuda 1987). From the vantage point of minority groups we might therefore ask: what has the impact of redress and reparations been on the institutional and legal structure of government power to restrict fundamental freedoms of minorities in the United States, especially in the context of military and national security matters? An examination of this question might shed additional light on the benefits and limitations of reparations for movement towards institutional "restructuring for freedom."

GOVERNMENT/MINORITY GROUP POWER RELATIONS

Derrick Bell's interest-convergence theory suggests that dominant groups will only concede "rights" to minorities when the exercise of those rights benefits the dominant groups' overall interests (1990: 518, 523).[3] According to this theory, a government is likely to make reparations only at a time and in a manner that furthers society's dominant interests. Those interests are furthered by preserving existing power structures during times of stress. "Rights" are conferred as "safety valves" to relieve accumulating pressure for fundamental structural changes (Delgado 1987; Gordon 1982: 286).

Does the interest-convergence theory illuminate aspects of redress and reparations? At a minimum, the theory casts an interesting light on certain events and people and raises poignant questions.[4] In most situations, even when a strong moral case is made for reparations, the government opposes them.[5] Stated practical reasons include inordinate cost and the impossibility of redressing all historical transgressions against all groups: "if we do it for one group we've got to do it for all, and we can't afford that." Stated legal reasons for government opposition to reparations include the existence of circumstances justifying the transgression, the difficulty of identifying perpetrator and victim groups, the lack of sufficient connection between past wrong and present claim, and the difficulty of calculating damages (Matsuda 1987: 373-74). Indeed, the Reagan administration for a long time opposed reparations to WW II Japanese-American internees ostensibly for these practical and legal reasons, and vigorously if not bitterly fought to dismiss the reopened *Korematsu* case.

So why did President Reagan and candidate Bush later acquiesce to reparations legislation? Explanations abound. None involve a desire to restructure government power. One explanation is that their tepid and belated support was an attempt to temper the anti-civil rights aura of ultraconservative Republicans in order to attract moderate voters.[6] An explanation for broader governmental support is that, domestically, in the context of increasingly volatile minority group criticisms about continuing disenfranchisement, reparations afforded decision makers an opportunity to point to a model minority that survived and flourished despite hardship, conveying the message that the system works, things historically wrong are made right, and things now are fine. Internationally, reparations enabled decision makers to enhance somewhat the United States' image as a country committed to human rights, bolstering an ostensible moral foundation for military incursions abroad, for mediation of Middle East conflicts, and for continuing struggle with the former Soviet Union.

From these simplified generalizations emerges a specific question: has reparations resulted in a reshaping of the amorphous structure of government military and national security power over citizens that led to the imprisonment of innocent Americans on the basis of their race? If the interest convergence theory is accurate, the answer is probably "very little." If very little restructuring of institutional power has occurred, then reparations may have unforeseen ill-effects for Japanese Americans and all minorities. The criticism is not that reparations are insignificant for recipients. The criticism is that they can lead to an "adjustment of individual attitudes" towards the historical injustice of the internment without giving current "consideration to the fundamental realities of power" (Edmonds 1991; Peller 1985). The "danger lies in the possibility of enabling people to 'feel good' about each other" for the moment "while leaving undisturbed the attendant social realities" creating the underlying conflict (Edmonds 1991: 15).[7] According to this view, redress and reparations could in the long run "unwittingly be seduced into becoming one more means of social control that attempts to neutralize the need to strive for justice" (Edmonds 1991; Delgado 1987).

It is therefore important to ask: has reparations fundamentally altered the structure of governmental relations with minorities, especially in the context of military and national security matters, or has it enabled society to feel better about itself without addressing issues of domination and oppression, power and injustice?

Consider the following: In 1991, during the Gulf War, the FBI undertook an aggressive campaign of interrogation of Iraqi Americans in the U.S., implying by manner and style a presumption of disloyalty by reason of race. In several recent cases, the United States Supreme Court affirmed the government's power to restrict or suspend completely the civil rights of citizens in the interest of national security, without any showing of necessity. Those cases involved discrimination against gays, women, political speakers, and assertedly subversive citizens seeking to travel abroad.[8] The Court's value judgments in those cases, and its deference to unsubstantiated government assertions of necessity, resemble the Court's disastrous approach in *Korematsu* in 1944.

The danger of that approach—the "distortion of the Constitution" in the interest of expediency, according to former Justice Jackson—is illustrated by President Bush's 1989 proposed executive order concerning uniform security clearance procedures for people working with or for the government. The proposed order denied due process rights for citizens in many instances. It also authorized revocation of the procedural safeguards that did exist whenever an agency head perceived the safeguards to be "inconsistent with national security interests of the United States" (Yamamoto 1986: 30-41; Dycus et al 1990).[9]

Consider also the following, which specifically concerns the structure of governmental relations with Asians in the United States in the context of national security matters: In 1988, the U.S. Coast Guard embarked on a program of selective enforcement of a prohibition against noncitizen offshore fishermen. The Coast Guard, which never before had enforced the 100-year old prohibition, targeted only permanent resident Vietnamese fishermen. The Coast Guard targeted those refugee fishermen only after fielding complaints from competing American fishermen. The Coast Guard justified its selective enforcement policy on national security grounds. The Vietnamese fishermen, however, were not representing foreign fishing fleets and, as permanent residents, were eligible to serve in the United States armed services and even the Coast Guard. As in the *Korematsu* case, the government offered no evidence of any threat to national security.

When the U.S. Ninth Circuit Court of Appeals heard the Vietnamese fishermen's legal challenge, Judge Noonan observed that the government's position on national security "would open the way for placing aliens 'in concentration camps' and making citizenship a condition of release" ("Case Against the U.S. Coast Guard" 1991: 2).

In 1990, Marine officer candidate Bruce Yamashita leveled charges of continuing racism against Japanese Americans in the armed services. Specifically Yamashita charged, and has since supported with independent witness testimony, that Marine training officers directly violated Marine nondiscrimination regulations. They subjected Yamashita to constant racial taunting and ultimately dismissed him from the program under the pretext of "lack of leadership." The initial perfunctory internal investigation found no violation ("Bruce Yamashita's Story" 1991: 4-5).

In 1990, the amended Immigration Act responded in part to the perception that "Asian and Latinos have 'overused' the preference system to the detriment of Europeans and others" ("Congress Passes New Immigration Law" 1991: 4). One of the amended act's apparent goals was to preserve the racial "balance" in the United States by excluding Asians, who altogether comprised 3% of the United States population. Support for the amendment eerily resembled cries of "yellow peril" in the early 1900s in Hawai'i and California—the Asian threat to the country's culture and security—which led then to Asian exclusion legislation (Congressional Commission 1983: 28-36).

This greatly simplified description of events, of course, paints an incomplete picture. It nevertheless lends general support to the critical view that reparations for WW II Japanese-American internees has not necessarily entailed a fundamental restructuring of governmental relations with Asian Americans particularly, or with minorities generally, especially concerning governmental exercises of national security power.

LESSONS FOR THE FUTURE

We now return to the question initially posed. What early lessons about restructuring for freedom might be learned from redress and reparations for WW II Japanese-American internees? I have outlined in simplified fashion salutary views, some perhaps overly bright, and critical views, some perhaps overly dark. Both have some legitimacy. Both point to societal benefit and to hidden danger.

It is not enough, however, to say that people differ, that their situations differ, and that understandably observer viewpoints differ. In looking forward we must ask: what lessons might we draw from reparations for Japanese Americans to transcend these colliding views, to realistically enhance future efforts at restructuring public and private institutions, and to change societal attitudes to assure citizens freedom from governmental abuses of power?

If government, mainstream America, and Asian Americans choose to embrace only the salutary views of reparations, then little fundamental change will occur in the structure, operation, and output of policy-making bodies, bureaucracies, and businesses. Reparations may come to mean part redress for human rights violations and part buy-out—remedying harm for specific past injuries for some while perpetuating the military and national security power structures and societal attitudes that gave rise to those group-based injuries.

But reparations may come to mean something different domestically and internationally if Asian Americans critically self-assess their model minority status, vowing not to be used (Matsuda 1990: 7); if they and others scrutinize and challenge government exercises of national security power that restrict civil liberties, especially the freedoms of minorities; if they along with others challenge power structures and attitudes fostering continuing discrimination against racial and religious minorities, women, gays, and the handicapped in the United States; and if they activate political organizations and employ lobbying, media, and legal skills developed during the reparations drive to join in addressing broad-based problems affecting all minorities in the United States and, to some extent, throughout the world. The politicization of former internees and larger segments of the public, the development of organizations for political education and action, and the creation of interethnic group links are salient aspects of the recently completed reparations process. They hold promise beyond the particular Japanese-American WW II internees' reparations effort. They hold potential for reassessing values, reaffirming political commitments, and pushing for reallocation of decisional power not only in legislatures, courts, and bureaucracies, but also in schools, workplaces, and homes.

A principal early lesson therefore is that redress and reparations by government should result over time in a restructuring of the institutions and relationships that gave rise to the human rights violation. Otherwise, as a philosophical and practical matter, a reparations program cannot be (a) effective in addressing root problems of government power abuse and citizen freedom, (b) offered as a meaningful model for other countries concerned about justice in redressing past wrongs committed against their own citizens, or (c) integrated into a country's moral foundation for urging or demanding other countries to restructure for freedom.

A second lesson is that restructuring those institutions and changing societal attitudes will not flow naturally and inevitably from a government reparations program for a particular group. Government and dominant private interests, it appears, will cast redress and reparations in ways that tend to perpetuate existing power structures and dominant group/minority group relationships. Those benefiting from reparations must draw upon the political insights and commitments derived from their particular reparation process and join with others to push for bureaucratic, legal, and attitudinal restructuring. Their efforts must extend beyond reparations.

Whether Asian Americans collectively will participate in that restructuring, whether they will choose a path connecting Asian Americans with others, or whether they will choose the separatist path of a seemingly now-healed model minority, are open questions. Of course, Asian Americans are not a singular, homogeneous group. Several paths will likely be followed. But will one path predominate in the hearts and minds of Asian Americans and in the perceptions of other minorities, of government decision makers, of mainstream America? No clear answer has emerged.

Yet consider the following: The permanent resident Vietnamese fisherman selectively prohibited from offshore fishing by the U.S. Coast Guard ostensibly for national security reasons recently achieved a Congressional repeal of the underlying 100-year-old statute. They did so through strong lobbying by and support from political and legal networks developed during the Japanese-American reparations process. These broad networks also endeavored to reveal and challenge the anti-Asian "yellow peril" premises of the Immigration Act of 1990. They spoke out against the FBI interrogation program launched against Iraqi-Americans during the Gulf War. They intervened in the Yamashita Marine racial harassment case, coordinating protests that resulted in the reopening and publicizing of the military investigation. They joined in protest of the President's proposed, and later withdrawn, security clearance executive order. They also helped explain to local prosecutors the racial underpinnings of anti-Asian violence, resulting recently in criminal trials and public understandings markedly different from those connected with Vincent Chin's murder a few years earlier.

On a broader scale, Asian-American groups joined with the NAACP and other minority groups to push for the Civil Rights Acts of 1990 and 1991 to counteract the effects of recent Supreme Court decisions. They also joined in the efforts of African-American leaders to mediate increasingly intense neighborhood conflicts between Asian immigrants and African Americans. They are lending support to Native Hawaiian reparation efforts.

These efforts, of course, do not mean that Asian Americans collectively have chosen one path over the other. They do indicate, however, that the political organizations, insights, and commitments derived from the process of struggling for redress and reparations have not withered. They hint at an evolving social value of reparations with potential for transcending colliding salutary and critical views— a meaning of some promise for continuing the struggle toward restructuring for peace with freedom.

NOTES

AUTHOR'S NOTE: My thanks to Edie Feldman and Cathy Takase for their assistance.

1. Pub. L. No. 100-383 (1988) authorizes a $20,000 payment to each surviving former internee.

2. The history of the Japanese-American redress and reparations movement is well documented.

3. The "principle of 'interest convergence' provides: The interest of blacks in achieving racial equality will be accommodated only when it converges with the interests of whites." As an example, Bell observes that *Brown v. Board of Education's* rejection of the separate-but-equal doctrine served U.S. interests internationally by enabling the U.S. to claim the moral high ground in its Cold War against communism. Racial remedies may be the "outward manifestations of unspoken and perhaps subconscious judicial conclusions that the remedies, if granted, will secure, advance, or at least not harm societal interests deemed important by middle and upper class whites."

4. "Some thoughtful victim group members are inclined to reject reparations because of the political reality that any reparations award will come only when those in power decide it is appropriate" (Matsuda 1987: 396).

5. See, for example, the Native Hawaiian Study Commission Minority Report (1986). The majority report by Republican-appointed commissioners found reparations unwarranted.

6. Some might say that President Bush revealed his true colors after the election. He then unsuccessfully attempted to scuttle funding for reparations payments.

8. Edmonds discusses the limitations of the multicultural conflict resolution concept of "bias reduction."

8. The cases of interest are *Webster v. Doe*, 486 U.S. 592 (1988) (gays); *Rostker v. Goldberg*, 453 U.S. 57 (1981) (women); *United States v. Albertini*, 105 S. Ct. 2987 (1985) (political speakers); and *Regan v. Wald*, 104 S. Ct. 3026 (1984) (citizen travelers).

9. Yamamoto 1986: 30-41 compares value judgments underlying the Supreme Court's approaches to national security restrictions of civil liberties.

REFERENCES

Bell, Derek. 1990. "Brown v. Board of Education and the Interest Convergence Dilemma." *Harvard Law Review* 93, no. 3 (January): 518-34.

"Bruce Yamashita's Story Could Be About All Asian Americans." 1991. *Leading the Way* [Newsletter of the Honolulu Chapter, Japanese-American Citizens League] 1, no. 1 (May): 4-5.

"The Case Against the U.S. Coast Guard." 1991. *Asian Law Caucus Reporter* 13, no. 1 (January 9): 2.

"Congress Passes New Immigration Law." 1991. *Asian Law Caucus Reporter* 13, no. 1 (January 9): 4.

Congressional Commission on Wartime Relocation and Internment of Civilians. 1983. "Personal Justice Denied." Report of the Commission. Washington, DC.

Delgado. 1987. "The Ethereal Scholar: Does Critical Legal Studies Have What Minorities Want?" *Harvard Civil Rights and Civil Liberties Law Review* 22: 301-304

Dycus, Stephen, Arthur L. Berney, William C. Banks, and Peter Raven - Hansen. 1990. *National Security Law*. Boston: Little, Brown.

Edmonds. 1991. "Beyond Prejudice Reduction." *MCS Conciliation Quarterly* (Spring).

Gordon, Robert W. 1982. "New Developments in Legal Theory." In *The Politics of Law: A Progressive Critique*. Ed. David Kairys. New York: Pantheon.

Hohri, William Minor. 1988. *Repairing America*. Pullman, WA: Washington State University Press.

Irons, Peter H. 1985. *Justice At War*. New York: Oxford University Press.

_____. 1988. *Justice Delayed*. Middletown, CT: Wesleyan University Press.

Matsuda, Mari. 1987. "Looking to the Bottom: Critical Legal Studies and Reparations." *Harvard Civil Rights and Civil Liberties Law Review* 22: 323-390.

_____. 1990. "We Shall Not Be Used." *Asian Law Caucus Reporter* 12, no. 1 (July).

Peller, Gary. 1985. "The Politics of Reconstruction." *Harvard Law Review* 98, no. 4 (February): 863-81.

Yamamoto, Eric. 1986. "Korematsu Revisited: Correcting the Injustice of Extraordinary Government Excess and Lax Judicial Review: Time for a Better Accommodation of National Security Concerns and Civil Liberties." *Santa Clara Law Review* 26, no. 1 (Winter): 1-62.

Part III

Peace With Justice

13

Peace and Development in the Post-Cold War Era

BJÖRN HETTNE

A NEW WORLD ORDER

The Gulf War was waged in and contributed to an emerging international context often referred to as a "new world order." It is true that the world will never be the same after this brief but extremely destructive war, but to what extent is the concept of world order applicable to this new situation? What is in it for the Third World? What is meant by the concept of world order in the first place?

In international political economy (IPE) theory, world order usually refers to that international political arrangement that provides the necessary framework for transactions in the world economy. More recently the concept has been used as a political propaganda phrase, either by Washington with reference to the post-Cold War era and in particular to the enlarged role of the UN and the U.S. in that era, or more ironically, with reference to the new role of military violence as a means of solving political problems, and particularly to the mess this method has led to in the Middle East.

In the Third World the concept is contrasted to that of the New International Economic Order so much discussed in the 1970s. This never implemented and now probably nonimplementable world order expressed the Third World preference for authoritative, as opposed to more market-oriented, modes of allocation (Krasner 1985). The implication is that the Third World has lost whatever room for maneuvering it might have possessed. The special message to emerging regional powers, particularly those with nuclear plans, is that their ambitions could be frustrated in a "surgical" hi-tech war. Radical Third World regimes will find it hard to survive the new order.

It is difficult to assess the Third World opinion about the Gulf War, but it is crystal clear that nowhere could the euphoria manifested in the U.S. be found ("Asia Asks: War for Whom" 1991; Rake 1991). A general pattern, particularly in Muslim countries, is that the governments reluctantly supported the war, while their people demonstrated against the West. Typical examples are Pakistan and Bangladesh in Asia, and Mali and Nigeria in Africa. Thus, the meaning of "new world order" is a matter of perspective.

In this chapter I shall stick to the stricter use of the term in international political economy as the political structure of the international economic system, which in principle could be unipolar, bipolar, or multipolar. The "new world order" debate implies a unipolar structure, a conclusion which may be rash.

Despite current U.S. military dominance, there are (basically economic) indications that, with the ending of the Cold War, a more multipolar world is taking shape, facilitating the development of a new kind of regionalism as a possible structural pattern of a new world order. It is my argument that this process has been triggered by the European integration process, and that Europe both serves as a positive example for offensive regionalism and as a threat leading to a defensive regionalism in other areas. This will first take the form of protective trading blocs, but in a longer perspective a new regionalism may emerge, based on multidimensional cooperation and even constituting embryonic regional states.

This new structure would also include the Third World, where regionalism seems to be on the rise, although very unevenly and rather embryonically in comparison with Europe. However, there is in the post-Cold War order a new freedom to act and no really important external constraints for the "new regionalism." The problems are rather specific to each region: economic problems, regional hegemonism creating suspicions among states, national conflicts, and ethnic rebellions influencing regional security systems. The regions of the world have not become more peaceful in the post-Cold War era; rather some old problems frozen in the Cold War complex are emerging.

The "new regionalism" may in fact provide solutions to many of these problems:

1. collective self-reliance, which was never viable on the national level for most countries, but may be a feasible development strategy on the regional level;
2. collective bargaining, which on the regional level could improve the economic position of Third World countries in the world-system;
3. collective strength, which could make it easier to resist political and strategic pressures from the North;

4. certain conflicts between states, which could be more easily solved within an appropriate regional framework without being distorted by old Cold War considerations; and

5. ethnic conflicts—the way states commonly deal with these issues, which often spill over into neighboring countries and are seen as threats to national security, is normally the most certain way of making them permanent; therefore a regional solution is often the only realistic option.

But are there existing or emerging world regions to fill an emerging power vacuum, or will an eventual trend towards multipolarism lead to an intensification of anarchic conditions? A political transformation of dormant world regions into acting subjects also implies substantial changes within the regions.

One essential precondition for the process of regionalism from below to gain momentum is increased political and economic homogenization among the countries of a particular region. In the present global context this homogenization would imply market rule and further democratization. After Latin America the time has now come for Africa.

In the formation of regions the security imperative, both in its negative and positive impacts, is of particular importance. In a "regional security complex" (Deutsch 1957), the national securities of the involved states are interwoven (Buzan 1983) for better or worse, mostly the latter. This is the negative imperative. To the conventional dimensions of security should be added ecological regional security complexes, for instance, hydropolitical complexes (Ohlsson 1991). The problem of water scarcity is now seen as one of the major conflict-generating issues of the 1990s, but it could also be seen as an important imperative for regional cooperation and as an impetus for development towards a "mature" security complex or a security community.

By definition institutional development in a regional security complex has eliminated even the thought of force as a means of conflict resolution. Perceptions of threats are homogenized and externalized. Thus, in order to be a factor for peace, the regional organization should coincide with the security complex as a whole, not just with a particular subcomplex (which may even need interregional conflict to maintain its own coherence). Furthermore, the regional organization should provide some balance to the local great power so that it does not become an instrument of exploitation and control.

The positive and negative aspects of the security imperative thus operate simultaneously, as integration within a region can be both positively related to cohesive factors within the region and negatively related to threats outside the region. If integration is defined by its predominantly voluntary character (Haas 1970), it cannot be caused by coercive factors within the region, since that would imply empire building rather than regional integration. This again underlines the need for a certain balance of power and a reduction of threat factors within the region.

The history of regional integration after World War II shows many disparate and conflicting impulses at work. In the first wave, regional cooperation was largely hegemonically superimposed within the context of the Cold War. Gradually regionalism became a force propelled mainly by internal factors (Väyrynen 1984). This internal dynamic is the most important precondition. However, regional formations necessarily operate in the context of a global system, and thus one cannot be understood without the other. In particular it is important to note the impact of European unification on world order.

THE ROLE OF EUROPE

What will be the European role in other regions? Will it be a new aggressive hegemonic superpower or a Fortress Europe closing its doors to the Third World? Or will it become a responsible actor organizing massive transfers of resources, as argued in the Brandt commission reports (Brandt 1986)?

It is true that the EC, or rather its commission, is spreading the gospel of regional integration over the globe, but Europe's role will have to change substantially if a new, better, and more symmetrical interregional exchange pattern is to take form. Not only must the content of the interregional relations between Europe or subregions within Europe, on the one hand, and various Third World regions, on the other, change, but Europe must also take a more active part in promoting regional cooperation and integration in the Third World. The regional dialogue carried out by the EC is explicitly intended to stimulate regionalism in the Third World. The rationale behind this dialogue comes out clearly in the following statement by Roy Jenkins: "From the formation of ASEAN we in the Community have always sought to treat ASEAN as a region since we from our own experience have learnt that an external stimulus can often support internal cooperation" (Edwards and Regelsberger 1990: 151). However, as long as the world order remained hegemonic the whole exercise was symbolic.

In a posthegemonic world order, on the other hand, the Cold War pattern of cultivating friendly regimes and intensifying and creating divisions within different regions could be replaced by a more forceful policy of promoting resolutions of indigenous and region-specific conflicts on the regional level, and stimulating regional cooperation through region-based development programs.

Looking Back

One must conclude that, on the whole, the role of Europe in promoting regional cooperation in the Third World has left much to be desired.

—In Asia, regional groupings tend to reflect the East-West division. ASEAN is one case in which the EC regional dialogue has played a role, and it is even cited as a "success story."

—In Africa, the division along lines of allegiance to one superpower or another has been a major obstacle to continental unity.

—In the Middle East, Europe has failed to take a distinct, constructive role. The EC-Arab dialogue has so far led to little.

—In Latin America, the European presence increased substantially through the 1970s, which raised Latin American expectations for a diversification of the continent's external relationship away from dependence on the United States. However, Western Europe so far has failed to develop a political strategy in its relationship with Latin America; and Eastern Europe no longer has a Third World policy.

Looking to the Future

The external effect of the process of Europeanization differs depending on alternative "domestic" developments. Consider the following scenarios.

The European Superstate scenario views Europe as an extroverted regional state, inspired by a mixture of liberalism and some elements of mercantilism, as well as social democracy nurtured by the moderate left. Internally it will be organized in the form of concentric circles, with a core, semiperiphery, and periphery. Externally the new superstate centered on the core will aspire to a hegemonic position, or at least a shared, trilateral hegemony. This means that Europe should take a more active role as a world police force, relying on its own security/coercive structure. It will cultivate selective relations with the more dynamic parts of the Third World, such as the emerging regional powers. It will also continue to provide some development assistance within the Lomé framework.

The Neo-Atlanticist scenario perceives Europe as a more open trading system consisting of sovereign nation-states protected by a modified Atlantic security system: NATO with a European leg. The economic inspiration for this scenario comes from neoliberalism, the dominant development ideology of the 1980s, particularly in its British "new right" form, and in Reaganism, combining a belief in market miracles with jingoist nationalism. The Gulf War (or Anglo-Iraq War) was a revival of this project after a decline beginning in 1989. The major international contradiction according to this worldview is "Euro-America" vs. "Islamistan." This Europe will create an unstable situation, which sooner or later will transform itself into one of the other scenarios, depending on which social forces emerge in which countries.

The European Home scenario views Europe as an introverted regional state in a world of regional blocs, and as a neomercantilist state inspired largely by the values of left-liberal, social democratic, and Euro-communist welfare ideologies. It thus includes an element of interventionism as well as supportive links to poor Third World regions. Such links would primarily promote collective self-reliance, such as the so-called Nordic initiative towards the Southern African Development Consideration Conference (SADCC).

The Greening of Europe scenario envisions Europe as a loose, undefined, informal structure of regions and local communities within a world order of similar decentralized structures characterized by "third system politics." The role of the state would be drastically reduced in this rather anarchistic scenario, which judging from recent elections and polls has lost some of its attraction.

The Orwellian scenario of Fortress Europe perceives Europe as a regional security state, inspired by autarchic mercantilism, in latent or manifest conflict with other regional systems. A European fortress will build fences against a "thirdworldized" Europe and a possible "great march" from a marginalized Third World. There will be increasing pressure from migration from the poor parts of the Third World, further enforcing the trend towards Fortress Europe. Many European newspapers have concluded that the drama of the Albanian refugees in Italy could be a mere foretaste of the future. I call this scenario Orwellian, because of its similarity to Orwell's future world in 1984. It is a darker conception of "Fortress Europe" than simply increased protectionism, although a connection is often made.

A North-South structure is now emerging within Europe. This undoubtedly means that the importance of the Third World will diminish in economic as well as political terms, to some extent depending on social and political forces within Europe. In this context I am referring to the European Community and European Free Trade Association (EFTA). As far as the Third World is concerned, the former Eastern Europe has disappeared as an actor. Evidently the EC will take note of human rights records in dealing with individual developing countries, namely the 68 Africa-Caribbean-Pacific (ACP) countries. Environmental concerns will play an increasing role. Further obstacles are created by the EC's antidumping policies. Reciprocity will be a key issue in EC trade policy ("Business Barometer" 1990). In the immediate future at least, poor Third World countries will have to rely more on their own resources. EFTA contains a core of like-minded countries with a tradition of generous assistance, but EFTA is rapidly harmonizing Euro-South relations to EC standards. One obvious response to this emerging situation is Third World regionalism: South-South cooperation and collective self-reliance.

THE ROLE OF THE EX-SUPERPOWERS

Based on its more multidimensional hegemonic power, the U.S. has provided the general rules for the world economy. These rules are summed up in what is usually referred to as the Bretton Woods system, which has constituted the framework for economic interdependence for the last couple of decades. Consequently, a decline in U.S. hegemonic power seems to imply a world governance crisis, for instance, in the form of nationalist and protectionist policies, challenging the existing rules of the game and fragmenting the world economy (Gilpin 1987; Keohane 1980, 1984; Kennedy 1987)

The U.S. and Soviet hegemonies were altogether different species: liberal vs. imperial. Soviet hegemony rested on the ideological primacy of the Communist Party of the Soviet Union within the socialist world system, but this primacy was backed by the militarized Soviet state. That situation was more akin to the old type of imperial dominance, and in fact there was a striking continuity between the czarist empire and the now-dissolved bolshevik state. Although described as a "socialist federation" which included the right to secession, there was no procedure for how this could be realized, simply because it was not meant to happen. Nevertheless it ultimately did.

The Emergence of NAFTA

The thesis of U.S. decline has been questioned by quite a few observers, from different perspectives (Huntington 1988; Strange 1988; Russet 1985). The concept as such is complex and multidimensional and opinions are therefore bound to differ. The Gulf crisis in 1990 and the subsequent war in 1991 certainly demonstrated that the U.S. is the only state with a global military reach, but they also showed the financial difficulty of sustaining such power, raising the problem of imperial overstretch. Quite apart from the costs of running the Iraq war (which have been more than recovered), the U.S. is a debtor country with both social problems and a degenerating infrastructure.

The cracks in the alliance behind the UN military action in the Gulf, and particularly in the messy aftermath of the war, illustrate the limitations of U.S. ideological leadership. Neither Japan nor Germany felt the military action was really necessary, and both had reason to suspect that U.S. dominance in the Middle East also implied dominance over them, in view of their oil dependence. France at times acted against the U.S. strategy, but remained isolated in the European context. A lot of rethinking is going on in Europe regarding a common security policy, ultimately leading to European military cooperation. The Grand Alliance with the U.S. as undisputed leader is thus explained by unique political circumstances, and not likely to be repeated.

Similarly, the opinion in the U.S., as has happened before, is split between isolationists and globalists. The latter argue in favor of a unipolar world with the U.S. unilaterally imposing solutions consistent with its "national interest" to various regional conflicts (Krauthammer 1991). For the isolationists the prospect of a North America region consisting of the U.S., Canada, and possibly Mexico (NAFTA) would be a proper response to a European fortress. The U.S.-Canadian free trade pact was signed in January 1989, and formal U.S.-Mexican negotiations were started in the summer of 1991 under protests from various lobbies: in the U.S., textile unions; in Mexico, the traditionally anti-U.S. left ("Mexico and Central America" 1991a). In spite of assurances that NAFTA will be "consistent with the GATT, the new fortress in the making is already creating concern in East and South East Asia" ("Enter the Latin Dragon" 1991: 43) As a bloc, however, it will be weak due to internal heterogeneity, indebtedness, and reliance on the dollar. Rather the strategy is to negotiate a fair deal with the other blocs, to intermediate between them, or combine with one of them against the other.

The Soviet Region: An Eastern EC?

Homo Sovieticus is a disappearing species. Instead there are emerging nations. In order to avoid economic fragmentation and political tensions, they will have to sort out their relations within some kind of regional framework. As in Europe, there needs to be a balance between one major regional power and smaller subregional groupings. Therefore, in the future, we will perhaps look upon the former Soviet Union as an Eastern EC. Devolving substantial authority from the center to the republics and regions seems to be the only way to save some kind of federation or confederation (Kux 1990). This method may not necessarily succeed, but then there is no solution apart from war. The confusing negotiations about the new union contributed to the failed coup in August 1991, and this in turn paved the way for a confederative solution, a loose grouping of sovereign republics.

There is nevertheless a great likelihood that what already has happened to the external empire will now happen to the internal. Countries of the external empire will presumably escape the region by "de-easternization" and consequently join the more wealthy "Western EC," but for most countries in the internal empire, a poorer Eastern version of the EC is the best they can hope for. Economic nationalism on the level of the fifteen republics would be a catastrophe for most of them. Direct trade relations among individual republics must therefore be a cornerstone in the structural reform and "renewal" of the federation.

A loose economic commonwealth based on political decentralization would be an obvious solution. The EC in fact is explicitly used in the internal reform debate as a model to copy. Obviously the Eastern EC will become more introverted, like an expanded Western EC, and in the long run the two will probably form part of a larger, more or less spontaneous integration process. Europe will ultimately become a "house" if not a "fortress," but either way a solution must be found to the increasing instability within the former Soviet region. Moscow may learn to prefer friendly neighbors to restive republics, and the smaller countries must somehow come to terms with geopolitical realities and a highly interdependent economy. There are strong reasons to find a better balance between function and territory, but provincial autarky is no option. The somewhat utopian project is to build a new union, based on new foundations, one of them being a functioning civil society.

REGIONALISM IN THE THIRD WORLD

Regional integration outside Europe has not been a great success so far. Two reasons are evident:

1. The structure of the world economy, under hegemonic control, has tended towards interdependence rather than regionalization; and

2. The common-market concept of regional cooperation, in a situation of asymmetry, has reintroduced the global hierarchy of dependency relations in the regions.

A positive turn for a different sort of regional cooperation in the Third World is therefore overdue. The trend until recently has been increasing regional conflicts accompanied by regional arms races: the Horn of Africa, Southern Africa, Central America, and of course the Middle East. Often these conflicts have been related to more or less aggressive plans of local influentials, the regional great powers: for instance, Iran, Iraq, India, Vietnam, Brazil, and South Africa.

Many regional cooperative arrangements have been partly caused by conflicts in the regions, and thus do not reflect an emerging regional identity, but rather the persistence of regional divisions. ASEAN was in fact a response to the communist threat from former Indochina; SADCC was a collective protection from South African destabilization; and SAARC (South Asian Association for Regional Cooperation) was an effort by the smaller states to balance the dominance of India. Other arrangements were destroyed by internal conflicts, such as the attempts to create common markets in East Africa, Central America, and the Caribbean. The West African experiment ECOWAS was hampered by the asymmetric relations between the Nigerian giant and the many small economies worrying about their national autonomy.

Latin America: Defensive Regionalism

At present, Latin America is becoming marginalized, or as some would say, "Africanized," in the world economy. Its crisis is both a debt and development crisis (Griffith-Jones and Sunkel 1986). The disappearance of the socialist alternative means that Latin America will become even more dependent on the U.S., and will be even more arrogantly treated. Not only is the Soviet counterweight evaporating, but also the European (Castaneda 1990). As shown by the recent U.S. intervention in Panama, the end of the Cold War will not change the pattern of dominance, merely the pretexts for intervention.

Some even argue for a Fortress America as the best scenario Latin America can hope for. Mexico, which had some potential for becoming a regional power (Hettne and Sterner 1988), now seems to have concluded that joining North America is the only possible way out of stagnation. There are signals that Mexico is abandoning the Third World concept, so important for some of its previous presidents ("Mexico and Central America" 1991b). Thus Central America is tilting north. To the extent that they are not already part of North America, the smaller Central American states will have little choice but to follow Mexico's example.

Central America has strong incentives for regional cooperation, and the change of regime in Nicaragua has increased the political homogeneity of the region. The crucial issue is whether the small countries can develop a common approach to the emerging U.S.-Canada-Mexico bloc, or whether they will join this bloc as individual client states.

The economic and geopolitical change in northern Latin America puts a certain pressure on the Southern Cone. The treaty signed by Argentina and Brazil in 1985 put fresh life into the integration process in the region. In March 1991 a free-trade agreement was signed between those two countries and Uruguay and Paraguay (MERCOSUL). This new kind of cooperation, designed to prevent further marginalization of Latin America in the world economy, is modelled on the EC. MERCOSUL will enable free circulation of goods, services, capital, and labor. It will gradually reduce custom tariffs and other barriers in the member countries. These countries will also coordinate certain aspects of macroeconomic and foreign currency policy, as well as their economic relations with third countries. The treaty is open to other Latin American countries. For instance, Chile, at present vacillating between North and South, is expected to join, as is Bolivia. The comparative strength of the new organization is that it will only contain members committed to the integration project. It is thus a case of regionalism from below.

In Latin America, the Argentina-Brazil rapprochement is one of the factors stimulating the discussion of a new concept of regional security: Seguridad Democratica Regional. This is a major geopolitical change. It is significant that Brazil, the alleged regional bully, is taking a rather low profile, thus preventing the traditional concern with regional hegemonism. This in turn has made it possible to initiate a disarmament process and provide a much needed peace dividend.

The Caribbean: A Case of Microregionalism

The Caribbean region has a 500-year relationship with Europe, which formed and continues to form it as a region (Thomas 1988). Earlier attempts at regional cooperation occurred in a colonial context, one reason for its failure. The Caribbean Free Trade Association (CARIFTA) arrangement of 1968 was a minimal form of integration, since its principal integration mechanism was the phased freeing of interregional trade. It was replaced in 1973 by the more ambitious Caribbean Community (CARICOM), which had from the start an explicit political element, namely, coordination of foreign policy. This idea seems to have grown out of experiences of negotiating with the EC (Thomas 1988: 317). There were statements condemning destabilization and criticism of the CBI, but after the invasion of Grenada controversial foreign policy issues have been avoided.

CARICOM has 13 regional members but fewer than 6 million people. The European market provides the incentive both for a more integrated market and for enlargement. There are 32 million people in the greater Caribbean. Still this remains a case of microregionalism, and there are great fears that the Caribbean could be marginalized in a world of large trading blocs. In the Caribbean, the privileged treatment of some countries in a position to play the geopolitical card will disappear. They will have to cooperate regionally while competing internationally. Regionalism of course cannot be the sole approach.

South Asia: Shared Civilization—Conflicting States

In South Asia, world powers such as the U.S., the Soviet Union, and China promoted their interests by forging alliances with local states. The region is internally dominated by one regional power, although Pakistan and India had a kind of competitive relationship before the splitting up of Pakistan in 1971. Since then India has been predominant, but without the luxury of a very secure position, while Pakistan, with the help of foreign aid, has become increasingly militarized and possibly possesses an "Islamic bomb."

The division of Pakistan further destabilized the region, transforming it into an arena of superpower competition, as a weakened Pakistan received support from both China and the U.S., while India entered into a treaty with the Soviet Union. As a culture and civilization with a special capacity for diversity and contradiction, India was and still is a giant. The problem of regional hegemonization is thus present.

Size is not always a source of power. The process of modernization in India creates more problems than it solves. The resulting conflicts are a great strain on India as a centralized nation-state, in contradistinction to India as a decentralized civilization. In the former sense India may not survive in its present state, since the internal forces of disintegration are now tremendous and the dominant political trend is Hindu chauvinism. The domestic situations in Pakistan and Sri Lanka also reveal similar weaknesses in national integration, while the ethnically more homogeneous Bangladesh suffers from general economic and political decay. These ominous trends are bound to have security implications both regionally and for the political systems concerned (Hettne 1988).

Thus, the security situation in South Asia cannot be understood without careful consideration of the ethnic, regional, and religious conflicts within the states and the way these affect interstate relations. Given India's geopolitical dominance, ethnic strife, secession, and disintegration could be the main vehicles for changes in the interstate system. Over the years the security situation has grown more and more complicated (Buzan and Rizvi 1986). India's position is strengthened by the growing regional disorder, but this also means a high risk of external penetration. Regional cooperation would mean a change for the better, at least as far as economic security is concerned. But the economic rationale is not overwhelming at present; it has to be created (Adiseshiah 1987).

The traumatic India-Pakistan conflict until recently prevented all efforts towards regionalism. Furthermore, after the assassination of Sheik Mujibur Rahman in 1975, Bangladesh's relations with India were characterized by distrust and hostility (Rahman 1985). However, in 1985, after five years of preparation, South Asia at last got its own organization, SAARC. The initiative originated from Bangladesh, and India was rather lukewarm, but the smaller countries strongly felt the need for it (Mishra 1984; Muni 1985). Thus, regional cooperation has been initiated as a counterforce to regional hegemonism.

It is both a strength and a weakness that SAARC is made up of all the South Asian states: India, Pakistan, Bangladesh, Sri Lanka, Bhutan, Nepal, and the Maldives. It is a weakness because the conflicts in the region will paralyze SAARC for a long time to come, confining its scope to noncontroversial marginal issues such as tourism and meteorology. It is a strength precisely because controversial problems can be handled within one organization and because at least a framework for regional conflict resolution has been created. Put differently, the regional organization coincides with the regional security complex and can be seen as an embryo of a security community.

If the internal power structure becomes more balanced by a weakening of Delhi and by greater political autonomy for the regions of India, there may also be a trend toward political homogenization in the form of democratic openings in Pakistan, Bangladesh, and Nepal. India may also opt for a more open economy due to pressures from the International Monetary Fund (IMF), thus reducing the gap in economic policies between India, with its tradition of import substitution, and the smaller, more extroverted states.

Southeast Asia: Transcending Bloc Politics?

Southeast Asia, like Europe, has been divided into two economic and political blocs: ASEAN (Indonesia, Thailand, Singapore, Malaysia, the Philippines and, since 1984, Brunei) and the Indochinese area (Vietnam, Kampuchea, and Laos). The latter subregion is under communist rule with Vietnam exercising subregional hegemony. Vietnam is also an actor in the East Asian region and can thus be seen as a bridge between the two regional complexes.

Vietnam, and behind it the Soviet Union, has been seen as a threat by the ASEAN countries, which is precisely why ASEAN as a regional organization has worked rather well. The source of common cause and identity is negative, thus it is a case of negative rather than positive peace. As in Europe, the dismantling of the Cold War system will change the pattern of conflict rather than eliminate conflicts. We can expect more relaxation between the two subregions and more conflicts within them.

The countries in ASEAN could be described as economically capitalist and politically conservative. The organization has existed since 1967, but assumed importance as a regional organization only after 1975, reflecting increasing political uncertainties in the region. The economic integration that has taken place so far is rather modest, and intraregional trade accounts for only about 20%. The external dependence on Japan is felt to be problematic.

The national economies are outward-oriented, and the political systems are formally democratic, but in practice more or less authoritarian. Problems on the international market usually reinforce domestic authoritarianism, due to the strong two-way causal relationship between economic growth and political stability. Economic growth and redistribution is a precondition for ethnic peace, and political stability a precondition for international capital to have economic confidence in the region.

However, peace in the larger region, which now seems to be under way, would change the basic parameters of the way ASEAN operates. As the superpowers pull out, old rivalries are emerging at the same time as the objective preconditions are improving for long-range cooperation encompassing the whole region.

East Asia and the Japanese Dilemma

East Asia is the most dynamic of the world regions, containing a hegemonic contender (Japan), an enormous "domestic" market (China), three NICs (South Korea, Taiwan, and Hong Kong), and a socialist autarky (North Korea) preparing itself for major changes which may alter the pattern of cooperation within the region. A reunification of Korea, a democratization of China, and a more independent Japanese role would release enormous potential. These changes will not be immediate, but they are quite feasible.

Korean unification is, of course, the key to regional cooperation. Considering the economic superiority of South Korea and the political lag in North Korea, it will probably be a spontaneous process of the German type—an Anschluss. The timing will be determined by the health of Kim Il Sung.

South Korea and the other NICs face changes in the objective conditions that originally made them NICs, and their strategy in the 1990s will probably involve betting on the domestic market, preferably a regional market. The regional framework is still, however, in flux. South Korea and Taiwan are traditionally dependent on Japan, but may have more to gain by orienting themselves towards Southeast Asia.

The ending of the Cold War opened up new possibilities for intersubregional contacts, widening the potential for regional cooperation.

China will continue the long road towards a more open economy in spite of what seems to be a temporary isolation following the Tiananmen Square killings. In the West the image of China is quickly improving due to China's stand in the Gulf crisis and its willingness to find a peaceful solution to the Cambodian political quagmire. As far as Japan is concerned, the separation of politics from economics has been national policy. Japan therefore took a rather understanding position vis-a-vis Peking.

Perhaps the most complex issue in the region is the future international role of Japan: will it remain number two in Pax Americana or take a more independent global role? The latter and perhaps more likely option would imply the accumulation of military strength and a break with the introverted Japanese worldview. The former course presupposes that the U.S. itself does not turn to isolationism, which would create great confusion as far as Japan is concerned (Tamamoto 1990). The Gulf War tended to speed up developments, as it triggered a minor crisis in U.S.-Japan relations.

Pressure on Japan has also increased due to the regionalist trend in the world economy. Malaysia has invited Japan to act as a leader of an East Asian Economic Grouping (EAEG), which would create an East Asian and Southeast Asian superbloc with a Sino-Japanese core. It would be a response to the European and North American "fortresses" and could very well embrace security matters as well. The idea is very controversial in a region extremely dependent on unhindered world trade, and the debate is carried out largely in terms of an "insurance policy" ("Asia: Trade" 1991: 52).

If this were to be the main trend, Japan, so far rather negative to the idea, would appear as a regional power in more than one sense, which would create suspicions in the region. Some countries hold the Greater East Asian Co-Prosperity Sphere in vivid memory and even today the Japanese attitude towards Asia is not free from arrogance. It has a rather weak identity as an Asian power. This is the Japanese dilemma. Its future path depends on the development of Japanese-U.S. relations, as well as the process of regionalization elsewhere.

Africa: The Post-Apartheid Scenario

In Africa there has been little regional integration, simply because there is so little to integrate. Only 5% of the continent's trade is inter-African. The need is rather for "integrated economic development" on the regional level (Thisen 1989), an element conspicuously lacking in

Africa's Structural Adjustment Programmes ("International Opportunity for Progress" 1991). Regionalism, however, has been a highly politicized issue, which tends to create suspicion in the national centers of decision-making in Africa. Little remains today of Nkrumah's pan-Africanism. Nevertheless, what was then a dream has now become a necessity, and not only for economic reasons. Ethnic conflicts, for instance, cannot be resolved within the nation-state framework, particularly as the unsuccessful nation-building project is in fact the main cause behind these conflicts. Also of importance is the ongoing democratization of Africa, including South Africa, which will increase the political homogeneity of the region and in the long run provide foundations for an African security community. Similarly economic policies are "harmonized" due to the general dependence on the IMF and the World Bank. "A new wind is bringing multi-party democracy" ("Wind of Democracy" 1991: 8). The arguments for the one-party state may have been theoretically right, but in reality they have been a cover for authoritarianism.

At the OAU summit in Abuja it was repeatedly stressed that the ongoing integration of Europe called for a collective response from the member states in the form of an African Economic Community (AEC). The theme of the summit was the threatening marginalization of Africa and regionalism was seen as the remedy. Many initiatives have been taken in this direction, for instance the Lagos Plan of Action in 1980, but undoubtedly the issue now has a special urgency. The implementation of the AEC may take three decades, and the first 5-year period will be devoted to the strengthening of existing regional economic communities.

The most important experience in terms of declared objectives is the SADCC, whose main function originally was to reduce dependence on South Africa, a regional power with evident designs on regional control. Thus, it is a fairly clear example of the "new regionalism," not simply based on the common-market concept, but having wider political objectives. With the elimination of apartheid in South Africa, the agenda for regional cooperation in southern Africa will change fundamentally—and the incentives will perhaps become positive rather than negative. Much depends on the character of a post-apartheid regime, not only for southern Africa but for all sub-Saharan Africa.

The prospects for regional cooperation are beginning to look brighter, partly as a result of the weakening of the nation-states as the dominant political institutions. Even in the case of the troubled ECOWAS, which has been more or less paralyzed by lack of resources, now that the organization has passed its 15th anniversary, there are positive signs of a political homogenization and a somewhat more active regionalism. National repressive regimes are crumbling; the "socialist" experiments are over; and even old "liberal" autocracies such as the Ivory Coast are slowly democratizing. The delinking of the state apparatus from elite interests may lead to strengthening on the regional as well as the local level—the regional because of the development imperative, the local because this is where the democratic forces are. The regional, or in the case of Africa subregional structures, however weak, will play an increasing role in conflict resolution.

In the summer of 1990, in the shadow of the Kuwait crisis, ECOWAS intervened in the Liberian civil war with the explicit purpose of preventing a general massacre of the population. Although not fully backed by the whole region and not highly successful—it led to a division of the country—the operation was unprecedented in the history of African regional cooperation. The shared view was that "the ECOWAS states cannot stand idly by and watch a member state slide into anarchy" ("ECOWAS Summit" 1991: 1075). From now on the more stable regimes within a specific region may feel obliged to interfere through regional institutions in countries heading toward anarchy.

The Maghreb: Peace and Development

In the Maghreb region harsh realities, both in terms of interstate conflicts and social and economic problems, have led to new attempts to stimulate regional integration. In February 1989 the five-country Arab Maghreb Union was created in order to tackle both peace (the Western Sahara conflict) and development (the debt crisis). There is great fear that the traditional European markets will close after 1992. At one stage Morocco even signalled an interest in joining the EC. The aim of the Maghreb Union is to stimulate trade between member states, increase nontraditional exports, and cut imports. The southern European countries are greatly concerned about the stability of Arab North Africa and have developed a Conference on Security and Cooperation in the Mediterranean (CSCM), modeled after the Conference on Security and Cooperation in Europe, but based on an even broader concept of security, including such issues as water scarcity as a security risk. This is significantly different from the U.S.-Middle East paradigm (Hadar 1991).

The Middle East: The Search for a Balance of Power

The Middle East region is in many ways the most complex. Regionalism there is bound to emerge in different manifestations. It covers territories in two geographical continents, Asia and Africa, and while extremely diverse ethnically, it is largely dominated by one religion and one linguistic culture. Therefore it is no coincidence that great ambitions towards regional unity coexist with constant conflicts between states and ethnic groups. Of some importance is the recent, frustrated, yet surviving idea of an Arab Nation, nurtured especially by minorities and politically articulated in Ba'athism. The present political boundaries are quite recent. They were externally imposed by European colonial powers and lack emotional significance, since they have so often been changed in the past. Urban centers such as Cairo, Damascus, Baghdad, and Istanbul have all possessed a regional significance far beyond their present national roles. It is the region of "realist thinking" par preference. The artificial boundaries and the lack of democratic tradition make the power play between heavily armed states as close to Machiavelli's world as one can come. Superpower involvement has followed the same cynical logic. Allies have been sought without the least regard for their domestic records.

The problem of regional hegemonism has a long historical tradition. Several competing major states have a potential for regional leadership or hegemony, but they also have decisive handicaps in performing that particular role. Iraq was the strongest candidate before the war crippled it. Syria and Egypt, the remaining Arab contenders, have become much too involved with the West to be credible. Turkey is an outsider, with ambitions to become a European state. Iran is feared throughout the region as non-Arab and Shi'ite. A recent cooperative agreement between Turkey, Iran, and Pakistan (ECO) is one example of the many possible, but until now short-lived, regional initiatives within this region of diversity.

For obvious economic and strategic reasons, superpower involvement in the region has been deep. During the most recent political crisis, triggered by Iraq's occupation of Kuwait in August 1990, attempts at finding a regional solution—not very realistic anyway—were halted by U.S. intervention, leading to a polarization within the region between conservative and radical currents. As the Soviet Union opted out, the U.S., with the help of frustrated potential regional influentials, established itself in the region. Nobody knows how long this will last, since the threatening breakup of Iraq could be the beginning of a long struggle for regional power in which external interests headed by the U.S. will play a major role. The Gulf crisis meant a backseat for Europe. To restore its image and counter U.S. influence, their strategy now involves a major role for Iran, where anti-U.S. feelings are strongest. Similarly, the intervention of regional influentials such as Egypt, Turkey, and Syria was unpopular among their people, which opens the door for unexpected domestic repercussions. The regional alliance is already breaking up, as the smaller Gulf countries seem to define their security in terms of the presence of the U.S., while the major players have their own schemes.

It is thus very difficult to foresee what a new security system in the Middle East might look like. The so-called peace process initiated in the summer of 1991 gives few clues. Ironically, Saddam Hussein is still needed, since no alternative military government is coming forward to guarantee the fragile balance of power, and what now binds the countries together is the fear of Iraq as the regional hegemonic power. The problems to be solved are many: first, to contain the power and influence of Iran, to find a solution to the Palestinian question, and to reduce the gap between the rich Gulf states and the poor Arab masses. Then there are a host of minority and human rights problems, of which the most urgent is the Kurdish question. A regional democratization wave, such as the one going on in Africa, would be needed to create a more solid civil society on which to base regional initiatives.

CONSTRUCTIVE FRAGMENTATION

Taking the continuation of the trend towards multipolarity as its point of departure, this chapter has explored the potentials of a world order beyond hegemonism. Such a perspective is different from the "new world order" presently in vogue because long-run economic trends are seen as more important than a show of force based on military dominance. What is clear is that market exchange has established itself as the dominant mode of economic integration. If we take the Polanyian view that market expansion implies processes of disintegration and conflict, the new situation is not at all the "end of history," but raises enormous problems of order, both in the sense of economic regulation and conflict control. There is also the theoretical possibility of a multilateral order based on interstate cooperation, but it seems more likely that some kind of fragmentation of the world economy will take place, a fragmentation that could be constructive as well as destructive.

One rather obvious and already visible pattern of fragmentation is the development of a few major trading blocs, such as the EC, NAFTA, and the EAEG proposed by Malaysian Prime Minister Mahathir Mohamad. The term blocs suggests an internal homogeneity within these groupings which, apart from the EC, simply does not exist. Both NAFTA and the EAEG are economic security measures, and not the dominant strategy. Trade wars between competing regional blocs could be quite destructive, as could other types of conflicts between different combinations of the three blocs. The Orwellian scenario comes to mind here. This chapter has dealt mainly with the possibility of a less conflictive regionalized world order, that is, a new regionalism, emphasizing the implications for the Third World. My approach is "guarded normativism:" regionalism is considered to be a potentially positive factor, but it is not taken for granted.

New Regionalism may also be conceived of as "extended nationalism" (Seers 1983). It could be compared to traditional nation building without a coercive political/administrative center. Its emergence is related to imperatives in the international political economy, including ecological concerns. For instance, water conflicts and the need for regional systems of water control will be in the center of world politics in the next decade.

The regionalization process evolves by its own internal logic, and unevenly in different regions. It is far advanced in Europe, where the trend now is toward a regional state, but with an unknown political orientation. There are several competing "social projects," some with an inward-looking bias, others with the clear intention of reestablishing European hegemony. Linked to this is the increasingly controversial issue of deepening versus enlarging the European Community. The Yugoslavian conflict represents the real test for a regional order: the capacity for internal conflict resolution.

Other regions may want or become forced to follow the European example of internalizing the sources of growth, and make use of a "domestic" regional market, although there may be a much more gradual step to security cooperation.

Latin America has traditionally been characterized by its "open veins." Import substitution in the 1950s and 1960s was generally carried out as a national strategy, in spite of futile efforts to create a regional framework for industrialization. A new inward orientation, this time on the regional level, in combination with a diversification of dependence, is an alternative to a "Fortress America" with a subordinate Latin-American role. However, different Latin American states will probably choose different routes. Mexico, Central America, and the Caribbean are becoming "North Americanized," while the Cone is developing a Latin alternative. The possibilities for a regional peace order are nevertheless relatively good.

The most inward-looking world region is South Asia, where geopolitical changes are presently increasing India's leverage, leading to intensified conflict with Pakistan and suspicions among the smaller countries. The regional great power has in this case traditionally emphasized self-reliance, while the small countries, for the same security reasons, encourage external links. However, there is also a potential homogenization, reflecting the shared Indic civilization. The elimination of the traumatic Indo-Pakistan conflict will make all the difference as far as further regionalization is concerned.

In Southeast Asia, because of the strong export orientation of the individual countries, ASEAN has a high stake in interdependence. However, the new situation in the world economy makes it necessary to develop regional complementarities and also to expand the organization to cover the whole region. The resolution of the Cambodian conflict is crucial here.

Japan and the East Asian NICs also have a strong commitment to interdependence. The Pacific region is in fact becoming a center for a new pattern of global interdependence, where the regional identity is rather weak, mainly because of the aloofness of the major power, Japan, and the suspicions its expansion creates within the region. Here the established interests in interdependence are the strongest.

In spite of numerous subnational identities, the Middle East has a certain regional identity, but it is too much a part of the world economy to be left to itself. More economic differentiation within the region and less Western dependence on oil are necessary prerequisites for Middle East regionalism, which in any event is bound to emerge in different manifestations. Democratization would contribute to the elimination of cynical power politics and struggles among the despots. Of major importance is the resolution of the Palestinian problem.

Africa is special, since the issue rather is to initiate a process of regionally integrated development. Judging from recent OAU meetings, this goal is now widely recognized. Democratization is on the agenda. The political climate today does not favor petty despotism, of which there has been an excess since the decline of the first generation of highly visionary but impatient leaders, victims of the Western concept of quick modernization. Thus in spite of the pathetic state of Africa today, there are reasons for optimism in the long run.

Although the preconditions for "extended nationalism" differ substantially between regions, I would nevertheless bet on this neomercantilist scenario of constructive fragmentation as the best order the world can hope for. Many probably feel uneasy about this concept. Mercantilism is the ideological expression of the nation-state logic, operating in the economic arena and violating the liberal principle that free trade in the long run is for the benefit of all. Neomercantilism retains the same suspicion the old mercantilists harbored against free trade. It transcends the nation-state logic in arguing for a segmented world-system, consisting of self-sufficient blocs large enough to provide "domestic" markets and to make use of economies of scale and specialization in production, on the one hand, without falling prey to the anarchy of the world market, on the other.

regionalized world system would be large enough to have a reasonable degree of economic efficiency, in accordance with the principles of comparative costs, economies of scale, and other conventional economic efficiency arguments. On the other hand, perversions generated by excessive specialization and an overly elaborated, and therefore vulnerable, division of labor could be avoided. Interregional trade will of course continue, but it will be subordinate to the territorial principle of the new regionalism, rather than the functional principle of the world market.

REFERENCES

Adiseshiah, Malcolm S. 1987. "The Economic Rationale of SARC." *South Asia Journal* 1, no. 1 (July-September): 29-42.

"Asia Asks: War for Whom?" 1991. *Far Eastern Economic Review* 151, no. 4 (24 January): 10-16.

"Asia: Trade." 1991. *Far Eastern Economic Review* 153, no. 30 (25 July): 52.

Brandt, Willy. 1986. *Arms and Hunger*. New York: Pantheon.

"Business Barometer." 1990. *South* 117 (November): 8.

Buzan, Barry. 1983. *People, States, and Fear: A Conceptual Introduction to the Role of Foreign International Relations*. Chapel Hill, NC: University of North Carolina Press.

Buzan, Barry and Gowher Rizvi, eds. 1986. *South Asian Insecurity and the Great Powers*. London: Macmillan.

Castaneda, Jorge G. 1990. "Latin America and the End of the Cold War." *World Policy Journal* 7, no. 3 (Summer): 469-93.

Deutsch, Karl W. 1957. *Political Community and the North Atlantic Area*. Princeton, NJ: Princeton University Press.

"ECOWAS Summit." 1991. *West Africa* no. 3851 (July 1): 1075.

Edwards, Geoffrey, and Elfriede Regelsberger, eds. 1990. *Europe's Global Links: The European Community and Inter-Regional Cooperation*. London: Pinter.

"Enter the Latin Dragon." *Far Eastern Economic Review* 153, no. 28 (July 11): 42-43.

Gilpin, Robert. 1987. *The Political Economy of International Relations.* Princeton, NJ: Princeton University Press.

Griffith-Jones, Stephany, and Osvaldo Sunkel. 1986. *Debt and Development Crisis in Latin America.* Oxford: Clarendon.

Haas, Ernst B. 1970. "The Study of Regional Integration: Reflections on the Joy and Anguish of Pretheorizing." *International Organization* 24, no. 4 (Autumn): 607-48.

Hadar, Leon T. 1991. *Extricating America from Its Middle Eastern Entanglement.* Washington, DC. Cato Institute.

Hettne, Björn. 1986. "An Inventory of European Social Projects for Peace and Development." In *Europe in the Contemporary World.* Ed. Ervin Laszlo. New York: Gordon and Breach.

_____. 1988. "India." In *Newly Industrializing Countries and the Political Economy of South-South Relations.* Eds. Jerker Carlsson and Timothy M. Shaw. London: Macmillan.

_____. 1989. "Regional Integration in a Security Complex: The Case of Europe." In *Case Studies of Regional Conflicts and Conflict Resolution.* Ed. Leif Ohlsson. Gothenburg, Sweden: Padrigu Papers.

_____. 1990. *Development Theory and the Three Worlds.* London: Longman.

Huntington, Samuel P. 1988. "The U.S.—Decline or Renewal?" *Foreign Affairs* 67, no. 2: 76-96.

"International Opportunity for Progress." 1991. *West Africa* no. 3854 (22 July): 1207.

Kennedy, Paul. 1987. *The Rise and Fall of the Great Powers.* New York: Random House.

Keohane, Robert O. 1980. "The Theory of Hegemonic Stability and Changes in International Economic Regimes, 1966-77." In *Change in the International System.* Eds. Ole R. Holsti, Randolph M. Siversen, and Alexander L. George. Boulder, CO :Westview.

_____. 1984. *After Hegemony: Cooperation and Discord in the World Political Economy.* Princeton, NJ: Princeton University Press.

Krasner, Stephen D. 1985. *Structural Conflict: The Third World Against Global Liberalism.* Berkeley and Los Angeles: University of California Press.

Krauthammer, Charles. 1991. "The Unipolar Movement." *Foreign Affairs* 70, no. 1: 23-34.

Kux, Stephen. 1990. "Soviet Federalism." *Problems of Communism* 39, no. 2 (March-April): 1-20.

"Mexico and Central America." 1991a. *Latin American Regional Report*. June 13.

_____. 1991b. *Latin American Regional Report*. July 15.

Mishra, K. P. 1984. "South Asia's Quest for an Identity and SARC." *India Quarterly* 40, nos. 3-4 (July-December): 314-22.

Muni, S. D. 1985. "SARC: Building Regions from Below." *Asian Survey* 25, no. 4 (April): 391-404.

Ohlsson, Leif, ed. 1991. *Regional Case Studies of Water Conflicts*. Gothenburg, Sweden: Padrigu Papers and Sando/U-centrum.

Rahman, Atiur. 1985. *Political Economy of SARC*. Dhaka, India: University Press.

Rake, Alan. 1991. "Africa and the Gulf." *New African* 282 (March): 30.

Russet, Bruce. 1985. "The Mysterious Case of Vanishing Hegemony; or Is Mark Twain Really Dead?" *International Organization* 39, no. 2 (Spring): 207-32.

Seers, Dudley. 1983. *The Political Economy of Nationalism*. Oxford: Oxford University Press.

Strange, Susan. 1988. *States and Markets*. London: Pinter.

Tamamoto, Masaru. 1990. "The Japan That Can Say Yes." *World Policy Journal* 7, no. 3 (Summer): 493-520.

Thisen, J. K. 1989. "Alternative Approaches to Economic Integration in Africa." *Africa Development* 14, no. 1.

Thomas, Clive Y. 1988. *The Poor and the Powerless: Economic Policy and Change in the Caribbean*. London: Latin American Bureau.

Väyrynen, Raimo. 1984. "Regional Conflict Formations: An Intractable Problem in International Relations." *Journal of Peace Research* 21, no. 4: 337-59.

"Wind of Democracy." 1991. *New African* 286 (July): 8-10.

14

Brave New World Order
or Fair New World Order?

HOLLY SKLAR

In a special "Survival Guide" for the 1990s, *Newsweek* declared, "we ushered in the decade celebrating the end of the cold war. . .The gulf crisis shows the world has been made safe again for the use of all-out military force" ("Age of Anxiety" 1990).

We are experiencing the wrong kind of global warming. The 1980s ended with the crumbling of the Berlin Wall and the U.S. occupation of Panama—one superpower shedding its empire in an effort to salvage its Union of Soviet Republics, the other seeking a resurgent Pax Americana. The expected post-Cold War American peace dividend was quickly rolled over into banking bailouts and war dividends.

The world of the 90s is not just post-Cold War, it is increasingly post-Soviet. It remains to be seen whether demagoguery or democracy will reap the whirlwind in the former Soviet Union. But without a fundamental change of course in Washington, the yellow ribbon U.S. military budget will continue wasting lives and resources in the "new world order."

ENGULFED

The Brave New World Order of President Bush, a past director of the Central Intelligence Agency (CIA), rests on double standards and doublespeak. Children are supposed to learn that two wrongs don't make a right. Iraq's annexation of Kuwait was wrong. So was the U.S. rush to reverse it through war rather than sanctions and diplomacy.

Sanctions and negotiated settlements require time, tact, and proportionality regarding ends and means. Too often there is obstruction by powerful nations, as in the case of U.S. and British circumvention of various South Africa sanctions since 1963 (NARMIC 1982; Minter 1986). In Iraq's case, sanctions should have worked relatively quickly, setting a positive precedent, because most countries were united in enforcing them (Johansen 1991). As journalist Bob Woodward belatedly disclosed, the chairman of the U.S. Joint Chiefs of Staff Colin Powell felt sanctions were "working. An extraordinary political-diplomatic coalition had been assembled, leaving Iraq without substantial allies . . . Intelligence showed that economic sanctions were cutting off up to 95 percent" of Iraq's imports and nearly all exports (Woodward 1991: 299). However, a negotiated withdrawal from Kuwait, leaving a militarily unscathed Saddam Hussein in power in Iraq, was seen as the "nightmare scenario" by Bush policymakers.

Ultimatums were substituted for diplomacy, and diplomacy was widely dismissed as an annoyance or appeasement. Here's how CBS News anchorman Dan Rather depicted Soviet peace proposals on February 12, 1991: "If you consider this a kind of Iraqi-Soviet Scud-- diplomatically . . . [presidential spokesman] Marlin Fitzwater at the White House has fired what amounts to a diplomatic Patriot at it."

Washington also wanted to avoid the "nightmare" of a post-Hussein Iraq without a reliable authoritarian regime to keep it whole and pro-West. While cynically urging and pressuring Iraqis to overthrow Hussein—through CIA-sponsored radio, for example—U.S. (and Saudi) officials privately acknowledged they wanted a military coup, not successful popular rebellions by Shi'ites and Kurds (Moyers 1991; Hunter 1991: 25; Hubbell 1991). The Kurds earlier had met disaster as U.S. pawns during 1972-1975, when the CIA and the Shah of Iran armed them as a "card to be played" against Iraq and then betrayed them. When former Secretary of State Henry Kissinger was asked about these events by staff of the congressional Pike Committee investigating the CIA, he declared: "Covert action should not be confused with missionary work" (Blum 1986: 278; Moyers 1991).

Washington continues playing the endlessly changing lethal game, "the enemy of my enemy is my friend" or "the enemy of my old friend turned enemy is my friend at least until my enemy becomes my friend . . ." Yesterday tilting toward Iraq; today, toward Iran and Syria. As the U.S. tilts, the Middle East teeters atop powder kegs of militarism and subjugation—territorial, ethnic, religious, gender, and economic.

RHETORIC AND REAL ESTATE

The Cold War era saw frequent hot wars. Nearly all of 130 wars since World War II were fought in the Third World. About 22 million women, men, and children suffered war-related deaths; by the late 1980s, three-fourths of the dead were civilians (Sivard 1989). How many millions more will die if the world has been made "safe again for the use of all-out military force"?

The post-Cold War era has brought an intensification of North-South conflict. Twentieth century U.S. intervention in the Third World was not a sideshow to the anti-Soviet crusade. Washington used the Cold War to justify long-running economic, political, and military intervention in the Third World.

Beneath all the rhetoric about freedom and democracy, most U.S. intervention revolves around a simple proposition: what's mine is mine, what's yours is mine. That was clearer with colonialism. Then came neocolonialism, allowing nations their own flags but not their own economies. As then U.S. Secretary of State George Shultz described occupied Grenada in 1984: "The terrain is more rugged than I imagined, but it is certainly a lovely piece of real estate" (Taubman 1984).

Generally, when the U.S. intervenes in other countries, government officials don't proclaim, "We're off to secure lovely pieces of real estate, with their lovely beaches, cheap labor and resources." Instead, the imperial right to intervene is promoted with propaganda taking two basic forms: we must protect civilization from the barbarians, and we must civilize the barbarians. During colonization the official barbarians were Africans, Arabs, Asians, and the indigenous peoples of the Americas. For much of the 20th century, the official barbarians have been the Soviet Union and its alleged communist-international-terrorist offspring in the Third World.

For the New World Order, Third World people are being granted more independent official barbarian status under convenient categories such as Narcoterrorist (used as a cover for counter insurgency abroad and civil liberties rollbacks at home), Castroite terrorist, Ecoterrorist, and Arab Hitler. Dictator clients like Panama's Manuel Noriega and Saddam Hussein are transformed instantly with the help of racism into dictator barbarians. The *New York Times*, for example, ran an unusually large cartoon titled "The Descent of Man" across the top of its op-ed page on February 1, 1991 (Levine 1991). It showed in descending order Clark Gable, a guerrilla, a monkey, a snake, and a fly-infested Saddam Hussein.

The United States has a long history of portraying nonwhite enemies as less than human—from Indian "savages" to Vietnamese "gooks" to Iraqi "camel jockeys" and "sand niggers," an even more disgusting term when you consider the high number of African-American Gulf veterans (Drinnon 1990). U.S. soldiers, following Vietnam War practice, commonly referred to the Gulf battlefield as "Indian country" or "Injun country." Jingoism abroad fuels racism at home. Japanese-Americans were rounded up into detention camps during World War II. Half a century later, Arab-Americans were subjected to blanket FBI suspicion and harassment and increased racist violence (as documented by the Washington-based American-Arab Anti-Discrimination Committee and the New York-based Movement Support Network of the Center for Constitutional Rights). War brings out the worst kind of "love it or leave it" politically correct patriotism. Many Americans saw no contradiction in applauding press censorship and telling antiwar protesters to shut up because the soldiers in the Gulf were defending their right to free speech.

SMART BOMBS, DUMB BOMBS, AND DOUBLESPEAK

In the euphemistic language of the Pentagon, often parroted by the media, weaponry is described in more human terms than people. U.S. missiles are "smart" and have names like "Tomahawk Cruise" and "Patriot." Dead and wounded civilians are "collateral damage," or as *Time* magazine put it during the first week of the war, it's "a term meaning dead and wounded civilians who should have picked a safer neighborhood" ("War in the Gulf" 1991: 14).

In Pentagon-speak there is no war zone, but a KTO or Kuwaiti Theater of Operations. For many Americans, especially those without friends or family in the Gulf, the war was a 6-week Desert Storm miniseries or a Smart Bomb Super Bowl. A May 27, 1991, *People* magazine story on Democratic presidential hopeful Paul Tsongas, asserted, "A lot of [people] will want to know that in the event of war, he can be counted on to provide more great Persian Gulf-style TV."

News was manipulated to serve propaganda and profit. A Gannett Foundation Media Center report concluded, "Often reporters and news organizations, with a few exceptions, lapsed into cheerleading the war effort instead of striving for more balanced news and historical perspective" (Dennis et al. 1991: xi). Fairness and Accuracy in Reporting (FAIR) noted that "in an effort to increase ad sales, CBS executives 'offered advertisers assurances that the war specials could be tailored to provide better lead-ins to commercials. One way would be to insert the commercials after segments that were specially produced with upbeat images or messages about the war, like patriotic views from the front'" (FAIR 1991: 10).

The Pentagon's home front propaganda experts know that television loves a good photo opportunity—however censored—and first images leave lasting impressions. So they packaged the opening of the Gulf war as a Top Gun video game with dramatic shots of supposedly civilian friendly "smart bombs" whizzing through doors and down air vents. Many reporters made it appear as if Tomahawk Cruise missiles were flying around Baghdad streets stopping to ask civilians, "Pardon me, is that the Air Force headquarters?" Examples of Orwellian doublethink abound. On January 20, NBC's Tom Aspell marveled over Tomahawk cruise missiles, "accurate to within a few feet," right after reporting that a missile had "hit the hotel employees' compound" (FAIR 1991: 5). The most publicized "collateral damage," the killing of hundreds of civilians, mostly women and children, when the U.S. bombed a public shelter, was blamed on Saddam Hussein and quickly forgotten lest Iraq reap "propaganda" benefit. Though publicly the Pentagon insisted it was a military command and control center, privately U.S. officials admitted it was targeted as a shelter used by high-level Iraqi officials and their families. Defense Secretary Richard Cheney later told reporters every Iraqi target was "perfectly legitimate," adding, "If I had to do it over again, I would do exactly the same thing" (Gellman 1991).

In the Pentagon's greatest hit videos, buildings and vehicles exploded and burned, not people. Other footage was censored by the military and news and photo agencies. For example, when long-time NBC stringer Jon Alpert "came back from Iraq with spectacular videotape of Basra and other areas of Iraq devastated by U.S. bombing, NBC president Michael Gartner not only ordered that the footage not be aired, but forbade Alpert from working for the network in the future" (FAIR 1991: 15; Hoyt 1991; Moyers 1991; Rogers 1991)

The War is Peace PR image of near perfect "surgical" smart bombing endures, undisturbed by reality. In fact, most of the bombs dropped by the U.S. military on Iraq and Kuwait were "dumb" bombs, with an acknowledged miss rate of 75%. Only about 7 % of U.S. bombs were "smart bombs," and many of them went off course. Smart-bomb accuracy estimates range from 60% to 90%. Laser-guided bombs, for example, are thrown off course when the laser beam hits smoke, dust, clouds or rain—hardly rare phenomena, especially in a war According to the Pentagon, the combined miss rate for smart and dumb bombs was 70% (Kaplan 1991a, b; Wicker 1991; Moyers 1991).

DELIBERATE DAMAGE

The U.S. military combines "smart" weaponry, with imperfect but improving accuracy, and conventional wide-area munitions such as cluster bomb units and fuel-air explosives, designed to have the destructive force of tactical nuclear weapons (Klare 1991; Walker and Stambler 1991). Superior air-land battle technology (including advanced radar, satellites, night vision, and electronic counter-measures) provides an unprecedented ability to pursue the strategic warfare objective of striking directly at the economic, military, and psychological cores of the opponent's society. When the U.S. dropped nuclear bombs on Hiroshima and Nagasaki, Truman propagandized: "The world will note that the first atomic bomb was dropped on Hiroshima, a military base. That was because we wished in this first attack to avoid, insofar as possible, the killing of civilians." In actuality, the U.S. sacrificed tens of thousands of civilians (and future generations) to speed Japan's unconditional surrender and preempt the Soviet Union (Zinn 1980: 413-15; LaFeber 1989: 414, 425-28).

After months of yellow ribbon victory celebrations, Pentagon officials acknowledged that civilian destruction in Iraq was deliberate policy. As reported in the *Washington Post:*

> Some targets . . . were bombed primarily to create postwar leverage over Iraq, not to influence the course of the conflict itself. Planners now say their intent was to destroy or damage valuable facilities that Baghdad could not repair without foreign assistance. Many of the targets in Iraq's Mesopotamian heartland . . . were chosen only secondarily to contribute to the military defeat of Baghdad's occupation army in Kuwait. Military planners hoped the bombing would amplify the economic and psychological impact of international sanctions on Iraqi society, and thereby compel President Saddam Hussein to withdraw Iraqi forces from Kuwait without a ground war. They also hoped to incite Iraqi civilians to rise against the Iraqi leader...
>
> The worst civilian suffering, senior officers say, has resulted not from bombs that went astray but from precision guided weapons that hit exactly where they were aimed—at electrical plants, oil refineries and transportation networks. Each of these targets was acknowledged during the war, but all the purposes and consequences of their destruction were not divulged (Gellman 1991).

In both letter and spirit the U.S. violated the laws of war regarding proportionality and the protection of noncombatants. Claiming to have adhered to the laws of war with "the most discriminate military campaign in history," the Pentagon acknowledged, "As a general principle, the law of war prohibits the destruction of civilian objects not imperatively required by military necessity and the intentional attack of civilians not taking part in hostilities" (Department of Defense 1991: 12-13).

Intentional damage to Iraq's civilian infrastructure caused mass death and misery. The thousands of direct civilian bombing casualties merged with the victims of U.S.-provoked epidemics, hunger, civil war, and displacement. Drawing on government sources, relief workers, and press reports, Greenpeace estimated that as of July 1991, there were 62,400 to 99,400 war-related Iraqi civilian deaths, including 5,000 to 15,000 during the air war. The estimated Kuwaiti total of civilian and military dead was 2,000 to 5,000 (Greenpeace 1991).

The U.S. military anticipated much higher civilian casualties—another indication of lack of proportionality. "According to a leaked copy of the 'civil affairs' annex to the Desert Storm war plan, the US military estimated in autumn that up to 40,000 Kuwaiti citizens would be killed in the war, and that another 100,000 would be injured [out of a population of 2 million]. But two thirds of the population fled Kuwait before the air war began" (Arkin et al. 1991: 45).

A May 1991 *Harvard Study Team Report* "conservatively" projected "that at least 170,000 children under five years of age will die in the coming year from the delayed effects of the Gulf Crisis." The report states:

> The immediate cause of death in most cases will be waterborne infectious disease in combination with severe malnutrition. . . . The incidence of water-borne diseases increased suddenly and strikingly during the early months of 1991 as a result of the destruction of electrical generating plants in the Gulf War and the consequent failure of water purification and sewage treatment systems (Harvard School of Public Health 1991: 1-3, 18).

A follow-up study reported that the child mortality rate was 380% greater than before the Gulf crisis (Neuffer 1991).

"Surgical" should not be confused with mutilation and accepted as a euphemistic term for bombing strikes, whatever their accuracy or inaccuracy. The only thing surgical about the U.S. bombing was the surgery used to save the wounded.

The Pentagon intentionally exaggerated Iraq's comparative strength—portraying the Iraqi army as one of the world's strongest, rather than as one of the Third World's strongest—both to mislead Iraq and to set the stage for a more heroic looking victory. Estimates of 100,000 to 200,000 dead Iraqi soldiers in 43 days reveal one-sided, rapid lethality reminiscent of the Gatling gun vs. the bow and arrow, but with even higher killing ratios. By official count, the U.S. lost 148 killed in action and its allies lost 192. U.S. pilots described the slaughter of an estimated 25,000 people on the Kuwait highways "to hell," jammed with Iraqis in full retreat, as "shooting fish in a barrel." Widely published photos of this carnage in the U.S. media showed only the corpses of vehicles.

RESTRUCTURING FOR WAR

Orwell told us in *1984*, "Who controls the past, controls the future: who controls the present, controls the past."

U.S. officials rewrote old history as they produced a censored version of new history. "By God," said Bush, "we have kicked the Vietnam Syndrome once and for all" in the desert sands because, unlike Vietnam, "we didn't fight this war with one arm tied behind our back." The U.S. lost in Vietnam, the official story goes, because the antiwar movement and the supposedly adversarial media prevented the military from winning, not because the war was wrong and many U.S. soldiers knew it. The official story has become the only story for many Americans born since the 1960s.

Newspapers juxtaposed photos of U.S. helicopters evacuating the American embassy in Saigon and landing marines on the embassy in Kuwait City. The Vietnamese had the compelling cause of national liberation and terrain less favorable to one-sided air war than the desert. Still, this supposedly one-armed war took 2 million Vietnamese and 58,000 American lives. Napalm, B-52 carpet bombing, and "Only we can prevent forests" Agent Orange—with its continuing chain of destruction from Vietnamese birth defects to high rates of cancer in American veterans and their children—turned such a large portion of Vietnam into wasteland that environmentalists called it ecocide.

In reality, the only arm tied during Vietnam was nuclear, and even that was seriously considered by American war planners. The "nuke Vietnam back to the stone age" attitude was expressed by Ronald Reagan in October 1965: "We should declare war on North Vietnam . . . We could pave the whole country and put parking strips on it, and still be home by Christmas." According to a CNN-Time poll taken shortly after the Gulf War began, 45% favored and 45% opposed using nuclear weapons.

Presidents Reagan and Bush paved the way to Iraq through Grenada, Libya, and Panama. The public rationales have grown more Orwellian: hostage rescue operation, punishing terrorism—by bombing a capital city in a failed attempt to assassinate a head of state and his family (Hersh 1987), and arresting a drug dealer. The Pentagon's enduring lesson from the Vietnam War is that if U.S. ground troops are used in combat, they should not be deployed gradually, but with overwhelming force to rapidly crush the opponent.

Now we're seeing a "Gulf syndrome" of jingoistic American military triumphalism, where many will assume the morality, legality, necessity, and low-risk winnability of future offshore wars. American dissidents will find it much harder to prevent, protest, and reverse the next war. It will be harder to warn that a war might bring high American casualties, much less argue against U.S. self-righteousness and the immorality of slaughtering others. As the motto painted on a U.S. armored vehicle put it, "Killing is our business, and business is booming" (*Boston Globe* photo, March 22, 1991).

RECOLONIZATION

Bush declared in his acceptance speech for the 1988 Republican nomination:

> This has been called the American Century because in it we were the dominant force for good in the world. We saved Europe, cured polio, went to the moon, and lit the world with our culture. Now we are on the verge of a new century, and what country's name will it bear? I say it will be another American Century.

The New World Order is a one-superpower order, with the U.S. as Top Gun. Washington is using militarism, as did the aging empires of old, in an attempt to humble the oil-poor economic superstars, Germany and Japan, and preserve U.S. preeminence in the increasingly hegemonic trilateral alliance among the U.S., Western Europe, and Japan (Sklar 1980). Perestroika has not been matched by "Yankeestroika." If trilateralism breaks down it is much more likely that the U.S. and Europe will ally against Japan (or, less likely, the U.S. and Japan against Europe), than that Japan and Europe will unite against the U.S. The hegemon for the foreseeable future will likely be a two-headed one: Pax Americana militarily, Pax Trilateral economically.

We are going back to the future: the recolonization of the Third World—legalized, if multinational corporate elites prevail, by a lopsided new GATT and Free Trade Agreements (Raghavan 1990), loansharked by the bankers' International Monetary Fund, disguised by pseudo-democracy, and policed by covert and open warfare.

Neocolonialism hid the interventionist principle: what's mine is mine, what's yours is mine. Now there's less pretense. An American T-shirt sold during the Gulf War shows a U.S. Marine pointing his rifle at an Arab on the ground, asking "How much is oil now?" Americans who easily claim Arab oil as "ours" would find it ludicrous if Arabs or anyone else asserted "That's ours" about Texas oil or Kansas corn.

Western policy has largely been set by those who see the world as their farm, factory, market, and playground. Women are the cheapest labor on the global assembly line stretching from the electronic firms of California and Mexico to the textile sweatshops of South Carolina and Korea (Fuentes and Ehrenreich 1983; Kamel 1990).

The former Soviet bloc has joined the global bidding war for corporations seeking the highest profits at the lowest wages.

To "develop" their countries as cash-crop plantations and export-platforms for multinational corporations, Western-backed Third World regimes went into heavy debt with multinational banks and agencies such as the International Monetary Fund. Like international loan sharks, the bankers encourage them to rob their people to service the debt. According to UNICEF, "Taking everything into account--loans, aid, repayments of interest and capital . . . [and] the effective transfer of resources implied in the reduced prices paid by the industrialized nations for [Third World] raw materials, then the annual flow from the poor to the rich might be as much as $60 billion each year" (UNICEF 1989: 15). The World Bank estimates that as many as 950 million people, nearly one out of five human beings, are "chronically malnourished." That is double the number of a decade ago.

MAKING THE WORLD SAFE FOR HYPOCRISY

The new Pax Americana harkens back to 19th century Manifest Destiny in the modern guise of Manifesto Democracy. To further its brand of political and economic correctness, Washington shores up repressive regimes with the flimsiest democratic facades and intervenes overtly and covertly in the most basic of internal affairs—the elections of other countries. The underlying attitude remains that expressed by U.S. Undersecretary of State Robert Olds in a 1927 Confidential Memorandum on the Nicaraguan Situation: "We do control the destinies of Central America . . . Until now, Central America has always understood that governments which we recognize and support stay in power, while those which we do not recognize and support fall" (Bermann 1986: 292-94).

Destabilization campaigns can culminate in invasions, as in Grenada in 1983; military coups, as in Guatemala in 1954 and Chile in 1973; or "electoral coups," as in Jamaica in 1980 and Nicaragua, where economic embargo, re-escalating contra war, and increased internal opposition to the Sandinistas prevailed in 1990. Angola may be next. Washington plans to help UNITA win elections in Angola, as it helped UNO in Nicaragua.

The main electoral manipulators of today are the CIA, the National Endowment for Democracy (NED), and an interlocking set of quasi-private organizations (Sklar 1988, 1989; Sklar and Berlet 1992). The National Endowment for Democracy—already involved in 77 countries from South Africa to New Zealand, Chile to Czechoslovakia—was established in 1983 as the public arm of "Project

Democracy," a mixed covert-overt intervention and propaganda operation coordinated by the National Security Council (NSC). The CIA-NED connection is personified by Walter Raymond Jr., a CIA officer who was detailed to the NSC in 1982 as Senior Director of Intelligence Programs. He resigned from the CIA in 1983 to become NSC director of International Communications and Public Diplomacy, overseeing NED, and later became deputy director of the U.S. Information Agency, where he focuses on Eastern Europe. In Eastern Europe, NED has followed in the CIA's footsteps in working with fascist and anti-Semitic forces, for example, Hungarian emigre Laszlo Pasztor, a convicted Nazi collaborator (Berlet and Sklar 1990; Sklar and Berlet 1992).

At the March 1990 NED board meeting, NED President Carl Gershman called the "victory of the democratic opposition in Nicaragua . . . a tremendous victory for the Endowment as well" (National Endowment for Democracy 1990: 6). Imagine the leaders of the Soviet Endowment for Perestroika or even the Swedish Endowment for Social Democracy claiming victory in U.S. elections It's not easy to imagine because U.S. law rightly prohibits foreign funding of U.S. candidates and such support could be politically suicidal.

The National Endowment for Democracy is busy making the world safe for hypocrisy. Freshly laundered, though, U.S. intervention in other nations' elections enjoys more political legitimacy now than before the CIA exposes of the 1960s and 1970s. Meanwhile, back in the U.S., you can buy a gun in many places more easily than you can register to vote.

NEW AMERICAN DISORDER

President Bush told the 1990 World Summit for Children, "I've learned that our children are a mirror, an honest reflection of their parents and their world." If the U.S. government were a parent, it would be guilty of child abuse.

The New American Order is marked by growing inequality, polarization, and violence—no model for collective security and sustainable development. American children are dying because the U.S. is the only industrialized nation besides South Africa without national health care protection. The U.S. has the world's number one military and economy, but ranks only 24th in infant mortality and child mortality. Washington, Detroit, and Philadelphia have higher infant death rates than Jamaica or Costa Rica. The United States is the poorest rich country in the world. Even by the government's understated figures, nearly one out of four children under six is born into poverty—

the highest rate of any industrialized nation—many with parents who have full-time jobs at the minimum wages of the working poor. Every day, one out of eight children under 12 goes hungry (Community Childhood Hunger Identification Project 1991).

Education, like health care, is rationed by income. Schools are becoming increasingly separate and unequal as affluent communities maintain decent schooling while others gut public education along with other government services. State university systems are being decimated. The proportion of the U.S. population attending college has begun to decline as reduced loans and grants means reduced access for lower-income students. Rising numbers of young people do not have equal opportunity except, as the recruiting slogan goes, to "Be all that you can be in the Army."

In the New American Order, more teenage boys, white and black, die from gunshots than all natural causes combined. More kids are killing and dying because society shows them violence is the way to settle disputes, via popular movies and popular wars, and makes guns more accessible than Head Start, health care, drug treatment, day care, job training, and college. A 1991 Senate Judiciary Committee report calls the United States, "the most violent and self-destructive nation on earth"—leading the world in per capita murder, rape, and robbery rates. The 1990 murder rate was more than twice Northern Ireland's and nine times England's. The rape rate was 15 times higher than England's, 26 times Japan's, and 46 times higher than in Greece (Committee on the Judiciary 1991a, b). The problem is not lack of prisons. The U.S. already has the world's highest per capita imprisonment rate.

The American Dream—always an impossible dream for many— is dying a slow death. Living standards are falling for younger generations for the first time since the Civil War. Average workers' wages are in a long-term depression, dropping 19% (after correcting for inflation) since 1973. Homelessness has become so visible it rouses little attention.

Wealth is not evaporating. It is being redistributed by and for the Truly Greedy. While average workers' wages are falling, for the richest 1% they more than doubled from 1977 to 1988 (after inflation). Between 1977 and 1988, the average aftertax income of the top fifth of the population rose by an estimated 34%, while the bottom fifth's share fell 10%. The richest 1% of all Americans now receive nearly as much income after taxes as the bottom 40%—in 1980, the top 1% received half as much as the bottom 40% (Shapiro and Greenstein 1991; Greenstein and Barancik 1990).

According to economist Robert Reich, were the personal income tax as progressive as it was in 1977, "in 1989 the top tenth would have paid $93 billion more . . . At that rate, from 1991 to 2000 they would contribute close to a trillion dollars more, even if their incomes failed to rise" (Reich 1991a, b: 51). In short, the Demon Deficit strangling social services, infrastructure repair, and other government responsibilities is a deficit of humanity, not money.

FAIR NEW WORLD ORDER

Each day, 40,000 children around the world die from poverty-related killers such as malnutrition, lack of clean water, and disease. Their deaths, and many adult deaths, are preventable with a shift in government priorities (Children's Defense Fund 1991). A Fair New World Order would be safe not for "all-out military force" and covert action, but safe for all-out smart diplomacy, disarmament, and international law. In a real new world order the United Nations would serve the cause of nonviolent conflict resolution and international peacekeeping, not selective veto-enforced, U.S.-directed police-keeping. The World Court would be strengthened so that international law judgments could be enforced evenhandedly (for example, in the case of *Nicaragua v United States*).

A Fair New World Order would be safe for human rights in their fullest sense, elaborated decades ago in the 1948 UN Universal Declaration of Human Rights, which embraced the right to an adequate standard of living, "including food, clothing, housing and medical care and necessary social services."

There are many steps to restructuring for peace with justice nationally and internationally:

1. Democratization of the American political system. We should abolish the globetrotting National Endowment for Democracy and endow participatory democracy in the United States, where corporate interests monopolize the "national interest" while workers, women, and others are dismissed as minority "special interests." Imagine a congress truly representative of the American people, more than half female, with an ethnic and racial mix more like the army's ground troops than the corporate boardroom. Essential elements of democracy include universal voter registration, free media for genuine debate among diverse candidates, and public financing for all campaigns at the local, state, and federal level.

2. Conversion of the U.S. military-industrial economy to a socially and ecologically responsible economy. Pentagon officials are helping convert the Soviet military-industrial complex to civilian use. They should set a good example at home. We should stop feeding the

NATO Cold War dinosaur, which consumes half the U.S. military budget, rather than develop it into a global rapid deployment force for recolonization. President Bush's September 1991 initiatives to eliminate some nuclear weapons had the militarily and politically expedient objectives of prompting the Soviets to dismantle their mobile tactical nuclear weapons based in different republics, while containing congressional moves to deeply cut the U.S. military budget. Bush's triage of redundant nuclear weapons is designed to preserve the triad of nuclear bombers, submarines, and inter-continental ballistic missiles under a Star Wars sky. Instead of Star Wars to shoot down nuclear missiles in flight, we need nonproliferation and disarmament to stop them before they get off the ground.

   3. Social and Environmental Compact. Responding to the speed-up in the globalization of the world economy, broad coalitions have formed nationally and internationally of farmers, workers, environmentalists, women, consumers, and others (the Third World Network, Free Trade Campaign, and Maquiladora coalition) (Kamel 1990; Brecher and Costello 1991). They emphasize the need for a social compact and sustainable development. The protection of earth's ecosystem is an essential element of security— personal, national, and international.

   In the words of Mexican opposition leader Cuauhtemoc Cardenas (1991), "Economic liberalization is not our objective, it is one of our tools. Development, social justice and a clean environment are our objectives."

REFERENCES

"Age of Anxiety." 1990. *Newsweek*. December 31. 14-16.

Arkin, William, Damian Durrant, and Marianne Cherni. 1991. *On Impact: Modern War and the Environment: A Case Study of the Gulf War*. Washington, DC. Greenpeace.

Berlet, Chip, and Holly Sklar. 1990. "The N.E.D.'s Ex-Nazi Adviser." *The Nation*. April 2: 450.

Bermann, Karl. 1986. *Under the Big Stick: Nicaragua and the United States Since 1848*. Boston: South End.

Blum, William. 1986. *The CIA: A Forgotten History*. Atlantic Highlands, NJ: Zed.

Brecher, Jeremy and Tim Costello. 1991. *Global Village vs. Global Pillage: A One World Strategy for Labor*. Washington, DC. International Labor Rights and Education Fund.

Cardenas, Cuauhtemoc. 1991. "The Continental Development and Trade Initiative." New York. February 8.

Children's Defense Fund. 1991. *Leave No Child Behind*. Washington, DC. Children's Defense Fund.

Committee on the Judiciary. 1991a. *Fighting Crime in America: An Agenda for the 1990's*. Majority Staff Report, U.S. Senate. March 12.

_____. 1991b. *Violence Against Women: The Increase of Rape in America 1990*. Majority Staff Report, U.S. Senate. March 21.

Community Childhood Hunger Identification Project. 1991. *A Survey of Childhood Hunger in the United States*. Washington, DC. Food Research and Action Center.

Dennis, Everette E., Craig LeMay, Martha Fitz Simon, and Jeanne Sahadi. 1991. *The Media at War: The Press and the Persian Gulf Conflict*. New York: Gannett Foundation Media Center, Columbia University.

Department of Defense. 1991. *Conduct of the Persian Gulf Conflict: An Interim Report to Congress*. Pursuant to Title V Persian Gulf Conflict Supplemental Authorization and Personnel Benefits Act of 1991 (Public Law 102-25). July.

Drinnon, Richard. 1990. *Facing West: The Metaphysics of Indian-Hating & Empire-Building*. New York: Schocken.

Fairness and Accuracy in Reporting (FAIR). 1991. *Extra*. May.

Fuentes, Annette and Barbara Ehrenreich. 1983. *Women in the Global Factory*. Boston: South End.

Gellman, Barton. 1991. "Storm Damage in the Persian Gulf: U.S. strategy against Iraq went beyond strictly military targets." *Washington Post Weekly*. July 8-14.

Greenpeace USA. 1991. "Deaths in the Gulf War at the One Year Mark." July.

Greenstein, Robert and Scott Barancik. 1990. *Drifting Apart: New Findings on Growing Income Disparities Between the Rich, the Poor, and the Middle Class*. Washington, DC. Center on Budget and Policy Priorities.

Harvard School of Public Health. 1991. *Harvard Study Team Report: Public Health in Iraq after the Gulf War*. May.

Hersh, Seymour M. 1987. "Target Qaddafi." *New York Times Magazine*. February 22. 16-27.

Hoyt, Michael. 1990. "Jon Alpert: NBC's Odd Man Out." *Columbia Journalism Review*. 29, no. 3 (September/October).

Hubbell, Stephen. 1991. "The Iraqi Opposition: From Babel to Baghdad." *The Nation*. April 15: 477-480.

Hunter, Jane. 1991. "Sowing Disorder, Reaping Disaster." *Covert Action Information Bulletin* 37 (Summer).

Johansen, Robert C. 1991. "Lessons for Collective Security." *World Policy Journal* 8, no. 3 (Summer): 561-79.

Kamel, Rachel. 1990. *The Global Factory: Analysis and Action for a New Economic Era*. Philadelphia: American Friends Service Committee.

Kaplan, Fred. 1991a. "Laser Bombs hit targets 60 percent of time, officials say." *Boston Globe*. January 29.

_____. 1991b. "General credits Air Force with Iraqi army's defeat." *Boston Globe*. March 16.

Klare, Michael. 1991. "High-Death Weapons of the Gulf War." *The Nation*. June 3. 738-742.

LaFeber, Walter. 1989. *The American Age: United States Foreign Policy at Home and Abroad Since 1750*. New York: W. W. Norton.

Levine, David. 1991 "The Descent of Man." *New York Times*. February 1. A-29.

Minter, William. 1986. *King Solomon's Mines Revisited: Western Interests and the Burdened History of Southern Africa*. New York: Basic Books.

Moyers, Bill. 1991. "After the War." Public Television. June 18.

NARMIC (National Action/Research on the Military Industrial Complex). 1982. *Automating Apartheid: U.S. Computer Exports to South Africa and the Arms Embargo*. Philadelphia: American Friends Service Committee.

National Endowment for Democracy. 1990. Draft Minutes of the Meeting of the Board of Directors. March 29.

Neuffer, Elizabeth. 1991. *Boston Globe*. October 23.

Raghavan, Chakravarthi. 1990. *Recolonization: GATT, the Uruguay Round and the Third World*. Penang, Malaysia: Third World Network.

Reich, Robert B. 1991a. "The REAL Economy." *The Atlantic Monthly*. February. 35-52.

_____. 1991b. *The Work of Nations*. New York: Knopf.

Rogers, Paul. 1991. "The Myth of the Clean War." *Covert Action Information Bulletin* 37 (Summer).

Shapiro, Isaac and Robert Greenstein. 1991. *Selective Prosperity: Increasing Income Disparities Since 1977*. Washington, DC. Center on Budget and Policy Priorities.

Sivard, Ruth. 1989. *World Military and Social Expenditures*. Washington, DC: World Priorities.

Sklar, Holly. 1980. *Trilateralism: The Trilateral Commission and Elite Planning for World Management*. Boston: South End.

_____. 1988. *Washington's War on Nicaragua*. Boston: South End.

_____. 1989. "Washington Wants to Buy Nicaragua's Elections Again." *Z*. December.

Sklar, Holly and Chip Berlet. 1992. "NED, CIA, and the Orwellian Democracy Project." *Covert Action Information Bulletin*. Winter.

Taubman, Philip. 1984. "Shultz Makes Quick Visit to Grenada." *New York Times*. February 8. A-3.

UNICEF. 1989. *The State of the World's Children 1989*. New York: Oxford University Press.

Walker, Paul and Eric Stambler. 1991. "Dirty Little Weapons." *Bulletin of Atomic Scientists* 47, no. 4 (May): 20-24.

"War in the Gulf." 1991. *Time*. January 21. 14-17.

Wicker, Tom. 1991. "An Unknown Casualty." *New York Times*. March 20. A-29.

Woodward, Bob. 1991. *The Commanders*. New York: Simon and Schuster

Zinn, Howard. 1980. *A Peoples History of the United States*. New York: Harper and Row.

15

Globalizing the Green Movement

PETRA K. KELLY

The chapters on restructuring for peace with freedom in Part II of this volume reminded me of all the frustrating, but also very rewarding human rights work I have done with the Green Party in the German Parliament since 1983, especially on the tragic situations in East Timor, Cambodia, China, Tibet, and many other forgotten parts of the world—especially those areas of the world where the First Peoples have lived and live and still suffer so much! They bring to mind many thoughts on the hypocrisy of Western human rights policy, a policy usually subservient to economic and strategic thinking.

I think, for example, of our relationship to China and how market and economic considerations always take top priority regardless of what type of human rights infringements and violations have occurred or are taking place there. I have worked in the past few years especially on the case of Tibet and have tried to chronicle the Chinese government's attempts to destroy the Tibetan people and their entire culture and way of life. Thankfully there is now a strong nonviolent campaign under way in many parts of the world to save what has been called the last Holy Land on earth. Let me cite these facts. Since the 1950s, when China invaded and occupied Tibet, more than a million Tibetans have been murdered or tortured to death and nearly all of the 6,000 monasteries in Tibet have been destroyed. For many years resolutions concerning Tibet have been lying in dusty desk drawers of the United Nations, and simply because Tibet has not been part of the superpower game, the nonviolent struggle of the Tibetan people and the Dalai Lama have been forgotten.

I have learned from all of my human rights work that human rights are indivisible. Whenever, wherever, and by whomever they are violated, public condemnation must follow, by everyone with a voice to raise. Silence is a betrayal of those who are suffering. When we talk about restructuring for peace with justice, we must of course never forget that human rights belong to that justice; individual, economic, and social human rights! It is very tragic that in our global village, the interest in developing economic, trade, and strategic relations with China's government clearly carry far more weight than the defense of international law and human rights, even though Western governments generally did not miss one opportunity to point out such violations in areas under Soviet communist rule. Tibet and Cambodia, East Timor, and other areas of the world where human rights have been violated are for me the cornerstones of morality in international politics.

An old saying has it that it is better to light a candle than curse the darkness. But it is very difficult at present in a united, intolerant Germany to light these candles, as it is very difficult to light them in greater Western and Eastern Europe. Western Europe is about to take off arrogantly as a future military, economic, and nuclear superpower, treating parts of Eastern Europe and the Soviet Union as newly won satellites and backyards for highly toxic chemical wastes and outdated, dirty technologies. These are given to the Europeans in Eastern Europe because they have increasingly become second and third class citizens by the way we are treating them.

RESTRUCTURING AND THE INDIGENOUS PEOPLES

The subject of restructuring for peace with justice is not only about radically restructuring the global political economy for peace or turning swords into plowshares. It is about converting a war economy into a peace economy, and this is quite a radical step. Let me add another dimension about restructuring for peace with justice. 1992 marks a year not of celebration but of mourning for the First Peoples of the Americas. In the 500 years since Columbus arrived, tragedy has taken its toll on the descendants of the continents' original inhabitants. Their numbers have been decimated (see Chapter 11). Indigenous peoples today are the most disadvantaged groups in society, suffering the worst health and receiving the least education. Indigenous peoples are among the very poorest. This is a time for indigenous peoples all over the world to reflect not only on the past but on the need for strategies for dealing with today's abuses. As environmental issues become increasingly urgent and Western models of development and economics daily become less sustainable, indigenous peoples will come to occupy a position of considerable influence. Their views on a union of development and conservation could become central to decision making. When I look at Hawai'i and see the intensive tourism industry, I realize how local inhabitants have been forced to give up their lands and traditional way of life and how tourism has ruined the environment. Many sacred native burial and archaeological sites have become restaurants or tourist parks. When we talk about restructuring the economy, we must act locally and think globally. In Hawai'i, this will be the challenge for the future. Tourist development here is mostly financed, owned, and controlled by foreign investors, while many native Hawaiians have low-paying jobs and little or nothing to say about the course of development of their islands.

I have had the privilege of meeting many Aborigines in Australia and Maoris in New Zealand, as well as many American and Canadian Indians, and I have had the chance to speak with First Peoples in Hawai'i. What I have learned from them is that they have been able to maintain a close living relationship to the land and that they have been able to live in a cooperative attitude of give and take, with a respect for the earth and the life it supports. We should not forget that superpower rivalry has brought even the most remote regions into the realm of military strategists. Whether in the Arctic homeland of the Inuit or the Dreaming Paths of the Aborigines of central Australia, military installations are now in place that continue to be the key targets in the event of even a regional nuclear war. In the industrialized countries, traditional indigenous lands have been misused for bases and military test sites, and in the developing countries these territories have often become killing grounds.

Let me cite one figure important to this debate. Although 80% of global military expenditure was accounted for by NATO and the Warsaw Pact, spending on arms and weapons in the developing world doubled between 1978 and 1988. It doubled also, of course, because we, the Western countries, exported those weapons and gave Third World countries the impression that they can only be an important member of the world community if they have enough weapons to deter others. In Third World countries, where indigenous peoples are concentrated, there are currently nearly 60 military regimes and over 20 major conflicts.

When we talk about peace with economic justice, let us also look at the example of the Amazon. Over the last 30 years, governments have earmarked the Amazon for economic expansion. Oil and plantation companies as well as ranches are flooding into the area. Nine oil consortiums have been granted concessions on Waorani land. In 1983, the Waorani were given title to 67,000 hectares of land, a fraction of their original territory. This entire area, plus a 250,000 hectare forest reserve set aside for their use, is now open to the petroleum industry. Also, let us not forget the example of Malaysia, which contains the world's oldest forests, dating back 150 million years. Every year 700,000 hectares of this ancient forest are logged, a rate of three hectares a minute. At this rate all natural forest, except for small areas of national parks, will disappear in the next 20 years. When the German parliament in Bonn discussed the logging in Sarawak, the government did not want to hear about the worries of the indigenous peoples living in those forests. They simply claimed that Malaysia wanted to cut down those precious ancient forests. There was no discussion about what happens when the trees come down and erosion damages the soils and water supplies become polluted and food sources disappear, and when all the introduced diseases breed new sickness.

A new strategy now emerging may light a candle in this darkness. A campaign to get the United Nations to proclaim a declaration of indigenous rights is now underway, and an alternative United Nations (UNPO) is being organized in Geneva and The Hague, an organization through which Tibetans, Hawaiians, American Indians, Kurds, and many others who are dispossessed of their economic, social, and individual human rights can come together and develop new strategies toward the United Nations. We need to find strategies to affirm First Peoples' rights to self-determination, to their land, and to their culture. Up to now I feel the United Nations has completely failed in this regard.

Talking about restructuring for peace with justice also means building new coalitions with indigenous peoples, who are themselves looking beyond their own individual struggles. The survival of the First Peoples rests wholly on a radical and holistic change in political, economic, and environmental conditions. The problem is not so much how to find solutions to all of these problems and crises, since there are many solutions already tested on local and regional levels. The problem is to find a strategy to form a global network for human survival that promotes human rights, economic justice, and a healthy environment for future generations. This global network needs to gain political power so that it can truly change political decisions, not only at the regional or local level, but also at the national and international level.

We all know that this world economy that we are living in is unsustainable, that the productivity rates are growing at an incredible speed, that consumption seems unending, and that the constraints of the natural environments are becoming more and more visible. We ourselves in the West must begin to learn from the indigenous peoples, who have become a very persistent voice of conscience, alerting us to the dangers of ecological destruction. When discussing economic justice in a global community let us not forget that there are 250 million indigenous peoples living in over 70 countries. The First, Second, and Third Worlds believe that the land belongs to the people; the Fourth World, the world of the indigenous peoples, believes that the people belong to the land. Perhaps that is the key to all of ecological understanding.

RESTRUCTURING THE MILITARY ECONOMY

Restructuring for peace with justice also has to do with radically transforming the permanent war economy. World military research and development have grown from $13 billion a year in 1960 to an estimated $90 to $100 billion in 1986. The two superpowers are responsible for about 85% of this total; China, France, the United Kingdom, and Germany (West) together form another 10%. We know much about the Western military industrial complex and its overkill capacities that exist to this very day, despite the fact that we all had hoped for a peace dividend because of the thaw in East-West relations. Only four days of total global military spending, about $8 billion, could finance a 5-year action plan to protect the world's remaining tropical forests. Up to now military and economic developments have dictated a global community of interests. The military has enjoyed a cornucopia while the civilian infrastructure has been starved of funds. The amount of capital devoted by the United States to building military power ($9.2 trillion between 1948 and 1988) exceeds the cumulative monetary value of all humanmade wealth in the United States (Renner 1989).

Countries are prepared to make considerable sacrifices in order to defend their national sovereignty and territory against foreign invaders. But they do not show an equal determination to guard against environmental threats, whether present dangers or future ones. Yet environmental degradation imperils the most fundamental aspect of a nation's security by undermining the natural support systems on which all human activity depends. According to the United Nations environment program, 35% of the earth's land surface, on which about one-fifth of the world's population depends for its livelihood, is threatened by desertification, a principal threat to the economic well-being of many countries. Particularly on the African continent, desertification has sapped food growing potential to the point where the livelihood of rural peoples is in acute jeopardy. Yet establishing an arms industry has been justified in many cases in the Third World as a shortcut to industrialization. The policy of stimulating civilian industry through arms production has been a real failure. As President Eisenhower stated, "every gun that is made, every warship launched, every rocket fired represents, in the final analysis, a theft from those who hunger and are not fed, who are cold and are not clothed." It would have been good if his policies had been in accord with that sentiment.

The American economy has been entrenched in military production for more than half a century. By the early 1980s, the military accounted for more than 30% of total U.S. goods consumed. The Pentagon's share of investment in plans and equipment from manufacturing in the United States was nearly 38% total during the 1980s. As of 1990, 20,000 major defense contractors and 100,000 subcontractors were working on Pentagon projects. According to the Center for Defense Information, in 1989 about 8 million Americans received pay checks associated with some form of military activity. Yet we and all policymakers must know that many ecologically desirable projects require the kind of funding granted up to now only to military programs. For the $100 billion cost of the Trident II Submarine and the F16 Jet Fighter programs, the U.S. government could clean up the 3,000 worst hazardous waste sites in the United States (Renner 1989). For the cost of the Stealth bomber program, estimated at $68 billion, the U.S. government could pay for two-thirds of the projected costs of the clean water program over the next 10 years. Two days of global military spending could finance a year's worth of efforts to halt Third World desertification. As Rifkin (1990) pointed out in the *Green Lifestyle Handbook,* the cost of one nuclear weapons test alone could pay for the installation of 80,000 hand pumps, giving Third World villages clean water. But here again I must curse the darkness. That peace dividend is now gone. The Gulf War cost West Asian states up to $800 billion and cost Kuwait and Iraq up to $600 billion. "To defeat a country with a GNP of Portugal required 75 % of all U.S. tactical aircraft and 40 % of its tanks" (Economist 1991: 15); all that plus President Bush's multiple auxiliaries, which reads like a who's who among the tyrants of the world, and the entire offensive capability of the Royal Air Force.

We are facing the first truly planetary environmental crisis in history, and we need ecologically desirable projects and ecological planning, but there is no alternative thinking whatsoever in the powerful Western military industrial complex. Just look at the agendas of past NATO meetings, while the entire Warsaw Pact was crumbling. There is, of course, still a Russian military industrial complex, even though the Warsaw Pact has disappeared, but if anything will tame that powerful complex, it will be the iron laws of economics. At least 500,000 skilled workers have left defense plants for civilian jobs as their salaries and privileges have eroded. Local conversion schemes are being worked out from pure economic necessity, not idealism. We know the threat of dictatorship has still not diminished in Russia.

RESTRUCTURING AND EASTERN EUROPE

We in Western Europe on the Green side of politics, who were in close touch with the various independent citizen action movements of Eastern Europe in the 1980s, in close communication with Solidarity, with Vaclav Havel, with Ecoglasnost, and with ecological and human rights groups in the former East Germany (CSFR), Hungary, and the Soviet Union, first learned the notion of a "civil society" from our friends in Eastern Europe. Civil society is what we all have been striving for in the alternative movements across Western and Eastern Europe. Civil institutions are the schools of democracy, and debates in Eastern Europe are about how to create democratic rules of law. We had hoped that after the revolutions in Eastern Europe the notion and vision of civil society, which was translated into concrete political action through Vaclav Havel and Jiri Dienstbier and Lech Walesa and others, would remain a constant factor in official politics. The political will and idealism in many cases is still there. But at the same time we find ourselves saddened by the fact that the Czech government sent a symbolic contingent of soldiers to aid the troops of General Schwarzkopf and that the radical plan to stop all armaments exports in Czechoslovakia was reduced down to no exports in areas of tension. Even under the respected President Havel, there are now plans to sell Czech tanks and other military items to Syria! Lech Walesa in Poland promised to buy U.S. military helicopters because U.S. Secretary of Defense Cheney stopped by to support Walesa in his presidential campaign. When Gert Bastian and I had the opportunity to speak at length with Jiri Dienstbier, now Czech foreign minister, someone for whom we had written many letters while he was in prison, we asked him why Green, ecological, and alternative economic concepts seemed to have no chance in the new liberated Czechoslovakia. He replied that the alternative models were missing because there were no Green think tanks in Czechoslovakia, there was little environmental expertise, and that many in the new Czech government had been imprisoned for many years and had missed the entire ecological and alternative economics debate about holistic societal transformation. Of course, he also mentioned another argument—that of jobs and more jobs, which were at risk and were the key priority in drafting economic policies. Thus there was no time for new idealistic experiments and new visions, but only for a quick turn to the West, so long admired for its culture of freedom and democracy, and a quick turn to the EC and other Western institutions, banks, and industries simply in order to begin to survive in postrevolutionary chaos!

On the one hand, there was momentous social upheaval that dismantled communism in the Eastern European countries, but on the other, there was hardly any time to think about what to do next and where to go next. One development chased another, while Western bankers and businessmen were lining up to invade Eastern Europe with ready-made old concepts and outdated economic and environmental solutions. It has become painfully clear that the civil society that we had dreamt of and about which we had spoken in the 1980s in the back rooms and kitchens of our dissident friends in the former East Germany and Czechoslovakia will not spring up overnight. The old repressive communist system that paralyzed so many people and the gentle revolutions, which had come overnight and had given so much hope, have left many in a state of shock.

Fears penetrates all levels of Eastern European society and many feel numb and powerless at the way in which the West has now invaded Eastern Europe, not in the interest of Eastern Europe, but as usual in self-interest! As Havel (1990) wrote:

> This is what Sisyphus might have felt if one fine day his boulder stopped, rested on the hilltop, and failed to roll back down. It was the sensation of a Sisyphus mentally unprepared for the possibility that his efforts might succeed, a Sisyphus whose life had lost its own purpose and hadn't yet developed a new one.

Or as Penn and Ross wrote:

> Communism had institutionalized the surrender of individual decision-making and problem solving capabilities to state control. Now that the authoritarian powers have stepped down, how can individuals unravel their culture conditioning and become free agents? This is particularly profound and sobering when we remember that two generations have grown up knowing no other way of life outside of an authoritarian system.

Gert Bastian and I had had so many discussions with our dissident friends in the 1980s in their small kitchens dreaming of what a civil society would be like once the revolutions would take place and dreaming about how civic participation would shape new social orders. This remains to be seen. Still in Eastern Europe there are many groups at the local level committed to continuing grass-roots social and nonviolent action. Many people believe that Havel's powerful concept of "living in truth" can generate more and more gentle revolutions. The old form of politics has been totally destroyed. That is why so many of our Eastern European friends speak rightly of the need for "antipolitics" and "antipoliticians," and perhaps we would all be better off if we shared more of that sense. The West, by which I mean Western banks and industries, in fact really did not give Eastern Europe any chance at all to consider what type of new society to build.

During the times of great repression in Eastern Europe under the communist system we always discussed the power of the powerless, meaning the power of our dissident friends' spirit and ideas. But is it possible to use that power of the powerless in a new and very difficult situation? Civil society always meant an open public life outside the sphere of government. Now, trying to create a civil society with all the capitalist pressures in and surrounding Eastern Europe is almost impossible. Eastern Europe has to create almost a new economic, financial, and even social infrastructure. To do it in an ecologically and socially just way, better than the West has done it, will be very difficult. Creating civil societies from the ground up in countries such as Albania and Romania will be the most difficult. In the case of Romania, there has never been an organized opposition or organized dissident movement. The few individuals who spoke up so bravely were usually isolated very quickly by the secret police. Thus we do not yet know how things will turn out there.

We also must not forget the issues of ethnic conflict and national rights in Eastern Europe, conflicts which also bring much darkness and little hope. When we think about the violent attacks on Hungarians in Romania or the attacks against the ethnic Albanian population in the province of Kosovo in Yugoslavia, we must also think about the terrible violence breaking out in the former Soviet republics, or about the Turkish minority in Bulgaria, and anti-Semitism in other parts of Eastern Europe. Ethnic prejudice is often just a surface issue, and behind it are problems of history, economic hardship, land, and long-term political resentments about to explode in a totally new world. Creating a multicultural and democratic state in the truest and most radical sense of democracy is difficult even for the strongest of Western democracies. It poses an even greater challenge for those countries which have to start from the ground up in building a civil society.

Restructuring for East-West justice also has to do with the way in which we treat Eastern Europe and the Third World, and it has to do with the environmental catastrophe Western governments and industries have not only aggravated and worsened, but have in fact caused in the Third World. With the end of tensions between East and West, the Third World will increasingly become the supplier of raw materials for the new unified North and the dump for its hazards and wastes. My Indian friend Vandana Shiva cites an African proverb: "When elephants make war, the grass gets trampled. When elephants make love, the grass gets trampled." The Third World environment and the Third World communities are the ones who have paid the highest

·price for the superpower rivalry of the past. The Cold War in Europe has always been translated into real and burning wars in the Third World, in Central America, Central Asia, and the Horn of Africa. Since 1945, 200 wars have been fought in the Third World. As the industrialized world now moves from an over-armed peace to a disarmed one, the military producers and traders merely find alternative markets in the Third World. As the superpowers withdraw from Afghanistan, the region of Kashmir goes up in flames, Pakistan and India become new markets for arms, and, of course, now the entire Middle East will become a new market for Western arms. Recently European Community defense ministers met and stated quite clearly that the time had come to start to harmonize European weapons production, and to start to think about export strategies to the Third World, as there was now little need to talk about more weapons production in an East-West context. This is a warning to us all about what lies ahead!

RESTRUCTURING AND THE ENVIRONMENT

As the Iron Curtain opened during the autumn of 1989, it revealed a land laid waste by industrial pollution. The environmental outrage of the people ran so high that it helped topple governments in several countries. The task in fact is daunting. Under the assault of air pollution and acid deposits, Eastern Europe's medieval cities are blackened and crumbling. Entire hillsides are deforested. Crop yields are falling. Rivers serve as open sewers and clean drinking water is rare. Life expectancies in the dirtiest parts of these regions are as much as five years shorter, and rates of childhood cancer, reproductive problems, and other illnesses are far higher than in other areas.

Restoring Eastern Europe's environment will be a massive undertaking. The estimates for cleaning up the former East Germany alone run as high as $300 billion. Just consider one example—a chemical plant in Halle, in the former East Germany, which discharges as much mercury in one day into nearby rivers as a comparable plant in the western part of the country spews in a year. Of course, we do not want any mercury spewing into any river, whether it be for a day or a year. Thousands of Bohemian school children must now wear breathing masks for their short walks to school. Pollution levels last winter in Czechoslovakia soared ten times past the internationally accepted safety limits. We know the reasons for this tragic damage: the lack of public accountability, central planning with high subsidies by the government, and the past heavy industry orientation.

But this should not blind us to the many urgent ecological problems existing in our market economies in the West. All too often now when we criticize our own ecological problems at home we are told to just look toward Eastern Europe and see how much worse it is there. But that is not how you solve environmental problems. You must start at home, regardless of whether it is worse elsewhere. Eastern Europe has a unique opportunity to leapfrog over the West by implementing only those ecological Western strategies that were successful and sidestepping those that did not work. Additionally, as obsolete factories in Eastern Europe are closed down, they could be replaced by ecological, safe, and socially useful industries and production. But this is simply not happening! The shift to Western market-oriented economies in Eastern Europe has involved little regard for clean industries, for as Western European businesses and governments send our old reactors and our old dirty industries to Eastern European countries, and to our own backyard in East Germany, we make it very clear that we have no intention of helping to make an ecologically sound Eastern Europe. Our industrialists and banks do not have any major ecological transformation in mind, either at home or in Eastern Europe. They simply see a new large market where they can sell our nicely and wastefully wrapped, asbestos-filled, and PVC-coated and leaded products at an even greater speed!

We had hoped for effective energy efficiency and energy conservation structures in Eastern Europe. Due to the removal of energy subsidies and the closing down of faulty old nuclear power plants, we are now witnessing exactly the opposite. We are witnessing the West building nuclear reactors in Eastern Europe that the Green movement and others had stopped at home in the West after years and years of nonviolent resistance. It's like a tragic boomerang. As Gorbachev told a group of German businessmen on his last visit to the region of Dusseldorf: "Give us the money we need and we will produce anything you want." Now that Russia is appealing to Washington and to Wall Street for a bailout of its crippled economy, there seems little hope left for a new third ecological way between repressive state socialism and aggressive capitalist economic development.

There is little hope for an ecological vision to become reality unless we realize that Western and Eastern air and water pollution spills across all borders, and that in fact we are all united in this one big mess together. One of the biggest impediments to cleaning up Eastern Europe is the huge debt load carried by most countries—hard currency spent on paying back debts is money unavailable for investments in environmental programs. Poland is saddled with a $42 billion debt, which represents 54% of its annual GNP, and Hungary carries an $18 billion debt, 65% of its GNP. Swapping debt for environmental protection, whereby debt is forgiven in exchange for a commitment to spend the money saved on environmental programs financed with local currency, is one creative way Western countries could help Eastern Europe out of its morass. One such swap has been made by the German government, which will wipe $60 million in debts off the books with Poland—at least one small modest step.

Another necessary step in creating more economic justice is setting up a system of ecological taxation. Market economies have failed miserably at taking environmental costs into account. The costs of pollution created by industrial processes are generally born by society as a whole, rather than by the consumer or producer of the item manufactured. To compensate for this and create an incentive to minimize pollution production, Eastern European movements at the grass-roots level are asking their governments to adopt ecotaxes similar to those now under consideration by Green Parties in the West. For example, emissions of harmful pollutants could be taxed at a level high enough to discourage the practice.

As new tax systems are put in place in Eastern Europe, Green levies could be incorporated from the very beginning. Of course, there must be strong regulations, including efficiency standards and prohibitions on carcinogenic chemicals, pesticides, and other harmful materials. Such strong regulations could steer Western investment in a different, environmentally helpful, direction. Thus, some grounds for optimism can be found in different Green movements developing and growing in Eastern Europe. We still face a considerable challenge in both Eastern and Western Europe, since people there search for jobs at any wage as unemployment rates rise sharply day by day. In the former East Germany, the Green Movement and Green Party had the worst electoral results in December 1990 in those areas with the most desperate environmental problems. As is well known, in a major upset, my own party, the West German Green Party, failed to capture any seats in the new united German parliamentary elections in December 1990, although a coalition of citizen action groups and East German Greens in former East Germany did win eight seats. But I emphasize, only eight seats. The fact that we lost the national elections in West Germany has had a very negative impact on our development as a Green Party and on our chances to get back into the national and European parliament in four years. At the same time we are very badly needed on a national level! We have put ourselves almost right out of history through our internal quarreling.

Ecological transformation and reconstruction in Eastern Europe is fundamental to societal transformation, but the Third World will have to bear the ecological cost of the new industrialism and consumerism in the North, including the cost of cleaning up Eastern Europe. East and

West will increasingly use the Third World as a dump for hazardous wastes. This is garbage imperialism. When the Third World is too far away, then the West will use its own backyard, Eastern Europe, for its dumping ground.

DEMOCRATIZATION

Restructuring for peace with justice also has to do with the need for radical democratization of our political and economic systems in Western Europe, including reforming the very undemocratic and exploitive European Community, which is about to become an embryo of a gigantic United States of Western Europe, the single largest trading block in the world! There's also a fortress in the making with the single Common Market that emerged in 1992. The environmental and economic dimensions and implications of the single Common Market simply make one dizzy. What is needed in present-day politics and international relations is a change in both form and content, a vision of holism rather than separation and compartmentalization. To heal the planet, we must end fragmentary problem solving. Moreover, we must change our daily consciousness about our own lifestyles and attitudes. We must be acutely aware of our own habits and behavior and the ways in which our personal actions can contribute to the perpetuation of the present unjust system. Just think, the 600 largest multinational corporations will control well over 40% of all planetary production by the end of this decade. The result of this monolithic mode of production is wastefulness, overdependence, and unnaturalness.

Is it not violence when we, the industrialized countries of the North, waste at least 60% of the energy we generate? Is it also not violence when we in the West overproduce, overconsume, and then dump our highly poisonous wastes and highly radioactive milk powder on developing countries? In the past three years alone, over 3.1 million tons of dangerous wastes were shipped from industrialized developing countries. Now there is a new target, the South Pacific. We have just gotten rid of the U.S. chemical weapons stock in West Germany. But once we celebrated that victory, we also realized that it was very short-lived, for all the U.S. chemical weapons stockpiles from Germany were sent to Johnston Atoll in the South Pacific.

The cash payments for accepting our wastes, whether civilian or military, are often large enough to tempt poor countries to consider mortgaging their public health and ecological integrity for much needed currency. Impoverishment in the South has been and continues to be related to the growth of the Western economies and to those new rich entities that help to keep them going. In 1990 about $50 billion was officially transferred from poor to rich countries in debt servicing and loan repayments. The environmental terrorism Saddam Hussein practiced in the Gulf War by the terrible oil spillage is viewed with skepticism by many Third World peoples, who have seen the West wage war on their environment since very early colonial days.

The deepening poverty of two-thirds of humanity and environmental degradation are not separate problems. It is the rich who are making the world poorer by their use of disproportionate amounts of the world's energy and resources. The earth is losing 24 billion tons of top soil a year and yet the world's farmers are now trying to feed 86 million more people annually. Let us look to the proposals of the South Commission, issued in Caracas in 1989, for a development strategy of self-reliance, its recognition that no country can be "developed" by outsiders, its determination to see people, their skills, creativity, and wisdom as instruments, as well as calling for an end to development.

One small proposal that I can offer is the setting up of an alternative credit system to the International Monetary Fund and the World Bank, perhaps a South Bank that a hundred or so countries of the South could devise as their own alternative. Some of us in the Green movement have called this kind of idea "counterdevelopment," which means disengaging where possible from the single, damaging present world system.

Where I cannot offer hope is on the issue of global warming. Now we in the West are calling upon the struggling countries of the Third World to reduce their carbon dioxide emissions, while the big polluters in the North refuse to do so. Yet it is we, the industrialized nations in the North, who are to blame for this threat to our planet. We have caused 90% of the greenhouse gas emissions to date and we must be responsible for cleaning it up, although it is far too late to undo the damage that we have already done to our atmosphere. From 1950 to 1985 alone, global energy consumption more than tripled and world carbon dioxide figures followed the same trend. Let me only remind you that every five years of delay in cutting pollution will lead to a 10% increase in global warming. The United States, Russia, China, West Germany, Japan, and the United Kingdom are the largest emitters of carbon dioxide. Between them they produce almost two-thirds of the world's CO_2. The German Green Party declared in 1983:

> A lifestyle and method of production which rely on an endless supply of raw materials and use those raw materials lavishly, also furnish the motive for the violent appropriation of raw materials from other countries. In contrast, a responsible use of raw materials as part of an ecologically sound lifestyle and

economy, reduces the risk that policies of violence will be pursued in our name. The pursuance of ecologically responsible policies within a society provides the preconditions for a reduction in tensions and increases our ability to achieve peace in the world.

This I believe is one of the most important messages that we have been able to send out to policymakers across the world. That is why I have to reiterate that to counter global warming, the North must bear the main burden and end its exploitation of both nature and the South. Vandana Shiva gets right to the point when she states that the Amazon is disappearing not because of the local inhabitants, but to supply cheap beef to Northern consumers and to supply charcoal for smelting iron for export. Southeast Asia's forests are disappearing to supply tropical hardwood to Japanese and European markets. As commodity prices fall and the debt burdens spiral, the Third World is increasingly trapped in the vicious cycle of exporting more to earn less. It is as if the sick and dying are giving blood transfusions to the healthy.

The prevailing model of economic activities and development has had a near catastrophic impact on the world's ecology. Growth, driven by the need of firms to expand based on unequal structures and principles of low economic costs and high profits, has heavily depleted the world's stock of nonrenewable resources such as oil, coal, minerals, and forests, and has eroded much valuable topsoil, eliminated genetic diversity, and contaminated the air, water, and soil. What in fact should grow is solidarity and care for the people on this globe and for the plants and animals of this planet. In Third World countries, ecological disruption is causing severe health and social effects. The disruption of the ecological balance is also affecting the climatic balance, with a high possibility that global warming will disrupt agricultural production and marine life and cause increased flooding. Just look at the tragic floods in Bangladesh and how we in the West are co-responsible for that tragedy due to our causing global warming.

The economic order itself and present economic policies must be radically transformed to minimize the use of nonrenewable resources and maximize resource conservation. We must minimize pollution and contamination of resources and prevent and minimize toxic wastes. We must cut down investment and consumption levels in the rich parts of the world that are not compatible with the sustainable use of resources. Ecological principles cannot be promoted in a vacuum; they have to be combined with the principles of social justice and the necessity to meet the basic and real needs of the poor. Income inequities worldwide have to be greatly reduced, along with the unsustainable consumption of the richer parts of the world. We need policies of equal justice and we need to realize the spiritual dimensions of our lives, of our interconnected planet earth, and of each other. We simply cannot feast on global resources while the world's poor struggle to survive on inhospitable lands. It is as simple as that.

UNIFIED GERMANY

The majority of the Greens opposed the speed of German reunification and the way in which it was done. We had hoped for a German confederation: two Germanys growing together slowly, with more dignity and respect for each other. We had hoped for a pacifist, nuclear-free, demilitarized, and socially just Eastern Germany, a new zone of peace in Europe, and we had hoped that the draft of a new German constitution with elements of pacifism, ecology, social justice, and feminist thinking prepared by the historic roundtable in the former East Germany could be a continuation of the short, first, real revolution on German soil! We had hoped for a multicultural society and for a new tolerance in German political thinking. But now we are united and I believe we are becoming a cause of real and renewed concern. Neo-Nazi street gangs attack Polish visitors at the border and harass foreigners on trams and subways. East and West German skinheads and hooligans threaten children coming from Chernobyl to East Germany for treatment and harass migrant workers and anyone not German. The call in Germany to be normal again is growing loud because we have regained our sovereignty and in trying to be normal again we define normality suddenly as being able to play a larger military role on a global scale. We're back to trying to send our boys to the front line so as not to be considered "cowards," or even worse, a pacifist country.

During the parliamentary debate on the unification treaty we did not even include one paragraph about the most unprecedented act of violence, the Holocaust. The Green Party was the only party attempting to include a passage about the Holocaust in the preamble to the unification treaty. Chancellor Kohl even spoke about his hope for a thousand years of German happiness and prosperity. Imagine, he spoke of a thousand years! We seem to have no problems returning to the terrible and for me very negative-spirited Reichstag building and we are now attempting to move our capital eastward to Berlin, near the Polish border. We also have a new formula in East Germany about who was responsible for all of the Communist misery. The one who did it all seems simply to have been Erich Honecker and a very few of his friends. The rest merely just went along and had no responsibility for the situation. Does this not sound familiar when one thinks back to the so called de-Nazification period after the war? The old East German judges and lawyers are now the new lawyers and the new judges of a unified Germany. In former East German factories, the workers at the bottom are sorted out and dismissed, while the former higher-paid officials at the top of the ladder remain. The economic situation in East Germany is growing worse day by day. The first to be fired and the last to be hired are single-parent mothers, pregnant women, or elderly handicapped people, and of course young people, who are left with no prospects at all.

Germany—economically the most powerful country now in Europe and on the whole growing stronger each day, while the former East Germany is kept as a sick man of Europe—should practice a policy of self-restraint and complete demilitarization and democratization. A policy of self-restraint could be the most important signal that Germany could give in this new and more powerful united Europe. The East German revolution was abruptly cancelled by West German politicians, West German banks, and West German businesses. Suddenly, nothing was of any value anymore in the GDR, or for that matter in all of Eastern Europe. The only thing that seemed to count was to "go West," which is in fact the name of a cigarette brand in Western Europe. Quickly politicians on the right in Germany reverted back to the German national rhetoric, and "being German" suddenly took on a special meaning again.

This is where I become most distrustful. The change in direction in East Germany from "we are the people" to "we are one people" was due to money, not conscience. The systematic Germanization of the European continent and the economic imperialism of the Germans (merchants of death) should not be underestimated. Just think how many German firms had no moral problems in exporting highly deadly materials and technical know-how for making chemical weapons to Iraq and elsewhere. Many, many German firms broke the United Nations embargo toward Iraq because they were out for business first and morality second. A German-led Europe, and also later I believe Japan, will carry out the task of "Latin Americanizing" most of the domains of the collapsing Soviet Empire, with the former Communist bureaucracy running the branch offices of foreign corporations. The rest of the Third World will be under Bush's new world order, Pax Americana, living the New American Century, and will be controlled by economic pressure if possible, or by high-tech force if necessary.

I have little hope at this moment as I do not see that any government at present is practicing sustainable development or ecologically sound policies. The North does not seem to be interested in changing its own lifestyle or consumerism, let alone in cutting back on consumption and exploitation patterns. The North does not seem interested in giving a greater voice to the South. This emerging pattern is already being seen in the South as environmental colonialism. The North uses coercive power to force outdated development models and economic structures on the South that enable the North to continue its way of life. This is an unstable order.

If only we could begin to realize that what we do to the world, we do to ourselves! Beginning to understand that global inter-dependence, beginning to learn that we are not outside of nature but a part of it, is our last chance to start healing what we are destroying.

REFERENCES

Economist. 1991. March. 9. 15

Havel, Vaclav. 1990. *Atlantic Monthly*. October.

Penn, Shana and Darien Ross. *Elmswood Newsletter*.

Renner, Michael. 1989. *National Security: The Economic and Environmental Dimensions*. World Watch Paper 89. Washington, D.C.: World Watch Institute.

Rifkin, Jeremy. 1990. *The Green Lifestyle Handbook*. New York: H. Holt.

16

A Third World Perspective on Global Justice and the New World Order

HERB ADDO

PURPOSE

This chapter takes a critical look at the declared New World Order (NWO), said to be succeeding the Cold War Order (CWO) of the post-World War II era. My intent is to examine the extent to which the fortunes of the Third World could change during the succession of CWO by NWO. I refer specifically to the ways in which global social justice, as it affects these countries, would become better or worse with the change in world orders.

CAVEATS

Some caveats are warranted. This chapter falls in the tradition of futures studies and hence is speculative. It raises more questions than it answers. That notwithstanding, we do not avoid the politics of possible futures; we engage them.

The Third World is not a homogeneous entity, but this motley collection of societies is characterized by a commonality: the paradoxical ability to generate capital and the simultaneous inability to accumulate the generated capital for the internal development and benefit of the societies. Many factors account for this phenomenon, but I hold that the impact of the capitalist world economy on these societies is largely responsible. As the South Commission sees the matter, "they exist on the periphery of the developed countries of the North. Most of their people are poor; their economies are mostly weak and defenseless; they are generally powerless in the world arena" (South Commission Report 1990: 1).

INITIAL QUESTION

Has a New World Order dawned upon us? What does that mean for the many different individuals and groups of individuals combined as regards race, class, creed, and gender?

This is the direct question. To answer it, we need to derive other, more subtle questions. The answers will depend on the mode and level of analysis. The quality of discourse will be defined by three pragmatic inclusions—what I call the Third World perspectives encompassing the trialectical approach—and the evaluation of the thrusts of historical episodes by the strict measure of increasing humanization, as operationalized by Galtung in terms of decreasing levels of direct and indirect violence, somatic violence, and structural violence (Galtung 1969). In essence I will be talking about global social justice in the irreversibly fluid and interdependent capitalist world-system, from a Third World point of view.

The NWO is not yet a historical event, but it may well be that the global structures and processes that can actualize it are forcefully gathering and shaping themselves. Chroniclers and journalists may be convinced that the NWO is unstoppably unfolding, not so much because President Bush said so, but because there are events to show it. The exhibits in favor are dramatic but few: the economic success of Japan and the four little dragons of South Korea, Taiwan, Singapore, and Hong King (Tu 1991, Chapter 20); the unexpected collapse of actually existing socialisms in the Soviet Union, Eastern Europe, and elsewhere (Addo,1990); the resolutions, or near resolutions of ideological wars in many parts of the world, such as Nicaragua, Kampuchea, Angola, Mozambique, Somalia, South Africa, and Ethiopia; the unnecessary Gulf War of 1991, which is seen by many as the very inauguration of the NWO (Addo 1991a);[1] and the emergence of larger liberal-capitalist trading blocs such as "Europe 1992" and the US-Canada Trade Agreement.

All this, however, is only part of an old and ambitious story. It is the very center of the height of Western European social philosophy— the universalized "end of history" on convenient European sociocultural terms, as Hegel had gleefully predicted after the battle of Jena in 1806; as Nietzsche despairingly noted with his sad "God is dead" metaphor; and as Marx invested and exhausted his immense genius and energy in convincing many of the termination of history in something called communism. It is the belief in a universalism of which Sartre is not the least of the apostles, and the legacy of a belief which Fukuyama wants not so much to claim for himself, as he wants to reiterate and validate by the demonstration of current affairs and "strange" events (Ado 1991b; Fukuyama 1989, 1990a, 1990b).

It is not surprising, therefore, that to many observers the NWO is once again the final arrival of the much-wanted closing of the "civilization gap." This is a sociocultural gap, the closing of which will remove any threat to European ideals and civilization, or even mere differences from them, in order that world history will end only on self-congratulatory Western European notes (Parkinson 1977).

If this cherished dream is to finally come true, are we not entitled to ask to whose eternal glory and, by implication, to whose eternal ignominy? Could this have anything to do with cultural violence, as Galtung describes it (Galtung 1990; Chapters 1 and 2)? Or is it just a simple case of sheer cultural arrogance? Could it even vaguely be that the periodic declaration of the end of history has something to do with a specific fascination with the permanent domination and exploitation of the entire world by a particular cultural part of it? Should it be that the end of history will finally come, in what global sociocultural form will it present itself to us and to perpetuity?

The answer is obvious. It will be the wished-for triumph of the globalization of the Thatcher-Major, Reagan-Bush, Kohl, and Mitterand crusade for conservative/liberal capitalism with all its well-known humanizing limitations, as admired and aspired to by the Gorbachev-Yeltsin conflicting tandem. The problem with this dangerous fantasy is that we are told that all this has nothing to do with the compulsive self-assertive triumphalism of Western civilization, presented to us all as the eventual victory of culturally sanitized conservative/liberal capitalism. Should this happen, Nietzsche's God would still be alive, thank God, but His supreme rule would have been shoved aside and replaced by the supreme rules of supply-side economics, debilitating mass alienation, unnecessary suppression, and the sacrifice of us all to the inhumanity of excessive bureaucracy, all united in the name and pursuit of the efficient accumulation of capital, and yet each seemingly independent, even though they all combine to exploit the majority, and in the process dehumanize all. In the peace research camp, we can only exclaim, "some end of history!"

How we come to understand the NWO can never be divorced from the master question from the social justice point of view: has the NWO dawned, and if so for whom? This is the question, but we need to work our way toward it systematically. First of all, what do we understand by the concept of change as it applies to historical time?

TIME

It was Immanuel Wallerstein, in his majestic essay on the "New International Order," who observed:

> It is often said that what distinguished so-called "traditional," premodern systems from the modern world is that the premodern systems were unchanging whereas the modern world-system makes . . . change its central focus. This is in fact false. Premodern societies were constantly changing, and the modern world has been, when all is said and done, a remarkably slow-changing world. Nonetheless there is an important difference between the two in their ideologies of change: in premodern systems, whenever there was real change it was justified by arguing that no change had occurred. In the modern world whenever real change does not occur, it is justified by asserting that change has in fact taken place (1984: 21-22).[2]

Is it, then, that in the cultural temporality of our capitalist world-system the very notion of systemic newness, in terms of the qualities of changing times, has itself become an absurd ideological device? For that reason we must approach the apparent willful pronouncements of the changingness of historical times within this specific capitalist historicity with severe skepticism.

Luckily there are other critical modes of conceiving of historical time and change which can be pressed into service here to clarify the ambiguities and uncertainties of global newness and change that the designation of NWO necessarily connotes.

In the same essay Wallerstein continues to argue, persuasively, that we should approach the subject of time and its changing newness cautiously, bearing in mind the meaninglessness of the invocation of newness and in what temporality it is said to be new. "For time is not singular. . . . There is more than one dimension of temporalities" (Wallerstein 1984: 22). He successfully focuses on two definitions of social time viewed in terms of historical change. First he suggests that we need to concentrate on Braudel's distinction between the *longue durée* and the *événementielle*. The former time form is "slow-moving, sometimes practically static, . . . conjunctural," which is the turn in a cyclical movement and is medium term. The latter time form is the episodic or short term, "the tempos of individuals, of our illusions and [convenient] rapid judgement . . . the chronicler's and journalist's time" (Wallerstein 1984: 22). Second is Paul Tillich's distinction between *chronos*, "formal time" and *kairos*, "the right time." The distinction derives from the position that time is not universal and absolute. "Time is an empty form only for abstract, objective reflection, a form that can receive any kind of content" (Wallerstein 1984: 22).

This understanding of time creates a choice. We can locate the so-called New World Order in the logic of the *longue durée*, in the *événementielle*, or in the *kairos* and *chronos*. We ought to recognize that from the transformational point of view, the mercurial *événementielle* is always the stuff of the *longue durée*. For without the episodic, the *longue durée* is not understandable by itself, since its very slow moving and near static nature befuddles determined analyses.

It is precisely in this context that statements so far made, questions raised, discourses engaged, and suggestions proferred usually can only point us to the time of chroniclers and journalists, bored as they must be by the monotony of Cold War dynamics and attracted as they should be to the speculative freeness of fin de siècle ruminations.

Real analysis demands that we see the *longue durée* as understandable only in reference to the subjective depictions of the apparent moments of the episodic and the short term. Even more significant to note is the fact that historical changes, no matter how benign, always bring with them different qualities of time. As I have expressed in detail elsewhere (Addo 1991c: ch. 7), the real meaning of change in historical times is the differential impacts of the historical momentum of historical change on individuals and groups of individuals as they affect the interconnecting parts of the world, in the categorical senses of creed, race, gender, and class, and in terms of their implied humanizing options and fortunes. Without this, there is nothing to the meaning of historical change, absolutely nothing!

So even though we know that the NWO is not yet discernible, let us assume for the moment that it may indeed be the presage of some real changes in the capitalist world-system as we knew it in the Cold War era. This being so, we need to raise some serious questions as to what the NWO could or could not be.

Without a clear sense of our methodological perspectives, the questions that we ask will mean little. What is it then that I mean when I refer to the Third World perspective?

PERSPECTIVES

The Third World perspective is an intense combination of inspirations and aspirations, with the intention to confront and overcome the dominating Eurocentric arrogance. That arrogance is inherent in the epistemological certainty that universality demands that the non-European parts, seen as nothing but underdeveloped Europe, have to be assiduously Europeanized at all costs and pretensions. It takes its inspiration from the belief that the real meanings of historical processes, the quality of historical moment, should be different for those at the bottom than for those at the top. Simply put, this perspective unabashedly arrogates to itself the representational rights of what should be the interests of the rapidly increasing number of underprivileged in the world. These interests are constantly talked about in the carpeted corridors and high offices of those who have the "right" to think and the power to decide. They always do so, but (except in rare cases) never appear to think or decide in favor of the underprivileged.

In other words, my perspectives view world history, the dynamics, and eventual effects of the capitalist world-system from the rarely articulated concerns of the majority of the people in the Third World countries, on whose behalf assorted capitalists, politicians, intellectuals, and bureaucrats never cease to make promises, pronouncements, and plans, while the people of the Third World continue to see and feel their humanizing fortunes dwindle from one world order to the next.

My perspectives revolve around two curiosities. The first is the problematic of why Third World societies, believing as they do that they have been dominated, suppressed, and exploited—in thought and deed—for so long by the remaining parts of the world, continue to allow themselves to be so dominated, suppressed, and exploited even in the immediate circumstances of the postindependence era in the history of world capitalism. The second curiosity is the efficacy of developmentalism. Essentially we ponder the capacity of Third World intellectuals to comprehend themselves and their societies as both have evolved over time in world history, and more important the adequacy of this knowledge to oppose and challenge the overwhelming Eurocentric dominance when it comes to the *problematique* of facing the demands of the present and the uncertainties of the future with respect to the unsurpassable grand project of systematically increasing global humanization.

Third World intellectuals are the undeniable and unenviable products of corrupt hybrid societies, where the weaknesses of their societies are augmented and their strengths are either overlooked or detracted from by force of the externally oriented source of their confidence. These Third World intellectuals, therefore, always emerge psychologically and sociologically bruised.[3] Their common condition has to be tragic, for while they have the ability to understand, they find it difficult to avoid the grave error of misapprehension, by virtue of their corrupt societal origins. They are always well schooled, they are always bereft, for they have yet to learn to think properly for themselves and their societies. Do not say anything! I am one of them, and therefore I must know!

From the Third World we produce exhausted intellectuals in the moulds of perfect mimics, persistent reactive moaners, and dynamic complainers, or fundamentalists given to preaching the ordained necessity of return to nativities.

It is for these reasons that this perspective betrays a massive disappointment with the contributions of the Third World's "best and brightest," the intelligentsia and the intellectuals, to the global debate that has been raging since the end of World War II. These contributions have not been grounded in fundamental criticisms led by a higher quality of narratives (Addo 1991c). The contributions have not been derived from radical, "rootsy" rereadings of the meaning of history, and therefore they have not been able to intimate to their societies what they should know about themselves in the world in order to improve their lot in the unfolding motions of history as subjects and not as permanent objects. The contributions have been superficial by being too protective of the weaknesses and insufficiencies of Third World societies, too sensitive to and overly dwelling on what the rest of the world is supposed to have done to us and are still doing to us, as if there could have been alternatives. Currently the vogue is to be angry at the World Bank, the International Monetary Fund, and multi-national corporations (MNCs) as imperialist agents of world-capitalism, exploiting for the capital benefit of the center the capital cost of the periphery, as if from our perspective these imperialist agents emerged for anything else but to do just that! The current manifestation of imperialist exploitation is nothing but what it is, the current form of an unbroken continuity of exploitation of modern historical duration, which from our perspective is the very essence of capitalist development, since the 16th century, as world-system adherents will have us rightly believe (Addo 1986a: ch. 7).

The problem is not that Third World intellects have not been intensely at work. We all know that they have. The problem is precisely that the intellects have been intensely at work on the wrong conceptions of the problem. They have defined the problem of development in the wrong context of imitating European past history.

I insist on employing a third dimension to the flat and bland dialectical approach. I call this the trialectical approach to the examination of what we see as the Third World debacle in the dynamics of modern world history. This approach entails deep auto-critical confrontation with actually existing reality in honest relationships to the practical deviations, betrayals, and other limitations in thought as history moves on, as our consciousness rises, and as our powers of observations and insights improve. The trialectical method of concentration derives directly from pragmatic methodology, in which the caution is to avoid the familiar evils of hasty and self-conscious over-idealism, on the one hand, and tardy self-praising overrealism, on the other. Here James would agree when I say that trialectics, while it rides among other things on deduced logical implications, cannot possibly stand by itself except with the help of hard-nosed pragmatism: "the Pragmatic method . . . is to try to interpret each notion by tracing its respective practical consequences" (James 1955: 42).

The notion of NWO is a prime candidate for pragmatic analysis, and it is indispensable for the discipline of peace research since the matter of social justice and its many concomitants are the center of the discipline's attention. The practical consequences of the NWO for our idea of the development of Third World societies must matter very much, because its proponents have said already that the NWO has in it a peace dividend to facilitate the development of the Third World, a long-standing Western European ideal dream of a universalized uniformity of a conception of future history for humankind. As I said earlier, this is the idea Fukuyama sees as having arrived finally but which arrives divided into compartments to accommodate those who fall into this history and those who fall outside it. The problem is precisely that we should always be worried about those said to fall outside this universal history in its current enactment as the NWO. What will happen to them?

When problems persist beyond the time span that make them novel and therefore interesting, we have the penchant to define them away. Or we define them in such ways that the problems lose their original meaning and importance by acquiring new forms and meanings that assure us that we need to move on to more important and challenging problematics. We do all this while the old problems persist and even intensify.

This is not to say that we lose interest in the initial problems altogether. It is to say that the hectic expectations of our times push us to attempt to solve problems much faster rather than taking time to understand their fundamentals. In the process we underplay the diagnostic necessity to know about deep structures, deep processes, and deep and enduring constancies of motives in the historical sense of continuities. Instead we highlight superficial analyses which in most instances lead to counter-final prescriptions. These compel more refined prescriptions and more acute counter-finalities result, each seemingly on its own, and each bearing nothing more than scant regard for the pragmatic object.

Global justice, or the lack of it, in the sense of worldwide equity, is rather a recent historical concern as an item on the agenda of our current self-conscious world totality, even though its causal roots go far back into the very beginning of the formation of our modern capitalist world-system (Parkinson 1977). In the rush to realize this agenda item, we have seen changes where none have really occurred; we have put too much store on the superficial diagnosis of developmentalist theories (Addo 1991c). Moreover, in the context of something called development, when counter-finalities stare us in the face, we have been quick to seek refuge in such counter-objectives as the fortuitous emergence of the New International Division of Labor (NIDL) and in the highly improbable efficacy of a fantasy called the New International Economic Order (NIEO), all in the pursuit of something that we see as the ideal of global social justice.

PROPOSITION

A proposition is a statement that we take to be more or less true. From our perspective the important proposition to consider here is that the current enactment of capitalist world-history, called the NWO, cannot possibly be the hoped-for *kairos*, since the most highly probable trends and vital tendencies inherent in the NWO point in the opposite direction from global social justice.

From my perspective, the immediate reaction to the prospect of the NWO should be one of deep suspicion. Third World experiences in the evolution of capitalist world-history should certainly tell us all one thing, loud and clear: that any "new" world order that has emerged in this history has assured Third World peoples and societies that the order would contain opportunities for them to improve their lot in terms of global social justice. Each time that things did not go as expected they had been assured, or they have come to believe, that the next order will promote their fortunes much better. This is not to say that many people in the Third World think that they have seen their *kairos* come true. It is to say that for the increasing majority, the *kairos* is ever receding and ever evasive. We do not want to go so far as to restate the thesis of "developmentalist impossibilism" (Addo 1991c: ch. 9); the fact is that the development of world capitalism, over its long course, has brought more people into misery and left them there than any other previous expansionist historical form (Wallerstein 1988: 98, 102; Carr 1961: 137)

This statement is easily verified by figures of all kinds (South Commission Report 1990: 55-76). Those who are happiest pursuing "facts" in quantitative terms are free to test this statement for themselves. Those who are as happy in the realm of value as they are in the realm of facts can proceed without doubt, because they can see and feel the mounting escalation of deteriorating misery and cruel deprivation, the historical legacy of historical capitalism. The end of history in the triumph of conservative supply-side liberal capitalism, as the celebration of free markets, can only make things worse. The historical foundation of this proposition has long been established in many places. For example, in *Imperialism: The Permanent Stage of Capitalism*, I argue that the continuity with which capital has leaked from the periphery to create the center of world-capitalism spans its entire history, from early mercantilism (1500-1640s), through mercantilism (1640s-1750s), classical capitalism (1750s-1870s), and monopoly capitalism (1870s-1950s), to the Transnational and New International Division of Labor capitalism (NIDL, 1950s-present) (Addo 1986a: 136).

Each of these phases of capitalism had its specific mechanisms of imperialist exploitation, and it is no less remarkable that the post-NIDL phase of capitalism coincides with the most severe debt burdens in modern history for the peripheral societies, where the burdens fall almost exclusively on the underprivileged majority (Stewart forthcoming; Eichengreen 1991). One of the principal engines of capitalist development has always been the ever-increasing efficiency of the leakage of capital from the periphery to the center.

By some calculations, in the 1980s the majority of the Third World has lost a mere decade. This is not at all true for the Third World. Deliberate attempts have been made to push it outside the speeding train of history, either by excessive exploitation and intensifying conscious marginalization, or by the sheer force of misplaced optimism and "innocent" misreadings of history itself. Why then should the NWO be different?

This is a good question!

THESIS

I posit here the speculative thesis that with the anticipated demise of the CWO and the suspected nascence of the NWO, developmentalist hopes that lingered on from the immediate postwar years through to the 1980s will be dashed for a variety of reasons, to be advanced in the brief discourse to follow.

Guided as it will be by the "end of history" wish, those who fall outside this disturbing history—the majority of Third World societies—will be offered a bizarre, historical choice: either to bend and be humble enough to kowtow to be allowed into this terminated history, or resist for a while until history itself, since it is presumed to be as universal as it is inevitable, will decide for its own reflexive good when the logic of the *longue durée* compels that those who appear to fall outside it ought to be pressured enough to allow themselves to be dragged screaming into it.

All this is to say that the philosophy of developmentalism has failed (Addo 1989). It has failed largely because the way it was constructed it was never intended to succeed, no matter how many New Orders occurred within its historic form. The road to global universalism, whatever that means, was never open to the majority in the Third World, and certainly will not be in the foreseeable future, which is as far ahead as we are allowed to see. It is clear that the optimism that developmentalism exuded was false. Thus we should fear that in trying to prove developmentalism to be the correct path, that the NWO in its unfolding will increase structural violence at the global and other levels, to the convenience of the common objectives of the comptrollers of the capitalist world-economy in its NWO mode.

Why should all this be so?

QUESTIONS

1. What precipitated the transition from the old CWO to the presumed NWO?

2. What are the deep global structures of the NWO that would support and contain its realization?

3. What are the deep processes that animate and propel the NWO toward its self-realization? How will the NWO proceed?

4. With reference to the dispensation of global social justice, how will the NWO perceive and treat the many Third World societies as regards its *événementielle* historical tendencies?

5. Will the deep structural continuities and processural predilections that survive the CWO in the NWO be fatigued enough to permit fresh imagination and renewed commitment to encourage genuine enhancement of the historical fortunes of the deprived majority in Third World societies?

6. How new then will the NWO be? From the Third World perspective, could the NWO possibly be a *kairos*, "the moment of transition," the moment of fullness of [transformational] time (Wallerstein 1984: 23)?

These are the questions that frame the brief discourse below, though not necessarily in the same order.

DISCOURSE

From the very beginning of capitalist world-history, as Parkinson convincingly tells us, something called a "civilization gap" was said to exist as the European civilization encroached and forced itself upon other civilizations (Parkinson 1977: ch. 1). This gap was and is the composite of differences between European and non-European cultural forms. The gap was thought to be dangerous to European civilization and therefore had to be bridged at all costs. To bridge the gap called for nothing less than the uncompromising Europeanization of the non-European environment, which in the process dominated and exploited it to Europe's own good. In fact, modern capitalist history is nothing less than the complex process of global Europeanization, as the negation of the non-European global environment (Addo 1986a: 1-4, 5, 11). This was justified by the firm belief that the non-European world was nothing but underdeveloped Europe which, once Europeanized, would usher in the uniformity of universal history, and remove any threat whatsoever to the precious European civilization.

As Europe became culturally greater, through the diasporic effect of permanent migrations and settlement, and as Europe became more and more capitalist in its cultural form, the gap was said to exist in the form of differences between capitalist and noncapitalist cultural forms. The problem became one of how to pursue the uniform goal of universal history as global capitalist culture. This problem has subparts to it: how the non-European cultures could assist Greater Europe so that it could become more secure as a capitalist culture; how the non-European, and hence the noncapitalist, cultures could be made to traverse the stages involved in becoming capitalist (Rostow 1960; Meier and Seers 1984), all in pursuit of creating universal history by closing the civilization gap; and, above all, how the Greater European powers could come to see that as self-acclaimed custodians of future world-history they needed to form a concert of sorts to police the world to make it safe for the capitalist ethos to thrive.

The 20th century presented itself, its latent potential, and its problems in clear and well-packaged forms. The first problem was the question of hegemony of the capitalist countries. The second was the threat posed by the socialist experiment in the Soviet Union and fascist departures in Italy, Spain, and Germany. The third was how to lead the so-called backward societies that were later baptized as the Third World countries into the comity of "civilized" nations. The potential was the confident self-affirmation of global capitalism as the master of the world.

By the end of the Second World War, these questions had largely answered themselves. Capitalist global structures and augmented processes were in place—the United Nations, the International Monetary Fund, the International Bank for Reconstruction and Development, and the General Agreement on Tariffs and Trade, among others. The United States was not only the hegemonic power of the capitalist part of the world, but also the richest and most powerful nation in the world, a superpower. The other superpower was the Soviet Union, the leader or vanguard of the socialist alternative to capitalist dominance and a pretender to global hegemony. The Third World countries were all about, busying themselves with the choice between capitalism and socialism, managing in a short space of time to corrupt and be corrupted by both.

This structure of the global political economy gave observers a field day, as their analyses fluctuated between bipolarity, multi-polarity, Third Worldism, the fear of war (nuclear war in particular), the construction of the developmentalist philosophy, and the mixing up of the superficialities of each. These were the ingredients of the Cold War era in the history of 20th century world-capitalism. The period was exciting in that it was paradoxically very unsure of itself and insecure in general, and yet very hopeful of the future.

The events and the thinking of the time related directly to the idea of expanding global social justice to cover everyone. Socialism and capitalism, with their developmentalist variations, were the main carriers of this belief. As we now know, the developmentalist idea failed, and failed miserably (Addo 1988). In particular, the socialist experiments under the auspices of the Soviet Union did not so much fail as collapse under the weight of their own feudal/modern contradictions.

The socialist form of social organization as implemented in the Soviet Union was never intended to be opposed dialectically to capitalism. It was meant as a shortcut to Westernize the Soviet Union. The Russian ambition to develop sufficiently to be accepted and respected by Western European nations as European and an equal partner is both as strong as it is old. As I argued in the "Collapse of Installed Ends" (1990), the pathetic collapse of Soviet socialism was caused principally by some specifically Russian cultural attributes which made straight capitalism or socialism unworkable, even contradictory. The Soviet Union was a feudal-controlled society, the veneer of superficial Western mimetics notwithstanding.

What therefore precipitated the transition from the CWO to the presumed NWO should not be a secret to anyone. The NWO, whatever it may or may not be, is the final outcome of the fruitless exhaustion of a long-standing conceptual misapprehension, even a conceptual lie: that, as forms of social organization, actually existing socialisms were dialectically opposed to actually existing capitalisms. In terms of the development of 19th century European social ideas (as Marx and Engels, Nietzsche, and Max Weber confronted and contested Hegel), socialism was supposed to oppose and supersede capitalism in the dialectical scheme of thought and practice. If this did not happen, historical fault does not lie with the idea as such but with the implementation of it, and perhaps even more so with the then contemporaneous historical contingencies: the circumstances of the encirclement immediately after the First World War in 1919 and the political response to it, and the irrefutable legacy of persistent Russian feudalism, vainly pursuing Western European modernness and superpower responsibilities while laboring under the incurable conviction of feeling besieged and wanting to be considered Western European.

The precipitation of the NWO is not due to the historical vacuity of the Marx-Engels factor but to the flawed crystallization of the socialist ideal. That ideal still lives with us as a real alternative, yet to be properly understood and implemented. Nor is it due to the admirable response of Reagan-Bush conservative capitalism or to the much-discussed US decline from its position of hegemonic power, measured as it is these days by the irrelevance of minor economic recessions and marginalist indicators (Frank 1991; Kennedy 1987). Nor is it due to the successful propaganda of the CIA and its creature Radio Free Europe. The cause of the rise of the NWO is the spectacular failure that has resulted from the Soviet consolidation of all that is vulgar in socialist Russia's feudal heritage.

We must also credit this final resolution with bringing about the real end to the long war of 1939-1985, for the Cold War was nothing but the continuation of the Second World War by ideological means (Addo 1991d). The spectacular failure of socialism surely does confer on the United States the undisputed title of the world's sole hegemon at least for the rest of the century. The American century lives on, even though the US is not as "heavy" as it used to be, not with Japan and Germany-led Europe stealing the march on the US in the economic sphere. But never mind, we have a long way to go yet in global history.

What will be new in the NWO for the Third World; and if nothing, why not? A lot will be new for the world, but a lot will be worse for Third World countries. This is why that must be so.

With the present eradication of socialism as a global organizational alternative, global capitalism has finally come into its own with the unimaginable confidence that it always claimed as its own. The NWO is building itself on strengthened conservative capitalist bases, all in the name of the singular, fundamental, and incurable motive of ever increasing efficiency of the accumulation of capital at the expense of, and without the interference of, the Third World.

In terms of structure—the constructional grooves and fibers through which daily processes run—the NWO will differ from the old world order largely because the NWO, being a post-Cold War phenomenon, will not have the overarching form of two competing hegemonic powers. Its structure will truly resemble the controlling board of directors of the capitalist world-economy. The global order is moving from the duopoly of superpower hegemony to a hegemonic concert of oligarchy in the NWO. The new system will be run by the same old powers forming nothing less than a veritable board of directors, a commanding corporate superintendent of the global capitalist enterprise. All will appear to have changed in the world with the NWO, but as long as the deep structures and deep processes that propel the world remain capitalist, the Third World's unenviable fortunes in global social justice will in fact dwindle further. The consolidation of control in the New World Order will facilitate this.

In other words, the NWO will be less rigid and inflexible in its dynamics. It will not be a nervous bipolarity but a confident concert of multiple powers, each operating its traditional sphere of influence, in the typical 19th century fashion of gunboat diplomacy and collective service as the board of directors of the developing capitalist world-system. The US will serve as the chairman of this board initially, with the unspoken understanding that changes in hegemonic leadership should not lead to wars between members of the board, because wars will be too devastating and, worse, unnecessary. Hegemonic ascendancy will not be inchoate and hence chaotic. Rather, it will be by a "gentle-states" agreement based on the accepted principle of hegemonic change or rotation.

The capitalist world-system has learned enough about itself for all this to be highly probable, until it burns itself out, as it finally will, but when and exactly how nobody can claim to know for sure, even though some try hard (Wallerstein 1988; Carr 1961).

Those procedurally imperfect spawns of the League of Nations— the UN, the World Bank, the IMF, and the General Agreement on Tariffs and Trade (GATT)—will stand even more ready, firm, and confident, to carry out the instructions of the Group of Seven to the letter. These institutions and many others will feel confident and strengthened to sing their masters' developmentalist tune fulfilling the historic theme of global capital generation and its accumulation in the center of world-capitalism and away from the periphery.

The NWO will attempt a "final solution" to the definitional problems of Third World societies by behaving as if these societies did not exist, or that even if they did, they would not matter much because they would fall outside the mainstream of history and by doing so would forfeit even the limited civil hearings and humane considerations that characterized the old CWO.

The NWO will differ from the CWO by being more openly contemptuous, brazenly oppressive, and heartlessly exploitative of the

Third World's attempts to participate in the making of world-history as history's inescapable subjects.

What we are seeing therefore is the essence of historical world-capitalism reasserting itself with the expected, but all the same historically fortuitous, resurgence in self-confidence at the height of its maturation and strengthening processes. Nevertheless, it is a world-system moving toward its own confrontation with its own final collapsing contradictions. I believe though that this is a long way in the future. This system is far from exhausting itself and we better know it and learn how to deal with it. It is still growing in depth, width, length, and height, while obviously awaiting its own eventual demise.

But until then what is there in the NWO for the Third World? Nothing good really. The capitalist world-system has come to learn so much and think so well of itself—its structural and procedural subtleties—that it can now rightly claim to govern itself, for itself, in the interest of the entire world. For the Third World, in the context of social justice, intensified suppression, direct and obvious exploitation, and inglorious neglect will reign supreme in the name of the "end of history" thesis. Such experimental schemes and phrases as autonomous development, delinking, "small is beautiful," socialism, and the return to atavistic fundamentalism, whatever they mean, will be met not with benign neglect but with direct and severe police action, with the 1991 war against Iraq a sinister portent of a regular routine to come.

It is said that we have never had a world government. This is true, of course, in the sense of a declared formal world government. But in the real sense of governance, it all depends on where we place the emphasis on our conceptual definition of government. In the final analysis, it all hinges on how we rank governmental structures, processes, and the effectiveness of governmental functional capabilities. All through the history of world-capitalism there have been some representations of structures, definite processes, and undeniable attempts at functional effectiveness. All through the history of world-capitalism hegemonic powers have behaved as though world governments existed. We are not talking about whether the structures of governance are discernible or the processes are detectable. To most people they are not. What is of more importance is the effectiveness of the functional pretensions at governance, because it is these pretensions that finally and immediately touch individuals and groups in their daily lives.

To come to the point, the rules of the global capitalist game all along have been used by the well-placed powers to manipulate the system to their own benefit and to bring some semblance of order to the system and to their primary good. This is unavoidably the case in any kind of system. Will the NWO be different? It will, and then again it will not. It will not be different because it is a "world-historical" system like any other in the past; but then it will be different in many crucial ways. I shall mention only two characteristics. They are a vastly improved self-knowledge and an assertive self-confidence, due to much more strengthened global structures and much more discernible processes, as well as a much more refined sense of purpose, and hence, much greater functional capabilities. Thus, while we can say that claims to hegemonic control of the capitalist world-system in the past were more pretentious than real, we can safely say the reverse will be the case with the NWO. It will be more real than pretentious. This will make the control of the system more conscious of itself and more determined in the pursuit of its purpose of the realization of the historic motive of ever increasing efficiency in the global generation of capital, and its compulsive and unfair accumulation in the center and away from the periphery. It is necessary to repeat this because it is the core of the master argument fashioned as the Third World perspective on the development *problematique*.

I see little in the NWO for most Third World societies other than a gloomy, replenished mixed bag of carrots and sticks, all wrapped up in a preservative bag of massive indifference, with the sticks more ready for use than the carrots. Simply put, the peace dividend will not materialize in the NWO. There is nothing to suggest that it would. It is not part of the capitalist scheme of things.

Some Third World countries will appear to benefit, but those will be false benefits. Some countries, by being considered "good," will have, among other things, their debts, like sins, forgiven, only to then be encouraged to commit more sins, to be more corrupted, to buy more armaments, so that they will fall more into debt at more exorbitant rates of interest in the future to facilitate the yet unavoidable dictates of global generation of capital and its sad, but destined, skewed accumulation in some parts and away from others.

However, we must not be too gloomy, for as they say, every dark cloud has a silver lining. The NWO will have its flashes of silver linings. At the minimum, while the NWO will continue to entrench such cruel regimes as Pinochet's Chile, Mobutu's Zaire, and Marcos's Philippines, it will discourage and even deter such vile excesses as Amin's Uganda, apartheid in South Africa, and other brutal regimes as exemplified by the last military regime in Argentina. Hopefully, the NWO will deter and discourage the installations of tin god fascists, banished from Western Europe, from continuing to reappear at will in non-European guises in the Third World. One does not have to agree with the invasions of Grenada, Panama, or Iraq to conclude that while they were wrong, they should have taught us lessons that we all better learn if we are going to be of any use in helping Third World societies, in the name of development, to understand the world-capitalist system well enough to accommodate themselves comfortably and respectably within its future history.

Many Third World seers, hearers, and sayers, and their sympathizers all over the world, have presented us with a long list of plausible, even viable, alternative paths to development: autonomous development, delinking, bottom-up strategies, self-reliance and its collective form, and the socialist path to development in its many permutations. All these alternatives were projected as plausible and they were all sincere in their intentions. But sincerity of intentions is not enough, and plausibility does not always equate with feasibility. The paltry effects of these alternative proposals can only leave us confused and disappointed

But why should this continue to be the case? As peace researchers we are involved in no less serious a matter than the attempt to connect the reality of the capitalist global-totality with the conception of development. Development is seen as the progressive process of systematically enhancing individual, as well as the second and third senses of human beings' security, identity, welfare, and freedom, all placed four-square in the problematic concreteness of the many corrupt cultural hybrids mentioned previously

Had alternative paths to development succeeded there might not have been any problems. But they failed. They failed because the Western European road to development (WERD), the functional handmaiden of the Eurocentric philosophy of developmentalism, and its achievements to date remain the implicit bases and objectives of these alternative paths. Like socialism, these alternative paths were seen not as negations but as clever shortcuts for Third World societies to reach where Western Europe had reached. The validity of the universalizing objective underlying the Western European philosophy of developmentalism was never questioned. As the Osagye fo Kwame Nkrumah of Ghana said to my then youthful ears, "We shall do in ten years what it took others a hundred years to do!" Such was the optimism in WERD. I believed him then, but sadly I no longer do.

Why? Because what the countries of Western Europe did to get to where they are, and to get all that they have, was largely done by developing their culture at the expense of other cultures. Third World societies will never get that opportunity. All they have is some internal parts to exploit other internal parts in order to realize *kairos* for some few, and for it to be postponed indefinitely for the vast majority. The success of the much advertised WERD, like any strategy, is its own announcement of its strategic unrepeatability and limitations.

We have seen the development process as the blind imitation of the dictates of WERD. When we came to conceive of development as transformation, we wrongly transposed the cultural and the merely social (Addo et al 1985).[4] Mistakenly we saw the social as incorporating the minor "lower case" cultural, understood as no more than different attires, cuisines, music, dances, mannerisms, and so on, when in fact the "upper case" cultural, the grand cultural, commanding the lower case cultural and the complex linkages among the core cultural factors of economic, political, religious, social, and intellectual styles, is what we should have been focusing on in our searches for understanding in the development *problematique*. The grand cultural is the maximum concept of the dynamic historical totality of historical transition in motion toward the realization of the historical project of increasing humanization.

So when we talk of development as "social" transformation, we really mean development as cultural transformation, for in the final analysis what we are dealing with is not the mimetic futility of attempting to catch up by way of WERD to bridge the mirage of the ever receding development gap. It is all about strivings at the proper reading of history, not as the endless narrations and celebrations of past pains and joy, nor of past defeats and victories, but as the storehouse of collective human experiences from which we take wisdom to explain the problems of the present so that we can constructively and consciously invoke a preferred world.

We are making some progress to be sure. As the recent report of the South Commission makes clear, we are now beginning to learn from the nonfulfillments of the developmentalist great expectations. This is good. But are we learning fast enough? No we are not. The humbug is that we sadly, but not strangely, continue to see development as the developmentalist "catch-up" proposition by means of WERD's emphasis on industrialization; and we continue to marvel at the fact that international capital does not rush to our aid, on fair terms, just when we need it. We lament that "Even the IMF and the World Bank are now net recipients of resources from the developing countries" (South Commission Report 1990: 3). These and many other capitalist institutions were created not to do anything else in the capitalist world-system but to respect the essence of capital and its singular reason for being capital: to use or risk as little capital as possible for optimum if not maximum returns—a simple case of using small bait to catch bigger fish.[5] No capital is ever set off to develop any part of the world for the benevolent sake of it. It is against the logic of its being and its very definition of itself.

The problem is precisely that the stercoraceous sediments of developmentalism and its obvious functionary, WERD, have settled like layers of volcanic dust and ashes on the minds of all of us otherwise thoughtful people, to be constantly swirled about. No matter how much we think we have transcended these intellectually burdensome limitations, these notions apparently remain part of our historical heritage of corrupt cultural hybrids.

What to do then? Nothing more, and certainly nothing less, than to start thinking seriously about really viable alternative paths to final arrivals at different development destinations, unconstrained and not misled by developmentalist chicaneries and shenanigans. The objective is to free the development mentality, that frozen ahistorical category of uncritical thought, that untrialectical, nonpragmatic, uncritical mode of thought, presented in the form of Eurocentric, undeviating, ontological givens.

Toward this end I propose what may be called development as disengaged cultural transformation (DCT) as the most viable alternative form of development. The aim is not merely to increase the range of possible alternative developmental paths, but to diversify its missions. I intend to bring in the future, deliver it, that is, by concrete and practical invocations; and in the process I cannot care much about being called impertinent or arrogant. This has to be so if we are to insist that to understand is to situate culturally, to discern historically and epistemologically. We are engaged in the deconstruction, the unpacking, of the present, avoiding its reinscription, so that we can enter the constructional realms of inquiries "into the epistemological construction of [viable futures]," as Inayatullah would say, through the critical analysis of the politics of meaning, always guided by the motto of the enhancing of human dignity (Inayatullah 1990: 116-17). Our intent is not to senselessly relativize the futures that could be inherent in the NWO at the expense of the politics of meaning or to move culture to a site outside criticism. It is to historicize just enough to enable us to deconstruct the present historically so that we can point to new epistemological spaces and possibly form viable alternative futures for the Third World.

ALTERNATIVES

DCT is an epistemological position that confronts the developmentalist WERD and pronounces it dangerous because it is futile and moribund as a historical project, in purpose and objective. It argues that WERD by its own logic is condemned to produce nothing better than counter-finalities of the worst possible kinds. What it produces in the Third World are societies that are induced to be externally oriented, societies encouraged to live not in themselves but outside themselves—societies therefore pathetically bound to lack the synergetic self-confidence that should have come with possessing souls of their own.

WERD preaches uncompromising Western Europeanization of Third World societies, where every capital city, through the agencies of authoritarian, tyrannic, corrupt, misled statisms and elitisms, is supposed to look like London, Paris, New York, Moscow, Chicago, or Toronto, complete with expensive highways, high rises, and universities, all ignoring their rural areas, all dominated by irrational bureaucrats and annoying accountants, all controlled by mercantilist exporters-importers who call themselves capitalist industrialists. In fact they are not, because they have yet to produce anything for the good of their societies by means of any serious industrialization processes in the capitalist world. We are always in search of models. Because there are so many models to choose from, DCT insists that there are no true models, only many false ones. Each society is its own model, an experiencing model onto itself.

Probable world-history begins to unfold now. The trialectical dictate insists that we recognize the obvious and the impossible: that because the world knows so much of itself by being so conscious of its irreversible interdependence, DCT does not cry out "stop the world, we want to get off!" It recognizes that there is nowhere to hide, no means of delinking to develop autonomously. DCT proposes that in the absence of universal WERD inevitability, we begin to conceive of development in terms of different cultural roads to modernity (DCRM). Each road is to be anchored in opposition to what history has endowed to date, in the foundations of what it is, of what exists; and it must be consciously ever critical of its own hybrid corruption.

If it is the corruptness of these societies that must be the focus of concern, then the logic of DCRM demands that primary attention should be directed away from externalities and destructive adventures. The NWO will not tolerate senseless confrontations with the hegemonic power, as Grenada 1983, Panama 1989, and Kuwait 1991 clearly show. This is not to say that Third World states, the Group of 77, should not collectively confront the giant Group of Seven to effect more social justice at the global level, nor does it mean that these states should abandon their assertiveness in such matters as demands for a NIEO, reforms in the World Bank, IMF, GATT, and the UN itself. What it means is that all these activities of global participation, while they must remain and even be intensified, should not be engaged in at the expense of the mandatory—the internal adjustments and reforms needed to facilitate the cultural transformation that DCT and its guiding idea of DCRM call for. Thinking must be domesticated enough to make trialectical sense of critical transformational thought, understood as grand cultural transformation. Instant revolutions have run out of constructive days and moments for years to come.

No social organization is as it will be forever. We are dealing with the openness of the future, complete with all the glories and the tragic conditions that it may entail. The future must be multiple and open or else we are all sunk.

The future is open in the sense that our trialectical approach admits some critical capacity to influence future formations in progress. It is multiple because the cultural formations the critical capacity relates to and informs are different in many fundamental ways. To say this is not to encourage a return to any historical, atavistic fossil of social organization. Our cultural approach is not one that "freezes time horizontally (across culture) and in the effort to be culturally sensitive, loses sight of the future" (Inayatullah 1990: 127). Caution is necessary, because the cultural approach has a way of defeating itself, in that there is the tendency to

> a depoliticization of power and time; preferences become simply eccentricities as opposed to hard fought economic, political, linguistic, and civilizational battles with alternative possibilities. The future while no longer objective, becomes terminally subjective so that inquiry and analysis are moribund. Without a grounding in critical analysis, what can emerge are futures, visions of the good that enslave the possible, and alternative cultures which merely repeat the terrible history of the past (Inayatullah 1990: 127).

The epistemological ends and destinations, the developmental conceptions of the good life, need not be the same for all cultural societies and there are, and always will be, cultures within cultures. The world-system of the future, whatever it is called, cannot erase the differences. They must and, in fact, ought to differ because cultures not only differ but also update themselves differently. It is the false and vulgar denial of these determined differences in transition routes that is the cause of the problem.

An illustration is called for at this point. As interesting as the economic success of Japan and the four little dragons may be, what is more interesting is the demonstration they provide to encourage us to start thinking seriously about the viability of DCRM. They show that to modernize one need not imitate or emulate Western European cultural forms to the hilt. What is occurring in these societies is not the perfect duplication of the WERD but the clever adoption of aspects of it, founded, scripted, and inked in their own specific cultural senses and contexts of transitions to their varied ends of modernity. In the unique circumstances of the CWO, the most favored political and economic protective considerations accorded Japan and the four little dragons by the West were fully grasped and used to anchor their development images in their cultural strengths, while perhaps amending their cultural weaknesses, not to substantiate the "end of history" thesis, but to show that their cultures can be modernized along roads different from WERD.

Of course, to modernize itself every society needs some external shocks or influences. What is being said here is that corrupt hybrids result when external shocks and influences overwhelm "informed" historical self-transformations of societies, the corruptive essence of which is best described as indulging in arrested transition politics away from historical transformations (Addo 1984: 268-71). Internal shocks and influences, while unavoidable, can also be harnessed along lines of valid transition policies toward authentic transformations to enhance internal social justice.

It is worth noting that Europe's so-called Dark Ages were not as dark as many presumed. It was during this long period, which Hegel would have preferred to leap over, that Europe learned to borrow and even steal from the rest of the world then known to it, and to lay the foundations of what we know today as Western European civilization. From the Roman relics and remnants, Europe's intellectuals reached back into the Greek classics, by way of translating Arabic translations, and then claimed Greek civilization to be their cradle. Western civilization did not give birth to itself. It used the cultural achievements of other civilizations—Greek, Islamic, Chinese, Indian, African, and so on—to create and build the foundations it would stand on later to realize its ambition of global reach and control.

This history cannot be repeated. What other cultures can do is learn just enough from cultural Europe to reform their own corrupt cultural hybrids into comparable and even preferred alternatives, which have their roots securely sunk in the strengths of their own cultures, which have the courage to recognize cultural weaknesses for what they are, and which use nothing more extraordinary than the benefits of historical hindsight and the advantages of rising global consciousness.

There are a lot of historical lessons here. They begin with the realization that there are some humanizing goods and bads in all cultures. Because of this, DCRM compels nonrigid internal orientations, which harness the developmental slogans referred to previously into concerted determinations to create societies that do not aim to be replicas of the so-called developed societies, but rather societies that are different, and yet do not lack basic creature comforts nor lag behind in the satisfaction of basic human needs. Constant trialectical surveillance is called for here.

The fulfillment of basic human needs, in a global context, is not out of reach for any society. But this will become clear only after updated intellectuals have learned from the limitations of Western European universalistic pretensions and have come to appreciate the potentials inherent in other cultures (Stauffer 1990).

NOTES

1. This war would not have happened had the Cold War been in full swing. Since it was not, the diplomatic path to conflict resolution was abandoned for the opportunity to demonstrate the reassertion of Western European gunboat diplomacy, in concert form, to indicate the shape of things to come following the abdication of the Soviet Union as pretender to the throne of superpowerhood.

2. Space does not allow further elaboration on the concept of time, but see also Inayatullah 1990, in particular 131-32.

3. These grave charges have not been made lightly. For a treatment of the issues involved, see my *Eurocentricity*, ch. 12 (1991c). I do not make these charges in order to exclude myself, but more to sing my own sad tale. I know. I must know. I am one of them. I admit it so that I can move on!

4. We also committed this fallacy of transposed contexts in this volume.

5. The cover picture on Wallerstein's *Historical Capitalism* reflects this idea very well.

REFERENCES

Addo, Herb, ed. 1984. *Transforming the World-Economy. Nine Critical Essays on the New International Economic Order*. London: Hodder and Stoughton.

_____. 1986a. *Imperialism: The Permanent Stage of Capitalism*. Tokyo: United Nations University.

_____. 1986b. "Contribution of Black Peoples to World-History Civilization." *Harambee* (Trinidad) 4: 1, 4, 5, 11.

_____. 1988. "Crisis in the Development Praxis: A Critical Global Perspective." In *Rethinking Caribbean Development*. Eds. George W. Schuyler and

Henry Veltmeyer. Issues in International Development Series No. 2. Halifax, Canada: St. Mary's University.

_____. 1989. "Development as Disengaged Cultural-Transformation." A paper presented at a Colloquium in honor of Raul Presbisch, Starnberger Institut. November.

_____. 1990. "The Collapse of Installed Ends: Origins of the Resolving Crises in the Soviet and East European Socialisms." Mimeograph. July

_____. 1991a. "Final Solution of the Crusades by an Unjust War." Mimeograph. March.

_____. 1991b. "Jottings on Fukuyama and His Benefactors: The End of History?" In *Essays on Topics in International Relations*. St. Augustine, Trinidad: Institute of International Relations, University of the West Indies.

_____. 1991c. *Eurocentricity: A Radical Methodological Treatise on Developmentalism.*

_____. 1991d. "The End of the Undoing of Yalta and Potsdam." Manuscript. Herb Addo et al. 1985. *Development as Social Transformation: Reflections on the Global Problematique*. London: Hodder and Stoughton.

Carr, E. H. 1961. *What is History?* Harmondsworth, England: Penguin.

Eichengreen, Barry. 1991. "Historical Research on International Lending and Debt." *Journal of Economic Perspectives* 5, no. 2 (Spring):149-69.

Frank, Andre Gunder. 1991. "Read My Lips! A Kinder Gentler Presidency? The Political Economy of New World Order in the Gulf." Mimeograph. April 20.

Fukuyama, Francis. 1989. "The End of History." *National Interest* 16 (Summer): 3-18.

_____. 1990a. "Are We at the End of History?" *Fortune* 121, no. 2 (January 15): 33-36.

_____. 1990b. "The End of History Debate." *Dialogue* 89, no. 3: 8-13.

Galtung, Johan. 1969. "Violence, Peace and Peace Research." *Journal of Peace Research* 6, no. 3: 167-91.

_____. 1990. "Cultural Violence." *Journal of Peace Research* 27, no. 3: 291-305.

Inayatullah, Sohail. 1990. "Deconstructing and Reconstructing the Future." *Futures* 22, no. 2 (March): 115-41.

James, William. 1955. *Pragmatism*. New York: Meridian.

Kennedy, Paul. 1987. *The Rise and Fall of the Great Powers*. New York: Random House.

Meier, Gerald M. and Dudley Seers, eds. 1984. *Pioneers in Development*. Washington, DC. World Bank.

Parkinson, F. 1977. *The Philosophy of International Relations*. Beverly Hills, CA: Sage.

Rostow, W. W. 1960. *States of Economic Growth: A Non-Communist Manifesto*. Cambridge: Cambridge University Press.

South Commission Report. 1990. *The Challenges to the South: An Overview and Summary*. Geneva: Imprivite S.A.

Stauffer, Bob. 1990. "After Socialism: Capitalism, Development, and the Search for Critical Alternatives." *Alternatives* 15 no. 4 (Fall): 401-30.

Stewart, Taimoon. (Forthcoming). "Debt Crises in the Periphery as Manifestations of the 'Continuity of Imperialism Thesis': The Specificity of the Industrializing Commonwealth Caribbean." Thesis in progress. University of the West Indies. St. Augustine, Trinidad.

Tu, Wei-Ming. 1991. "Cultural China: The Periphery as the Centre." *Daedalus* 120, no. 2 (Spring): 1-32.

Wallerstein, Immanuel. 1984. "An Historical Perspective on the Emergence of the New International Order: Economic, Political, Cultural Aspects." In Addo 1984: 21-32.

_____. 1988. *Historical Capitalism*. London: Verso.

Part IV

Peace With Community

17

A Paradigm of Community for the Post-Cold War World

MICHAEL HAAS

During the Cold War, paradigms of regional integration developed so that contiguous groupings of countries could build solidarity in case of a military challenge. Devastated from World War II, countries in Western Europe launched integrative schemes for joint economic development, whereupon academic theorists tried to construct scenarios that anticipated eventual political union from particularistic integrative efforts in the field of economics. These theories of regional integration proved embarrassing to their progenitors in the 1970s, when many oil-producing states broke the chains of dependency. The Third World then proposed a New International Economic Order (NIEO). Theorists of regional integration, fearful of NIEO, soon became apologists for First World dominance, advancing theories of world "interdependence." Since theories of integration were not theories of cooperation, interdependence theory soon became hegemony theory. When the Cold War ended, theorists of integration, having discredited themselves, had nothing new to offer.

Meanwhile, the Association of Southeast Asian Nations (ASEAN), which initially formed to guarantee a detente following fruitless bilateral military confrontations between Indonesia, Malaysia, and the Philippines, sought to build community rather than profit, achieving an unparalleled success. The six-nation ASEAN, whose other three members are Brunei, Singapore, and Thailand, thus emerged as one of the few "peace zones" in the world, perhaps the only one which evolved from a "confrontation zone" in so short a time. As such, ASEAN is a model for countries seeking to move from confrontation to cooperation, with cultural resilience rather than economic advantage as the primary motive. ASEAN is also unique in that group identity has been achieved through the negotiation process itself.

Earlier in my career I analyzed why decision makers chose violence over nonviolence in handling nearly three dozen policy dilemmas (M. Haas 1974a: part II). I discovered that the main predisposing factor was a perception of cultural dissimilarity between the decision maker and the object of the decision, provided that the decision was regarded as one of high priority and involved an inadequate processing of information. This model, which accounted for some 95% of the variance across the many decisions, prompted me to consider the conditions under which some leaders believe that others are so alien that they would rather deal with them in a violent manner than a peaceful one. I then embarked on a study of regional cooperation in Asia and the Pacific, from which I developed a new "communitarian paradigm" of international community (M. Haas 1989 a, b). The purpose of this chapter is to show that the new paradigm is applicable worldwide.

Paradigms of international community have an intellectual heritage that began in the 14th century. While Asia was relatively quiescent under the hegemony of China, various European thinkers from Dubois (1306) to Kant offered plans to build a larger European community. Both in his *Idea for a Universal History* (1784) and in *Perpetual Peace* (1795), Kant advocated a federal state composed only of constitutionally based republics, with a separation between executive and legislative power, which experience told him would be more peaceful than monarchical despotisms. Whereas each state would be independent in domestic matters, there would be a rule of law within the federation based on a common commitment to a just and rational social and political order. Kant thought that war would be seen as less profitable than the benefits of economic development.

Kant did not foresee that the forces of nationalism would unleash the bloody era of the Napoleonic wars. After Waterloo, the five major powers of Europe (Austria, Britain, France, Prussia, and Russia) formed the Concert of Europe to monitor events so that no more national uprisings would depose legitimate monarchs (Nicolson 1946). When England refused to go along, the so-called Holy Alliance formed among the remaining four states.

Over the centuries, while theorists penned plans for peace, extraordinary political events proceeded almost unnoticed. China's empire was peaceful for thousands of years without many displays of force, because its emperors showed restraint and most vassals cooperatively sent tribute without being exploited.[1] Independent polities in Europe grew in size, but none could impose hegemony on the system as a whole. European states, nevertheless, could cooperate to launch the crusades, and such cooperative interstate behavior entailed an acceptance of common norms of mutual respect that made possible the orderly exchange of goods among equals, thus providing the preconditions for modern capitalism as a world-system.

Wales agreed to merge with Scotland in 1215. France emerged out of separate provinces at the time of Jean d'Arc's struggle to drive out the English in the early 15th century. Castille expanded into most of Spain with the expulsion of the Arabs in 1492. The Swiss gave up the conquest of Lombardy and formed a confederation in 1515. Scotland merged with England in 1603, after the death of the childless Queen Elizabeth, and then made the union official in 1707. The federal United States of America replaced the weaker Confederate States of America in 1791.

While these instances of political unification showed that the formation of larger communities was possible through decisions to collaborate politically, some peoples were less fortunate. Italians, for example, lived under Austrian, French, and Spanish rule throughout the 18th century. Germans lived under Austrian, Danish, and French rule as well as in various independent states, such as Bavaria, Prussia, and Saxony. Unification of divided peoples was thus a motivating force, particularly after the rise of nationalistic sentiments triggered by the Napoleonic wars. When Giuseppi Mazzini's *The Duties of Man* (1860) called for the unification of the Italian states, he was challenging the Holy Alliance. Mazzini's nationalism was linked with the rise of romanticism (Barzun 1943), a current of thought that glorified the root cultures of the peasants and shopkeepers and thus had a democratic ideological underpinning. The rise of nationalism and the spirit of democracy thus served to delegitimize imperialist and dynastic rule first in Europe, then in the rest of the world as the ideas of Mazzini and others became known. Proponents of nationalism wanted to develop a community of like-minded peoples, who would cooperate to develop the cultural, economic, and political destiny of a government. A world of monoethnic separate states, possessing self-determination, would make for a more peaceful world, according to Mazzini. After national liberation would inevitably come human liberation. That was the promise of nationalism.

In Prussia, Chancellor Otto von Bismarck saw the task of piecing together a larger German state somewhat differently than Mazzini. By building the Prussian army into Europe's strongest, he could effect unification through conquest or the threat of war, despite the wishes of the peoples affected. The industrialists of Berlin then could sell their products to a wider market.

The legitimacy of nationalism is an accepted fact of contemporary world politics. The unification of Germany and Italy took place by 1871, although the German case was hardly peaceful. Other countries, such as Norway in Europe, Guyana in South America, India in Asia, and Fiji in the Pacific did not reach independent political status until the 20th century.

The formation of the League of Nations recognized that an international debating body might provide a more rational forum in which to air disputes than the imperfect diplomacy that failed in 1914. The League, however, gave each member a veto. Founded on the principle of national self-determination and equality of states, it could not cope with the totalitarian ambitions of Adolf Hitler to reunite Germans throughout Europe. Hitler's domestic and international obscenities discredited nationalism and imperialism as dangerous and parochial. When the United Nations formed to correct the defects of the League, decolonization was high on the agenda for global action.

Very few colonies exist today. Division is considered abnormal by the peoples who live in separate though adjacent states. China, Cyprus, Ireland, Korea, and Samoa are prominent among contemporary cases of divided countries. Examples of divided peoples without separate sovereignty include the Armenians, Kurds, and the Palestinians of the Middle East as well as the Moros of the former Sulu Sultanate (located in Mindanao, Sabah, and the archipelago between these two territories). Thus, for many peoples national liberation is still an unfulfilled goal.

A world of separate states poses a risk of endless war. Since very few states are monoethnic, many scholars and world leaders focus instead on ways in which peoples may transcend their boundaries through various modes of international cooperation to achieve human liberation, bypassing national liberation. If nations can unify, why not groups of states? Can a *Gesellschaft* (society) of states become a *Gemeinschaft* (community)? If so, how?

For our purposes, an international community exists when peoples in separate states cooperate to pursue common objectives; this leaves open the possibility that community is either a convergence in values or an economic joint product, such as a common market. International communities also may be single or multipurpose, short term or of longer duration. A weak international community, one that is of single purpose and short term, is certainly preferable to no community at all; peace follows when countries work together for a common goal instead of at cross purposes. Our task is to ascertain how to promote more international communities, preferably those that are multipurpose and long term.

The first modern agreement for economic integration between separate sovereign states was signed in September 1944, when Belgium, Luxembourg, and the Netherlands concluded a customs convention. Known as "Benelux," the arrangement came into effect on January 1, 1948. Although the original idea was for a complete economic union between the three countries, the target date of January 1, 1950 was postponed as another development was underway. The second breakthrough came in 1952 with the unification of a single industry under an intergovernmental organization, the European Coal and Steel Community (ECSC), in which the Benelux countries joined France, Italy, and West Germany. Five years later the six countries agreed to form the European Economic Community (EEC), popularly know as the European Common Market. The EEC and the European Atomic Energy Agency (Euratom) came into effect in 1958. These developments, in turn, triggered academic theorizing about how to advance the goal of international community building.

Although interest in international community can be traced to various plans for peace from Dubois to Kant, modern social science speculation about modes of international political integration may be traced to the year 1946, when British Prime Minister Winston Churchill delivered a speech in Zurich urging the development of "some kind of United States of Europe." The follow-up to Churchill's address was an increase in enthusiasm for the idea of European economic integration as a pathway to peace through political unification. Academic researchers began to construct paradigms that might advance the goal of European political unification, with Western European economic integration as their chief example (as shown in Table 1).

Two kinds of factors have been cited as crucial in determining whether peoples or states can reach various levels of international community—beliefs and ideas or economic and material realities. For some scholars, following the tradition of Mazzini, arguing that "ideas rule the world" (1860: 266), either elite opinion or public opinion, or both, must favor increased cooperation in two or more countries if there is to be any progress in forging community between the respective countries. Efforts to bring European countries together after World War II occurred because of an attitudinal consensus, whereupon various events unfolded accordingly. Another perspective was that the devastation of the war brought leaders of countries to the realization that their economic self-interests required cooperation, not competition.[2]

Paradigms of international community may be classified with reference to three foci or stages in the process of reaching greater

Table 1. Paradigms of International Community Building.

Theorist	Name of Paradigm	Focus	Ideology	Methodology
Deutsch	transactionalism	preconditionist transactionalist	pluralism	statistical; comparative
Mitrany	functionalism	developmentalist	amalgamationism	Verstehen
E. Haas	neofunctionalism	preconditionist	pluralism; later transactionalist	comparative amalgamationism
Etzioni	leadership	preconditionist	assimilationism or developmentalist	comparative amalgamationism
Olson	cost-benefit	preconditionist	pluralism	ideal-type; statistical
Lindberg & Scheingold	group pressure	developmentalist	pluralism, some	comparative amalgamationism
M. Haas	communitarian	developmentalist	amalgamationism	comparative; statistical

harmony between peoples and states (M. Haas 1974b). Some scholars are preconditionists, that is, they seek to determine factors required before more intimate cooperation, such as economic integration, can move from stage I to stage II, from stage II to III, and so forth. Transactionalists plot the rise and fall of trends in exchanges of mail, trade, and other forms of international traffic over time or over space, then often identify subclusters of countries with dense patterns of interaction. The nurturing of cooperative processes is a developmentalist approach. Institutional growth and cooperative negotiations in international organizations provide the focus. For example, does co-membership in alliances lead to increased economic integration or social transactions? If so, why?

Ideologies of community building are also relevant to our concerns. One ideology asserts that world peace ensues when weaker states assimilate to the system rules imposed by the hegemon (Gilpin 1981). Balance-of-power theorists, such as Rosecrance (1963), tend to advocate a pluralist view in which peace is enhanced when there is Wilsonian noninterference in the internal affairs of states based on the principle of self-determination. Proponents of regional or international community building as a pathway to peace usually espouse amalgamationist arguments that a union of states can build a new world culture that will supersede national cultures. These three ideologies permeate speculation on international community building.

Initially, the paradigms focused on "regional integration" as a prelude to a united world. Among the important scholars who have contributed to regional integration theory, we should note Deutsch (1953, 1954), Mitrany (1943), E. Haas (1958 a, b; 1964), Etzioni (1965), Olson (1965), and Lindberg and Scheingold (1970), who have used a variety of methodological approaches to support their claims. As I have reviewed their contributions in depth elsewhere (M. Haas 1991: ch 8), I need not repeat that task here. Instead, I note that they theorized primarily about events in Europe. Extension of the theories beyond Europe came later.

In the 1970s, Western European economic and political integration became stalemated. Galtung (1973) accused the European Community (EC)—which resulted in 1967 from a merger of ECSC, EEC, and Euratom—of seeking superpower status. He applied a structural violence paradigm and emerged with an assimilationist, hegemonistic explanation for Western European cooperation.

For E. Haas (1976), integration theories had become "obsolescent" (though not "obsolete") because the motivations of elites in Western Europe changed substantially. Integration theories were "becoming obsolete because they are not designed to address the most pressing and important problems on the global agenda of policy" (E.

Haas 1976: 178). He then shifted his focus from integration and unification to efforts to build international community by delineating issue-areas subjected to collective decisions. From 1957 to 1975, he claimed, the focus of attention in Western Europe shifted to such matters as energy self-sufficiency, competing with U.S. multinational corporations operating inside the Common Market, protection of the environment, and a redistribution of the benefits of the customs union into economic sectors neglected in earlier years (E. Haas 1976: 181-2). Haas found more stress on national self-interest, with issues less frequently approached from a joint incrementalist strategy. Accordingly, he felt that the organizing concept for studying European community building should shift from narrower "regional integration" to broader "global interdependence" through the concept of "fragmented issue linkage."[3] In due course Haas decided to study international regimes in such fields as ocean management (E. Haas 1982), where the question quickly became does the United States dominate decision making in functionally specific regimes? The concern for hegemony degenerated into a quest to enshrine the advantages of hierarchy under the cloak of supposed interdependence, rather than the virtues of community as an alternative to dependency. As economist Bergsten (1988) has noted, the three equally important economic units in the world today—the European Community, Japan and its Asian partners, and North America—will either cooperate or stay apart. The hegemony paradigm within studies of international regimes, thus, was a diversion from the need to build international community and was premised on a faulty pluralistic assumption that structures of power in one area of human activity do not pervade another.

Meanwhile, during the 1970s, the Third World began to reject one-sided decisions by hegemons. One response was to proclaim the dawn of a New International Economic Order in order to reverse regime hegemony.

Thus, regional integration theory seemed Eurocentric—relevant to Europe and irrelevant elsewhere. After agitating, fighting, and dying to achieve national independence (disintegration from European empires), states of the Third World did not want to reintegrate just to suit theories of integration developed for Western Europe. Greater regional cooperation, however, might be useful. For example, if subregions of Third World countries could agree to stop squabbling about border disputes and taking sides in the Cold War, they could devote their resources more fully to economic development.

Haas's neofunctionalism predicted that developed countries were more likely to build international communities because they were pluralistic democracies. Additional research on Latin American efforts at integration by E. Haas and two coauthors tended to support the compatibility of neofunctionalist conclusions regarding Europe versus Latin America (E. Haas and Schmitter 1966; Barrera and Haas 1969).

Etzioni (1965 :318-21) cited three reasons for the failure of Third World unification movements: (a) illiterate publics have a "restricted horizon;" (b) less developed economies neither require technical coordination nor have sufficient talent to administer regional bodies; and (c) domestic problems overshadow foreign policy adventures.

Hansen (1969) similarly noted three specific problems with Third World integration: (a) economic issues seem heavily politicized in the Third World, so it is absurd to predict that an economic union can lead to a political union through gradual politicization; instead, developing countries need to depoliticize economic issues before succeeding at economic unions; (b) challenging Etzioni's third point, the superpowers hamper the freedom of Third World countries to act autonomously by penetrating their economic and political systems; and (c) integrative efforts are impossible while developing countries are engaged in nation building.

During the 1970s these points were seriously questioned. In Asia and the Middle East literacy spread, and talented technocrats abounded. Foreign problems were considered the source of many domestic problems, as the dependency theorists argued convincingly (Frank 1967). Economic union was rarely an objective of groups of Third World states, which sought to advance their economic self-interest vis-a-vis the First World through joint cooperative efforts, such as those exemplified by the increased prices declared by the Organization of Petroleum Exporting Countries in the 1970s, the main event that triggered the call for NIEO. In the case of South Asia, the countries adjacent to India were so integrated economically with India that they resented their dependent status and sought to break free. The dependent status of the Third World on the First World prompted attention to the collective need for a less dependent status. Finally, the era of exclusivist nationalism was largely over. Organizations such as the Association of South East Asian Nations (ASEAN), which began in 1967, were successful in regional community building because Indonesia, Malaysia, the Philippines, Singapore, and Thailand wanted to prosper together rather than struggle separately. Thus a new paradigm was needed.

In 1971 I embarked on a tour of Asian regional organizations, armed with questions based on the paradigms delineated above. In due course the evidence indicated that Mitrany-style functionalism was more descriptive of progress in community building in Asia and the Pacific, since relatively unobtrusive, functionally specific intergovernmental organizations were far more successful than politicized forums (M. Haas 1989a; Schubert 1978). A later trip to the South Pacific confirmed the same judgment (M. Haas 1989b). In comparing some 75 regional institutions in Asia and the Pacific since the 1950s, I soon concluded that there was a need for a new paradigm to describe the process of increasing regional cooperation. While Mitrany believed that technocrats propel regional cooperation forward, Deutsch awaited new patterns of social communications from millions of ordinary people, and the remaining theorists expected political leaders to make the difficult decisions, these factors did not explain what was working in Asia and the Pacific. Instead, a communitarian paradigm emerged, which stressed the development of an amalgamationist attitudinal consensus on modes of interaction and an egalitarian distribution of benefits.

There is an identifiable causal pattern in which modest technical cooperation, pursued for joint economic gain, leads to the development of a communitarian culture of interaction (Tehranian 1990), which spills over into the building of a political community that is so firmly rooted in cultural affinity that economic collaboration proceeds and spillback becomes impossible. The sequence is as follows: (a) The first step is for ministers of education or other less politicized officials of countries at similar levels of economic development in a region to agree that their needs for technical assistance have to be pursued jointly, instead of independently (similar to functionalism but contrary to neofunctionalism). (b) Technocrats then build successful work programs, with private goods for all, in many modest technical organizations (as recommended by functionalists); social transactions among experts in the region increase considerably in the process (the reverse of transactionalism); and the number of tasks and scope of issues increase. (c) Next, foreign ministers form a broader politically oriented international organization but proclaim that their aim is to form a bloc to reach a collective good—building solidarity in the economic and political arenas and forums of the world to advance economic development in the region (as neofunctionalists expect). (d) Political leaders develop a new egalitarian operational code, similar to Lindberg and Scheingold's (1970) "community method." (e) Similar to Nye's (1971) analysis of Central American regional cooperation, foreign ministers develop a collective good—an egalitarian commitment to resolve intraregional conflicts or to put them into deep freeze. (f) The cooperative political venture then receives support from elites and the public. (g) Concrete if modest initial steps proceed toward increased economic harmonization, including preferential trading arrangements of various sorts. (h) The result is an increase in economic transactions among the peoples whose states belong to the innovating organization. Increased transactions come next, rather than the beginning of the process, as neofunctionalists argue. (i) At this point a deepening of economic cooperation carries its own momentum, but the countries are reluctant to open the organization to new members until economic arrangements are fully in place.

The primary example of communitarianism in *The Asian Way to Peace* (M. Haas 1989a) is ASEAN. The paradigm also incorporates lessons learned from organizations in Asia and the Pacific that failed. Member countries represented heterogeneous cultures in Asia, but the most consistent predictor of cooperation is similarity in economic development (Schubert 1985a: ch. 7). Technical organizations, such as the UN's Economic and Social Commission for Asia and the Far East (now the Economic and Social Commission for Asia and the Pacific), the Colombo Plan, the Asian Development Bank, and the Southeast Asian Ministers of Education Organization first proved that representatives of Asian countries could get along, including Indonesia and Malaysia, which were mobilized for war along each other's borders in the mid-1960s (M. Haas 1989a: ch. 2, 4-6, 8-12). Innovative programs enabled technocrats of the region to meet one another at a variety of conferences, workshops, and in other opportunities for intraregional technical assistance; cost-sharing arrangements were carefully balanced so that no country was exploited (Kim 1985: ch. 13). Tasks and issues grew (Schubert 1978). ASEAN, and other ambitious organizations formed next, after foreign ministers decided to pursue collective goods (Solidum 1974), then developed a distinctive operational code known as the "Asian way" (M. Haas 1989a: ch. l). Border disputes between ASEAN countries were then either routinized through border committees or dropped (Solidum 1974: ch. 3); conflicts were rarest among comembers of Asian regional organizations (Schubert 1985b: ch. 22). At this point, business elites agreed to cooperate under the ASEAN banner in order to identify joint projects. Frequent press stories on ASEAN projected a favorable image to the public (M. Haas 1989a: ch. 7). Public opinion, which Etzioni (1965: 319) thought unimportant in the Third World, rallied behind ASEAN and other successful political bodies, but destroyed the Asian and Pacific Council and the Southeast Asia Treaty Organization (SEATO) (M. Haas 1986). Thereafter, ASEAN embarked on tentative programs of regional joint ventures and tariff reductions (M. Haas 1989a: ch. 7). In 20 years mutual trade between ASEAN countries quadrupled from 5% to 20%, while cultural exchange skyrocketed. Sri Lanka and Vietnam have repeatedly applied to join ASEAN, but ASEAN has admitted as a new member only the oil-rich enclave of Brunei, which achieved independence in 1984. The South Asian Association of Regional Cooperation arose in the 1980s to emulate ASEAN (M. Haas 1989a: ch. 13), but by then, Asian regional cooperation had become ASEANized (M. Haas 1989a: ch. 14). Thus, the principles of the "Asian way" have been institutionalized. The formation of the intergovernmental Asian Pacific Economic Cooperation framework in 1989, composed of ASEAN plus Australia, Canada, Japan, New Zealand, South Korea, and the United States, suggest that the outlook is for even more intensive economic cooperation in the future.

The principles of the "Asian way" were developed through discussions among leaders of the ASEAN countries. Contrasting as they do with Western modes of diplomacy, they represent a modern syncretic innovation more than a reliance on archaic cultural norms (as shown in Table 2). There are six "Asian way" principles. ASEAN foreign ministers prefer to engage in equalitarian socializing at an informal level before moving to more formal concerns. Whereas Westerners seek to maximize gains from diplomacy, deriving the best deal, the Asian way stresses the need to build consensus, starting from areas of agreement before venturing into areas of possible disagreement. Western diplomacy too often seeks blueprints—grand designs such as a "new world order"—while Asians prefer to move incrementally, that is, step by step. The discourse of Western diplomacy is to "grasp the nettle" and move quickly to details; Asians prefer to reach an agreement on principles, leaving their implementation as a bureaucratic detail outside diplomacy. The Western penchant for universalistic nostrums contrasts with the idea of "Asian solutions for Asian problems" in which an agreement is tailored to the situation.

Finally, the Western preoccupation with regional integration has been regarded in Asia as a return to the evils of colonialism. One of the secrets of ASEAN is that it sought regional cooperation before intruding into each other's internal affairs. Leaders of countries can cooperate by achieving more economic integration, but they must also be prepared to cooperate by dismantling regional integration whenever necessary.[4]

Table 2. Principles of the Asian Way.

Asian Way Principles	Western Diplomacy
equalitarian socializing before diplomacy	businesslike diplomacy
consensus building	maximization
incrementalism	blueprintism
values have primacy	details have primacy
unique solutions	universalistic solutions
multilateral cooperation	integration

Elements of the communitarian paradigm have been around for some time, but they have not been combined into a dynamic perspective. For example, Angell's *Peace on the March* (1969) showed the link between increased transnational communications and attempts to effect a peaceful resolution of international differences. Kegley and Raymond (1982, 1984) have demonstrated that international conflicts decrease when disputants establish common norms. Some of the same points were made in the initial paradigms, but the order of steps differed. Etzioni, who founded the journal *The Responsive Community: Rights and Responsibilities*, has also given support to the need to develop a community-oriented alternative to the "me-ism" critiqued in Hirsch's *The Social Limits to Growth* (1976). We will doubtless be hearing more about communitarianism, which may develop many variants.

Theorists of international community seek a future world in which individuals, peoples, and states will have a greater sense of community. Deutsch would let ordinary people decide with whom they want to interact; he wanted governments to stop interfering in the social lives of the people. Mitrany had faith that technical experts could build a peaceful world without interference from politicians. Olson opposed exploitation, and suggested that ordinary persons should opt out of exploitative relationships; the communitarian paradigm makes the same claim about governments. All the theorists expect officeholders to play key roles in bringing about international communities, with the public playing a reactive (Etzioni, E. Haas, Lindberg, Scheingold) or vetoing (M. Haas) role.

Theorists of European integration, while insisting on concrete results heading toward eventual political unification, appear to have missed the basic point in postwar European intergovernmental cooperation, losing track of a theoretical literature that began seven centuries earlier. The point is that no states in Western Europe took up arms with any other after World War II. When the Benelux countries agreed to form a customs union, they were cooperating. When they decided not to go ahead to a trilateral common market, they were also cooperating. After the European Economic Community began, a cooperative spirit prevailed; bickering was routinized. During the 1970s the European Community demurred in regard to ambitious undertakings, but cooperation reigned supreme. Charles de Gaulle's veto of Britain's admission to the community was one of the very few examples of noncooperation. Rather than having a fetish about integration as an unquestioned objective, the world awaits a coherent method for promoting international cooperation, whether the form of the cooperation embarks on integration or retracts integration (cf. Morrow 1990; Yesilada and Wood 1990). The aim of regional cooperation is peace, not cooperation or integration for its own sake.

Olson's effort to understand why humans cooperate in economic terms may have been answered by Hirsch, who advanced the need for collective over individualistic decision making before civilization degenerates. Hirsch's argument may be extended to explain why countries following Asian way principles are advancing so rapidly today.

There is nothing unusual about finding new foci for study after a field of research has been delineated. The Cold War has come and gone. An Asian paradigm that developed to steer confrontationist diplomacy in Southeast Asia into a cooperative mode is an example of a successful post-Cold War method of community that worked at a regional level. Communitarianism can work at the global level as well.

NOTES

1. Vietnam, although culturally Sinicized, refused political subordination to China. After 1,000 years of war, China ceased trying to subjugate Vietnam in the year 1428.

2. There are ontological differences between these idealist and materialist approaches. For more details see M. Haas 1991: ch. 8.

3. Etzioni (1965: 6 n.8) defined "interdependence" as narrower than "integration."

4. Similar principles of a "Pacific way" are found in M. Haas 1989b: ch. 1.

REFERENCES

Angell, Robert Cooley. 1969. *Peace on the March: Transnational Participation*. New York: Van Nostrand Reinhold.

Barrera, Mario and Ernst B. Haas. 1969. "The Operationalization of Some Variables Related to Regional Integration: A Research Note." *International Organization* 23 (Autumn): 150-60.

Barzun, Jacques. 1943. *Romanticism and the Modern Ego*. Boston: Little, Brown.

Bergsten, C. Fred. 1988. *America in the World Economy: A Strategy for the 1990s*. Washington, DC. Institute for International Economics.

Deutsch, Karl W. 1953. *Nationalism and Social Communication: An Inquiry Into the Foundations of Nationality*. New York: Wiley.

_____. 1954. *Political Community at the International Level: Problems of Definition and Measurement.* Garden City, NY: Doubleday.

Deutsch, Karl W., Lewis J. Edinger, Roy C. Macridis, and Richard L. Merritt. 1967. *France, Germany and the Western Alliance: A Study of Elite Attitudes on European Integration and World Politics.* New York: Scribner's Sons.

Dubois, Pierre. [1306] 1956. *The Recovery of the Holy Land.* New York: Columbia University Press.

Etzioni, Amitai. 1965. *Political Unification: A Comparative Study of Leaders and Forces.* New York: Holt, Rinehart, and Winston.

Frank, Andre Gunder. 1967. *Capitalism and Underdevelopment in Latin America: Historical Studies of Chile and Brazil.* New York: Monthly Review Press.

Galtung, Johan. 1973. *The European Community: A Superpower in the Making.* Oslo: Universitetsforlaget.

Gilpin, Robert. 1981. *War and Change in World Politics.* Cambridge: Cambridge University Press.

Haas, Ernst B. 1958a. "The Challenge of Regionalism." *International Organization* 12 (Autumn): 440-58.

_____. 1958b. *The Uniting of Europe: Political. Social. and Economic Forces, 1950-1957.* Stanford, CA: Stanford University Press.

_____. 1964. *Beyond the Nation State: Functionalism and International Organizations.* Stanford, CA: Stanford University Press.

_____. 1976. "Turbulent Fields and the Theory of Regional Integration." *International Organization* 30 (Autumn): 173-212.

_____. 1982. "Words Can Hurt You; or, Who Said What to Whom About Regimes." *International Organization* 36 (Spring): 207-43.

Haas, Ernest B. and Philippe C. Schmitter. 1964. "Economics and Differential Patterns of Political Integration: Projections About Unity in Latin America." *International Organization* 18 (Autumn): 705-37. Revised in *International Political Communities: An Anthology.* Ed. Amitai Etzioni. Garden City, NY: Doubleday, 1966.

Haas, Michael. 1974a. *International Conflict.* Indianapolis, IN: Bobbs-Merrill.

_____. 1974b. "International Integration." In *International Systems: A Behavioral Approach*. Ed. Michael Haas. San Francisco: Chandler.

_____. 1986. "Comparing Regional Cooperation in Asia and the Pacific." In *Toward a World of Peace: People Create Alternatives*. Ed. Jeannette P. Maas and Rober t A. C. Stewart. Suva, Fiji: University of the South Pacific. 149-68.

_____. 1989a. *The Asian Way to Peace: A Story of Regional Cooperation*. New York: Praeger.

_____. 1989b. *The Pacific Way: Regional Cooperation in the South Pacific*. New York: Praeger.

_____. 1991. *Polity and Society: Philosophical Underpinnings of Social Science Paradigms*. New York: Praeger.

Haas, Michael, ed. 1985. *Basic Documents of Asian Regional Organization* vol. 9. Dobbs Ferry, NY: Oceana.

Hansen, Roger D. 1969. "Regional Integration: Reflections on a Decade of Theoretical Efforts." *World Politics* 31 (January) :242-71.

Hirsch, Fred. 1976. *The Social Limits to Growth*. Cambridge, MA: Harvard University Press.

Kant, Immanuel. 1784. *Idea for a Universal History*. Reprinted in *The Philosophy of Kant: Immanuel Kant's Moral and Political Writings*. Ed. Carl J. Friedrich. New York: Modern Library, 1949.

_____. [1795] 1939. *Perpetual Peace: A Philosophical Essay*. New York: Columbia University Press.

Kegley, Charles W., Jr. and Gregory A. Raymond. 1982. "Alliance Norms and War: A New Piece in an Old Puzzle." *International Studies Quarterly* 26 (December): 572-95.

_____. 1984. "Alliance Norms and the Management of International Disputes." In *Quantitative Indicators in World Politics: Timely Assurance and Early Warning*. Eds. J. David Singer and Richard Stoll. New York: Praeger.

Kim, Kook Chin. 1 985. "The Political Economy of Asian International Organizations: Collective Goods, Burden-Sharing, and Benefits." In M. Haas, ed. 1985.

Lindberg, Leon N. and Stuart A. Scheingold. 1970. *Europe's Would-Be Polity: Patterns of Change in the European Community*. Englewood Cliffs, NJ: Prentice Hall.

Mazzini, Giuseppe. [1860] 1907. *The Duties of Man and Other Essays*. London: Dent.

Mitrany, David. [1943] 1966. *A Working Peace System*. Chicago: Quadrangle.

Morrow, James D. 1990. "Modelling International Regimes." Paper presented to the annual convention of the American Political Science Association, San Francisco, August 30.

Nicolson, Harold. 1946. *The Congress of Vienna: A Study in Allied Unity, 1812-1822*. New York: Harcourt, Brace.

Nye, Joseph S. 1971. *Peace in Parts: Integration and Conflict in Regional Organization*. Boston: Little, Brown.

Olson, Mancur, Jr. 1965. *The Logic of Collective Action: Public Goods and the Theory of Groups*. Harvard Economic Series 124. Cambridge, MA: Harvard University Press.

Riesman, David. 1990. *Theories of Collective Action: Downs, Olson and Hirsch*. London: Macmillan.

Rosecrance, Richard N. 1963. *Action and Reaction in World Politics: International Systems in Perspective*. Boston: Little, Brown.

Schubert, James N. 1978. "Toward a 'Working Peace System' in Asia: Organizational Growth and State Participation in Asian Regionalism." *International Organization* 32 (Spring): 425-62.

_____. 1985a. "Compatibility and Cooperation: Preconditions to Functional Integration in Asia." In M. Haas, ed. 1985.

_____. 1985b. "Cooperation and Conflict in Asia: A Comparative Analysis." In M. Haas, ed. 1985.

Solidum, Estrella D. 1974. *Towards a Southeast Asian Community*. Quezon City, Philippines: University of the Philippines Press.

Tehranian, Majid. 1990. "Communication, Peace, and Development: A Communitarian Perspective." In *Communicating for Peace: Diplomacy and Negotiation*. Eds. Felipe Korzenny and Stella Ting-Toomey. Newbury Park, CA: Sage.

Yesilada, Birol, and David Wood. 1990. "Reassessment of Regional Integration Theory for Europe." Paper presented at the annual convention of the American Political Science Association, San Francisco, August 30.

18

Restructuring as a Political Process: Ethnicity as a Case Study

JOHN BURTON

RESTRUCTURING AS A CONTINUING PROCESS

Restructuring of societies has always been an ongoing evolutionary process. Civilizations have adapted to changes in circumstances, as for example, the restructuring in response to inventions that gave rise to industrialization; the global restructuring that was a response to exploration, discovery, and expansionism that gave rise to colonialism; the restructuring that followed struggles for independence and gave rise to many new nation-states in the global system; and, generally, the restructuring throughout history as a consequence of wars and alterations in power balances.

Other types of restructuring have been less an evolutionary response to circumstances and more the result of deliberate intent, such as the French Revolution, the introduction of communism in the Soviet Union, and the contemporary endeavors of religious fundamentalists to determine political policies (see Chapter 19).

Both the evolutionary and the more deliberate restructuring have been hit or miss—only by chance they may have led to some improvement in quality of life. Both provoked resistances, giving rise to conflict between restructured authorities and those over whom authority was exercised, inviting more restructuring. Indeed, we can reasonably look at the history of politics within societies as a continuing restructuring, as is natural evolution; however, with an element of deliberate intent not present in natural evolution.

Behind this continuing restructuring we can assume some drives that spring from human nature and the societies in which humans live. We can assume that the many conscious attempts at restructuring, from revolutions to religious movements, are reactions to and symptoms of experienced frustrations. The powerful have not always had their way. "The power of human needs" (Coate and Rosati 1988) has at times been stronger than authoritative and military power, as was demonstrated in the Vietnamese war of postcolonial independence. While the power political process has dominated, over the long term there has also been restructuring that favors those who do not have authoritative or military power.

The restructuring process has, therefore, been adversarial—both for and against change. It is these adversarial institutions and processes that we have inherited, and which now control our political and legal institutions.

THE GOALS OF RESTRUCTURING

If restructuring for peace is to avoid this adversarial inheritance, the aggressive and defensive elements of historic change, the self-defeating and inadequate elements in ideological change, and the built-in resistances to further change (for every new structure carries within it a predilection to maintain its own status quo), then this restructuring has to have, first, goals that are precisely defined and universally sought, and second, processes that reliably achieve these goals. Political goals are frequently put forward without consideration of processes. In the absence of practical processes goals may be no more than wishful thinking.

Goals. It is not useful to define goals in general terms such as peace, justice, or other concepts. These are meaningless when it comes to determining means. Peace through strength? Peace through strategic peace-keeping forces? Peace through "justice" (without some definition of "justice")? Nor can there be restructuring for just one purpose or value. Restructuring for peace cannot be allowed to compete with restructuring for development, employment, quality of life, and other values: all are part of each other. Restructuring for peace is a restructuring for a total way of life sought universally and with consensus. Restructuring based on some personal ideology or immediate goal in some particular culture will lead to problems that are likely to invite violent responses.

Processes. Goals in practice include the processes by which they are to be attained. If restructuring for peace is to be more successful than past attempts, evolutionary or deliberate, the question on which we should concentrate is: can we evolve a political philosophy, a political process, a political system, that is not ideological and adversarial, but problem solving and cooperative?

RESTRUCTURING AS A DECISION-MAKING PROCESS

Indeed, restructuring for peace could be rephrased as restructuring of decision-making processes, for the reality is that restructuring for peace, or any other goal, is dependent on a decision-making process. Generally people, societies, and nations would like to live in a condition of peace. But how can they get there by peaceful means? And where is "there"? What kind of peace, what kind of institutions, would satisfy all and thereby create a condition of peace? Clearly decision making within a power frame that imposes some "solution" on people cannot create conditions of peace. No imposed ideology or innovative idea can create a condition of peace. The issues involved are too complex for simple solutions: the ultimate solution will be the result of a process through which policies, responses to policies, and responses to responses move societies in the direction of peaceful relationships.

Decision making is a recent study, despite its crucial role. The reason is that there was little interest in decision-making processes in the power frame that is our inheritance. It was only 30 years ago that Modelski sought to model political decision making—and it was power political decision making that he was modelling (Modelski 1962). He drew a diagram as simple as stimulus-response. At that time this simple reaction model could be translated into power and distribution of power, meaning that the resource input of societies was power, and the resource output was its distribution in the pursuit of various objectives. The input-output diagram had a dot between the two, presumably indicating no interest in the decision-making process that connected the two. This reflected consensus thinking and practice at the time.

Civilizations are only now moving from adversarial power politics, that is, structures and policies imposed by the powerful, toward a system that could be called thoughtful rather than powerful. In the same year Modelski was describing current realities, Deutsch (1962), influenced by techniques that enabled pilots to anticipate and avoid turbulence, drew attention to the possibility of political decision-making processes that would take into account the likely responses of those affected by decisions and adjust accordingly, rather than rely wholly on enforcement power. This was called the feed-back or cybernetic model.

An extension of this model is to have decision makers and those to be affected interacting before the decision is taken to ensure that decisions do not have self-defeating consequences. In this way interests and universal human aspirations and needs would be included in the decision-making process, ensuring agreement on goals and on the means of achieving them, and, most important, ensuring alteration in goals and the means of achieving them as conditions alter.

CONFLICT PROVENTION

The next logical development in decision making is *provention* of conflict or attainment of peace by policies based on a cybernetic process. In this model there is an analysis of the situation in the context of an adequate theory of human behavior, one that takes into account universal human needs and aspirations, and decision making is based on this analysis. Street violence could be avoided or *pro*-vented by educational, housing, employment, and other conditions that avoid the alienation that leads to street gangs and street violence. Ethnic problems could be avoided by ensuring that tribal and ethnic boundaries allowed personal identity with relevant autonomous identity groups. I use *pro*-vent rather than *pre*-vent to stress the paradigm shift involved: prevention implies constraints and coercion (Burton 1990).

It needs to be stressed that provention is a special feature of conflict resolution usually not present in other studies. We cannot afford not to give attention to means of proventing crime, strife, community, industrial, and other problems. Just dealing with particular incidents is tantamount to putting a finger or two in the hole while a flood threatens the very fabric of the dike.

THE HUMAN DIMENSION

The processes of analytical problem solving are more than processes toward some defined goal, such as peace. They in fact define the goal, alter the goal, accommodate to changing circumstances, and in so doing become a political and decision-making process, with the potential of creating a conflict resolution system in place of contemporary adversarial systems.

Only by such a process can there be deliberate restructuring likely to achieve its goals. When we talk about restructuring, we must have in mind a restructuring that is no less than the introduction of a new philosophy and a new political system, one that is a continuing consensual problem-solving process.

It must be noted, however, that restructuring as a political system requires decision makers with extensive knowledge at all levels and in all capacities—political, diplomatic, industrial, community, and all others.

This is not just knowledge of some special techniques of mediation or other interventions. It requires an extensive knowledge of human behavior. There has to be an awareness of the human dimensions involved. Some behaviors can be controlled by the normal means of threat and coercion, some cannot. Examples of the former are driving on a designated side of the road, turning up at school on time, and a whole host of social and legal norms of behavior featured in our everyday living, including most commercial relationships and transactions. These touch upon social norms and interests. There can be negotiation and compromise where differences occur. Such differences can be termed "disputes." Because there can be compromise and adjustments in behavior, differences can be "settled," by enforcement processes if necessary, hence we have "dispute settlements."

Examples of behaviors that cannot be so controlled, that is, behaviors for which there cannot be negotiation and compromise, are those that seek personal recognition and identity, security of personal autonomy, and the recognition and identity of groups with which the person identifies as a last-resort protection once personal recognition is denied. For example, a wage claim could well be not just a demand for increased wages, but for compensation for treatment that denies identity within the workplace, and which cannot be negotiated within normal working conditions. Blacks in South Africa seek their tribal identities and not merely their black identity. Street gangs and violence in cities deny control by police and the threat or experience of jail. The chief of police in New York observed in April 1991 that maintenance of law and order was now beyond the capacity of police, and that it was time politicians took the necessary steps to eliminate the causes of violence. Where there is denial of human needs, there is "conflict" that cannot be settled by coercive means and which must be "resolved" in ways that fully satisfy the human needs involved— hence "conflict resolution." Techniques are derived from the theoretical frame that explains the problem. Courts and arbitration are relevant in dispute situations. But arbitration, mediation, and many related techniques are not appropriate in conflict resolution where what is required is an analysis of the problem by the parties concerned, with the help of a facilitator or consultant with insights into the nature of human behavior and conflict.

PROBLEM-SOLVING PROCESSES

The starting point of problem-solving decision making is the discovery of the sources of the problem, for it is only after sources are discovered, communicated, costed, and agreed upon that constructive policies can be advocated and adopted.

Costing is particularly important, especially when there are power differences between parties. The analytical process and the realistic costing of policy consequences effectively eliminate power in the facilitating process. To hope for political and social change is unrealistic until the costs and consequences of the status quo are realistically assessed. If the costs of conflict are not yet experienced, they are not politically significant, unless there can be convincing prediction. This requires a meaningful explanation or theory by which to make a prediction. Such a theory is also the basis of proventive policies. In short, unacceptable costs of the present or of the predictable future, together with the demonstration of credible alternatives, are required before there can be politically acceptable change.

These processes have been set out elsewhere (Burton 1987, 1990). What requires emphasis is that this process, applied on a large scale, becomes in itself an alternative political philosophy and an alternative political system. Predictive decision making, based on a theory of behavior that takes into account human needs that cannot be compromised, problem solving, and problem avoidance, takes the place of power political decision making.

THE POWER CULTURE AND A PARADIGM SHIFT

Several scholars have pointed to these different behaviors, notably Sites (1973). There is now a "conflict series" based on needs theory and the appropriate practices of conflict provention and resolution (Burton and Dukes 1990). This thinking represents a paradigm shift of great social and political significance. The assumption within all behavioral disciplines has been that the person is wholly malleable and can be socialized into required behaviors. The "needs theory" approach, and daily experience internationally and on the streets of major cities, suggests that this traditional power view is false. There are behaviors that cannot be controlled by threat and coercion, and that may be altered only by solving the problems that have led to the denial of individual identity and group autonomy. It was not Iraqi madness that led to the U.S. failure to predict defiance of its overwhelming threat. It was the false power theory of human behavior that determined U.S. policy.

It is understandable that behavioral disciplines would make this basic assumption. Our heritage is feudalism, and most of our institutions are feudal and we-they in character. Industry is of this order. Underlying all our institutions is the Augustinian assertion that, to use the terms of Lloyd (1964), there are those who have a right to expect obedience and others who have a moral duty to obey. Indeed, it is this assumption that is at the heart of the power political frame within which so-called civilized societies operate. The assertion that there are behaviors not subject to coercion is challenging to all behavioral disciplines, and to traditional thinking and policies.

Out there in the political arena there are people whose job it is to legislate and to determine policies. Because of the influence of tradition, and the simplicity of power, they follow the popular power approach. Police are expected to deal severely with law breakers, such as gang members or thieves, without questioning the reasons for those behaviors. The public and those who legislate and manage are not attracted by any alternatives designed to get to the roots of problems. On the contrary, these may be seen as weakness in leadership, and as a threat to law and order and to existing institutions.

We live in the power culture. Power in this context means the ability to coerce, manipulate, and impose behaviors on others. At the family level, power is typically with the male, and violence has, until very recently, been socially accepted. Management is more powerful than employees in industry, with far-reaching consequences affecting the identity and autonomy of the person. Nevertheless, despite its destructive effects, the exercise of power is admired and emulated. It is accepted that political power is exercised by powerful elites, even though they represent small minorities. Leadership status, like boxing status, rises with the successful employment of power.

Alternatives to power are not welcome in this power culture. When these alternatives are put forward in vague and ambiguous ways, they are inevitably put in the category of "do-goodism" and not taken seriously. Unless they are presented clearly as long-term political "realism," more politically realistic than power from the point of view of attaining social and political goals, they cannot be credible.

The assertion that there are behaviors that cannot be controlled by threat and coercion implies a different political philosophy. In place of power political controls, the need for problem-solving processes that require adjustments of institutions and policies to meet the human needs of people, rather than people being socialized or coerced into conformity with institutions and policies, is asserted.

No country, not even the most developed, is coping with the exponential rise in social crime and social strife, much of which is associated with class and cultural clashes, reflecting alienation from the rest of society. We could reasonably argue that this exponential rise in violence is inevitable given the means that are employed to control disputes and conflicts. They are based on coercion and containment and do not get to the source of the problem. They deal with symptoms, not causes. Indeed, the rise in violence will increase as populations increase at a similar exponential rate—the world population will now double in 40 years or less—and as environmental conditions make access to raw materials even more competitive.

Despite many, many examples of policy mistakes, there has been little learning. But now it is becoming increasingly clear that coercion by majority governments, a legitimate policy in traditional democracies, is no answer. Minorities, whether class, cultural, or ideological, once organized, are prepared to suffer great costs over long periods of time rather than give up their struggle for separate recognition and autonomy. This has been demonstrated in Sri Lanka, Northern Ireland, the West Bank, more recently in Iraq, and now throughout both the communist and the Muslim regions.

Human needs that must be met, and the problem-solving decision making that this implies, are political realities. Societies are now faced with this reality. But if conflict resolution is to be accepted as an alternative to power, it must be defined precisely, separating it from the mass of peace studies generally, and placed firmly in the consultative, decision-making, proventive area of studies.

IDEALISM OR POLITICAL REALITY?

This is not necessarily as impossible as it might seem. At the academic level, which usually reflects trends and precedes practice, there is now a growing interest in problem-solving conflict resolution processes. There are many universities with appropriate courses and degrees. There is a growing literature and official interest.[1] Courts are moving toward procedures designed to take into account human factors. Parliaments are relying more and more on committee procedures that cut across political parties. There are many examples of parties to an international conflict being brought together into an analytical problem-solving frame (Fisher 1991). The movement exists of necessity.

SPECIAL CASES: ETHNICITY

Restructuring is sought by persons and groups who are struggling for their development and the satisfaction of their human needs. They belong to social classes or to religious, tribal, ethnic, or other identity groups. In the historic process of restructuring, unintended and unanticipated problems emerge, giving rise to even more minority protests.

There could be no more typical case of a need for restructuring for peace than the ethnicity problem. The ethnic problem is now almost universal because of past colonialism. Boundaries were drawn by conquest, sometimes through tribal areas. After independence, the new indigenous elites were reluctant to give up territory. At an early meeting of the Organization of African Unity it was decided that there would be no alterations in the old African colonial boundaries. Hence, there are today a great number of unsolved tribal, language, and ethnicity problems.

More recently, the postcolonial problem has been aggravated by extensive migrations, most frequently resulting from violence in postcolonial regions. Britain had no option but to accept as nationals many from Africa and Asia who felt alienated as a result of changes in political leadership, and who could claim British citizenship. The U.S. had an obligation to accept as nationals many whose future was put into jeopardy by American interventions into postcolonial struggles for independence, and subsequent struggles to oust regimes established by the outgoing colonial powers, as was the case in Vietnam.

Can there be a deliberate restructuring that would deal with this problem? In other words, can there be attempts at restructuring directed to particular problems within an overall frame that makes such restructuring part of a more comprehensive social restructuring?

PROBLEMS WITH TRADITION

Western political thought is not appropriate for resolving socio-political problems in nations in which there is more than one culture. The reason is simply that for historical and philosophical reasons, democracy in the Western tradition is defined as one-person-one-vote leading to majority government. When the notion of democracy was first entertained in Greece, there were few minority populations within the society, and majority government could be called democratic or representative of the population, though, let it be noted, in this tradition slaves and females were excluded from the electorate.

In present-day societies workers and females are not as readily excluded. But there are typically different cultural and ethnic minorities that are effectively unrepresented or underrepresented in a majority system. Minorities have no redress against discrimination, and perceive themselves as second-class citizens. If this source of unrest is to be avoided, some system is required that is not majority government, but that would effectively meet the felt needs of minorities for their recognition as social equals.

It is difficult to find a multiethnic, or even a multicultural society, that is integrated and harmonious. The "melting pot" idea is wishful thinking, as inhabitants of the major cities in the U.S. know.

Sometimes the problem could be resolved by giving separate state status to ethnic communities, which is the de facto position in Cyprus, though in this case the altered condition was brought about by violence, not by any decision-making process by the majority government.

In many situations of ethnic conflict the minorities are scattered throughout the larger society, and separation would not be possible without extensive movements of peoples from one location to another, with all the hardships associated with this.

ANOMALIES

However, any generalization asserting that ethnicity is the source of what we perceive and refer to as ethnic conflict is misleading. There are several anomalies which should cause us to rethink this assertion.

There appear to be few difficulties in relationships among people of different ethnic origin within the diplomatic and academic communities, and to some extent within the business community. Where people have had the opportunity to develop as individuals and feel secure in themselves, relationships across ethnic divisions are easier. It would seem that primary identity with a group—cultural, religious, or ethnic—is important mainly for any who do not have this sense of security, which is the general condition of peoples in modern societies. This would suggest that ethnicity is not so much a cause of conflict, but a symptom of social conditions that fail to promote individual development.

There is another anomaly or example that leads us to believe that ethnic struggles and conflicts may have a source in social conditions rather than in ethnicity itself. We are beginning to see that the same struggles for autonomy occur among underprivileged groups who are frustrated in their quest for more adequate representation. This takes many forms, and is frequently associated with ethnicity, because of the same experience of long-standing opportunity differences. In the typical Western type of so-called democracy, leaders and representatives may be elected by no more than 20% of the population. Sometimes 50% of the electorate do not vote. This seeming lack of interest is probably a response more of alienation and despair than of indifference. The despair leads to forms of protest at the workplace, at the local community level, and ultimately, to a rejection of the legal and social norms of society. As an example of this phenomenon, we have gang warfare, even between gangs of the same ethnic origin.

One could conclude that whether sociopolitical unrest has bases in ethnicity or class, the fundamental source is a sense of frustration and despair. The two different allegiances, ethnicity and class, could well be fundamentally the same, based in a sense of lack of recognition of the person and the group with which the person identifies.

In most developed countries, economic policies designed to stimulate the economy are resulting in the rich getting richer and the poor poorer. In the unrest and increased violence that can be predicted, conflict based on ethnicity and class will increasingly become one and the same phenomenon, leading to the same kind of escape tactics.

While sometimes separation may seem to be the practical remedy to the ethnicity case, perhaps such separation and its costs to persons involved in transferring to a new location could be avoided if the equal opportunities that are demanded by those involved in class situations were available.

The political reality, however, is that such equal opportunities in the class case are not likely to occur. Power elites and those whom they represent usually seem to be prepared to meet the costs of violence rather than give away some of their special system privileges, at least until the costs become too high and threaten the system and its privileges. As ruling power elites are in a position to maintain a special status, usually only violent revolt can bring about change. By that time the system is likely to be in a state of chaos, and migrations or separation are likely to be the option sought by any ethnic minority involved.

These options are not always available to members of underprivileged classes. Certainly migrations will be less and less available for such people. However, underprivileged classes that are located in one area, as, for example, within some regions within states in the U.S., finding that they cannot expect support from the nation-state authorities, could well come to the conclusion that they would be better off doing their own thing even in defiance of central authorities.

We have a pressing and almost universal problem, that is, alienation caused by lack of acceptance in society due to ethnicity and/or lack of social and economic achievement. While all authorities and societies are fully aware of the existence of the problem, there appear to be no remedies other than traditional means of socialization and containment. Our task as academics is to find viable and politically acceptable options.

ALTERNATIVES TO SUPPRESSION OF ALIENATED PEOPLE

Separation is probably ideal for alienated ethnic groups. Most are underprivileged and would get satisfaction out of going it alone. Cyprus is a good example. It is also an example of how majority elites seek to prevent any lessening of their jurisdiction. If there is to be separation, there must be a process by which it can be brought about that avoids the costs of violence and the hardships of misplaced persons.

One form of separation, which would probably have been the outcome in Cyprus had there been a peaceful process, would be separate autonomies brought together in agreed upon functional transactions and constant interactions under a shared president who had no powers other than facilitating transactions. This could also be an ideal system for South Africa. One-person-one-vote in South Africa would effectively exclude whites and some black tribes from the decision-making process, making it worse than Sri Lanka or Northern Ireland. There could be ten or so states designed to accommodate different identity groups, in each of which one-person-one-vote would be appropriate, all brought together in functional cooperation encouraged by a common president— the traditional British Commonwealth model.

But such separation and autonomy is not possible where ethnic populations are spread throughout the society. There are some concentrations of blacks and other minorities in the U.S. that could operate as separate states, and looking to the future maybe this will happen. But this would leave many in mixed communities, and the problem would not be solved.

Are there options by which there could be harmony rather than violence, and a real democracy rather than the present Western frame? How do we go about finding that option? Socialism was designed to overcome just these problems. It has never been tried, but a first step in that direction, communism, failed because there were no processes of change built into the system, which became an elite-driven one. What are the processes by which an appropriate system can be discovered and implemented step by step?

TRANSITION

Logically we could advocate the elimination of courts, arbitration, negotiation, mediation and such techniques (differently interpreted by different people) in handling social problems relating to ethnicity. They need to be replaced by legislation and social norms that remove the source of the ethnicity problem. But in this environment of growing conflict, the greatest possible use must be made of whatever facilities are available for settling disputes and conflicts, even by coercive and manipulative means, and even though these means can be faulted theoretically and in practice.

If civilizations survive long enough, many of these traditional institutions will give way to processes and policies designed to provent ethnic conflicts. By provent I mean decision making based on an understanding of the problem, and policies designed to accommodate it in constructive ways. Some lawyers are moving in this direction. Little by little, as knowledge of the nature of conflict spreads, disputes will be defined either as negotiable differences or symptoms of more fundamental conflicts. Conflicts will be defined either as nonnegotiable differences or the sources of what may appear to be disputes. They will be clearly seen as different phenomena with separate treatments— not a continuum of varying intensities of strife.

We are not looking to some dramatic revolutionary process which brings about some new system. Attempts to do this have failed consistently. We are looking for a transition from the present to the future, brought about by insights into behavior and the nature of institutions required to satisfy human needs.

This will be a slow and gradual process, perhaps helped by an increasing number of students from many walks of life making careers of such facilitation and advising. Already practical realities are forcing changes. Some judges in the U.S. refuse to observe sentencing norms and seek to make the punishment fit the crime, and also fit the individual who committed the crime. Two crimes of the same type may result in two different sentences. There are the beginnings of attempts to find the source of crime by judges working with sentencing attorneys. Judges acting alone do not have the facilities by which to be analytical about problems of relationships, but appropriate adjuncts can assist.

There has not yet been even the beginning of attempts to analyze problems of relationships at the international level. There was no attempt by the U.S. or the UN to find the reasons for Iraq's invasion of Kuwait, still less to find the reasons for internal repression of minorities. What would be an American president's response to ethnic demands for separate autonomy in Chicago or Washington, D.C.? What have Britain's responses been to Irish Republican Army demands for recognition of their autonomy? Israel seems to be so preoccupied with preserving its own autonomy, with U.S. assistance, that it has not taken into account the same human drives among Palestinians. Costing has not been undertaken because there is still the same assumption that military threat and power can control behaviors.

PEACE STUDIES

I would like to observe, finally, that "peace studies" still fall mostly within the traditional power frame. They range from peace through security and peace-keeping forces to peace through disarmament. Almost all are concerned with peace as an international phenomenon, brushing aside the source of the majority of violence in the world society, that is, relationships within each nation, and neglecting the human needs element which is the source of conflict. It seems convenient to ignore the reality that international conflict is a spillover of domestic problems (Burton 1984). The ethnicity problems faced by leadership in Iraq, and system problems faced by leadership in the U.S., led to a confrontation that gave both leaderships a temporary boost in legitimacy. The problems each faced should have been dealt with years ago. But great powers did not favor ethnic autonomy in Iraq and are reluctant to face up to their own internal problems. Thinking Americans should realize that the U.S. and its "new world order" is part of the problem and not the solution, as was a Soviet Union that sought to deny autonomy to ethnic and cultural identities. To discover sources of conflict between systems and deal with them, we have to look inside systems. Peace studies has not done this. Restructuring for peace begins at home, and with the satisfaction of fundamental, nonnegotiable human needs.

NOTES

1. Volume Four of *The Conflict Series* (Burton and Dukes 1990) contains an annotated bibliography of the literature. The official interest is reflected in the publications of the Foreign Service Institute of the U.S. Department of State, in particular, McDonald and Bendahmane 1987.

REFERENCES

Burton, John W. 1984. *Global Conflict: The Domestic Sources of International Crisis.* Brighton, England: Wheatsheaf.

_____. 1987. *Resolving Deep-Rooted Conflicts: A Handbook.* Lanham, MD: University Press of America.

_____. 1990. *Conflict: Resolution and Provention.* New York: St. Martin's Press.

Burton John W. and Frank Dukes. 1990. *The Conflict Series.* 4 volumes. New York: St. Martin's Press.

Coate, Roger A. and Jerel Al Rosati, eds. 1988. *The Power of Human Needs in World Society.* Boulder, CO: Lynne Reiner.

Deutsch, Karl. 1962. *The Nerves of Government.* London: Free Press.

Fisher, Ronald. 1991. Toronto: Canadian Institute of International Affairs.

Lloyd, Dennis. 1964. *The Idea of Law.* London: MacGibbon and Kee.

McDonald, John W. and Diane B. Bendahmane. 1987. *Conflict Resolution: Track Two Diplomacy.* Center for the Study of Foreign Affairs. Washington, DC. Foreign Service Institute, U.S. Department of State.

Modelski, George. 1962. *A Theory of Foreign Policy.* New York: Praeger.

Sites, Paul. 1973. *Control: The Basis of Social Order.* New York: Dunellen.

19

Competing World Orders and the New Nation-State

MARK JUERGENSMEYER

A persistent theme in this volume—of which the very title is a cue—is that we are currently witnessing a shaking up of the political and social structures of national societies on a global scale. Whereas scarcely 10 years ago the world was still held in the grip of a Cold War between two forms of secular ideologies, one Marxist and one capitalist, today the most imposing ideological confrontation is between the secular state and a virulent new traditionalism. The worldwide rise of religious politics (sometimes, I think mistakenly, called "fundamentalism") is the symbol of a clash between two competing frameworks of social order, and although the results of this clash are often destructive, this confrontation also offers possibilities for accommodation.

The political career of India in this century offers a modern parable. In 1909, the first decade of this century, Mohandas Gandhi argued in *Hind Swaraj* (arguably his best—and only sustained—treatise on political theory) that modern civilization and its nation-states contained a "sickness" that an emerging Indian nationalism would do well to avoid. Instead, Gandhi argued, India should look to its own cultural heritage for its formative political concepts. When Gandhi became a leader of India's independence movement in the 1920s and 1930s, members of India's Muslim minority took his Hindu nationalism seriously, and Mohammed Ali Jinnah led the demand for a Pakistan: a nation of secular justice in which his Muslim compatriots could have equal rights. Jinnah, as it turned out, need not have bothered. In an irony of history, it was Pakistan that became increasingly theocratic and India, at least initially, secular. It was not Gandhi's vision that triumphed at the time of India's independence in

1947, but Nehru's. Nehru looked toward the shining models of capitalist America and socialist Russia and decided that these secular visions of nation-states defined the future. If Nehru was India's most noble exponent of this vision, his daughter, Indira Gandhi, was its most self-serving, its most desperate proponent. When she was assassinated in 1984, it was a symbol of the decaying of the dream. When her son Rajiv was killed in the savage burst of a bomb in 1991, it was an emblem of the final obliteration of his grandfather Nehru's vision of a Western-style modernity for modern India. It was as if the experiment with modernity had failed, and Gandhi, in 1909, had been right all along. His compromise between modernity and tradition may yet provide a useful model for helping us to move beyond the tensions that currently devastate so many parts of the world.

THE COMPETITION BETWEEN TWO IDEOLOGIES OF ORDER

How should we describe this political competition between modernity and tradition? Our choice of terms is important, because they color how we think about what is currently occurring around the globe. It might be easy to characterize the confrontation as one between "religion" and "nationalism." I have no quarrel with that characterization as long as we are careful to explain what we mean by the "religion" and the "nationalism" that are in competition, and how they are related.

By putting traditional religion and modern nationalism in juxtaposition, we imply that they are both subsets of a general category—a "genus" of which religion and nationalism are the two competing "species." What should that genus be called? Smart (1983) has suggested "worldviews" as the common term. His choice has the benefit of including a wide range of concepts, from attitudes toward sexuality and natural science to views about the cosmos, and explicitly includes both what we call religion and what we call nationalism. Since our discussion is focused on conceptual frameworks that legitimate authority, however, I prefer something with a more political connotation, such as "ideologies of order."

I use the word "ideology" with a certain amount of trepidation, knowing that it comes loaded with meanings attached to it by Marx and Mannheim, and a great deal of controversy still lingers over its interpretation today.[1] I find the term useful for our purposes, however, because it originated in the late 18th century in the context of the rise of secular nationalism. A group of French *ideologues*, as they called themselves, were attempting to build a science of ideas based on the theories of Francis Bacon, Thomas Hobbes, John Locke, and Rene

Descartes that would be sufficiently comprehensive to replace religion. According to one of the *ideologues*, Destutt de Tracy, whose *Elements of Ideology* introduced the term to the world, "logic" was to be the sole basis of "the moral and political sciences" (Cox 1969: 17). The French originators of the term would be surprised at the way it has come to be redefined, especially in contemporary conversations where it is often designated as an explanatory system that is specifically "non-scientific" (Giddens 1979: 184). But in posing their own "science of ideas" as a replacement for religion, the ideologues were in fact putting what they called ideology, and what we call religion, on an equal plane.

Perhaps Geertz, among all of the modern users of the term, has come closest to its original meaning by speaking of ideology as a "cultural system" (1964). Geertz includes religious cultural systems and political cultural systems within this framework, as well as the many cultural systems that are unified and do not make religious and political distinctions. Religion and nationalism may easily be considered cultural systems in Geertz's sense of the word, and hence, as he uses it, they are ideologies.

I would prefer, then, to call both religion and nationalism "ideologies" and have done with it. But to make clear that I am referring to the original meaning of the term and not "political ideology" in a narrow sense, or a Marxist or Mannheimian notion of ideology, I will call them "ideologies of order." Both religious and nationalistic frameworks of thought conceive of the world around them in coherent, manageable ways; they both suggest that there are levels of meaning beneath the day-to-day world that give coherence to things unseen; and they both provide the authority that gives the social and political order its reason for being. In doing so, they define for the individual the right way of being in the world, and relate him or her to the social whole.

Nationalism, as an ideology of order, locates an individual within the universe. It ties him or her to the larger collectivity of individuals associated with a particular place and a particular history. A number of social scientists have recently explored this phenomenon and, in general, they link nationalism with individuals' innate need for a sense of community. Deutsch (1966) has pointed out the importance of systems of communication in fostering a sense of nationalism. Gellner (1983: 140) argues that the political and economic network of a nation-state can only function in a spirit of nationalism that draws upon a homogeneous culture, a pattern of communication, and a common system of education. Other social scientists have stressed the psychological aspect of national identity: the sense of historical location that is engendered when individuals feel they are part of a larger, national history (A. D. Smith, 1979: 3; Doob 1964).

Behind these gentle feelings of community is a more stern image of order, however, for nationalism also involves the assent to an authority over the whole of a given society (Breuilly 1982).[2] Giddens describes nationalism as the "cultural sensibility of sovereignty" (1985: 219), implying that the awareness of being subject to an authority—an authority who has been invested with the power of life and death—is part of what gives nationalism its potency. It is not only an attachment to a spirit of social order, it is the act of submission to an ordering agent.

Recent attempts by social scientists to define religion also stress the importance of order, albeit in a conceptual more than a political sense. In providing its adherents with a sense of conceptual order, religion often deals with the fundamental problem of disorder. The disorderliness of ordinary life is contrasted with the more substantial, unchanging reality of the divine. Geertz, for instance, sees religion as the effort to integrate messy everyday reality into a pattern of coherence that takes shape on a deeper level.[3] Bellah also thinks of religion as the attempt to reach beyond ordinary reality in the "risk of faith" that allows people to act "in the face of uncertainty and unpredictability" on the basis of a higher order of reality (1969: 907). Berger specifies that such faith is an affirmation of the sacred, which acts as a doorway to a more certain kind of reality (1980: 37; 1967). Dupre prefers to avoid the term "sacred," but integrates elements of both Berger's and Bellah's definitions in his description of religion as "a commitment to the transcendent as to *another* reality" (Dupre 1976: 26).[4] In all of these cases there is a tension between this imperfect, disorderly world, and a perfected, orderly one to be found at a deeper level of reality, in a transcendent state, or in a cumulative moment in time. As Durkheim, whose thought is fundamental to each of these thinkers, was adamant in observing, religion has a more encompassing force than can be suggested by any dichotomization of the sacred and the profane. To Durkheim, the religious point of view includes both the notion that there is such a dichotomy, and that the sacred side will always, ultimately, reign supreme.[5]

From this point of view religion, like nationalism, is the glue that holds together broad communities, each of which has a tradition of sharing a particular worldview in which the essential conflict between appearance and deeper reality is described in specific and characteristic cultural terms.[6] This "deeper reality" holds a degree of permanence and order quite unobtainable by ordinary means, and the conflict between the two levels of reality is what both religion and nationalism are about: the languages of each contain images of both grave disorder and tranquil order, and often hold out the hope that, despite appearances to the contrary, order will eventually triumph and disorder will be contained.

Since both religion and secular nationalism are ideologies of order, they are potentially rivals. Either one could claim to be the guarantor of orderliness within a society; either could claim to define the ultimate authority for social order. Such claims carry with them an extraordinary degree of power, for contained within them is the right to give moral sanction for life and death decisions, including the right to kill. When either nationalism or religion assumes that role by itself, it reduces the other to a peripheral social role.

Earlier in history it was religion that denied moral authority to secular politicians, but in recent centuries it has been the other way around. Political authorities now claim to have the sole authority to sanction violence. They did this long before the advent of the nation-state, of course, but usually in collusion with religious authority, not in defiance of it. Seldom in history has the state so vehemently denied the right of religious authorities to be ultimate moral arbiters as in the modern period, and seldom before has it so emphatically taken on that role for itself. The state and the state alone is given the power to kill, albeit for limited purposes: military defense, police protection, and capital punishment. Yet all of the rest of the state's power to persuade and to shape the social order is derived from these fundamental powers. For that reason Max Weber is able to define the modern state as that agency which has the monopoly of legitimate violence in a society. This was not always so, and in challenging the authority of the state, religious activists, wherever they assert themselves around the world, often assert the traditional right of religious authorities to say when violence is moral and when it is not.

Religious wars are one indication of the power of religion to sanction killing. The parties in such a war may claim a higher degree of loyalty to their sides than parties in a purely political war. Their interests can subsume national interests. It is interesting to note, in this regard, that the best known incidents of religious violence throughout the contemporary world have occurred in places where there is difficulty in defining or accepting the idea of a nation-state. Palestine, the Punjab, and Sri Lanka are the most obvious examples, but the revolutions in Iran, Nicaragua, and Eastern Europe also concern themselves with what the state should be like and what elements of society should lead it. In these instances, religion provides the basis for a new national consensus and a new kind of leadership.

It may be easy to think of Islam and Christianity as rivals to nationalism, and less easy to think of Buddhism in this sense. To many Western observers, Buddhism has come to stand for an interior, ascetic, spiritual discipline that is far from nationhood—the province of a large-scale social authority. Yet even that way of putting it reveals that the notion of order is a common thread that runs between the two. When the bhikkhus I recently interviewed in Sri Lanka spoke of the need for discipline in political life, and the necessity for having a religious impulse to provide it, they were speaking about an essential and compatible quality of both religious and national identity. Sri Lanka, of course, has had a long and glorious precolonial history of Buddhist rulers and Buddhist revolutionaries. This is so in other Theravada Buddhist societies as well. In Thailand, for instance, the king must first be a monk before assuming political powers—he must be a "world renouncer" before he can become a "world conqueror," as Tambiah (1976) puts it.[7] Burmese leaders have established a Buddhist socialism, guided by a curious syncretic mix of Marxist and Buddhist ideas, and even the current revolution against that order in Burma has a religious character. Many of the demonstrations in the streets are led by Buddhist monks (D. E. Smith 1965; Sarkisyanz 1965; Bechert 1974: 147-167).[8]

Thus it is that in most traditional religious societies, including Buddhist ones, "religion," as D. E. Smith puts it, "answers the question of political legitimacy" (1971: 11). In the modern West, that legitimacy is provided by a sense of nationalism, a secular nationalism. But even there, religion continues to have the potential of legitimizing and providing a basis for national politics and of challenging a notion of nationalism based on secular assumptions. Perhaps nothing indicates this more than the persistence of an American "civil religion" in the 20th century and the rise of politically active religious fundamentalists in the 1980s.[9] Like secular nationalism, religion can provide a faith in the unitary nature of a society such that it can authenticate political rule.

HOW NATIONALISM FAILED TO ACCOMMODATE RELIGION

Where nationalism, rather than religion, has become the dominant paradigm in society, religion is shunted to society's periphery. Nothing illustrates this more dramatically than the club-like "church religion" common to the United States. Yet even in America there have been attempts to assimilate some aspects of religion into the national consensus. The reasons for doing so are varied: co-opting elements of religion into nationalism keeps religion from building its own antinational base of power; it provides religious legitimacy for the state; and it helps to give nationalism a religious aura. To accomplish these goals, national leaders may borrow various elements of a society's religious culture. In the United States, secular nationalism is to some extent influenced by a religiosity such as this, as Bellah has pointed out in his analysis of what he calls "civil religion" sprinkled throughout the inaugural addresses of American presidents and the rhetoric of other public speakers (Bellah 1970).

Despite these attempts to co-opt it, and despite its relegation to the periphery of society, church religion persists in the West, and it is not always easy to contain politically. In the United States, what Krejci calls "the American pattern" of "ethno-political relationships" occasionally breaks down (Krejci: 39). This was seen dramatically in the civil rights era, when the black church and the black clergy became central to the movement. In a different way the rise of fundamentalist politicians is a new assault on the presumptions of secular nationalism in America. In what Krejci calls "the European pattern" of strong ethnic and religious communities, which are supposed to be insulated from political life, the insulation sometimes wears thin. The recent events in Eastern Europe are cases in point.

So, the West has found that religion does not stay as tightly leashed as secular nationalists might wish. But if accommodating religion has been difficult for the West, the new nations' problems in bridling religion have been a thousand times greater. There the need to accommodate religion is much more obvious. Given religious histories that are part of national heritages, religious institutions that are sometimes the most effective systems of communication in the country, and religious leaders who may be more devoted, efficient, and intelligent than the government's own staff, religion cannot be ignored. Attempts to accommodate it, however, have not always been successful.

In Egypt, following the revolution of 1952, Nasser was caught in a double bind. His support came from both the Muslim Brotherhood and the modern elite, and he was expected to create a Muslim state and a modern secular state at the same time. His approach was to create the image of an Egypt which was culturally Muslim and politically secular, and he cheerfully went about "Egyptizing along with modernizing," as a professor in Cairo put it (el-Hamamsy 1989). The compromise did not work, and especially after Nasser attempted to institute "scientific socialism," which the Muslim Brotherhood regarded as anti-Islamic, it became Nasser's foe. The Brotherhood attempted to overthrow his government, and Nasser jailed its members and executed its leader, Sayid Qutb.

Nasser's successor, Anwar al-Sadat, repeated the pattern, which turned out to be a tragic and fatal mistake. Like Nasser, Sadat raised Muslim expectations by currying favor with the Muslim Brotherhood, and in 1971 he released many of them from jail. But by 1974 he and the

Brotherhood were at loggerheads and again the organization was outlawed. Sadat attempted to wear the trappings of Islam by giving himself a Muslim title, revealing that his first name was really Mohammad rather than Anwar, and promoting religious schools. None of this really worked. His wife was regarded as something of a floozy, and Sadat himself was thought to be a Muslim turncoat. With this thought in mind, a member of the al-Jihad, a radical fringe group of the Muslim Brotherhood, assassinated Sadat in 1981. His successor, Hosni Mabarak, tries to steer more of a middle course, making no promises to the Muslim activists, but no new secular or socialist departures as well (Ibrahim 1989).

In India, three generations of prime ministers in the Nehru dynasty—Jawaharlal, his daughter Indira Gandhi, and her son Rajiv—all tried to accommodate religion as little as possible. Yet there have been times when they were forced to make concessions to religious forces almost against their wills. Nehru seemed virtually allergic to religion, putting secularism alongside socialism as his great political goal. Nonetheless, the Indian constitution and subsequent parliamentary actions have given a great deal of public support to religious entities.[10] Special seats have been assigned in the legislature for Muslims and other minority religious communities, religious schools have been affiliated with the state, and temples and mosques have received direct public support. In general the government's notion of secularism has not been indifference to religion, but an attempt to treat and foster each religion equally. As Embree puts it, "advocates of secularism in India always insisted . . . that far from being hostile to religion, they valued it" (1990: 88).

Even so, these concessions have not been sufficient to stem the tide of religious politics in India. The 1980s was a decade of tragedy in that regard. Hindu nationalists wanted more and then more access to power, prompting defensiveness on the part of Muslim and Christian minorities and a vicious rebellion on the part of the Sikhs. The assassinations of Prime Minister Indira Gandhi in 1984 and former Prime Minister Rajiv Gandhi in 1991 did not put an end to their sense of dissatisfaction, and it is fair to say that religious politics are ready to flare up again in India at any time over the slightest pretext.

In Sri Lanka following independence, the urbane and educated leaders of the new nation realized that they would have to give a Sinhalese Buddhist aura to secular politics in order for it to be widely accepted. Perhaps no Sri Lankan leader attempted to give in to Buddhist demands as much as S. W. R. D. Bandaranaike, but even he lost his life at the hands of an irate Buddhist monk who felt that he had not gone far enough.

There have been attempts to create a "civil religion" for Sri Lanka: a national religion that borrows elements from several of the religious traditions in the country without favoring any one of them. Perhaps the Adam's Peak flag would have served as an apt symbol of such a syncretic religious point of view. In the current climate of communal enmity, a syncretic view of Sri Lankan society might provide something of a leavening influence, and many thoughtful people have advocated that their fellow citizens adopt such a perspective. The Colombo office of the International Centre for Ethnic Studies, for example, has attempted to provide a public service by producing a series of television programs that have as their theme the notion of "unity through diversity" in Sri Lankan society. The producers have described, with striking visuals, the complex historical and theological interdependencies of Hinduism, Buddhism, and other religious traditions of Sri Lanka. The Hindu god, Vishnu, for instance, is shown to be frequently worshipped at Buddhist Temples, and the distinctly Sri Lankan god, Kataragama, is seen to be venerated equally by Buddhists and Hindus alike.

Syncretic religious nationalism—a Sri Lankan civil religion—seems not to have caught on, however, at least not among the Sinhalese portions of society. Where it has become the pattern of nationalism is in Tamil areas, where it is not a syncretic religious nationalism embracing the whole of Sri Lankan society, but only the Tamil-dominated portions of it. The nationalism of Thamil Eelam, the goal of the separatists, is one in which religious identities—specifically Hindu and Christian—are alleged not to be important. As one separatist writer explained, "the original link between Tamil ethnicity and the Hindu religion has come to be severed" (Ponnambalam 1983: 31). Instead a sort of Tamil religiosity has replaced Hinduism as the national religion of Tamils. As a result, some of the most active participants in the Tamil separatist movement have been Christians, even Christian clergy.

Although in the Tamil provinces of Sri Lanka religion (Hinduism) has not yet played a legitimizing role, in the rest of the country it has (Sinhalese Buddhism). While trying at the same time to preserve its secular nature, each of the country's prime ministers have tried to outdo the others in endorsing the religious character of their country's majority. An emphasis on Buddhist culture and Sinhalese language was the vehicle on which Bandaranaike and his Sri Lanka Freedom Party rode into power, and in 1956 they went to the limits of supporting legislation that made Sinhala the sole official language of the nation. As soon as the bill was passed, they backed away from the extreme implications of it in order to protect Tamil minority interests, but in doing so they alienated some of their Buddhist supporters (such as the Rasputin-like monk, Buddharakkhita) and left an opening for political rivals—including one of Bandaranaike's successors, J. R. Jayewardene—to gain Sinhalese support by claiming that the SLFP had reneged on its promises.

The present rulers face the same dilemma that their predecessors did: they need Sinhalese support, but they feel they cannot go so far as to alienate the Tamils and other minority communities. They would like to achieve what might be an impossibility: a national entity that is both Buddhist and secular. They attempt to use the trappings of Buddhism in order to appeal to Sinhalese, and a secular political ideology to legitimize their rule in the eyes of all. This dual policy has led to such flamboyant displays of support for Buddhist culture as the rebuilding of grounds around the Dalada Maligawa, "the Temple of the Tooth." This is the temple that houses one of the most important relics in Buddhism, a tooth said to have been taken from the Buddha's funeral pyre in 543 BCE, the only remains of the Enlightened One's physical being. How it got to Sri Lanka and eventually to Kandy is a long story, but there it is, and the temple that houses it is the central shrine of Sinhalese Buddhism. For that reason no politician can afford to ignore it. In 1987, when the United Nations proclaimed "the international year of housing" to encourage the building of shelters for the world's poor, the first thing that the prime minister housed with the money he collected from international sources was the tooth: he built a roof over the temple and layered it with a gold sheath that can be seen throughout the city. It shimmers in the sunlight by day, and gleams in floodlights by night.

In housing the tooth, the prime minister was responding to a dilemma faced by many sensitive citizens of Sri Lanka. They want to affirm that there is something distinctively Buddhist about their national identity, and yet they also want to affirm that ultimately there is a secular Sri Lankan nationalism that surmounts any particular religious expression of it. This dilemma is particularly acute among those who come from minority communities—Christians, Muslims, even Hindu Tamils—who would like very much to identify with the national culture, even it if is Buddhist, and yet not lose what is distinctive about their own religious traditions. An Anglican pastor and scholar in Colombo spoke movingly about how he had come to embrace the Christ of Buddhism, and how his own research in Buddhist theology had brought him more closely in touch with his Christian sensibilities (Fernando 1988). The Harvard anthropologist, Stanley Tambiah, a Tamil who was raised and educated in Sri Lanka, writes in a personal epilogue to his essay on what he calls "ethnic fratricide" in his native homeland, that his interest in studying Buddhist culture—which has become the center of his professional career—began with a feeling of being excluded from Sinhalese nationalism during the ethnic riots of 1958. By studying Buddhist society in Thailand, Tambiah writes, he was able to "study with the double posture of rapport and distance in someone else's country" many of the things that he "could not aspire to do, or do well, in Sri Lanka" (1986: 137). His ambivalent relationship to Buddhism, and his ambiguous feelings of Sri Lankan national identity, remain.

The problem with these forms of accommodation is that they lead to a double frustration: those who attempt to follow them are sometimes considered traitors from both a spiritual and a secular point of view. Moreover these accommodations presume a basic separation between religion and politics, which most religious activists see as a capitulation to secularism at the outset. After that, no accommodation is possible. In both Muslim and Jewish cultures the common slogan is that religion and politics simply cannot be separated. The same sentiment is voiced in Buddhist quarters. The bhikkhu I interviewed in Sri Lanka rejected the notion out of hand: "It is not possible to separate religion from politics," he said, adding that "politics needs religion to give people the motivation for obeying laws, otherwise they would only do it out of fear. That's not enough." The head of the largest Buddhist monastic order in Sri Lanka, the Mahanayake of Asgiriya, affirmed this point of view, saying that religion gives the two things necessary for a political system to function: a sense of discipline and a respect for civil order (Chandrananda 1988). Moreover, he said, only a religiously guided leader in Sri Lanka would be willing or capable of upholding Sinhalese Buddhist culture.

CAN RELIGION ACCOMMODATE THE NATION-STATE?

As nationalism's unhappy attempts at accommodating religion have shown, religion is not easily placated. Religious activists are well aware that if a nation starts with the premises of secular nationalism, religion is often made marginal to the political order. This is especially onerous from many revolutionary religious perspectives, including the Iranian, the Sikh, and the Sinhalese, because they regard the two ideologies as unequal: the religious one is far superior. Rather than starting with secular nationalism, they would begin with the notion of religious nationalism.

According to one Sinhalese writer, whose booklet, *The Revolt in the Temple*, was published shortly after independence and was influential in spurring on the Buddhist nationalist cause, "it is clear that the unifying, healing, progressive principle" that held together the entity known as Ceylon throughout the years has always been "the

Buddhist faith." The writer goes on to say that religion in Sri Lanka continues to provide the basis for a "liberating nationalism," and that Sinhalese Buddhism is "the only patriotism worthy of the name, worth fighting for or dying for" (Vejayavardhana 1971: 105).

The implication of this way of speaking is that religious rather than secular nationalism is the appropriate premise on which to build a nation-state. The question is whether what we think of as a modern nation—a unified, democratically controlled system of economic and political administration—can be accommodated within religion.

It is an interesting question, and one to which many Western observers would automatically say no. Even as acute an interpreter of modern society as Giddens regards most religion as a syncretism between "tribal cultures, on the one hand, and modern societies, on the other" (1985: 71).[11] Yet by Giddens's own definition of a nation-state, the Islamic revolution in Iran has solidified not just a central power but a systemic control over the population that is more conducive to nationhood than the monarchical political order of the Shah. In the case of the Iranian revolution, a new national entity came into being that was quite different from the old Muslim rule and from the Shah's inept attempt at nationhood. The Shah had dreamed of Ataturk's Turkey and what he perceived as the instant modernity that was brought to that country by its leader, and he too wanted instantly to create a modern state. Ironically it was Khomeini, his integrative religious ideology, and his grassroots network of mullahs that was ultimately able to accomplish the task.

Does religion lose something in accommodating modern politics? Some Muslims think that it does. In Egypt several critics have accused Khomeini of making Islam a political ideology and reducing it to the terms of the modern nation-state (Schleiffer 1989). Moreover, Lewis (1988) claims that most Islamic rebellions are aimed in the opposite direction: to shed Islam of an alien nation-state idea. While I agree that that is their aim, one of the curious consequences of their way of thinking is to appropriate many of the most salient elements of modern nationality into an Islamic frame of reference. Rather than ridding Islam of the nation-state, they create a new synthesis.

It was precisely this synthesis of modernity and tradition that Gandhi envisioned in *Hind Swaraj* over 80 years ago. What he hoped for was the evolution of a moral politics, the development of a new form of modernity that overcame the alienation and exploitation of modern organizations through the sensitivity that traditional values give to the spiritual bases of human societies. Gandhi was not a Luddite, however; he did not advocate the demolition of what modern civilizations have wrought. Rather, he advocated that modern factories and institutions be held "in trust" for the benefit of all.

Gandhi's religious politics is one grand compromise between the opposing "ideologies of order." Reinhold Niebuhr's Christian-based view of structures of justice for Western institutions is another. The Ayatollah Khomeini's vision of Islamic revolution may yet emerge as a third.

While opening up hopeful possibilities for a compromise between the two great ideologies of order, there is also a significant caveat: the radical accommodation of religion to nationalism may not necessarily be a good thing. A merger of the absolutism of nationalism and the absolutism of religion might create a rule so vaunted and potent that it would be destructive to itself and to its neighbors as well. The experience of Iran in the 1980s and Iraq in 1990 warrants some of those fears. When a society's secular state and its religious community are sufficiently strong and independent, the power of life and death that is commanded by any absolute authority—be it secular or religious—may be held tenuously in check. Without that balance, an absolute power of the worst sort could claim its most evil deeds to be legitimate moral duties.

NOTES

1. For major statements, see Marx and Engels 1939, and Mannheim 1936. The contemporary meaning of ideology is discussed in Apter 1964 and Waxman 1964.

2. A general overview of the subject is found in A. D. Smith 1971.

3. Geertz defines religion as "a system of symbols which acts to establish powerful, pervasive and long-lasting moods and motivations in men by formulating conceptions of a general order of existence and clothing these conceptions with such an aura of factuality that the moods and motivations seem uniquely realistic" (1972: 168).

4. Berger's and Dupre's definitions are discussed by Douglas 1982: 1-19.

5. Durkheim describes the dichotomy of sacred and profane in religion in the following way: "In all the history of human thought there exists no other example of two categories of things so profoundly differentiated or so radically opposed to one another. . . . The sacred and the profane have always and everywhere been conceived by the human mind as two distinct classes, as two worlds between which there is nothing in common. . . In different religions, this opposition has been conceived in different ways" (1976: 38-39). Durkheim goes on to talk about the sacred things that religions encompass; but the first thing he says about the religious view is the perception that there is this dichotomy.

6. Although I think one can use the term "religion" (as in "the Christian religion") if one is careful to define it, in general I am in agreement with W. C. Smith, who suggested some years ago that the noun "religion" might well be banished from our vocabulary, and that we restrict ourselves to using the adjective "religious" (1962: 119-153).

7. For a useful overview of Theravada society, see Swearer, 1981; for the role of monks in Thai politics, see Suksamran 1982.

8. For a somewhat opposing point of view—that there is relatively little Buddhist influence on Burmese nationalism—see the chapter on Burma in von der Mehden 1963 and von der Mehden 1974: 49-66.

9. For references on "civil religion," see Bellah's (1970) influential article; and for references on fundamentalism, see Balmer 1989 and Lawrence 1989.

10. D. E. Smith (1963) details the many concessions the government has made.

11. He goes on to deny that most religions outside the West have much to do with day-to-day morality and the social order (p. 73). It is an astoundingly inaccurate observation, and shows that Giddens is unaware of the importance of such ethical and social notions as dharma in Hinduism, shari'a in Islam, and li in Chinese religion.

REFERENCES

Apter, David. ed. 1964. *Ideology and Discontent*. New York: Free Press.

Balmer, Randall. 1989. *Mine Eyes Have Seen the Glory*. New York: Oxford University Press.

Bechert, Heinz. 1974. "Buddhism and Mass Politics in Burma and Ceylon." In Religion and Political Modernization. Ed. Donald E. Smith. New Haven, CT: Yale University Press.

Bellah, Robert. 1969. "Transcendence in Contemporary Piety." In *The Religious Situation: 1969*. Ed. Donald R. Cutler. Boston: Beacon Press.

_____. 1970. "Civil Religion in America." In *Beyond Belief: Essays on Religion in a Post-Traditional World*. Ed. Robert Bellah. New York: Harper and Row.

Berger, Peter. 1980. *The Heretical Imperative*. New York: Doubleday

Breuilly, John. 1982. *Nationalism and the State*. Manchester, England: Manchester University Press.

Chandrananda.   1988.   The   Venerable   Palipanna   Chandrananda,   the Mahanayake of the Asgiriya order. Interview with the author. Kandy. February 3, 1988.

Cox, Richard H.   1969.   *Ideology, Politics. and Political Theory*.   Belmont, CA: Wadsworth.

Deutsch, Karl.   1966.   *Nationalism and Social Communication*.   Boston: MIT Press.

Doob, L.   1964.   *Patriotism and Nationalism*.   New Haven, CT: Yale University Press.

Douglas, Mary. 1982. "The Effects of Modernization on Religious Change." *Daedalus* 111, no. 1 (Winter): 1-19.

Dupre, Louis.   1976.   *Transcendent Selfhood: The Loss and Rediscovery of the Inner Life*. New York: Seabury.

Durkheim, Emile. [1915] 1976. *The Elementary Forms of the Religious Life*. Trans. Joseph Ward Swain. London: George Allen and Unwin.

Embree, Ainslee.   1990.   *Utopias in Conflict: Religion and Nationalism in Modern India*. Berkeley and Los Angeles: University of California Press.

Fernando, Rev. Kenneth. 1988. Interview with the author. Colombo. January 27, 1988.

Geertz, Clifford. 1964. "Ideology as a Cultural System." In Apter 1964.

_____. 1972. "Religion as a Cultural System." In *Reader in Comparative Religion: An Anthropological Approach*.   Eds. William A. Lessa and Evon Z. Vogt. New York: Harper and Row.

Gellner, Ernest. 1983. *Nations and Nationalism*. Oxford: Basil Blackwell.

Giddens, Anthony. 1979. *Central Problems in Social Theory: Action, Structure and Contradiction in Social Analysis*.   Berkeley and Los Angeles: University of California Press.

_____. 1985. *A Contemporary Critique of Historical Materialism*. Vol. 2. *The Nation-State and Violence*. Berkeley and Los Angeles: University of California Press.

el-Hamamsy, Leila.   1989.   Interview with the author.   American University, Cairo. January 10, 1989.

Ibrahim, Saad. 1989. Interview with the author. Cairo. January 10, 1989.

Krejci, Jaroslav. 1982. "What is a Nation?" In *Religion and Politics in the Modern World*. Eds. Peter Merkl and Ninian Smart. New York: New York University Press.

Lessa, William A. and Evon Z. Vogt, eds. 1972. *Reader in Comparative Religion: An Anthropological Approach*. 3rd ed. New York: Harper and Row.

Lawrence, Bruce B. 1989. *Defenders of God*. San Francisco: Harper and Row.

Lewis, Bernard. 1988. *The Political Language of Islam*. Chicago: University of Chicago Press.

Mannheim, Karl. 1936. *Ideology and Utopia*. New York: Harcourt, Brace and World.

Marx, Karl and Friedrich Engel. 1939. *The German Ideology*. Ed. R. Pascal. New York: International.

von der Mehden, Fred R. 1963. *Religion and Nationalism in Southeast Asia: Burma, Indonesia, the Philippines*. Madison, WI: University of Wisconsin Press.

_____. 1974. "Secularization of Buddhist Polities: Burma and Thailand." In *Religion and Political Modernization*. Ed. Donald E. Smith. New Haven, CT: Yale University Press.

Ponnambalam, Satchi. 1983. *Sri Lanka: National Conflict and the Tamil Liberation Struggle*. Thornton Heath, Surrey, England: Tamil Information Centre.

Sarkisyanz, E. 1965. *Buddhist Backgrounds of the Burmese Revolution*. The Hague: Martinus Nijhoff.

Schleiffer, Abdullah. 1989. Interview with the author. American University, Cairo. January 7, 1989.

Smart, Ninian. 1983. *Worldviews: Crosscultural Explorations of Human Beliefs*. New York: Charles Scribners Sons.

Smith, Anthony D. 1971. *Theories of Nationalism*. London: Duckworth.

_____. 1979. *Nationalism in the Twentieth Century*. London: Duckworth.

Smith, Donald E. 1963. *India as a Secular State*. Princeton, NJ: Princeton University Press.

_____. 1965. *Religion and Politics in Burma.* Princeton, NJ: Princeton University Press.

Smith, Donald E., ed. 1971. *Religion. Politics. and Social Change in the Third World: A Sourcebook.* New York: Free Press.

Smith, William Cantwell. 1962. *The Meaning and End of Religion: A New Approach to the Religious Traditions of Mankind.* New York: Macmillan.

Suksamran, Somboon. 1982. *Buddhism and Politics in Thailand: A Study of Socio-Political Change and Political Activism of the Thai Sangha.* Singapore: Institute of Southeast Asian Studies.

Swearer, Donald K. 1981. *Buddhism and Society in Southeast Asia.* Chambersburg, PA: Anima.

Tambiah, S. J. 1976. *World Conqueror and World Renouncer: A Study of Buddhism and Polity in Thailand against a Historical Background.* Cambridge: Cambridge University Press.

_____. 1986. *Sri Lanka: Ethnic Fratricide and the Dismantling of Democracy.* Cambridge: Cambridge University Press.

Vejayavardhana, D. C. [1953] 1971. "The Revolt in the Temple: Composed to Commemorate 2,500 Years of the Land, The Race, and the Faith. " In Donald E. Smith, 1971: 105.

Waxman, Chaim I., ed. 1964. *The End of Ideology Debate.* New York: Simon and Schuster.

20

Core Values and the Possibility of a Fiduciary Global Community

TU WEI-MING

The sense of crisis confronting our human community, occasioned not only by the threat of nuclear annihilation and the disintegration of the ecosystem, but also by the troubling awareness that our species may not even be viable, challenges us to examine the core values that have for decades sustained our form of life. The fact that we now share the perspective of the astronaut, that we can see in graphic detail the shape of our "lifeboat" and even the depth of the air surrounding the blue earth, compels us to think globally and to address the issue of human survival in realistic terms. For the first time in human history, the question of the viability of our race permeates our corporate critical self-awareness: we have never been outside life, but we have been outside the earth; we have yet to probe the mystery of life, but we have observed in awe the fullness and vulnerability of our lived universe.[1] Our newly informed common sense dictates that we accept the sanctity of the earth as a guiding principle for our life.[2]

The end of the Cold War may have lessened the threat of nuclear annihilation, but the concern about the deterioration of the environment, notably the quality of the air we breathe and the water we drink, intensifies as pollution and deforestation continue at an alarming rate. Yet, the fundamental issue is not only what can we do and how should we do it but also, given our understanding of the human condition, who we are and who we ought to become. Sartre instructs us that, for human beings, "existence precedes essence" and that we authenticate who we are by living dangerously in shaping the form of life most meaningful to us. The current crisis demands that we reflect on the "things at hand" so that the choices we make individually and communally will not lead to an irreversible disaster, destroying our life-support system as well as our race. The question of human essence is not merely speculative; it has profound practical significance.

For more than a century, the Enlightenment mentality of the modern West has been the dominant ideology in defining the human project. Virtually all the major spheres of interest in the world today are indebted to this mentality: market economy, democratic polity, science and technology, mass communication, institutes of higher learning, transnational corporations, metropolitan centers, central and local bureaucracies, and so forth. Furthermore, the values underlying these spheres, such as individualism, freedom of the press, speech, thought, religion, assembly, human rights, and due process of law have also been widely hailed throughout the world as aspirations for the human community as a whole. The proponents of these values have occupied prominent positions in academies, business, and government all over the world; as a result, these broadly defined "liberal democratic" ideas are now universally accepted as defining characteristics of modernity (Tu 1989).

Understandably the modernizing process, which originated in Western Europe and flourished in North America, is in practical terms, Westernization with a European and American imprimatur. The conflict between capitalism and socialism, seen in this light, has been a conflict within the hegemonic discourse of the modern West. The power of this discourse is amply shown in the fact that the whole world has been engulfed in this conflict for the last four decades. The end of the Cold War, in this sense, does not necessarily signal the beginning of a new era. The triumph of capitalism, in Weberian terms, indicates the renewed dominance of instrumental rationality in economy, polity, society, and culture. The modernizing process, which Weber defined as rationalization, continues to shape the human project despite the collapse of European and Soviet communism.

Ironically, while Weber characterized the spheres of interest and their attendant values mentioned above as manifestations of the spirit of capitalism, he did not celebrate the advent of the modern age as human liberation. Instead, he deeply worried that the excessive accumulation of wealth would lead to human misery. The horrifying image of a light cloak transforming into an iron cage signifies that the seemingly innocuous quest for material possession, as a result of this-worldly asceticism, may eventually lead to self-inflicted imprisonment.[3]

It is certainly farfetched to suggest that the Enlightenment mentality in itself was responsible for this development. The dynamism of the modern West was not the result of instrumental rationality alone. It involved not only cool, calculating technique but also the passion to explore, to know, to subdue, and to conquer that made the modern West wealthy and powerful. The anthropocentrism fueled by a Faustian drive to expand and informed by the Social Darwinian necessity to compete provided both justification and motivation for knowledge to become power. We need not appeal to Marxist rhetoric to acknowledge the unprecedented destructive forces in the modern West: imperialism, colonialism, and more recently fascism, communism, and some would also add, capitalism.

The recognition that the modern Western paradigm, specifically the Enlightenment mentality, has been the most influential ideological and practical force shaping the human project for more than a century is the first step toward a redefinition of who we are and who we ought to become. The full acknowledgement that we are both beneficiaries and victims of the modern West enables us to perceive our human condition both as a constraint to overcome and as an instrument that we must use. The spheres of interest and their attendant values are the *sine quo non* for our existence in the modern age. We are beneficiaries of the Enlightenment mentality because it provides the conceptual apparatus as well as the material foundation and institutional structure for our practical living. Yet we are also its victims, because we are critically aware that the form of life that has been shaped by this mentality, whether Western European, North American, or more recently East Asian, is, in the long haul, neither exportable nor sustainable.

If this is not self-evident, it should become obvious as we ruminate on our own situation in the United States. The euphoria felt by American policymakers, opinion leaders, academic experts, and business executives, that the Cold War was over and that capitalism had triumphed, was short-lived. A sober reflection on the necessity of formulating a new structure of order and a solemn realization of the enormous difficulties involved (i.e., the Middle East peace process) now characterize the mood of American political, academic, and business communities. Despite a deceptively simple solution to the Gulf War, it is widely recognized that advanced military technology cannot be readily applied to other serious concerns of American society, such as education, economy, environment, energy, child care, crime, drugs, and racial tension. Underlying this recognition is a genuine willingness to explore new ways of building and rebuilding complex mass societies. The rationale and the modus operandi of modernization which have served us well since the end of the Second World War in restructuring global community modelled on the American way are now outmoded. While we celebrate the spheres of interest and the underlying values characteristic of the vitality of our society, we are critically aware that much of what we take for granted is not available, or in many cases, even imaginable in most parts of the world.

Nevertheless, it is vitally important to note that much of the practical idealism in world politics, articulated in both international and national forums, is still shaped by the American experiment. The success of the American system continues to provide a standard of inspiration for the global community. We need to repeatedly remind ourselves what the United States, as contrasted with the Soviet Union, for example, really stands for:

> The American belief system [as compared with that of the Soviet Union] emphasized the rights of the individual. American society embraced free enterprise and then tried to soften its edges. America believed in the market system. America believed that government should not guarantee wealth but opportunity. Individuals and corporations should compete in the private sector. Those who won should be taxed fairly so that those who lost the economic competition would not suffer. The market was never perfect and in times of war it gave way to state control. Still, Americans in economic matters trusted self-reliance more than solidarity.
>
> But Americans have believed in more than the market. We have believed in personal mobility and the free flow of ideas. We have believed in an openness of spirit and a range of possibility unheard of anywhere at anytime in history. We have believed in the proposition that self-government was possible in a world of monarchies and dictatorships.
>
> The genius of the Founders was to construct a system in which participation could be broadened and each generation could create America anew. The vote was the fulcrum of democracy, the press its conscience, and the prospect of a better life for your children its driving motivation. Americans fought two world wars in the 20th century defending those values.[4]

While we appreciate this impassioned articulation of the American belief, the American experience, as an exemplification of the spirit of the modern West, clearly shows the dilemma of the most recent phase of the human project shaped by the Enlightenment mentality: with all its ostentatious display of wealth and power, its soul is sick and its morality corrupt. The ideology built on the hierarchy of relationships and centering on the security and self-interest of the United States as a supreme value has lost much of its persuasive power in the international arena. The myth of continuous prosperity as a natural consequence of economic vitality generated by profit maximization is no longer convincing in the domestic market.

Indeed, the idea of unlimited growth, continued progress, or linear development is itself dissolved. As we move from a bipolar world to a multifaceted, international order, the faith in the rightness of the American way of life is also lost. The assertion that Pax Americana has finally arrived is no more than wishful thinking. The end of European and Soviet communism also exposes the weakness and impotence of capitalism in dealing with newly emerging as well as perennial global issues.

As beneficiaries and victims of the modern West and, by implication, of communism and capitalism, we need a more sophisticated and integrated approach to the human condition. We cannot allow the anthropocentrism embedded in the Enlightenment mentality to be the guiding principle for our action. We cannot uncritically subscribe to the transformative power of instrumental rationality. Nor can we afford to be driven by the Faustian spirit to realize our human potential. The task before us is how can we creatively transform the Enlightenment mentality of the modern West so that we can continually benefit from it without being its victim.

The point of departure for initiating such a task is to firmly grasp a fascinating paradox characteristic of our current human condition: the coexistence, the interaction, and indeed the mutuality of global consciousness and local commitment.

Thanks to modernization, the "global village" is upon us not as a utopian vision but as a lived reality. The sense of interconnectedness and interdependency of the global community is strong and pervasive. Despite geographic, national, linguistic, ethnic, religious, and cultural boundaries, the world is increasingly and irreversibly shrinking. Mass media, trade, tourism, entertainment, and scholarly exchange seem to have penetrated all imagined and real barriers against human communication. As material goods, sounds, colors, tastes, and ideas circulate around the world, there is a quantum leap in local, national, regional, and international networking. The density of communication is a defining characteristic of the Information Age.

However, we are acutely aware that as the world shrinks, it does not necessarily become more integrated. On the contrary, the world has never been so divided by wealth, power, and influence; the accessibility to goods, services, and information is so unequally distributed that the global community is fragmented at all levels, from local to international. Actually the complexity and variability of the modern experience are such that people sharing the same neighborhood may belong to a radically different economic class, political affiliation, social position, and symbolic universe, with a differing access to information and even sense of time. It does not take a cynic to recognize that what the "global village" consists of is difference, differentiation, and discrimination.

In recent decades, the upsurge of interest in searching for roots in highly industrialized as well as developing societies fundamentally challenged the naive thesis that modernization entails homogenization. Racial tension in the United States, linguistic conflict in Canada, Belgium, and India, the struggle to reclaim or preserve ancestral homes in North America as well as in the Middle East, the resurgence of fundamentalist religious movements in Judaism, Christianity, Islam, and Hinduism, and feminist restructuring of the workplace throughout the world are some examples of the staying power of primordial ties in the modernizing process.

The common practice of lumping these primordial ties together and subsuming them under the category of nationalism and localism is dangerously misleading. The assumption that these are mere aberrations in the universalizing tendencies of modernization is seriously flawed. Ethnicity, gender, language (mother tongue), ancestral home (fatherland), class, and religious faith are constitutive parts of our human condition. They define who we are and provide the necessary resources for us to become what we choose to be. They each address an essential dimension of humanity. Together they contain the bulk of what any sensible human project ought to incorporate.

The penchant to characterize concerns for primordial ties as manifestations of provincialism is predicated on the strong belief that modernization as universalization inevitably undermines particularities in cultural orientation. The inability of even the most articulate modernists to take cultural diversity into serious consideration accounts for much of the poverty of thought in modernization theories. The failure to assign proper weight to primordial ties leads to the false conclusion that universalism will eventually prevail over particularism. Unfortunately, the universalism abstracted from the modern West is itself a reflection of the Enlightenment mentality. Athough this value orientation has been the predominant world ideology for more than a century, it is historically and culturally rooted in Western Europe and North America.

When we begin to probe the modern West and pay special attention to its primordial ties from the perspective of cultural pluralism, we see that the conceptual apparatuses derived from the Enlightenment mentality are also deficient. The more we appreciate the cultural diversity of the modern West, the more we recognize the inadequacy of applying abstract universalism to the global situation. However, while we celebrate cultural diversity, we are deeply concerned about the danger of pernicious relativism. We strongly believe that there are normative standards transcending the existing linguistic and cultural areas of the world; we firmly subscribe to minimum requirements for the civilized conduct of modern states including respect for human rights; and we continually hope that the Enlightenment values we cherish such as liberty, equality, fraternity, and due process of law will become universally available.

The coexistence of the general awareness that, as members of the global community, we are inexorably interconnected and interdependent, and the focused concern for our own specificity (ethnicity, gender, language, ancestral home, class, and religion) is so pervasive throughout the world, that we must recognize this as a defining characteristic of the current human condition rather than a reflection of a developmental stage in the modernizing process. In fact, the interaction between the felt necessity that the global crisis demands that we have a transcending vision and the strong desire to search for our own roots at the expense of a sense of national, let alone regional or international community, features prominently in virtually all troubled areas of the world.

However, the apparent conflict between global consciousness and local commitment indicates the complexity of our modern human condition rather than being an unresolvable problem in the global community. The conceptual framework informed by the exclusive dichotomy of universalism and particularism is partly responsible for our inability to wrestle with this intriguing phenomenon. In other words, if we insist upon an either-or choice between global consciousness and local commitment, we—self-styled cosmopolitan citizens of the world under the influence of the Enlightenment mentality—are prone to condemn all alien forms of quests for roots as narrow-minded and dangerous particularisms. Curiously, at the same time, our own commitment to ethnicity, gender, mother tongue, fatherland, class, and faith often compels us to take radically exclusivist positions despite our avowed cosmopolitanism. This schizophrenia is so readily observable throughout the world, among our countrymen, our respected intellectuals, our otherwise sensitive friends and colleagues, and ourselves that we must acknowledge not only its existence but its destructive power.

I, therefore, recommend that the global consciousness and local commitment which coexist and interact ought to be recognized as also forming an intimate mutuality. This view, easily criticized as a stoic endurance of apparent contradiction, is predicated on the assumptive reason that if we move beyond the exclusive dichotomy of either-or and employ the inclusive dichotomy of both-and, we may be in possession of an adequate conceptual resource in dealing with the intriguing phenomenon characteristic of the human condition today. Notwithstanding the danger of explaining the conflict away, my considered opinion is that a choice between global consciousness and local commitment is neither desirable nor necessary. Specifically, our task is not to choose between them but to capitalize on the creative tension generated by their continuous dialectic interaction so that the destructive potential between them can be minimized. This has to work at the international, regional, and national levels as well as in the local and personal contexts.

It is perplexing to note that in this crucial arena of human endeavor the nuanced modes of moral reasoning in the local and personal contexts are sharply contrasted with the vague styles of ideological pronouncements at the international, regional, and national levels. Core values may function as guiding principles in our daily living, but they are seldom evoked in any national discussion. Societies in Western Europe and North America, assuming that they are the originators, executors, and judges of the civilized world defined in terms of the Enlightenment mentality, never feel the need to justify the existing geopolitical structure beyond occasionally employing the rhetoric of human rights and co-prosperity. Since the rhetoric so far has not, in actuality, significantly undermined those power relationships in which the supremacy of the modern West is unquestioned, there is little urgency to mobilize any spiritual resources other than the appeal to values such as security and self-interest.

I should clarify the main thrust of my critical reflection, lest my deliberate cynicism gives the impression that I have been venting Third World or communist sentiments against capitalistic imperialism. While I believe there is a measure of truth in the seemingly outmoded Third World and Communist polemics against the advanced industrial economies, I do not think that they have adequately addressed the human condition at all. Indeed, they have been so much seasoned in the language of wealth and power that their articulation is often a pale reflection of what they intend to reject. It is certainly not persuasive to demand a transfer of assets from the "haves" to the "have-nots" simply because of blatant inequality; the justificatory scheme as well as the practical mechanism must be worked out case by case. Moreover, since any comprehensive form of planetary bargaining is at most an imagined possibility, the tasks can only be accomplished through existing international agencies, such as those sponsored by the United Nations. This requires an entirely different analysis. Rather, my main purpose is to show that in regard to core values, the evocation of security and self-interest in the international arena is not persuasive.

At a minimum, the principle of the Christian and Confucian (*Analects* 15:23) golden rule stated in the negative must be observed: "Do not do unto others what you would not want others to do unto you." Simply put, if we desire security and self-interest, we must make sure that our enemies as well as our friends are not adversely affected by our action. We should ensure that our well-being is not built on the misery of the rest of the world. Unfortunately, as regards the depletion of natural resources, not to mention the displacement of great civilizations and genocidal threats against primal peoples, the modern West, including its most successful contemporary exemplar, the United States, is profoundly guilty. This, however, should not be the reason to relegate the whole discussion on core values to the background. For one thing, we—the inheritors of the Enlightenment mentality—although implicated in the unintended negative consequences of our intellectual forefathers, are also the victims of our own environment. Moreover, the real purpose of our self-criticism is not to blame the past but to anticipate the future. This requires that we explore the spiritual resources available to us here and now.

At least three kinds of spiritual resources are still available to us as we reflect upon our own human condition at the present moment. First, those spiritual resources that have contributed to the rise of the modern West and yet have been instrumental in continuously generating creative responses to the dark side of the Enlightenment mentality, notably the Hebrew prophetic vision, Greek philosophical wisdom, Christian faith, and Roman law. Second, the non-Western world religions, notably Buddhism, Islam, Hinduism, Confucianism, and Taoism. And third, the primal traditions such as Shintoism, shamanism, tribal forms of life, and Native American, Maori, Hawaiian, and Alaskan spiritualities (Tu 1991).

In the 1970s, Parsons defined modernity in terms of two major spheres of interest and a central value in the modern West: market economy, democratic polity, and individualism (Parsons 1977). In light of the spiritual resources just enumerated, what Parsons seems to have failed to recognize is twofold: the continuous presence of tradition in modernity and the authentic possibility for the modernizing process to take on different cultural forms. At the level of core values, the assertion of individualism as an inseparable aspect of modernity appears to be particularistic, indeed idiosyncratic.

When we juxtapose the Parsonian vision of modernity with the shared concerns of all three kinds of spiritual resources, including those instrumental in the rise of the modern West, the most thought-provoking realization is the divergent attitude towards community. It is even more striking to note that among the three great Enlightenment values espoused by the French Revolution, "fraternity," both in theory and practice, seems to have been least realized in the modern West. Understandably, modern political scientists are surprised to learn that family, perhaps the most important and enduring institution in human history, is hardly a subject of discussion in the voluminous writings of modern Western political theorists.[5] On the contrary, community features prominently in Hebraic, Greek, Hindu, Confucian, Christian, Islamic, and virtually all primal traditions.

When Parsons characterized modernity in terms of market economy, democratic polity, and individualism, he may have had the inevitable triumph of capitalism over communism in mind. The implicit contrast with the socialist system is not difficult to miss: planned economy, centralized polity, and collectivism. If the range of possibilities provided by the modern West had exhausted all the available models for human development, any investigation into our spiritual resources would appear to be a mere exercise in futility. However, the rise of industrial East Asia (Japan, South Korea, Taiwan, Hong Kong, and Singapore) as the most vibrant economic region in the world for the last four decades suggests not only the plausibility of a second case of capitalism but also the reality of an alternative form of modernity. To be sure, these societies have been thoroughly Westernized, but their ability to develop a less individualistic, less adversarial, and less legalistic approach to modernity is truly fascinating. Given the examples of Japan and the Four Mini-Dragons, it is not at all farfetched to suggest that communalism, a government-monitored market, democracy shaped by meritocratic elitism, and family-centered society can also become salient features of modernity (Tu 1988).

Nevertheless, as the matter now stands, what industrial East Asia symbolizes is no more than a mixed blessing. As far as we can determine, the motivational structure underlying its economic dynamism is the same modernist will to power, wealth, and influence, if not the functional equivalent of the Faustian drive to subdue and conquer. Whether or not we label Japan and the Four Mini-Dragons mercantilist states, what they have exhibited is the capitalization of their comparative advantages in the economic game of Social Darwinian competition. Needless to say, they may have successfully outmaneuvered their competitors in international trade, but what they have demonstrated is as much the dark side of the modern West as a liberating alternative to the negative consequences of the Enlightenment mentality.

The implications of the industrial East Asian development model for the global community is truly far-reaching. Suffice it to note that the two most densely populated nations in the world, India and Mainland China, each produces a total domestic economic output comparable to only about 10% of that of Japan. This kind of asymmetry in the Asia-Pacific Rim is unlikely to sustain well into the 21st century. If, like Southeast Asia, Mainland China and India also follow an aggressive model of economic development, their role in restructuring the power relationships of the world will be substantial. Already Mainland China's favorable balance of trade with the United States has surpassed all other nations except Japan. The need for some understanding based on the principle of reciprocity is obvious.

In addition to the principle of reciprocity—the golden rule stated in the negative—another moral dictum must be added to make the idea of a global community a real possibility: "Wishing to establish oneself, one establishes others; wishing to enlarge oneself, one enlarges others" (*Analects* 6:28). Strictly speaking, this is not altruism but the natural consequence of perceiving the self as the center of relationships. We—persons, societies and states—are networks of human relatedness, not isolated individual entities. Once the negative injunction not to impose on others what we would not want others to impose on us is augmented by the positive recommendation to bring others sequentially into our own orbit of human flourishing, our table of conversation is gradually enlarged and the agenda for discussion becomes extended beyond security and self-interest. For security then means, among other things, the sanctity of the earth and self-interest, properly understood in the global community, must transcend selfishness, nepotism, ethnocentrism, chauvinistic nationalism, and anthropocentrism.

Surely each community, large or small, must make the local commitment to articulate its own configuration of core values. It is highly unlikely that a list of artificially constructed core values can be applied to all communities. Yet, a communal effort, at all levels, to address the common ground based on shared and practicable core values is not only desirable but necessary.

The concerted effort of the Indonesian government to resort to *Pancasila* (the Five Principles) for building national consensus in the last two decades and the recent attempt of the People's Action Party in Singapore to define core values for the entire society may have been occasioned either by the perceived threat of religious fundamentalism or by feared racial and language conflicts in a multiethnic and multilingual society, but the central issue they have raised is universal, namely, how can we commit ourselves to the core values specific to our community in an increasingly pluralistic cultural context (Quah 1990: 24-30, 91-105).

It seems that multiculturalism is not only an emerging phenomenon but also an enduring feature of modernity. However, we must observe the principles of reciprocity and human flourishing as constitutive parts of our local commitment. Our global consciousness demands that we do not impose our standards prematurely and that we invite an ever expanding circle of the human community to take part in our own establishment and enlargement. This may provide an opportunity to explore ways to help us to define anew who we are and who we ought to become. The Biblical question, What is man that thou art mindful of him, must not be replied to by a limited and limiting Greek answer: "Man is the measure of all things!"

NOTES

1. The technological breakthrough enabling us to acquire a holistic vision of our habitat is unprecedented. The Wittgensteinian mode of questioning, which was perhaps intended to reject any possibility of providing a proper answer to issues such as the meaning of earth or life, takes on new significance as our knowledge about the ecosystem, the mystery of life, and the structure of the brain has substantially increased in recent decades. However, it has become obvious that as our knowledge expands, our awareness of our ignorance also intensifies. It is a humbling experience to learn about our vulnerability as a result of our scientific ingenuity. The Baconian dictum, "Knowledge is power," must now be supplemented by the common sense that wisdom helps us to appreciate our fallibility, indeed our powerlessness.

2. Thomas Berry's (1988) earth-centered theology provides an eloquent argument for the sanctity of the earth as a primary datum for any form of theological reflection.

3. Max Weber comments in "Asceticism and the Spirit of Capitalism:" In Baxter's view the care for external goods should only lie on the shoulders of the "saint like a light cloak, which can be thrown aside at any moment." But fate decreed that the cloak should become an iron cage (Weber 1976: 181).

4. Senator William Bradley's remark on the occasion of the confirmation hearing of Robert Gates' nomination as the CIA Director (*Congressional Record*, U.S. Senate, Washington, D.C., November 4, 1991), S 15838.

5. Samuel P. Huntington's (1991) recent concern for the idea of community is a notable example.

REFERENCES

Berry, Thomas. 1988. *The Dream of the Earth*. San Francisco: Sierra ClubBooks.

Huntington, Samuel P.   1991.   *Third Wave: Democratization in the Late Twentieth Century*. Norman, OK: University of Oklahoma Press.

Parsons, Talcott. 1977. *The Evolution of Societies*. Ed. Jackson Toby. Englewood Cliffs, NJ: Prentice Hall.

Quah, S. T., ed. 1990. *In Search of Singapore's National Values*. Singapore: Times Academic Press.

Tu, Wei-ming.   1988.   "A Confucian Perspective on the Rise of Industrial East Asia."   1687th Stated Meeting Report.   *Bulletin of the American Academy of Arts and Sciences* 42, no. 1 (October): 32-50.

_____. 1989.   "The Enlightenment Mentality and the Chinese Intellectual Dilemma."   Paper presented to the Four Anniversaries Conference. Annapolis, Maryland. September 11-14.

_____. 1991.   "The Challenges in Contemporary Spirituality."   In *Ancient Wisdom and Local Knowledge*.   Ed. Steve Friesen.   Dialogue of Civilization Project.   Honolulu: Institute of Culture and Communication, East-West Center.

Weber, Max. 1976. *The Protestant Ethic and the Spirit of Capitalism*. Tr. Talcott Parsons. New York: Charles Scribner's Sons.

21

Conclusion

MAJID TEHRANIAN

The future often catches the futurologists by surprise. Who could have predicted the dramatic world events of 1989-91? Brought about by a global information explosion through international telecommunication networks, as well as a domestic implosion of repressed historical forces, history accelerates, making prediction a hazardous task (Tehranian 1990). The end of the Cold War, the outbreak of the Gulf War, the demise of the Soviet Union, the unleashing of repressed ethnic forces, and the economic decline of the United States as a superpower despite its military success in the Gulf War—each has reinforced accelerating global transformations whose future remains unknown.

Fortunately, however, this book is not about futurology. The project began from a different premise: that there is no determinable past or future, only *present* constructions of the past and the future. Every generation reconstructs history to fit its own *present* images of the past, often reading into it present preoccupations and prejudices. Every generation also projects its own *present* visions of the future, often extrapolating current trends while neglecting unforeseen natural or social forces. Normative preferences and prescriptions are thus firmly built into our constructions of the past and future. By thinking and acting in terms of our constructed pasts and futures, every generation thus engages in restructuring the future in order to mould its contours to its own image.

This book will thus be read in the 21st century as the chronicle of a project in which 27 peace scholars from around the world projected into the future the fears and hopes of their own defining moment in history. It can be also read as an act of intervention in the processes of shaping that future by raising consciousness, proposing policies, and inviting action on behalf of certain preferred futures. Since the project was conceived and born at a point when the postwar world system was being actively restructured, its perspectives are shaped by a uniquely fluid period of history.

The fluid contradictions of the world situation currently contain too many uncertainties to allow for any safe predictions. The Cold War has come to an end, yet its stockpiles of weapons of mass destruction are still with us. The arms race has come to a relative halt in the United States, Europe, and the former Soviet Union, but it is continuing in Asian- Pacific and Middle East regions on a pace with their respective high rates of economic growth and low levels of mutual trust. The Gulf War has put the United Nations system of collective security through what some may consider a successful test, but it has left grave moral and political questions on the limits and consequences of military intervention. The world's last major empire, the Soviet Union, has collapsed but it has left behind a legacy of economic disaster and political turmoil in a loosely defined Commonwealth of Independent States. Europe has entered into a new economic and political union, but its future role and leadership in world affairs remain problematical. Japan and Germany have achieved the status of economic superpowers, yet their political and military roles in the world remain uncertain and worrisome. The ideological rivalries between capitalism and communism, with their universalist pretensions, have mercifully subsided, but the vacuum has opened up a new era of ethnic consciousness and nationalist revival promising bloody civil and interstate wars. The world therefore continues to be a dangerous place.

This concluding essay cannot go into the substance of each of these emerging conflicts and their possible peaceful resolutions. It merely recapitulates the main themes and perspectives of this volume on the problems of restructuring for a durable and just peace in the post-Cold War era. It also proposes a research agenda on the problems of restructuring for positive world peace.

RESTRUCTURING FOR POSITIVE PEACE

This book reflects some of the diversity of cultural, ideological, and disciplinary perspectives which characterize the field of peace studies. But it also reflects the common core of values which unify the field. The book is thus organized around the four generally acknowledged, democratic principles of *security, freedom, justice,* and *community* as the foundations for restructuring for a more peaceful and just world system. In its four different sections, the book has thus focused on how to build the institutions of a positive peace—an international system based on pacific settlement of disputes for mutual security, respect for human rights, social and economic justice, and communitarian autonomy and cooperation.

As the different chapters of this book have amply demonstrated, the world is far from such an international system. True, the tensions of the Cold War have come to an end, but the emerging conflict formations outlined by Galtung in Chapter 2 are shaping new contradictions and tensions. The world system seems to be moving in opposite directions. On the one hand, the democratic revolutions of the postwar period have finally reached the bastions of racism in parts of the First World (notably South Africa), communism in the Second World (notably in Central and Eastern Europe), and militarism in the Third World (notably in Latin America). On the other hand, new counterdemocratic formations in the shape of military regimes, fundamentalist religious movements and dictatorships, and extreme nationalism and racism continue to threaten old and new democracies (Tehranian 1992a, b).

Similarly, in the field of *security*, two contradictory trends characterize the emerging polarities of power. On the one hand, the Gulf War demonstrated how a Pax Americana could replace the bipolar world with a combination of U. S. military power and allied financial support. A debate between "the declinists," led by Kennedy's *The Rise and Fall of Great Powers* (1987), and "the revivalists" led by Nye's *Bound to Lead* (1990), has presented the major arguments for and against the possibility of Pax Americana. The United States, Kennedy has argued, is following the pattern of past empires, with an economic decline brought about by its overextensions of power. With no other superpower candidates in sight, Nye has countered, the United States is "bound to lead" because it has the necessary combination of global economic interests, military power, and political will that it takes to be a superpower. The emergence of Japan and Germany as the leaders in two powerful regional formations in East Asia and Western Europe, however, challenges the leadership of an economically declining and politically divided United States. In the medium run, the likely outcome, as Sklar argues in Chapter 14, is the emergence of a Pax Trilateral—a U.S.-Japan-European hegemony. In the long run (as Galtung, Hettne, Haas, and Tehranian argue), other regional groupings such as ASEAN, the Arab world, and the South Asian Association of Regional Cooperation will perhaps develop their own autonomous security regimes. In the meantime, it is highly desirable to develop a broader world security system that encompasses ecological security (Stephenson), disarmament in both conventional and unconventional weapons (Graham), an expanded role for the UN in peacekeeping (Knippenberg), and a greater role for nongovernmental agencies in peacebuilding (Smoker).

In the field of *freedom* and human rights, the legal remedies are necessary but not sufficient. Many of the violations of basic human rights are structural in nature, resulting from such conditions as poor prenatal care, infant mortality, malnutrition, lack of access to educational and public health facilities, and denial of cultural and political rights of full citizenship. The world pronouncements on political, economic, social, and cultural rights expressed in the Universal Declaration of Human Rights and its ancillary documents are more a testament to world aspirations than achievements. The main problem is how to translate these international norms into the human rights practices of states both domestically and at the international level. The chapters in Part II all focus, in one way or another, on the interface between domestic and international protection of human rights. That appears to be the weakest link in the process of applying international legal norms to domestic situations. The proposals that emerge from Chapters 7-12 include the establishment of regional and subregional human rights commissions such as LAWASIA (Hyndman); the creation of national, regional, and global forums for redressing the violations of previous regimes (Van Dyke & Berkley); the provision of international rights of humanitarian intervention in a domestic situation when flagrant violation of basic human rights occur (Nanda); the establishment of Nuremburg-style international trials and procedures for the war crimes of political leaders (Newman); the provision of full sovereignty rights of indigenous peoples (McGregor); and the payment of compensation for the redress of past wrongs committed against specific ethnic or racial groups (Yamamoto).

The central problem of peace with *justice* in the contemporary world lies in the growing income gaps within and between nations. The chapters in Part III focus on this problem by highlighting the connections among peace, justice, and development. Hettne, Sklar, Kelly, and Addo present a highly differentiated world, divided into a hierarchy of regions incorporating the world centers and peripheries. Although the relations have become more complex, the development of the centers has historically meant the underdevelopment of the peripheries, resulting from declining international terms of trade and economically corrupt and misguided domestic regimes. The relationship between the centers and peripheries has thus generally been one of dependency, in which the latter have provided the former with sources of raw materials, cheap labor, consumer markets, and investment opportunities.

First, at the apex of this hierarchy stands North America, with its peripheries in South and Central America. Second, catching up and occasionally surpassing North America in per capita income is Western Europe, with its old colonial peripheries in Asia and Africa and its new potential peripheries in Central and Eastern Europe. Third, aspiring to the top position is Japan together with its peripheries in East Asia, some of whom are out-Japanizing the Japanese by remarkable rates of economic growth driven by export development strategies. These include South Korea, Taiwan, Hong Kong, and Singapore, trailed by Malaysia, Indonesia, and Thailand. Fourth, Russia in the new Commonwealth of Independent States presents a new periphery for Western, Japanese, and North American investment, while acting as a center in relation to its own Asian peripheries. Fifth, China plays a similar role for Japan as a source for Japanese transfers of technology and capital, while acting as a center in relation to its less developed regions such as Mongolia, Tibet, and the eastern provinces. Sixth, India is acting as a center for its multilingual empire, as well as the smaller nations of South Asia, although itself vulnerable to Western penetration. Seventh, the ASEAN region stands out as a unique combination of countries united in common efforts to attain economic growth and avoid periphery status through regional cooperation (see Chapter 17). Eighth, the Arab world, despite a unity of language and culture, presents a less successful effort at the same objectives. A strategic military location, the possession of oil resources by some and not others, and traditional national and tribal rivalries have divided and weakened the Arabs in their efforts towards such unity. Ninth, Latin America, with its wealth of population and resources, presents yet another periphery united by a common Hispanic-Portuguese culture, divided by different types of political regimes, and holding the promise of regional collaboration for development. Tenth, and finally, stands the vast continent of black Africa south of the Sahara, with its dark history of white exploitation, famines, tribal conflicts, sluggish growth, and current awakening to a new need for regional cooperation. To this complex picture, we must add the hierarchies of inequality within nations in which women, minorities, and immigrant laborers are often placed at the bottom of the structures of injustice and violence.

There are no panaceas to remedy these injustices. However, as the four authors of Part III eloquently point out, the most appropriate measures call for fundamental changes in the prevailing strategies of development, away from a focus on *having* to *being*, from efforts to satisfy the insatiable greed for material objects to the development of the potentials of human beings. This, in turn, calls for devolution of power, decentralized decision making in the allocation of resources, and a new balance between market incentives, government regulation, and civic intervention whenever market and government forces fail to perform their proper functions. Both systems of market and government management of the economy have failed in important respects. In the socialist camp, there is a cry for market incentives to break through centralized and bureaucratic planning, while in the capitalist camp, there is an urgent demand for industrial policy and government re-regulation to sustain a more balanced growth and employment. While the Greens and the communitarian democratic movements have presented alternative economic policies for ecologically and socially responsible development strategies (see Chapters 14 and 15), there is no doubt that real economic solutions to social problems will have to come about as a result of trial and error, experimentation and adjustment, destruction and creativity. The pain and suffering of this process unfortunately will be with us as we move towards the 21st century, but it could be lessened by a new development philosophy that recognizes the natural and social limits to economic growth.

Last but not least are the emerging world calls for a renewed sense of *community* at the local, national, and global levels. There is, however, an increasing tension between the growing global interdependence directed by the power centers and a groping for cultural, political, and economic autonomy by the repressed national, ethnic, racial, and gender peripheries. Each of the four chapters in Part IV calls for a different set of responses to this challenge. Burton calls for peace rather than power politics to deal with the resolution of the nonnegotiable and deep-seated ethnic conflicts emerging in many parts of the world. Juergensmeyer cautions against the secularist disdain of religious politics by pointing out the need for spiritually informed polities, cultural identity, and community. Haas calls for a communitarian, regionalist strategy by the peripheries, such as the ASEAN countries, to achieve development through cooperation and collective self-reliance. Tu calls for "fiduciary" responsibility for an economically interdependent and culturally diversified globe. A global sense of community can come about only through respect and celebration of these diversities while developing common core values.

RESTRUCTURING FOR POSITIVE PEACE RESEARCH

The opening of a new century has always served as a symbolic turning point in human history, and the 21st century is no exception to this rule. The world stands at a historical juncture between the roads to self-destruction and self-renewal. On the one hand, an environmental catastrophe, a nuclear holocaust, a war among fragmented ethnic groups or potentially insular regional blocs (Fortress North America vs. Fortress Western Europe vs. Fortress East Asia), a population explosion of unprecedented magnitude, a division of the world between islands of riches in an ocean of dehumanizing poverty, and a protracted terrorist war between the two camps all seem to be disturbing possibilities. On the other hand, human achievements in science, technology, education, and social organization have opened up magnificent new horizons for reaching new heights in human civilization. The conquest of ignorance and poverty, the achievement of a new harmony among nations and between nature and humanity, and the development of a new sense of world community for the exploration of the outer and inner spaces also seem within human reach.

Peace scholars can contribute to the process of positive peacebuilding by envisioning a world without violence, poverty, and ignorance while conducting policy research towards its fulfillment. This requires a global network of concerned scholars bringing together, through electronic networking or face-to-face communication, experts from all walks of life to address the urgent problems facing the human family. In a world of narrow specializations, it calls for broader perspectives and holistic approaches to human problems. It needs common grounds rather than divisive fetishisms. It demands a scientific method sensitive to global community interests rather than any particular ideological or sectional agendas.

The end of the Cold War and its ideological simplifications clearly call for fresh approaches to social policy, in which choices are not dichotomized between either/or: communism or capitalism, equality or freedom, planning or market, development or environment, urban or rural, secular or religious. The great challenges we face call for ideological emancipation, human imagination, and social creativity. They also call for a sense of social responsibility towards the common heritage and destiny of humankind. They demand what some authors in this volume have called a "communitarian" approach in which loyalty to the human community is made central to all levels of aggregation, from local to global.

For its own part, the Matsunaga Institute for Peace (MIP) at the University of Hawai'i is launching one such multinational, collaborative, and future-oriented research, publication, and educational project focused on strengthening the institutions of cooperation in the Asia-Pacific community. Titled *Pacifica*, the project has a second purpose to develop and institutionalize a network of peace scholars and policy analysts for continuing collaboration. A third purpose is to define and plan for the facilitating role of Hawai'i as a bridge of understanding between Asia, the Pacific, and North America.

This project has grown out of the "restructuring for peace" project of the Institute, which has led to conferences in Honolulu and New York, a monograph, *Restructuring for Peace and Security in the Asia-Pacific Region* (Kamo 1992), and two edited books, the present volume and *Restructuring for Ethnic Peace: A Public Debate at the University of Hawai'i* (Tehranian 1991). The project has been cosponsored by the

United Nations University, Matsunaga Peace Foundation, Institute of Culture and Communication of the East-West Center, and the Global Land Authority for Development of Peace Zones.

In view of the emerging importance of the Asia-Pacific as a zone of potential conflict in the post-Cold War era, the project will now focus on the processes of conflict and cooperation among the nations of the Asia-Pacific community, with a particular emphasis on the roles of Japan and the United States. Following the development of a conceptual and methodological framework, the project will be divided into several interlocking phases to study Pacific conflict and cooperation in a number of sectors. These include peace and security, tourism, telecommunications, multicultural education, indigenous peoples' rights, urbanism, health and environment, and arts and culture. Within a comparative multinational framework, each sector will be studied for the problems and prospects of its contributions to the building blocks of a Pacific Community. The project will conclude with the development of policy proposals for the strengthening and creation of institutions of cooperation among the nations of the Asia-Pacific community in order to enhance *security, trade and development, free and balanced news and information flows, education for cultural diversity, democracy and social justice, urban planning, health and ecological preservation, art and creativity.* The research output of the project will be made available to policymakers and the broader public through books, monographs, seminars, conferences, and the mass media.

MIP extends its hand to other peace, policy, and futures research institutes for collaboration in this and similar projects extending into other regions of the world. Three central concepts can integrate the diversity of problems, perspectives, and methodologies that inevitably have to be faced in such a grand venture. These concepts have served as a unifying theme in this volume. First, the concept of "community," broadly understood to mean a common core of interests, values, fears, and hopes that can bring a potentially quarrelsome group of people together in a common venture in life. Second, the concept of "restructuring," to mean a belief in the possibility of human agency in the processes of envisioning, negotiating, and designing our common futures. Third, the concept of "peaceful development," as an expression of a determined hope to abolish violence and achieve cooperation in improving the material and spiritual lives of the over 5 billion inhabitants of this Spaceship Earth.

The melodic voice of Sting in the lyrics of his song *Fragile* tells it all:

If blood will flow when flesh and steel are one
Drying in the colour of the evening sun
Tomorrow's rain will wash the stains away
But something in our minds will always stay.
Perhaps this final act was meant
to clinch a lifetime's argument
That nothing comes from violence
and nothing ever could
For all those born beneath an angry star
Lest we forget how fragile we are.

REFERENCES

Kamo, Takehiko. 1991. *Restructuring for Peace and Security in the Asia-Pacific Region.* Occasional Paper 5. Honolulu: Matsunaga Institute for Peace.

Kennedy, Paul. 1987. *The Rise and Fall of the Great Powers.* New York: Random House.

Nye, Joseph S. 1990. *Bound to Lead: The Changing Nature of American Power.* New York: Basic.

Tehranian, Majid. 1990. "Communication, Peace, and Development: A Communitarian Perspective." In *Communicating for Peace: Diplomacy and Negotiation.* Eds. Felipe Korzenny and Stella Ting-Toomey. Newbury Park, CA: Sage.

_____. 1992 a and b. "Fundamentalisms, Education, and the Media: An Introduction." and "Islamic Fundamentalism in Iran and the Discourse of Development." In *Fundamentalism and Society.* Eds. Martin Marty and Scott Appleby. Chicago: University of Chicago Press.

Tehranian, Majid, ed. 1991. *Restructuring for Ethnic Peace: A Public Debate at the University of Hawai'i.* Honolulu: Matsunaga Institute for Peace.

Works By The Editors

Books of Katharine Tehranian

A Study of Housing in Nine Low Income Communities in Tehran. Tehran, 1973.

An Annotated Bibliography of the Persian Cities of 5th-10th Centuries. Tehran, 1978.

The City as Discourse: The Origins of American City Planning. Cresskill, NJ: Hampton Press. Forthcoming.

Images of American Landscape. Forthcoming

Books of Majid Tehranian

The Middle East: It's Governments and Politics, with A. Al-Marayati et al. Belmont: Duxbury Press, 1972.

Towards a Systemic Theory of National Development. Tehran: Industrial Management Institute, 1974.

Communications Policy for National Development: A Comparative Perspective, edited with F. Hakimzadeh and M. L. Vidale. London: Routledge, Kegan, Paul, 1977.

Socio-Economic and Communication Indicators in Development Planning: A Case Study of Iran. Paris: UNESCO, 1981.

Technologies of Power: Information Machines and Democratic Prospects. Norwood, NJ: Ablex, 1990.

Letters from Jerusalem. Honolulu: Matsunaga Institute for Peace, 1990.

Deconstructing Paradise: Dependency, Development, and Discourse in Hawai'i. Honolulu: Department of Communication, 1990.

Restructuring for Ethnic Peace: A Public Debate at the University of Hawai'i. Ed. Honolulu: Matsunaga Institute for Peace. 1991.

Publications of the Matsunaga Institute for Peace

The Matsunaga Institute for Peace publishes scholarly and creative works on peace in all media. The publications are available from the Institute (Matsunaga Institute for Peace, University of Hawai'i, Porteus Hall 717, 2424 Maile Way, Honolulu, Hawai'i, USA 96822; 808-956-7718, FAX 808-956-5708).

Solving Conflicts: A Peace Research Perspective, by Johan Galtung. In conjunction with the University of Hawaii Press. 1989. 62 pp. $8.

Peace and Development in the Pacific, by Johan Galtung. In conjunction with the University of Hawaii Press. 1989. 68 pp. $8.

Nonviolence and Israel/Palestine, by Johan Galtung. In conjunction with the University of Hawaii Press. 1989. 79 pp. $10.

Peace Studies: The Evolution of Peace Research and Peace Education, by Carolyn Stephenson. Occasional Paper 1. 1990. 19 pp. $2.

War and Children's Survival, by George Kent. Occasional Paper 2. 1990. 33 pp. $2.

Letters from Jerusalem, edited by Majid Tehranian. Occasional Paper 4. 1990. 87 pp. $4.

Restructuring for Peace and Security in the Asia-Pacific Region, by Takehiko Kamo. Occasional Paper 5. 1992. 18 pp. $2.

Engulfed in War: Just War and the Persian Gulf, edited by Brien Hallett. 119 pp. $5.

Restructuring for Ethnic Peace: A Public Debate at the University of Hawai'i, edited by Majid Tehranian. 1991. 187 pp. $5.

Implementing the Rights of Children in Armed Conflict, by George Kent. Working Paper 1. 20 pp. Fall 1991.

In addition, the Institute distributes the following publications from the Center for Global Nonviolence Planning Project of the University of Hawai'i:

Nonviolence and Hawaii's Spiritual Traditions, edited by Glenn D. Paige and Sarah Gilliatt. 1991. 112 pp. $5.

Buddhism and Nonviolent Global Problem-Solving, edited by Glenn D. Paige and Sarah Gilliatt. 1991. 176 pp. $10.

Nonviolence Speaks to Power, by Petra Kelly. 1992. 183 pp. $5.

INDEX